BEST EUROPEAN
CITY WALKS
& MUSEUMS

LONDON

AMSTERDAM

PARIS

VENICE

FLORENCE

ROME

MADRID

DCH

Rick Steves & Gene Openshaw

AVALON
TRAVEL

CONTENTS

INTRODUCTION   **1**

    Art History 4

    Artists & Dates 11

LONDON   **17**

    Westminster Walk 18

    British Museum 29

    National Gallery 51

    British Library 69

    Westminster Abbey 78

PARIS   **87**

    Historic Paris Walk 89

    Louvre 112

    Orsay 136

    Versailles 160

AMSTERDAM   **179**

    Amsterdam City Walk 181

    Rijksmuseum 199

    Van Gogh Museum 216

    Anne Frank House 227

VENICE   **235**

    St. Mark's Square 237

    St. Mark's Basilica 246

    Doge's Palace 262

FLORENCE 277

Renaissance Walk 279
Uffizi Gallery 296
Bargello 316

ROME 325

Colosseum 327
Roman Forum 334
National Museum of Rome 347
Pantheon 360
St. Peter's Basilica 363
Vatican Museum 379

MADRID 407

Madrid City Walk 409
Prado Museum 419
Guernica 449

MODERN ART 453

INDEX 467

INTRODUCTION

Mona Lisa, David, Big Ben, the Colosseum....

Europe's cultural treasures can be exhilarating—for some, even life-changing. Its world-class museums open up the world of our ancestors, letting us understand past generations by seeing objects they considered beautiful. But Europe's masterpieces aren't confined to museums. A walk through the great cities shows us a world as modern as our own, though still quite different, tinged with centuries of history. Standing face-to-face with Europe's timeless wonders, many travelers have eye-opening epiphanies.

Beforehand

Rip up this book. Before your trip, rip out, staple bind, and pack just the individual chapters you'll use. (If this really bugs you, send all the pieces and $5 to Europe Through the Back Door, 130 Fourth Avenue North, Edmonds, WA 98020, and we'll send you a new copy. Really.)

Read ahead. Scan the chapter before your visit to get a sense of what you'll want to concentrate on.

Check the "Orientation" material. The first page of each chapter lists the museum hours, cost, availability of information, tips on avoiding crowds, and more. Avoid tactical problems by planning ahead.

At the Sight or Museum

Use the maps and written directions to get your bearings. Our maps are purposely simple and schematic to help you quickly get the layout of the sight or museum.

Keep the big picture. Scan the room for the common characteristics of the art. Next, study the specific example mentioned in the text. Then browse, trying out what you have learned.

Partners, take turns acting as guide. It's easier if one looks while the other reads.

For more information: Serious art lovers might want to supplement this book with an audioguide or guided tour at the museum. Audioguides, available at many museums (for about $5), are handheld devices that give English commentary as you walk through a museum. Audioguides are usually pretty dry, repeating the names and dates you'll read in this book, but occasionally they're excellent.

Some museums offer guided tours (sometimes free but usually at a cost of $6 or more). In France, Italy, and Spain, tours in English are most likely to occur during peak season. The quality of a tour depends on the guide's knowledge, fluency, and enthusiasm.

Watch For Changes

Museums change. Paintings can be on tour, on loan, out sick, or shifted at the whim of the curator. Even museum walls are often moved.

To adapt, pick up any available free floor plan as you enter. Let the museum's information person glance at this book's maps to confirm locations of paintings. If you can't find a particular painting, ask any museum worker where it is. Just point to the photograph in this book and ask, "Where?": in Italian, *"Dove?"* (DOH-vay); in French, *"Ou est?"* (oo ay); in Spanish, *"¿Dónde?"* (DOHN-day).

Museum hours change. Especially off-season (and in Italy), you'll want to confirm by telephone or at the city tourist office upon arrival.

General Museum Policies

Last entry: Many museums have a "last entry" 30–60 minutes before closing. Also, guards usher people out before the official closing time.

Photography: Cameras are normally allowed, but no flashes or tripods (without special permission). Flashes damage oil paintings and distract others in the room. Even without a flash, a handheld camera will take a decent picture (or buy postcards or posters at the museum bookstore). Video cameras are usually allowed.

Baggage check: For security reasons, you're often required to check even small bags. Every museum has a free checkroom at the entrance. They're safe. Check everything (except this book) and enjoy the art.

Food: Museum-going stokes appetites. Most museums have cafeterias with reasonable prices and decent food. Consult the "Orientation" information at the beginning of each chapter for any recommendations.

Toilets: WCs are free and better than the European average.

Museum bookstores: These sell cards, prints, posters, slides, and guidebooks. Thumb through a museum guidebook to be sure you haven't overlooked something of particular interest to you.

No Apologies

This book drives art and history snobs nuts. Its gross generalizations, sketchy dates, oversimplifications, and shoot-from-the-hip opinions will likely tweeze art highbrows. This book isn't an art history text; it's a quick taste of Europe's fascinating but difficult sights and museums. Use it as an introduction—not the final word. From this point on, "we" (your co-authors) will shed our respective egos and become "I." Enjoy.

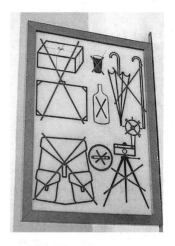

A victim of the Louvre

ART HISTORY

FIVE MILLENNIA IN SIX PAGES

Egypt: 3000–1000 B.C.

Tombs and mummies preserved corpses and possessions for the afterlife. Statues of pharaohs were political propaganda. Statues and painted figures were stiff and unrealistic, perpetually standing at attention. Little changed in 2,000 years. You'll find examples in the:
- British Museum (statues, mummies, and the Rosetta Stone)
- Vatican Museum
- Louvre

Greece: 700 B.C.–A.D. 1

Greece was the foundation of our "Western" civilization—science, democracy, art, and the faith that the universe is orderly and rational.

Archaic: 700–500 B.C.

In a time of wars the creative Greek spirit was beginning to show itself. Stiff statues reflect their search for stability and order amid chaos. Sculptors showed keen interest in, but no mastery of, the human body.
- "Kouros" statues (in Louvre and British Museum)

Golden Age: 500–325 B.C.

Athens ruled a coalition of city-states in the days of Socrates, Pericles, Plato, and Aristotle. The Greek gods were portrayed as ideal human beings. Statues look natural, but their balanced poses show the order found in nature. Nothing in extreme.

- *Apollo Belvedere* (Vatican Museum, see photo)
- Elgin Marbles from the Parthenon (British Museum)
- *Venus de Milo* (Louvre)
- *Venus de' Medici* (Uffizi)

Hellenism: 325 B.C.–A.D. 1

Alexander the Great conquered Greece and spread Greek culture around the Mediterranean. They produced restless statues of people in motion, struggling against other people, animals, and themselves. Everything in extreme.

- *Laocoön* (Vatican Museum, see photo)
- *Winged Victory* (Louvre)

Rome: 500 B.C.–A.D. 500

The Romans conquered Greek lands and absorbed their culture and gods. The result: Greek style, with a "bigger is better" attitude. Romans were engineers, not artists. Using the arch and concrete, they built unprecedented grand structures, decorated with Greek columns and statues. Realistic portrait busts of the emperors reminded subjects who was in charge.

- Colosseum (see photo), Forum, and Pantheon (Rome)
- Greek-style statues (Vatican Museum, Louvre, and British Museum)
- Portrait busts (Vatican Museum and Louvre)

Medieval Europe: A.D. 500–1400

Rome fell, plunging Europe into "dark" centuries of poverty, war, famine, and hand-me-down leotards. The church was the people's refuge, and heaven was their hope. Art served the church—Bible scenes, crucifixes, saints, and Madonnas

(Mary, the mother of Jesus) decorated churches and inspired the illiterate masses. Gothic architects used the pointed arch to build tall, spired churches with walls of stained glass.

Art was symbolic, not realistic. Saints float in a golden, heavenly realm, far removed from life on earth. Humans are scrawny sinners living in a flat, two-dimensional world.

- Altarpieces in many museums and churches
- Notre-Dame and Sainte-Chapelle (Paris)
- Illuminated manuscripts (British Library)

Byzantine: A.D. 300–1450

The Eastern half of the Roman Empire, centered in Constantinople (Istanbul), lived on after Rome fell, remaining Christian, Greek-speaking, and enlightened while Western Europe was mired in medievalism. Byzantium preserved the classical arts and learning through the Dark Ages. These ideas reentered Europe via Venice.

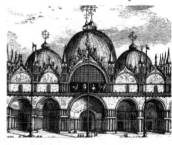

- St. Mark's Basilica—mosaics, domes, and treasures (Venice)
- Icon-style gold-leafed paintings (many museums)

Italian Renaissance: 1400–1600

The Renaissance was the "rebirth" of the arts and learning of ancient Greece and Rome—democracy, science, and humanism. Architects built balanced structures with Greek columns and Roman domes and arches. Sculptors used 3-D realism to glorify human beings like Greek nudes. Artists used mathematical laws of perspective to capture the 3-D world on a 2-D canvas. They saw God in the orderliness of nature and the beauty of the human body. Art was no longer tied to the church. Art for art's sake was OK.

Florence: 1400–1520

In this city, the birthplace of the Renaissance, Greek-style sculpture and Roman-style architecture were revived. Pioneering 3-D painting, artists placed statuelike people in spacious settings.

- Michelangelo's *David* (Florence's Accademia)
- Botticelli's *Birth of Venus* (Uffizi, see photo)
- Brunelleschi's dome (Florence)
- Dontello's sculpture (Bargello)

- Leonardo da Vinci, Giotto, and Raphael (Uffizi and other museums)

Roman Renaissance: 1500–1550

The city of Rome was grandly rebuilt by energetic, secular-minded Renaissance popes.

- Sistine Chapel, Michelangelo (Vatican Museum, see photo)
- St. Peter's Basilica, with dome by Michelangelo (Vatican City)
- Raphael paintings (Vatican Museum)

Venetian Renaissance: 1500–1600

Big, colorful, sensual paintings celebrate the Venetian good life, funded by trade with the East. Whereas Florentine painters drew their figures with heavy outlines, Venetians "built" figures out of patches of color.

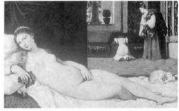

- Titian (see photo), Veronese, and Tintoretto (many museums)
- Best museum: Madrid's Prado
- Doge's Palace (Venice)

Northern Protestant Art: 1500–1700

Art was bought by middle-class merchants, not popes and kings. Everyday things were painted on small canvases in a simple, realistic, unemotional style, with loving attention to detail. Rather than painting Greek gods and heavenly Madonnas, they concentrated on portraits, landscapes, still lifes, and wacky slice-of-life scenes.

- Rembrandt (many museums)
- Vermeer (see photo, Amsterdam's Rijksmuseum)
- Dürer (National Gallery, Uffizi)
- Bosch (Prado)
- Best museums: Rijksmuseum and Prado

Baroque: 1600–1700

This style of divine-right kings (Louis XIV) and the Counter-Reformation Catholic Church was meant to impress commoners. Baroque is big, colorful, and ornamented, though based on Renaissance balance. Featuring exaggerated beauty and violence, Baroque specializes in Greek gods, fleshy nudes, and pudgy, winged babies.

- Palace of Versailles
- St. Peter's Basilica
- Rubens (many museums, see photo)

Rococo: 1700–1800

Baroque's frilly little sister was smaller, lighter, and even more ornamented, with pastel colors, rosy cheeks, and pudgier winded babies. In architecture, the oval replaced the circle as the basic pattern. Aristocratic tastes were growing more refined and more out of touch with the everyday world.

- Versailles' interior decoration
- Boucher (see photo), Watteau, and Fragonard (Louvre)

Neoclassical: 1750–1850

With the French Revolution, Rococo became politically incorrect. Neoclassical was yet another rebirth of the Greek and Roman world. It was simpler and more austere than Renaissance and Baroque versions of the classical style. Reflecting its era, neoclassical was the art of democracy and the "Age of Reason."

- J. L. David (Louvre)
- Ingres (Louvre and Orsay, see photo)
- Paris' Pantheon

Romanticism: 1800–1850

Reacting against the overly rational neoclassical and Industrial Age, Romanticism was a return to Nature and Man's primitive roots. Dramatic, colorful art expresses the most intense inner emotions. Both individuals and nations struggle to be free.

- Goya (Prado, see photo)
- Delacroix (Louvre)

Impressionism and Post-Impressionism: 1850–1900

Quick "impressions" of everyday scenes (landscapes, cafés) are captured with a fast and messy style. The thick brush strokes of bright colors laid side by side on the canvas blend at a distance, leaving the impression of shimmering light.

- Monet, Manet, Degas, and Renoir (see photo, Orsay)
- Van Gogh (Van Gogh Museuem, Orsay)
- Gauguin, Cézanne, and Rodin (Orsay)
- Best Museums: Paris' Orsay and London's National Gallery

Modern Art: 20th Century and Beyond

The 20th century—accelerated by technology and shattered by wars—produced art as chaotic as the times. There was a wide variety of art styles ("-isms") and many new media. Many artists abandoned photorealism to paint abstract, colorful patterns (Abstract art, Cubism, Abstract Expressionism). Others distorted reality to give a new perspective or express a larger truth (Surrealism, Expressionism, Pop art). Most modern artists mixed these two strains.

But what does it *mean*? Modern art offers an alternative to our normal, programmed McLives. It's a wild, chaotic jungle that you'll have to explore and tame on your own. *Grrr.*

- Picasso (Cubism and many other styles, see photo)
- Dali (Surrealism)
- Mondrian (Abstract)
- Warhol (Pop art)
- Pollock (Abstract Expressionism)
- Chagall (mix of various styles)
- Museums: London's Tate Modern, Paris' Pompidou Center, Amsterdam's Stedelijk, Venice's Peggy Guggenheim, Madrid's Centro Arte de Reina Sofia, and more.

Artist Timeline: 1300—2000

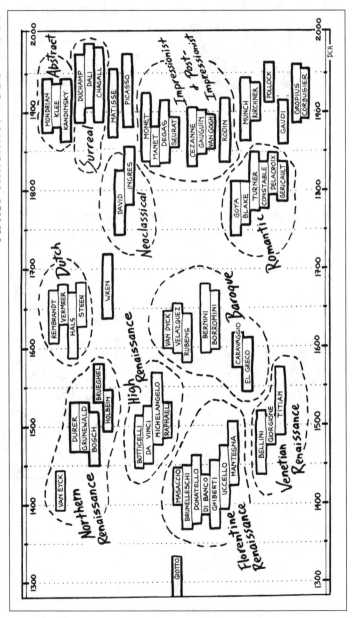

ARTISTS & DATES

Avercamp, Hendrick (AH-vehr-kahmp), 1585–1634—Dutch slice-of-life scenes.

Baldung Grien, Hans (BAHL-dung green), 1484–1545—Northern student of Italian Renaissance techniques.

Bellini, Giovanni (bel-LEE-nee), 1430–1516—Colorful soft-focus Madonnas.

Bernini (ber-NEE-nee), 1598–1680—Baroque grandeur, exuberance, emotion, and flesh.

Blake, William, 1757–1827—Mystical visions.

Bosch, Hieronymous (bosh), 1450–1516—Crowded, bizarre scenes.

Botticelli, Sandro (bot-i-CHEL-lee), 1445–1510—Delicate Renaissance beauty.

Boucher, François (boo-shay), 1703–1770—Sensual Rococo scenes for French aristocrats.

Brancusi, Constantin (brahn-KOO-zee), 1876–1957—Smooth, shiny, abstract statues.

Braque, Georges (brock), 1882–1963—Cubist pioneer.

Brueghel, Pieter (BROY-gull), ca. 1525–1569—Netherlands, peasant scenes.

Brunelleschi, Filippo (broon-uh-LES-key), 1377–1446—First great Renaissance architect.

Calder, Alexander, 1898–1976—Abstract mobiles.

Canaletto (kah-nah-LET-toh), 1697–1768—Misty Venetian overviews.

Caravaggio (kar-ah-VAH-jee-oh), 1573–1610—Shocking ultra-realism.

Cellini, Benvenuto (chel-LEE-nee), 1500–1571—Renaissance metal statues.

Cézanne, Paul (say-zahn), 1839–1906—Bridged Impressionism and Cubism.

Chagall, Marc (shah-GAHL), 1887–1985—Fiddlers on roofs, magical realism.

Cimabue (chee-MAH-bway), c. 1240–1302—Experimented with Renaissance techniques and influenced Giotto.

Claudel, Camille (cloh-del), 1864–1943—Rodin's protégé.

Constable, John, 1776–1837—Rustic English country scenes.

Courbet, Gustave (coor-bay), 1819–1877—Unglamorized Realism.

Cranach, Lucas (KRAH-nakh), 1472–1553—Northern Renaissance plus sensuality.

da Vinci, Leonardo (dah VINCH-ee), 1452–1519—A well-rounded Renaissance genius who also painted.

Dalí, Salvador (DAH-lee), 1904–1989—Surrealist showman.

Daumier, Honoré (dohm-yay), 1808–1879—Caricatures of pomposity.

David, Jacques-Louis (dah-veed), 1748–1825—Chronicler of heroic Napoleonic era (neoclassicism).

Degas, Edgar (day-gah), 1834–1917—Impressionist snapshots, dancers.

Delacroix, Eugène (del-ah-kwah), 1798–1863—Colorful, emotional, exotic Romanticism.

Donatello, (doh-na-TEL-oh), ca. 1386–1466—Early Renaissance sculptor.

Dürer, Albrecht (DEWR-er), 1471–1528—Renaissance symmetry with German detail; "the Leonardo of the north."

El Greco (el GREK-oh), 1541–1614—Spiritual scenes, elongated bodies.

Fabriano, Gentile da (fah-bree-AH-noh), 1370–1427—Medieval master of colorful detail.

Fra Angelico (frah ahn-JEL-lee-koh), 1387–1455—Renaissance techniques, medieval piety.

Fragonard, Jean-Honoré (frah-goh-nar), 1732–1806—Rococo candy.

Gainsborough, Thomas, 1727–1788—Relaxed portraits of English upper crust.

Gauguin, Paul (go-GAN), 1848–1903—Primitivism, native scenes, bright colors.

Géricault, Théodore (zher-ee-koh), 1791–1824—Dramatic Romantic.

Ghiberti, Lorenzo (gee-BEHR-tee, hard "g"), 1378–1455—Pioneer of Renaissance 3-D in bronze relief.

Giacometti, Alberto (jee-ah-koh-MET-tee), 1901–1966—Stick-figure sculptures, modern art.

Giorgione (jor-JONE-ee), 1477–1510—Venetian Renaissance, mysterious beauty.

Giotto (JOT-oh), 1266–1337—Proto-Renaissance painter (3-D) in medieval times.

Goya, Francisco (GOY-ah), 1746–1828—Three stages: frilly court painter, political rebel, dark stage.

Guardi, Francesco (GWAHR-dee), 1712–1793—Postcards of Venice.

Hals, Frans (halls), 1581–1666—Snapshot portraits of Dutch merchants.

Hogarth, William, 1697–1764—Stage-sets of English life.

Ingres, Jean Auguste Dominique (ang-gruh), 1780–1867—Neoclassical.

Kandinsky, Wassily (kahn-DIN-skee), 1866–1944—Colorful, abstract squiggles and shapes.

Kirchner, Ernest Ludwig (KIRSH-ner), 1880–1938—Expressionist critic of society in jagged shapes and lurid colors.

Klee, Paul (klay), 1879–1940—Simplified, playful, childlike forms.

Lorrain, Claude (loh-ran), 1602–1682—Glorious sunsets over classical architecture.

Leger, Fernand (leh-zhay), 1881–1955—Cylinder-shaped cubism ("tubism").

Lippi, Fra Filippo (LIP-pee), 1406–1469—Young, pretty virgins.

Manet, Edouard (mah-NAY), 1823–1883—Forerunner of Impressionist rebels.

Mantegna, Andrea (mahn-TAYN-yah), 1431–1506—Renaissance 3-D and "sculptural" painting.

Matisse, Henri (mah-TEES), 1869–1954—Decorative "wallpaper," bright colors.

Michelangelo (mee-kel-AHN-jel-oh), 1475–1564—Earth's greatest sculptor and one of its greatest painters.

Millet, Jean-François (mee-yay), 1814–1875—Realist painter in Academic society.

Miró, Joan (mee-ROH), 1893–1983—Childlike, simplified forms.

Mondrian, Piet (MAHN-dree-ahn), 1872–1944—Abstract, geometrical canvases.

Monet, Claude (moh-NAY), 1840–1926—Father of Impressionism.

Murillo, Bartolomé Esteban (moo-REE-yoh), 1617–1682—Sugar-coated Catholic images.

Newman, Barnett, 1905–1970—Big, empty, abstract canvases.

Parmigianino, 1503–1540 (par-mee-jee-ah-NEE-noh)—Mannerist exaggeration, elongated bodies.

Picasso, Pablo (pee-KAHS-soh), 1881–1973—Master of many modern styles, especially Cubism.

Pissarro, Camile (pee-SAHR-roh), 1830–1903—Grainy Impressionism.

Pollaiuolo, Antonio (pohl-eye-OH-loh), 1432–1498—Influential studies of human anatomy.

Pollock, Jackson (PAHL-luck), 1912–1956—Wild drips of paint.

Poussin, Nicolas (poo-san), 1594–1665—Calm, balanced, classical themes.

Raphael (roff-eye-ELL), 1483–1520—Epitome of the Renaissance—balance, realism, beauty.

Rembrandt (REM-brant), 1606–1669—Greatest Dutch painter, brown canvases, dramatic lighting.

Renoir, Auguste (ren-wah), 1841–1919—Impressionist style, idealized beauty, pastels.

Reynolds, Sir Joshua, 1723–1792—English academic in classical style.

Robert, Hubert, 1733–1808—Classical ruins.

Rodin, Auguste (roh-dan), 1840–1917—Classical statues with rough "Impressionist" finish.

Rossetti, Dante Gabriel (roh-SET-tee), 1828–1882—Pre-Raphaelite earnestness.

Rothko, Mark (RAWTH-koh), 1903–1970—Blurry, two-tone rectangles.

Rouault, Georges (roo-oh), 1871–1958—Stained glass–style paintings.

Rousseau, Henri (roo-soh), 1844–1910—Exotic scenes in children's-book style.

Rubens, Peter Paul (ROO-buns), 1577–1640—Baroque, fleshy women, violent scenes.

Seurat, Georges-Pierre (suh-rah), 1859–1891—Bright works made with dots of color (pointillism).

Simone Martini, 1284–1344—Sienese medieval altarpieces.

Steen, Jan (stain), 1626–1679—Slice-of-life everyday Dutch scenes.

Stubbs, George, 1724–1806—Horses.

Tiepolo, Giovanni Battista (tee-EP-oh-loh), 1696–1770—3-D illusions on ceilings.

Tintoretto (tin-toh-RET-oh), 1518–1594—Venetian Renaissance plus drama.

Titian (TEESH-un), 1485–1576—Greatest Venetian Renaissance painter.

Toulouse-Lautrec, Henri de (too-loose-loh-trek), 1864–1901—Posters and scenes from seedy French nightclubs.

Turner, Joseph Mallord William, 1775–1851—Messy "proto-Impressionist" scenes of nature.

Uccello, Paolo (oo-CHEL-oh), 1396–1475—Early 3-D experiments.

Van der Weyden, Rogier (van dehr WAY-den), 1400-1464—Northern master of detailed altarpieces.

Van Dyck, Sir Anthony (van dike), 1599–1641—Flemish portraitist of Europe's aristocrats.

Van Eyck, Jan (van ike), 1390–1441—Northern detail.

Van Gogh, Vincent (van GO, or, more correctly, van HOCK), 1853–1890—Impressionist style plus emotion.

Velázquez, Diego (vel-LAHS-kes), 1599–1660—Objective Spanish court portraits.

Vermeer, Jan (vehr-MEER), 1632–1675—Quiet Dutch art, high-lighting everyday details.

Veronese, Paolo (vehr-oh-NAY-zee), 1528–1588—Huge, colorful scenes with Venetian Renaissance backgrounds.

Verrochio, Andrea del (vehr-ROH-kee-oh), 1435–1388—Leonardo's teacher in painting and sculptures.

Watteau, Jean-Antoine (wah-toh), 1684–1721—Scenes of Louis XIV's court.

London Sights

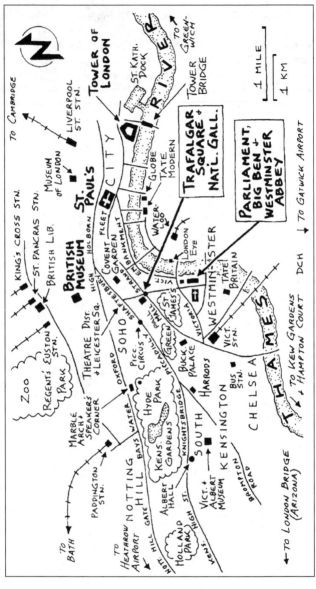

LONDON

London—a city of nine million people from every nation on earth—is a microcosm of the planet's culture. Get an overview of the grand city by taking the Westminster Walk from Big Ben to Trafalgar Square. Tour ancient Egypt, Assyria, and Greece at the British Museum. Westminster Abbey contains the piety of the Middle Ages. Then see the ancient world "reborn" in the Renaissance paintings of the National Gallery, which brings art history right up to the brink of the modern world. Finally, page through 2,000 years of history, from Bibles to Beatles, in the manuscripts of the British Library.

Westminster Walk   **18**

British Museum   **29**

National Gallery   **51**

British Library   **69**

Westminster Abbey   **78**

WESTMINSTER WALK

From Big Ben to Trafalgar Square

London is the L.A., D.C., and N.Y. of Britain. This walk starts with London's "star" attraction, continues to its "Capitol," passes its "White House," and ends at its "Times Square"…all in about an hour.

Just about every visitor to London strolls the historic Whitehall Boulevard from Big Ben to Trafalgar Square. This quick eight-stop walk gives meaning to that touristy ramble. Under London's modern traffic and big-city bustle lie 2,000 fascinating years of history. You'll get a whirlwind tour as well as a practical orientation to London.

Start halfway across Westminster Bridge (Tube: Westminster; take the Westminster Pier exit).

❶ On Westminster Bridge
Views of Big Ben and Parliament

• *First look south (upstream), toward the Parliament. (Note that, though the Thames runs generally west to east, here it makes a jog to the north.)* Ding dong ding dong. Dong ding ding dong. Yes, indeed, you are in London. **Big Ben** is actually "not the clock, not the tower, but the bell that tolls the hour." However, since the 13-ton bell is not visible, everyone just calls the whole works Big Ben. Named for a fat bureaucrat, Ben is scarcely older than my great-grandmother, but it has quickly become the city's symbol. The tower is 320 feet high, and the clock faces are 23 feet across. The 13-foot-long minute hand sweeps the length of your body every five minutes.

Big Ben is the north tower of a long building, the **Houses of**

Westminster Walk

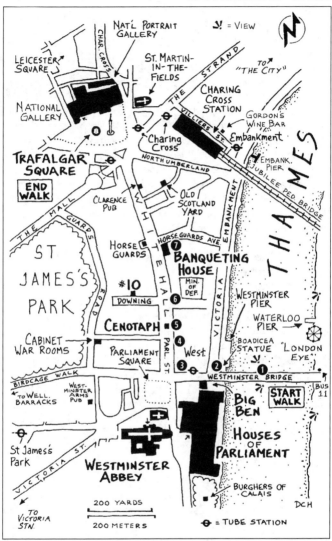

Parliament, stretching along the Thames. Britain is ruled from this building, which for five centuries was the home of kings and queens. Then, as democracy was foisted on tyrants, a parliament of nobles was allowed to meet in some of the rooms. Soon, commoners were elected to office, the neighborhood was shot, and the royalty moved to Buckingham Palace. The current building, though it looks medieval with its prickly flamboyant spires, was built in the 1800s

after a fire gutted old Westminster Palace. Its horizontal
symmetry is an impressive
complement to Big Ben's
vertical.

Today, the **House of
Commons,** which is more
powerful than the queen and
prime minister combined,
meets in the north half of the
building. The rubber-stamp **House of Lords** grumbles and snoozes
in the south end of this 1,000-room complex and provides a tempering effect on extreme governmental changes. The two houses are
very much separate: Notice the riverside tea terraces with the color-
coded awnings—royal red for lords, common green for commoners.
If a flag is flying from the Victoria Tower, at the far south end of
the building, Parliament is in session.

Views of the London Eye Ferris Wheel, The City, and the Thames

• *Now look north (downstream).*
Built in 2000 to celebrate the millennium, the London Eye—known
to some as "the London Eyesore"—stands 443 feet tall and slowly
spins 32 capsules, each filled with 25 visitors, up to London's best
viewpoint (up to 25 miles on a rare clear day). Aside from Big Ben,
Parliament, St. Paul's Cathedral, and the wheel itself, London's skyline is not overwhelming; it's a city that wows from within.

Next to the wheel sprawls the huge former **County Hall building,** now a hotel and tourist complex. Shut down a decade ago, this
bastion of London liberals still seems to snarl across the river at the
home of the national government.

The London Eye marks the start of the **Jubilee Promenade,** a pleasant one-hour riverside walk along the "South Bank" of the Thames, through London's vibrant, gentrified arts and cultural zone. Along the way, you have views across the river of St. Paul's stately dome and the financial district, called "The City."

London's history is tied to the **Thames,** the 210-mile river linking the interior of England with the North Sea. The city got its start in Roman times as a trade center along this watery highway. As recently as a century ago, large ships made their way upstream to the city center to unload. Today, the major port is 25 miles downstream.

Look for the piers on the Thames. A 50-minute round-trip **cruise** geared for tourists departs from Waterloo Pier near the base of the Ferris wheel. On the other side of the river, at **Westminster Pier,** boats leave for the Tower of London, Greenwich, and Kew Gardens.

Lining the river, beneath the lamp posts, are little green copper **lions' heads** with rings for tying up boats. Before the construction of the Thames Barrier in 1982 (the world's largest movable flood barrier, downstream near Greenwich), high tides from the nearby North Sea made floods a recurring London problem. The police kept an eye on these lions: "When the lions drink, the city's at risk."

Until 1750, only London Bridge crossed the Thames. Then a bridge was built here. Early in the morning of September 3, 1803, William Wordsworth stood where you're standing and described what he saw:

> *This city now doth like a garment wear*
> *The beauty of the morning; silent, bare,*
> *Ships, towers, domes, theaters, and temples lie*
> *Open unto the fields, and to the sky;*
> *All bright and glittering in the smokeless air.*

• *Walk to Big Ben's side of the river. Near Westminster Pier is a big statue of a lady on a chariot (nicknamed "the first woman driver"...no reins).*

❷ Boadicea, Queen of the Iceni

Riding in her two-horse chariot, daughters by her side, this Celtic Xena leads her people against Roman invaders. Julius Caesar had

been the first Roman to cross the Channel, but even he was weirded out by the island's strange inhabitants, who worshiped trees, sacrificed virgins, and went to war painted blue. Later, Romans subdued and civilized them, building roads and making this spot on the Thames—

"Londinium"—into a major urban center.

But Boadicea refused to be Romanized. In A.D. 60, after Roman soldiers raped her daughters, she rallied her people and "liberated" London, massacring its 70,000 Romanized citizens. However, the brief revolt was snuffed out, and she and her family took poison rather than surrender.

• *There's a civilized public toilet down the stairs behind Boadicea. Continue past Big Ben, one block inland to the busy intersection of Parliament Square.*

❸ Parliament Square

To your left is the orange-hued **Parliament.** If Parliament is in session, the entrance is lined with tourists, enlivened by political demonstrations, and staked out by camera crews interviewing Members of Parliament (M.P.s) for the evening news. Kitty-corner across the Square, the two white towers of **Westminster Abbey** rise above the trees. And broad Whitehall (here called Parliament Street) stretches to your right up to Trafalgar Square.

This is the heart of what was once a suburb of London—the medieval City of Westminster. Like Buda and Pest, London is two cities that grew into one. The City of London, centered near St. Paul's Cathedral and the Tower of London, was the place to live. But King Edward the Confessor decided to build a church (minster) and monastery (abbey) here, west of the city walls—hence Westminster.

And to oversee its construction, he moved his court here and built a palace. The palace gradually evolved into a meeting place for debating public policy, which is why to this day the Houses of Parliament are known to Brits as the "Palace of Westminster."

Across from Parliament, the cute little church with the blue sundials, snuggling under the Abbey "like a baby lamb under a ewe," is **St. Margaret's Church.** Since 1480, this has been *the* place for politicians' weddings—such as Churchill's.

Parliament Square, the small park between Westminster Abbey and

Big Ben, is filled with statues of famous Brits. The statue of **Winston Churchill,** the man who saved Britain from Hitler, shows him in the military overcoat he wore as he limped victoriously onto the beaches of Normandy after D-Day. According to tour guides, the statue has a current of electricity running through it to honor Churchill's wish that if a statue were made of him, his head shouldn't be soiled by pigeons.

In 1868 the world's first traffic light was installed on the corner here where Whitehall now spills double-decker buses into the square. And speaking of lights, the little yellow lantern atop the concrete post on the street corner closest to Parliament says "Taxi." When an M.P. needs a taxi, this blinks to hail one.

• *Consider touring Westminster Abbey (see page 78). Otherwise, turn right (north), walk away from the Houses of Parliament and the abbey, and continue up Parliament Street, which becomes Whitehall.*

❹ Walking Along Whitehall

Today, Whitehall is choked with traffic, but imagine the effect this broad street must have had on out-of-towners a century ago. In your horse-drawn carriage, you'd clop along a tree-lined boulevard past well-dressed lords and ladies, dodging street urchins. Gazing left, then right, you'd try to take it all in, your eyes dazzled by the bone-white walls of this man-made marble canyon.

Whitehall is now the most important street in Britain, lined with the ministries of finance, treasury, and so on. You may see limos and camera crews as an important dignitary enters or exits. Political demonstrators wave signs and chant slogans about issues foreign to most Americans. Notice the security measures. Iron grates seal off the concrete ditches between the buildings and sidewalks for protection against explosives. London was on "orange alert" long before September 2001. As the N.Y., L.A., and D.C. of Britain, London is also seen as the "Babylon" of a colonial empire whose former colonies sometimes resent its lingering control.

The black, ornamental arrowheads topping the iron fences were once colorfully painted. In 1861 Queen Victoria ordered them all painted black when her beloved Prince Albert ("the only one who called her Vickie") died. Possibly the world's most determined mourner, Victoria wore black for the standard two years of mourning—and tacked on 38 more.

• *Continue toward the tall, square, concrete monument in the middle of the road. On your right is a colorful pub, the Red Lion. Across the street, a 700-foot detour down King Charles Street leads to the Cabinet War Rooms, the underground bunker of 21 rooms that was the nerve center of Britain's campaign against Hitler (£7, daily April–Sept 9:30–18:00, Oct–March 10:00–18:00).*

❺ Cenotaph

This big white stone monument (in the middle of the boulevard) honors those who died in the two events that most shaped modern Britain—World Wars I and II. The monumental devastation of these wars helped turn a colonial superpower into a cultural colony of an American superpower.

The actual cenotaph is the slab that sits atop the pillar—a tomb. You'll notice no religious symbols on this memorial. The dead honored here came from many creeds and all corners of Britain's empire. It looks lost in a sea of noisy cars, but on each Remembrance Sunday (closest to November 11), Whitehall is closed off to traffic, the royal family fills the balcony overhead in the foreign ministry, and a memorial service is held around the cenotaph.

It's hard for an American to understand the impact of the Great War (World War I) on Europe. It's said that if all the WWI dead from the British Empire were to march four abreast past the cenotaph, the sad parade would last for seven days.

Eternally pondering the cenotaph is an equestrian statue up the street. Earl Haig, commander-in-chief of the British army from 1916 to 1918, was responsible for ordering so many brave and not-so-brave British boys out of the trenches and onto the killing fields of World War I.

• *Just past the cenotaph, on the other (west) side of Whitehall, is an iron security gate guarding the entrance to Downing Street.*

❻ #10 Downing Street and the Ministry of Defense

Britain's version of the White House is where the current prime minister—Tony Blair—and his family live, at #10 (in the black-brick building 300 feet down the blocked-off street, on the right). It looks modest, but the entryway does open up into fairly impressive digs. Blair used his persuasive charm to build consensus between the Conservatives ("Tories") and Liberals ("Labour"), but his support for America's invasion of Iraq divided the country. There's not much to see here unless a VIP happens to drive up. Then  the bobbies (police officers) snap to and check credentials, the gates open, the traffic barrier midway down the street drops into its bat cave, the car drives in, and…the bobbies go back to mugging for the tourists.

The huge building across Whitehall from Downing Street is the **Ministry of Defense** (MOD), the "British Pentagon." This bleak place looks like a Ministry of Defense should. In front are statues of illustrious defenders of Britain. "Monty" is **Field Marshal Montgomery** of World War II, who beat the Nazis in North Africa (defeating "the Desert Fox" Rommel at El Alamein), giving the Allies a jumping-off point to retake Europe. Along with Churchill, Monty breathed confidence back into a demoralized British army, persuading them they could ultimately beat Hitler.

You may be enjoying the shade of London's **plane trees.** They do well in polluted London: roots that work well in clay, waxy leaves that self-clean in the rain, and bark that sheds and regenerates so the pollution doesn't get into their vascular systems.

• *At the equestrian statue, you'll be flanked by the Welsh and Scottish government offices. At the corner (same side as the MOD), you'll find the Banqueting House.*

❼ Banqueting House

This two-story neoclassical building is just about all that remains of what was once the biggest palace in Europe—Whitehall Palace, stretching from Trafalgar Square to Big Ben. Henry VIII started it when he moved out of the Palace of Westminster (now the Parliament) and into the residence of the archbishop of York. Queen Elizabeth I and other monarchs added on as England's worldwide prestige grew. Finally, in 1698, a roaring fire destroyed everything at Whitehall except the name and the Banqueting House.

The kings held their parties and feasts in the Banqueting House's grand ballroom on the first floor. At 112 feet wide by 56 feet tall and 56 feet deep, the Banqueting House is a perfect double cube. Today, the exterior of Greek-style columns and pediments looks rather ho-hum, much like every other white, marble, neoclassical building in London. But in 1620, it was the first—a highly influential building by architect Inigo Jones that sparked London's distinct neoclassical look.

On January 27, 1649, a man dressed in black appeared at one of the Banqueting House's first-floor windows and looked out at a huge crowd that surrounded the building. He stepped out the window and onto a wooden platform. It was King Charles I. He gave a short speech to the crowd, framed by the magnificent backdrop of the Banqueting House. His final word was "Remember." Then he knelt and laid his neck on a block as another man in black approached. It was the executioner—who cut off the King's head.

Plop—the concept of divine monarchy in Britain was decapitated. But there would still be kings after Cromwell. In fact, the royalty was soon restored, and Charles' son, Charles II, got his revenge here in the Banqueting Hall...by living well. His elaborate parties under the chandeliers celebrated the Restoration of the monarchy. But, from then on, every king knew that he ruled by the grace of Parliament.

Charles I is remembered today with a statue at one end of Whitehall (in Trafalgar Square at the base of the tall column), while his killer, Oliver Cromwell, is given equal time with a statue at the other end (at the Houses of Parliament).

• *Farther up Whitehall (left side) are the **Horse Guards**, dressed in Charge-of-the-Light-Brigade cavalry uniforms and swords. Until the*

Ministry of Defense was created, the Horse Guards was the headquarters of the British army. It's still the home of the queen's private guard. (Changing of the Guard Mon–Sat 11:00, 10:00 on Sun, dismounting ceremony daily at 16:00.)

*Continue up Whitehall, passing the **Old Admiralty**, headquarters of the British Navy that once ruled the waves. Across the street, behind the old Clarence Pub (serves lunch only, no dinner), stood the original Scotland Yard, headquarters of London's crack police force in the days of Sherlock Holmes. Finally, Whitehall opens up into the grand, noisy...*

❽ Trafalgar Square

London's Times Square bustles around the monumental column where Admiral Horatio Nelson stands 170 feet tall in the crow's nest. Nelson saved England at a time as dark as World War II. In 1805 Napoleon (the Hitler of his day) was poised on the other side of the Channel, threatening to invade England. Meanwhile, more than 900 miles away, the one-armed, one-eyed, and one-minded Lord Nelson attacked the French fleet off the coast of Spain at Trafalgar. The French were routed, Britannia ruled the waves, and the once-invincible French army was slowly worn down, then defeated at Waterloo. Nelson, while victorious, was shot by a sniper in the battle. He died, gasping, "Thank God, I have done my duty."

At the top of Trafalgar Square (north) sits the domed National Gallery and, to the right, the steeple of St. Martin-in-the-Fields, built in 1722, inspiring the style of many town churches in New England (free lunch concerts on Mon, Tue, and Fri at 13:05, and evening concerts for a fee at 19:30 Thu–Sat, box office tel. 020/7839-8362). In

Trafalgar Square

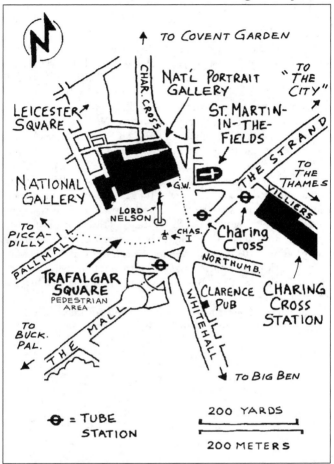

between is a small statue of America's George Washington, looking veddy much the English gentleman he was.

At the base of Nelson's column are bronze reliefs cast from melted-down enemy cannons, and four huggable lions, dying to have their photo taken with you. In front of the column, Charles I sits on horseback with his head intact.

Trafalgar Square is the center of modern London,

connecting Westminster, the City, and the West End. A recent remodeling of the square has rerouted some car traffic, helping reclaim the area for London's citizens. Spin clockwise 360 degrees and survey the city:

To the south (down Whitehall) is the center of government, Westminster. Looking southwest, down the broad boulevard called The Mall, you see Buckingham Palace in the distance. (Down Pall Mall is St. James' Palace, where Prince Charles lives when in London.) A few blocks northwest of Trafalgar Square is Piccadilly Circus. Directly north (2 blocks behind the National Gallery) sits Leicester Square, the jumping-off point for Soho, Covent Garden, and the West End theater district.

The boulevard called the Strand takes you past Charing Cross Station, then eastward to the City, the original walled town of London and today's financial center. In medieval times, when people from the City met with the Westminster government, it was here. And finally, Northumberland Street leads southeast to a pedestrian bridge over the Thames. Along the way, you'll pass the Sherlock Holmes Pub at 10 Northumberland Street, housed in Sir Arthur Conan Doyle's favorite watering hole. It sounds touristy (and has an upstairs replica of 221-B Baker Street), but it's frequented by government workers.

Soak it in. You're smack-dab in the center of London, a thriving city atop thousands of years of history.

BRITISH MUSEUM

In the 19th century, the British flag flew over one-fourth of the world. London was the world's capital, where women in saris walked the streets with men in top hats. And England collected art as fast as it collected colonies.

The British Museum is *the* chronicle of Western civilization. History is a modern invention. Three hundred years ago, people didn't care about crumbling statues and dusty columns. Nowadays, we value a look at past civilizations, knowing that "those who don't learn from history are condemned to repeat it."

The British Museum is the only place I know where you can follow the rise and fall of three great civilizations—Egypt, Assyria, and Greece—in a few hours with a coffee break in the middle. And, while the sun never set on the British Empire, it will on you, so on this tour we'll see just the most exciting two hours.

ORIENTATION

Cost: Free, but £2 donation requested. If you can afford it, donate.

Hours: The **British Museum** is open daily 10:00–17:30, plus Thu–Fri until 20:30 (but from 17:30–20:30, only selected galleries and the Reading Room are open). Rainy days and Sundays always get me down because they're most crowded (the museum is least crowded late on weekday afternoons).

The **Great Court**—the grand entrance with eateries, gift shops, an exhibit gallery, and the Reading Room—has longer hours than the museum (daily 9:00–18:00, Thu–Sat until 23:00).

British Museum Overview

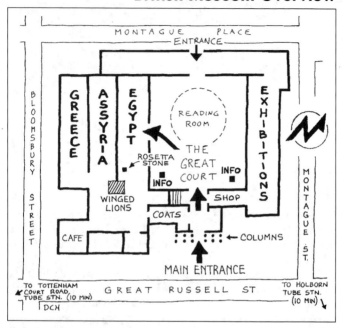

The **Reading Room,** located within the Great Court, is free and open to the quiet public. Computer terminals within the Reading Room offer COMPASS, a database of information about selected museum items; see "Information," below. The Reading Room viewing area opens at 10:00.

Getting There: The main entrance is on Great Russell Street. Take the Tube to Tottenham Court Road, four blocks from the museum. You have your choice of buses: #7, #8, #10, #19, #24, #25, #29, #38, #55, #68, #73, #91, #98, #134, #188, or #242. Taxis are reasonable if you buddy up.

Information: The information desk just inside the Great Court has museum plans. For a schedule of the museum's frequent tours (see "Tours," below), ask at the desk or call the museum (tel. 020/7323-8000, recorded information 020/7388-2227, www .thebritishmuseum.ac.uk).

For **books,** consider the main bookstore (just behind the Reading Room) or The Museum Bookshop (across the street at 36 Great Russell Street).

Computer terminals in the reading room are loaded with **COMPASS,** a free, fun, and user-friendly program allowing visitors to take a virtual tour of the British Museum, delving deeply into whatever is of interest to them. (To prepare ahead,

you can access the program at www.thebritishmuseum.ac
.uk/compass.)

Tours: Eye-Opener tours (free, nearly hrly, 50 min) are each different, focusing on one particular subject within the museum.
These leave throughout the day and can make the visit much
more meaningful. There are also three types of audioguide
tours: top 50 highlights (90 min, pick up at Great Court information desks), the Parthenon Sculptures (60 min, pick up at
desk outside Parthenon Galleries), and the family tour, with
themes such as "bodies, boardgames, and beasts" (length varies,
pick up at Great Court information desks). To rent an audioguide (£3.50), you'll need to leave a photo ID (and sometimes a
£10 deposit).

Length of This Tour: Two hours.

Cloakroom: You can carry a day bag in the galleries, but big backpacks are not allowed. If the line is long and not moving, the
cloakroom may be full (£1 per item).

Photography: Photos allowed without a flash. No tripods.

No-no's: No eating, drinking, smoking, or gum-chewing in the galleries.

Cuisine Art: You have three choices inside the complex. In the Great
Court, you'll find the Court Café (on the main level) as well as
the pricier Court Restaurant (on the upper floor). Within the
museum, the Gallery Café is located off Room 12 (the Greek
section). There are lots of fast, cheap, and colorful cafés, pubs,
and markets along Great Russell Street. No picnicking is
allowed inside the Great Court or the museum. Karl Marx
snacked on the benches near the entrance and in Russell Square.

Starring: Rosetta Stone, Egyptian mummies, Assyrian lions, and
Elgin Marbles.

THE TOUR BEGINS

Enter through the main entrance on Great Russell Street. Ahead is
the Great Court (with the round Reading Room in the center), providing access to all wings. To the left are the exhibits on Egypt,
Assyria, and Greece—our tour. You'll notice that this tour does not
follow the museum's numbered sequence of rooms. Instead, we'll try
to hit the highlights as we work chronologically.

Enjoy the Great Court, Europe's largest covered square, bigger
than a football field. This people-friendly court—delightfully out of
the London rain—was for 150 years one of London's great lost
spaces...closed off and gathering dust. Now, and since the year
2000, it's the 140-foot-wide glass-domed hub of a two-acre cultural
complex. Its centerpiece is the stately Reading Room, a study hall
for Oscar Wilde, Arthur Conan Doyle, Rudyard Kipling, T. S.
Eliot, Virginia Woolf, W. B. Yeats, Mark Twain, V. I. Lenin, and

The Ancient World

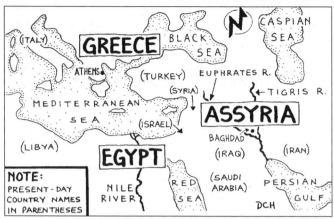

Karl Marx, who formulated his ideas on communism here while writing *Das Kapital.*

• *The Egyptian Gallery is in the West Wing, to the left of the round Reading Room. Enter the Egyptian Gallery and immediately turn left. The Rosetta Stone is at the far end of the gallery.*

EGYPT (3000 B.C.–A.D. 1)

Egypt was one of the world's first "civilizations," that is, a group of people with a government, religion, art, free time, and a written language. The Egypt we think of—pyramids, mummies, pharaohs, and guys who walk funny—lasted from 3000 to 1000 B.C. with hardly any change in the government, religion, or arts. Imagine two millennia of Eisenhower.

The Rosetta Stone (196 B.C.)

When this rock was unearthed in the Egyptian desert in 1799, it was a sensation in Europe. This black slab caused a quantum leap in the evolution of history. Finally, Egyptian writing could be decoded.

The writing in the upper part of the stone is known as hieroglyphics, indecipherable for a thousand years. Did a picture of a bird mean "bird"? Or was it a sound, forming part of a larger word, like "burden"? As it turned out, hieroglyphics are a complex combination of the two, surprisingly more phonetic than symbolic. (For example, the hieroglyph that looks like a mouth or eye is the letter "R.")

British Museum—Egypt

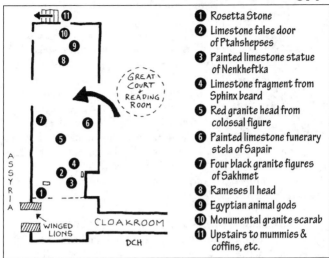

1. Rosetta Stone
2. Limestone false door of Ptahshepses
3. Painted limestone statue of Nenkheftka
4. Limestone fragment from Sphinx beard
5. Red granite head from colossal figure
6. Painted limestone funerary stela of Sapair
7. Four black granite figures of Sakhmet
8. Rameses II head
9. Egyptian animal gods
10. Monumental granite scarab
11. Upstairs to mummies & coffins, etc.

The Rosetta Stone allowed scientists to break the code. It contains a single inscription repeated in three languages. The bottom third is plain old Greek (find your favorite frat or sorority), while the middle is medieval Egyptian. By comparing the two known languages with the one they didn't know, they figured it out.

The breakthrough came when they discovered that the large ovals (e.g., in the sixth line from the top) represented the name of the ruler, Ptolomy. Simple.

• *Twenty steps down the gallery is a 10-foot-high, red-tinted, hieroglyph-inscribed wall labeled...*

Limestone False Door and Architrave of Ptahshepses (c. 2400 B.C.)

This "false door" was a ceremonial entrance (never meant to open) for a sealed building (a *mastaba*) that marked the grave of a man named Ptahshepses. The hieroglyphs of eyes, birds, and rabbits serve as Ptashepses' epitaph, telling his life story.

The deceased was mummified, placed in a wooden coffin that was encased in a stone coffin, then in a stone sarcophagus (like the nearby **red-granite sarcophagus with paneled exterior surfaces** from 2400 B.C.), and buried 50 feet beneath the *mastaba* in an underground chamber (see the **diagram on the wall** of a typical tomb).

In ancient Egypt, you *could* take it with you. They believed that after you died, your soul lived on, enjoying its earthly possessions—sometimes including servants, who might be walled up alive with

their master. (Remember that even the great pyramids were just big tombs for Egypt's most powerful.)

Mastabas like Ptahshepses' were decorated inside and out with **statues, stelas, and frescoes** like those displayed nearby. These pictured the things that the soul could find useful in the next life—magical spells, lists of the deceased's accomplishments, snapshots of the deceased and his family while alive (see the **stela of Sapair,** below), and secret passwords from the Egyptian Book of the Dead. False doors like this allowed the soul (but not grave robbers) to come and go.

• *Originally, this mastaba's door was decorated with a statue similar to the one in the glass case to the right...*

Painted Limestone Statue of Nenkheftka (2400 B.C.)

Standing in a "false door," this statue represented the soul of the deceased still active, going in and out of the burial place. This was the image of the departed that greeted his loved ones when they brought food offerings to place at his feet to nourish his soul. (In the mummification rites, the mouth was ritually opened to prepare it to eat soul food.)

Statues functioned as a refuge for the soul on its journey after death. The rich scattered statues of themselves everywhere, just in

case. Statues needed to be simple and easy to recognize, mug shots for eternity: stiff, arms down, chin up, nothing fancy. But this does have all the essential features, like the simplified human figures on international traffic signs. To a soul caught in the fast lane of astral travel, this symbolic statue would be easier to spot than a detailed one.

With their fervent hope for life after death, Egyptians created calm, dignified art that seems built for eternity.

• *Go past two tall columns that give a sense of the grandeur of the Egyptian temples. On the other side of the ramp is a glass case containing a...*

Limestone Fragment of the Beard of the Sphinx

The Great Sphinx—a statue of a pharaoh-headed lion—crouches in the shadow of the Great Pyramids in Cairo. Time shaved off the sphinx's soft-sandstone, goatee-like beard, and it's now preserved here in a glass case. The beard gives an idea of the scale of the six-story-tall, 200-foot statue.

The sphinx is as old as the pyramids (c. 2500 B.C.), built during the time known to historians as the Old Kingdom (2686–2181 B.C.), but this beard may have been added later, during a restoration (c. 1420 B.C., or perhaps even later under Ramesses II).

• *Find a huge head with a hat like a broken bowling pin.*

Red Granite Head from a Colossal Figure of a King (c. 1350 B.C.)

Art also served as propaganda for the pharaohs, kings who called themselves gods on earth. Put this head on top of an enormous body (which still stands in Egypt), and you have the intimidating image of an omnipotent ruler who demands servile obedience. Next to the head is, appropriately, the pharaoh's powerful fist—the long arm of the law.

The crown is actually two crowns in one. The pointed upper half is the royal cap of Upper Egypt. This rests on the flat, fez-like crown symbolizing Lower Egypt. A pharaoh wearing both crowns together is bragging that he rules a united Egypt. As both "Lord of the Two Lands" and "High Priest of Every Temple," the pharaoh united church and state.

• *On the wall to the right of the Red Granite Head, you'll see three painted stelas. The biggest of these is the...*

Painted Limestone Funerary Stela of Sapair (c. 1400 B.C.)

These people walk like Egyptian statues look—stiff and flat, like they were just run over by a pyramid. We see the torso from the front and everything else—arms, legs, face—in profile, creating the funny walk that has become an Egyptian cliché. But the stiffness is softened by a human touch. It's a family scrapbook; snapshots of loved ones from a happy time to be remembered for all eternity.

In the upper half, Mr. Sapair worships the god Osiris (with pointed hat). Below, tanned Sapair relaxes with his pale wife while their children prepare a picnic. At Sapair's feet, their tiny son sniffs a lotus flower (with a spiritual scent), and their daughter crouches beneath her parents—a symbol of protection. When Sapair's winged spirit finally left his body (very top of stela), he could look at this painting on the tomb wall and think of his wife just like this...with her arms around him and a smile on her face.

• *On the opposite wall are four black, lion-headed statues.*

Four Black Granite Figures of the Goddess Sakhmet (1400 B.C.)

This lion-headed goddess looks pretty sedate here, but she could spring into a fierce crouch when crossed.

The gods ruled the Egyptian cosmos like dictators in a big banana republic (or the American Congress). Egyptians bribed their gods for favors, offering food, animals, or money, or by erecting statues like these to them.

Sakhmet holds an ankh. This key-shaped cross was the hieroglyph meaning "life" and was a symbol of eternal life. Later, it was adopted as a Christian symbol because of its cross shape and religious overtones.

• *Pass by the "Limestone Dyad" of a husband and wife (1350 B.C.) waiting for the Eternity Express and continue on to the eight-foot-tall granite head and torso.*

Upper Half of Colossal Statue of Ramesses II of Granite (1270 B.C.)

When Moses told the king of Egypt, "Let my people go!," this was the stony-faced look he got. Ramesses II ruled 67 years (c. 1290–1223 B.C.) and may have been in power when Moses cursed Egypt with plagues, freed the Israeli slaves, and led them out of Egypt to their homeland in Israel (according to the Bible, but not exactly corroborated by Egyptian chronicles).

This seven-ton statue, made from two different colors of granite, is a fragment from a temple in Thebes. Ramesses was a great builder of temples, palaces, tombs, and statues of himself. There are probably more statues of him in the world than there are cheesy fake *David*s. He was so concerned about achieving immortality that he even chiseled his own name on other people's statues. Very cheeky.

Picture what the archaeologists saw when they came upon this: a colossal head and torso separated from the enormous legs and toppled into the sand—all that remained of the works of a once-great pharaoh. Kings, megalomaniacs, and workaholics, take note.

• *Say, "Ooh, heavy," and climb the ramp behind Ramesses, looking for animals.*

Various Egyptian Gods as Animals

Before technology made humans the alpha animal on earth, it was easier to appreciate our fellow creatures. Animals were stronger, swifter, or fiercer than puny *Homo sapiens.* The Egyptians worshiped animals as incarnations of the gods.

The powerful ram is the god Amun (king of the gods), protecting a puny pharaoh under his powerful chin. The clever baboon is Thoth, the gods' secretary, who gave writing to man. Horus, the god of the living, has a falcon's head. The standing hippo (with lion head) is Tawaret, protectress of childbirth. Her stylized breasts and pregnant belly are supported by ankhs, symbols of life. (Is Tawaret grinning or grimacing in labor?)

• *At the end of the Egyptian gallery is a big stone beetle.*

Monumental Granite Scarab (200 B.C.)

This species of beetle would burrow into the ground, then reappear—like the sun rising and setting, or dying and rebirth, a symbol of resurrection. Scarab amulets were placed on mummies' chests to protect the spirit's heart from acting impulsively.

Like the scarab, Egyptian culture was buried—first by Greece, then by Rome. Knowledge of the ancient writing died, condemning the culture to obscurity. But since the discovery of the Rosetta Stone, Egyptology has boomed and Egypt has come back to life.

• *You can't call Egypt a wrap until you visit the mummies upstairs. If you can handle 72 stairs (if not, return to the Rosetta Stone and start the Assyria section—below), continue to the end of the gallery past the giant stone scarab (beetle) and up the stairs. At the top, take a left into Room 61. Browse through Rooms 61–64, with glass cases full of...*

Mummies, Coffins, Canopic Jars, and Statuettes—The Egyptian Funeral

To mummify a body, disembowel it (but leave the heart inside), pack the cavities with pitch, and dry it with natron, a natural form of sodium carbonate (and, I believe, the active ingredient in Twinkies). Then carefully bandage it head to toe with hundreds of yards of linen strips. Let it sit 2,000 years, and...voilà! Or just dump the corpse in the desert and let the hot, dry,

bacteria-killing Egyptian sand do the work—you'll get the same results.

The mummy was placed in a wooden coffin, which was put in a stone coffin, which was placed in a tomb. (Remember that the pyramids were just big tombs.) The result is that we now have Egyptian bodies that are as well preserved as Dick Clark.

The internal organs were preserved alongside in canopic jars, and small-scale statuettes of the deceased *(shabtis)* were scattered around. Written in hieroglyphs on the coffins and the tomb walls (see the reconstructed murals on the museum walls) were burial rites from the Book of the Dead. These were magical spells to protect the body and crib notes for the waking soul, who needed to know these passwords to get past the guardians of eternity.

Many of the mummies here are from the time of the Roman occupation, when they painted a fine portrait in wax on the wrapping. X-ray photos in the display cases tell us more about these people.

Don't miss the animal mummies. Cats (Room 62) were incarnations of the goddess Bastet. Worshiped in life as the sun god's allies, preserved in death, and memorialized with statues, cats were given the adulation they've come to expect ever since.

• *Linger in Rooms 62 and 63, but remember that eternity is about the amount of time it takes to see this entire museum. In Room 64, in a glass case, you'll find...*

"Ginger" (Naturally Preserved Body)

This man died 5,400 years ago, a thousand years before the pyramids. His people buried him in the fetal position, where he could "sleep" for eternity. The hot sand naturally dehydrated and protected the body. With him are a few of his possessions: bowls, beads, and the flint blade next to his arm. His grave was covered with stones. Named "Ginger" by scientists for his wisps of red hair, this man from a distant time seems very human.

• *Head back down the stairs to the Egyptian Gallery and backtrack to the Rosetta Stone. Next to the stone are two huge, winged Assyrian lions (with bearded human heads) standing guard over the exhibit halls.*

ASSYRIA (900–600 B.C.)

Long before Saddam Hussein, Iraq was home to other palace-building, iron-fisted rulers—the Assyrians.

Assyria was the lion, the king of beasts of early Middle Eastern civilizations. This Semitic people from the agriculturally challenged

British Museum—Assyria

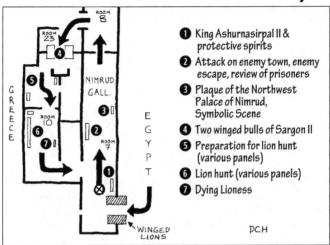

❶ King Ashurnasirpal II & protective spirits

❷ Attack on enemy town, enemy escape, review of prisoners

❸ Plaque of the Northwest Palace of Nimrud, Symbolic Scene

❹ Two winged bulls of Sargon II

❺ Preparation for lion hunt (various panels)

❻ Lion hunt (various panels)

❼ Dying Lioness

hills of northern Iraq became traders and conquerors, not farmers. They conquered their southern neighbors and dominated the Middle East for 300 years (c. 900–600 B.C.).

Their strength came from a superb army (chariots, mounted cavalry, and seige engines), a policy of terrorism against enemies ("I tied their heads to tree trunks all around the city," reads a royal inscription), ethnic cleansing and mass deportations of the vanquished, and efficient administration (roads and express postal service). They have been called "The Romans of the East."

Two Winged Lions with Human Heads (c. 870 B.C.)

These lions guarded an Assyrian palace. With the strength of a lion, the wings of an eagle, the brain of a man, and the beard of ZZ Top, they protected the king from evil spirits, and scared the heck out of foreign ambassadors and left-wing newspaper reporters. (What has five legs and flies? Take a close look. These quintupeds, which appear complete from both the front and the side, could guard both directions at once.)

Carved into the stone between the

bearded lions' loins, you can see one of civilization's most impressive achievements—writing. This wedge-shaped ("cuneiform") script is the world's first written language, invented 5,000 years ago by the Sumerians (of southern Iraq) and passed down to their less-civilized descendants, the Assyrians.

• *Walk between the lions, glance at the large reconstructed wooden gates from an Assyrian palace, and turn right into the narrow red gallery (Room 7) lined with brown relief panels.*

Nimrud Gallery (9th century B.C.)— Ashurnasirpal II

This gallery is a mini version of the throne room of King Ashurnasirpal II's palace at Nimrud. Entering, you'd see the king on his throne at the far end, surrounded by these pleasant sand-colored gypsum relief panels (which were, however, originally painted and varnished).

That's Ashurnasirpal himself in the **first panel on your right,** with braided beard, earring, and fez-like crown, flanked by his supernatural hawk-headed henchmen, who sprinkle incense on him with pine cones. The bulging forearms tell us that Ashurnasirpal II (r. 883–859 B.C.) was a conqueror's conqueror who enjoyed his reputation as a merciless warrior, using torture and humiliation as part of his distinct management style. The room's panels chronicle his bloody career.

Under his reign, the Assyrians dominated the Mideast from their capital at Nineveh (modern Mosul). Ashurnasirpal II proved his power by building a brand-new palace in nearby Nimrud (called Calah in the Bible).

The cuneiform inscription running through the center of the panel is Ashurnasirpal's résumé: "The king who has enslaved all mankind, the mighty warrior who steps on the necks of his enemies, tramples all foes and shatters the enemy; the weapon of the gods, the mighty king, the King of Assyria, the king of the world, B.A., M.B.A., Ph.D., etc...."

• *Thirty feet farther down, on your left, you'll find an upper panel labeled...*

Attack on an Enemy Town

Many "nations" conquered by the Assyrians consisted of little more than a single walled city. Here, the Assyrians lay siege with a crude "tank" that shields them as they advance to the city walls to

smash down the gate with a battering ram. The king stands a safe distance away behind the juggernaut and bravely shoots arrows.

• In the next panel to the right, you'll find...

Enemy Escape

Soldiers flee the slings and arrows of outrageous Assyrians by swimming across the Euphrates, using inflated animal bladders as life preservers. Their friends in the castle downstream applaud their ingenuity.

• Below, you'll see...

Review of Prisoners

The Assyrian economy depended on booty. Here, a conquered nation is paraded before the Assyrian king, who is shaded by a parasol. Ashurnasirpal sneers and tells the captured chief, "Drop and give me 50." Above the prisoners' heads, we

see the rich spoils of war—elephant tusks, metal pots, and so on. The Assyrians depopulated conquered lands by slavery and ethnic cleansing, then repopulated with Assyrian settlers.

• Notice the painted reconstruction of the palace on the opposite wall.

Plaque of the Northwest Palace of Nimrud, and Symbolic Scene Panel

The plaque shows the king at the far end of the throne room, shaded by a parasol and flanked by winged lions. (In the diagram of the palace's floorplan, the throne room is Room B.) The 30,000-square-foot palace was built atop a 50-acre artificial mound. The new palace was inaugurated with a 10-day banquet (according to an inscription), where the king picked up the tab for 69,574 of his closest friends.

The nearby relief panel labeled **Symbolic Scene** stood behind the throne. It shows the king (and his double) tending the tree of life while reaching up to receive the ring of kingship from the winged sun god.

• Exit the Nimrud Gallery at the far end, then hang a U-turn left (through Room 23). Pause at the entrance of Room 10 to see...

Two Winged Bulls from the Khorsabad Palace of Sargon II (c. 710 B.C.)

These marble bulls guarded the entrance to the city of Dur-Sharrukin ("Sargonsburg"), a new capital with vast palaces built by Sargon II (r. 721–705). The 30-ton bulls were cut from a single block, tipped on their sides, then dragged to their place by P.O.W.s. (In modern times, when the British transported them here, they had to cut them in half; see the horizontal cracks through the bulls' chests.)

Sargon II gained his reputation as a general subduing the Israelites after a three-year siege of Jerusalem (2 Kings 17:1–6). He solidified his conquest by ethnically cleansing the area, deporting many Israelites (inspiring legends of the "Lost" Ten Tribes).

In 710 B.C., while these bulls were being carved for his palace, Sargon II marched victorious through the streets of Babylon (modern Baghdad), having put down a revolt there against him. His descendants would also have to deal with the troublesome Babylonians.

• *Sneak between these bulls and veer right (into Room 10), where horses are being readied for the big hunt.*

Royal Lion Hunts

Lion-hunting was Assyria's sport of kings. On the right wall, see horses being readied for the hunt. On the left wall are the hunting dogs. And next to them, lions, resting peacefully in a garden, unaware that they will shortly be rousted, stampeded, and slaughtered.

Lions lived in Mesopotamia up until modern times, and it was the king's duty to keep the lion population down to protect farmers and herdsmen. This duty soon became sport, with staged hunts and zoo-bred lions, as the kings of men proved their power by taking on the king of beasts.

• *Enter the larger lion-hunt room. Reading the panels like a comic strip, start on the right and gallop counterclockwise.*

The Lion-Hunt Room (c. 650 B.C.)

They release the lions from their cages, then soldiers on horseback herd them into an enclosed arena. The king has them cornered. Let the slaughter begin. The chariot carries King Ashurbanipal, the great-grandson of Sargon II. The last of Assyria's great kings, he's ruled now for 50 years. Having left a half-dozen corpses in his wake, he moves on, while spearmen hold off lions attacking from the rear.

• *At about the middle of the long wall...*

The fleeing lions, cornered by hounds, shot through with arrows, and weighed down by fatigue, begin to fall. The lead lion carries on even while vomiting blood.

This low point of Assyrian cruelty is, perhaps, the high point of their artistic achievement. It's a curious coincidence that civilizations often produce their greatest art in their declining years. Hmm.
• *On the wall opposite the vomiting lion...*

Dying Lioness

A lioness roars in pain and frustration. She tries to run, but her body is too heavy. Her muscular hind legs, once the source of her power, are now paralyzed.

Like these brave, fierce lions, Assyria's once-great warrior nation was slain. Shortly after

Ashurbanipal's death, Assyria was conquered, and their capital at Nineveh was sacked and looted by an ascendant Babylon (612 B.C.). The mood of tragedy, dignity, and proud struggle in a hopeless cause makes this dying lioness simply one of the most beautiful of human creations.

• *Return to the huge, winged Assyrian lions (near the Rosetta Stone) by exiting the lion-hunt room at the far end. To reach the Greek section, exit Assyria between the winged lions and make a U-turn right, into Room 11. You'll walk past early Greek Barbie and Ken dolls from the Cycladic period (2500 B.C.). Continue into Room 12 (the hungry can go straight to the Gallery Café) and turn right, into Room 13, filled with Greek vases in glass cases.*

GREECE (600 B.C.–A.D. 1)

The history of ancient Greece could be subtitled "making order out of chaos." While Assyria was dominating the Middle East, "Greece"—a gaggle of warring tribes roaming the Greek peninsula— was floundering in darkness. But by around 700 B.C. these tribes began settling down, experimenting with democracy, forming self-governing city-states, and making ties with other city-states. Scarcely two centuries later, they would be a united community and the center of the civilized world.

During its "Golden Age" (500–430 B.C.), Greece set the tone for all of Western civilization to follow. Democracy, theater, literature, mathematics, philosophy, science, gyros, art, and architecture, as we know them, were virtually all invented by a single generation of Greeks in a small town of maybe 80,000 citizens.

British Museum—Greece

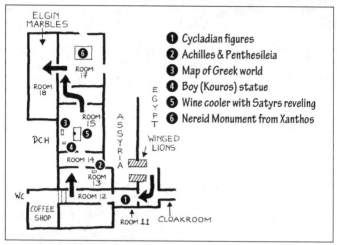

1 Cycladian figures
2 Achilles & Penthesileia
3 Map of Greek world
4 Boy (Kouros) statue
5 Wine cooler with Satyrs reveling
6 Nereid Monument from Xanthos

• *Near the middle of Room 13, find case #8, containing a...*

Black-Figured Amphora (Jar): Achilles and Penthesileia (540–530 B.C.)

Greeks poured wine from jars like this one, painted with a man stabbing a woman, a legend from the Trojan War. The Trojan War (c. 1200 B.C.)—part fact but mostly legend—symbolized Greece's long struggle to rise above war and chaos.

Achilles of Greece faces off against the Queen of the Amazons, Penthesileia, who was fighting for Troy. (The Amazons were a legendary race of warrior women who cut off one breast to facilitate their archery skills.) Achilles bears down, plunging a spear through her neck, as the blood spurts. In her dying moment, Penthesileia looks up and her gaze locks on Achilles. His eyes bulge wide, and he falls instantly in love with her. She dies and Achilles is smitten.

Pottery like this (and many others in the room), usually painted red and black, was a popular export product for the sea-trading Greeks. The earliest featured geometric patterns (8th century B.C.), then a painted black silhouette on the natural orange clay, then a red figure on a black background. On this jar, see the names of the two enemies/lovers ("AXILEV" and "PENOESIIEA") as well as the signature of the craftsman, Exekias.

• *Continue to Room 15, then relax on a bench and read, surrounded by statues and vases in glass cases. On the long wall, find a...*

Map of the Greek World (500–430 B.C.)

Athens was the most powerful of the city-states and the center of the Greek world. Golden Age Greece was never really a full-fledged empire, but more a common feeling of unity among Greek-speaking people.

A century after the Golden Age, Greek culture was spread still further by Alexander the Great, who conquered the Mediterranean world and beyond. By 300 B.C. the "Greek" world stretched from Italy and Egypt to India (including most of what used to be the Assyrian Empire). Two hundred years later, this Greek-speaking "Hellenistic Empire" was conquered by the Romans.

• *There's a nude male to the left of the map.*

Boy (Kouros) (490 B.C.)

The Greeks saw their gods in human form...and human beings were godlike. With his perfectly round head, symmetrical pecs, and navel in the center, this *Boy* exemplifies the divine orderliness of the universe. The ideal man was geometrically perfect, a balance of opposites, the "Golden Mean." In a statue, that meant finding the right balance between movement and stillness, between realistic human anatomy (with human flaws) and the perfection of a Greek god. This *Boy* is still a bit uptight, stiff as the rock from which he's carved. But—as we'll see—in just a few short decades, the Greeks would cut loose and create realistic statues that seemed to move like real humans.

• *In the glass case by the map, filled with decorated vases, find one in the center marked...*

Red-Figured Psykter (Wine Cooler) with Satyrs Reveling (490 B.C.)

This clay vase, designed to float in a bowl of cooling water, shows satyrs at a symposium, or drinking party. These half-man/half-animal creatures (notice their tails) had a reputation for lewd behavior, reminding the balanced and moderate Greeks of their rude roots.

The reveling figures painted on this jar (red on black) are more realistic, more three-dimensional, and suggest more natural movements than even the literally three-dimensional but quite stiff *Kouros* statue. The Greeks are beginning to conquer the natural world in art. The art, like life, is more in balance. And speaking of "balance," if that's a Greek sobriety test, revel on.

• *Carry on into Room 17 and sit facing the Greek temple at the far end.*

Nereid Monument from Xanthos (c. 400 B.C.)

Greek temples (like this reconstruction of a temple-shaped tomb) housed a statue of a god or goddess. Unlike Christian churches, which serve as meeting places, Greek temples were the gods' homes.

Worshipers gathered outside, so the most impressive part of the temple was its exterior. Temples were rectangular buildings surrounded by rows of columns and topped by slanted roofs.

The triangle-shaped roof, filled in with sculpture, is called the "pediment." The cross beams that support the pediment are called "metopes" (MET-uh-pees). Now look through the columns to the building itself. Above the doorway is another set of relief panels running around the building (under the eaves) called the "frieze."

Next, we'll see pediment, frieze, and metope decorations from Greece's greatest temple.

• *Leave the British Museum. Take the Tube to Heathrow and fly to Athens. In the center of the old city, on top of the high, flat hill known as the Acropolis, you'll find...*

The Parthenon (447–432 b.c.)

The Parthenon—the temple dedicated to Athena, goddess of wisdom and the patroness of Athens—was the crowning glory of an enormous urban-renewal plan during Greece's Golden Age. After Athens was ruined in a war with Persia, the city—under the

bold leadership of Pericles—constructed the greatest building of its day. The Parthenon was a model of balance, simplicity, and harmonious elegance, the symbol of the Golden Age. Phidias, the greatest Greek sculptor, decorated the exterior with statues and relief panels.

While the building itself remains in Athens, many of the Parthenon's best sculptures are right here in the British Museum—the so-called Elgin Marbles (pronounced with a hard "g"), named for the shrewd British ambassador who acquired them in 1816. Though the Greek government complains about losing its marbles, the Brits feel they rescued and preserved the sculptures. The often-bitter controversy continues.

• *Enter through the glass doors labeled The Parthenon Galleries.*

THE ELGIN MARBLES (450 b.c.)

The marble panels you see lining the walls of this large hall are part of the frieze that originally ran around the exterior of the Parthenon (under the eaves). The statues at either end of the hall once filled the Parthenon's triangular-shaped pediments. Near the pediment

British Museum—Elgin Marbles

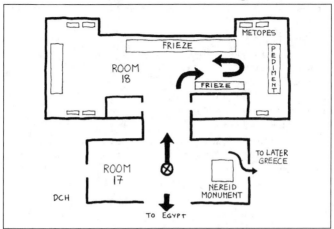

sculptures, we'll also find the relief panels known as metopes. Let's start with the frieze.

The Frieze

These 56 relief panels show Athens' "Fourth of July" parade, celebrating the birth of the city. On this day, citizens marched up the Acropolis to symbolically present a new robe to the 40-foot-tall gold-and-ivory statue of Athena housed in the Parthenon.

• *Start at the panels by the entrance (#136) and work counterclockwise.*

Men on horseback, chariots, musicians, children, animals for sacrifice, and young maidens with offerings are all part of the grand parade, all heading in the same direction—uphill. Prance on.

Notice the muscles and veins in the horses' legs (#130) and the intricate folds in the cloaks and dresses. Some panels have holes drilled in them, where gleaming bronze reins were fitted to heighten the festive look. Of course, all these panels were originally painted in realistic colors. Despite the bustle of figures posed every which way, the frieze has one unifying element—all the people's heads are at the same level, creating a single ribbon around the Parthenon.

• *Cross to the opposite wall.*

A three-horse chariot (#67) cut out of only a few inches of marble is more lifelike and three-dimensional than anything the Egyptians achieved in a freestanding statue.

Enter the girls (#61), the heart of the procession. Dressed in pleated robes, they shuffle past the parade marshals, carrying incense burners and jugs of wine and bowls to pour out an offering to the thirsty gods.

The procession culminates (#35) in the presentation of the robe to Athena. A man and a child fold the robe for the goddess while the rest of the gods look on. There are Zeus and Hera (#29), the king and queen of the gods, seated, enjoying the fashion show and wondering what length hemlines will be this year.

• *Head for the set of pediment sculptures at the right end of the hall.*

The Pediment Sculptures

These statues are nestled nicely in the triangular pediment above the columns at the Parthenon's main (east) entrance. The missing statues at the peak of the triangle once showed the birth of Athena. Zeus had his head split open, allowing Athena, the goddess of wisdom, to rise from his brain fully grown and fully armed, inaugurating the Golden Age of Athens.

The other gods at this Olympian banquet slowly become aware of the amazing event. The first to notice is the one closest to them, Hebe, the cup-bearer of the gods (tallest surviving fragment). Frightened, she runs to tell the others, her dress whipping behind her. A startled Demeter (just left of Hebe) turns toward Hebe.

The only one who hasn't lost his head is laid-back Dionysus (the cool guy further left). He just raises another glass of wine to his lips. Over on the right, Aphrodite, goddess of love, leans back into her mother's lap, too busy admiring her own bare shoulder even to notice the hubbub. A chess-set horse's head screams, "These people are nuts—let me out of here!"

The scene had a message. Just as wise Athena rose above the lesser gods, who were scared, drunk, or vain, so would her city,

Athens, rise above her lesser rivals.

This is amazing workmanship. Compare Dionysus, with his natural, relaxed, reclining pose, to all those stiff Egyptian statues standing eternally at attention.

Centaurs Slain around the World

Dateline 500 B.C.—Greece, China, India: Man no longer considers himself an animal. Bold new ideas are exploding simultaneously around the world. Socrates, Confucius, Buddha, and others are independently discovering a nonmaterial, unseen order in nature and in man. They say man has a rational mind or soul. He's separate from nature and different from the other animals.

Appreciate the folds of the clothes on the female figures (on the right half), especially Aphrodite's clinging, rumpled robe. Some sculptors would first build a nude model of their figure, put real clothes on it, and study how the cloth hung down before actually sculpting in marble. Others found inspiration at the *taverna* on wet T-shirt night.

Even without their heads, these statues, with their detailed anatomy and expressive poses, speak volumes.

Wander behind. The statues originally sat 40 feet above the ground. The backs of the statues, which were never intended to be seen, are almost as detailed as the fronts.

• *The metopes are the panels on the walls to either side. Start with "South Metope XXXI" on the right wall, center.*

The Metopes

In #XXXI, a centaur grabs a man by the throat while the man pulls his hair (see sidebar above). The humans have invited some centaurs—wild half-man/half-horse creatures—to a wedding feast. All goes well until the brutish centaurs, the original party animals, get too drunk and try to carry off the women. A battle ensues.

The Greeks prided themselves on creating order out of chaos. Within just a few generations, they went from nomadic barbarism to the pinnacle of early Western civilization. These metopes tell the story of this struggle between the forces of human civilization and animal-like barbarism.

In #XXVIII (opposite wall, center), the centaurs start to get the upper hand as one rears back and prepares to trample the helpless man. The leopard skin draped over the centaur's arm roars a taunt. The humans lose face.

In #XXVII, the humans finally rally and drive off the brutish centaurs. A centaur tries to run, but the man grabs him by the neck and raises his right hand (missing) to run him through. The man's folded cloak sets off his smooth skin and graceful figure.

The centaurs have been defeated. Civilization has triumphed over barbarism, order over chaos, and rational man over his half-animal alter ego.

Why are the Elgin Marbles so treasured? The British of the 19th century saw themselves as the new "civilized" race, subduing "barbarians" in their far-flung empire. Maybe these rocks made them stop and wonder—will our great civilization also turn to rubble?

The Rest of the British Museum

You've toured only the foundations of Western civilization on the ground floor, West Wing. Upstairs you'll find still more artifacts from these lands, plus Rome and the medieval civilization that sprang from it. Some highlights:

- Lindow Man (a.k.a. the "Bog Man") in Room 50. This victim of a Druid human-sacrifice ritual, with wounds still visible, was preserved for 2,000 years in a peat bog.
- The 7th-century Anglo-Saxon Sutton Hoo Burial Ship (Room 41).
- The only existing, complete cartoon by Michelangelo (Room 90).

But, of course, history doesn't begin and end in Europe. Look for remnants of the sophisticated, exotic cultures of Asia and the Americas (in North Wing, ground floor) and Africa (downstairs)—all part of the totem pole of the human family.

NATIONAL GALLERY

The National Gallery lets you tour Europe's art without ever crossing the Channel. With so many exciting artists and styles, it's a fine overture to art if you're just starting a European trip and a pleasant reprise if you're just finishing. The "National Gal" is always a welcome interlude from the bustle of London sightseeing.

ORIENTATION

Cost: Free.

Hours: Daily 10:00–18:00, Wed until 21:00.

Getting There: It's central as can be, overlooking Trafalgar Square, a 15-minute walk from Big Ben and 10 minutes from Piccadilly. The closest Tube stop is Charing Cross or Leicester Square. Take your pick of buses: #3, #6, #9, #11, #12, #13, #15, #23, #24, #29, #53, #88, #91, #94, or #109.

Information: The information desk in the lobby offers a free, handy floor plan. Find the latest events schedule and a listing of free lunchtime lectures in the complimentary "National Gallery News" flier. Drop by the Micro Gallery, a computer room even your dad would enjoy (closes 30 min earlier than museum); you can study any artist, style, or topic in the museum, and print out a tailor-made tour map (tel. 020/7839-3321, recorded information tel. 020/7747-2885, www.nationalgallery.org.uk).

Tours: Free one-hour overview tours are offered daily at 11:30 and 14:30 (also Wed at 18:30). Excellent audioguide tours (suggested £4 donation) let you dial up info on any painting in the museum.

Length of This Tour: 90 minutes.

Cloakroom: Free cloakrooms are at each entrance. You can take in a small bag.

Photography: Photos are strictly forbidden.

Cuisine Art: Crivelli's Garden Restaurant (first floor, Sainsbury Wing), while expensive, is a cool and classy place for a meal. Cheaper eateries abound in and around the museum. A block away, there's a good cafeteria in the crypt of St. Martin-in-the-Fields church (facing Trafalgar Square).

Starring: You name it—da Vinci, Raphael, Titian, Rembrandt, Monet, and van Gogh.

THE TOUR BEGINS

Of the two entrances that face Trafalgar Square, enter through the smaller building to the left (as you face it) of the main, domed entrance. Pick up the free map and climb the stairs. At the top, turn left and grab a seat in Room 51, facing Leonardo's *Virgin of the Rocks.*

The National Gallery offers a quick overview of European art history. We'll stay on one floor, working chronologically through medieval holiness, Renaissance realism, Dutch detail, Baroque excess, British restraint, and the colorful French Impressionism that leads to the modern world. Cruise like an eagle with wide eyes for the big picture, seeing how each style progresses into the next.

Leonardo da Vinci—*The Virgin of the Rocks* (1508)

Mary, the mother of Jesus, plays with her son and little Johnny the Baptist (with cross, at left) while an androgynous angel looks on. Leonardo brings this holy scene right down to earth, by setting it among rocks, stalactites, water, and flowering plants. But looking closer, we see that Leonardo has deliberately posed his people into a pyramid shape, with Mary's head at the peak, creating an oasis of maternal stability and serenity amid the hard rock of the earth. Leonardo, who was illegitimate, may have sought, in his art, the young mother he never knew. Freud thought so.

• *We'll circle back around to Leonardo in a couple hundred years. But first, turn your back on the Renaissance and cruise through the medieval world in Rooms 52, 53, and 54.*

Medieval and Early Renaissance (1260–1440)

Shiny gold paintings of saints, angels, Madonnas, and crucifixions floating in an ethereal gold never-never land. One thing is very clear: Medieval heaven was different from medieval earth. The holy wore gold plates on their heads. Faces were serene and generic. People posed stiffly, facing directly out or to the side, never in between. Saints are recognized by the symbols they carry (a key, a sword, a book), rather than by their human features.

Middle Ages art was religious, dominated by the Church. The illiterate faithful could meditate on an altarpiece and visualize heaven. It's as though they couldn't imagine saints and angels inhabiting the dreary world of rocks, trees, and sky we live in.

• *One of the finest medieval altarpieces is in a glass case in Room 53.*

Anonymous—*The Wilton Diptych* (c. 1395)

Three kings (left panel) come to adore Mary and her rosy-cheeked baby (right panel), surrounded by flame-like angels. Despite the gold-leaf background, a glimmer of human realism peeks through. The kings have distinct, down-to-earth faces. And the back side shows not a saint, not a god, not a symbol, but a real-life deer lying down in the grass of this earth.

Still, the anonymous artist is struggling with reality. John the Baptist (among the kings) is holding a "lamb of God" that looks more like a Chihuahua. Nice try. Mary's exquisite fingers hold an anatomically impossible little foot. The figures are flat, scrawny, and sinless, with cartoon features—far from flesh-and-blood human beings.

• *Walking straight through Room 54 into Room 55, you'll leave this gold-leaf peace and find…*

Uccello—*Battle of San Romano* (c. 1450)

This colorful battle scene shows the victory of Florence over Siena—and the battle for literal realism on the canvas. It's an early Renaissance attempt at a realistic, nonreligious, three-dimensional scene.

National Gallery Highlights

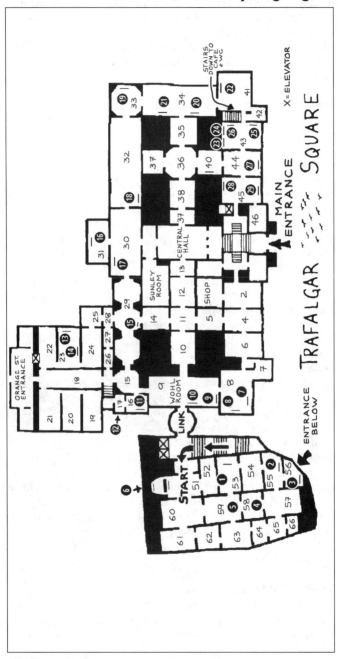

MEDIEVAL & EARLY RENAISSANCE
1. Wilton Diptych
2. UCCELLO Battle of San Romano
3. VAN EYCK Arnolfini Marriage
4. BOTTICELLI Venus and Mars
5. CRIVELLI Annunciation with St. Emidius

HIGH RENAISSANCE
6. LEONARDO DA VINCI Virgin and Child (painting and cartoon)

NATIONAL GALLERY MAIN BUILDING - HIGH RENAISSANCE
7. MICHELANGELO Entombment
8. RAPHAEL Pope Julius II

VENETIAN RENAISSANCE
9. TITIAN Bacchus and Ariadne
10. TINTORETTO Origin of the Milky Way

NORTHERN PROTESTANT ART
11. VERMEER Young Woman
12. "A PEEPSHOW"
13. REMBRANDT Belshazzar's Feast
14. REMBRANDT Self-Portrait

BAROQUE & ROCOCO
15. RUBENS The Judgment of Paris
16. VAN DYCK Charles I on Horseback
17. VELAZQUEZ The Rokeby Venus
18. CARAVAGGIO Supper at Emmaus
19. BOUCHER Pan and Syrinx

BRITISH
20. CONSTABLE The Hay Wain
21. TURNER The Fighting Temeraire
22. DELAROCHE The Execution of Lady Jane Grey

IMPRESSIONISM & BEYOND
23. MONET Gare St. Lazare
24. MONET The Water Lily Pond
25. MANET The Waitress (Corner of a Café-Concert)
26. RENOIR Boating on the Seine
27. SEURAT Bathers at Asnières
28. VAN GOGH Sunflowers
29. CEZANNE Bathers

Uccello challenges his ability by posing the horses and soldiers at every conceivable angle. The background of farmyards, receding hedges, and tiny soldiers creates an illusion of distance. In the foreground, Uccello the artist

actually constructs a grid of fallen lances, then places the horses and warriors within it. Still, Uccello hasn't quite worked out the bugs—the figures in the distance are far too big and the fallen soldier on the left isn't much bigger than the fallen shield on the right.
•*In Room 56, you'll find...*

Van Eyck—*The Arnolfini Marriage* (1434)

Called by some "The Shotgun Wedding," this painting of a simple ceremony (set in Bruges, Belgium) is a masterpiece of down-to-earth details. The solemn, well-dressed couple take their vows, with hands joined in the center.

Van Eyck has built a medieval dollhouse, inviting us to linger over the furnishings. Feel the texture of the fabrics, count the terrier's hairs, trace the shadows generated by the window. Each object is painted at an ideal angle, with the details you'd see if you were standing right in front of it. So, the strings of beads hanging on the back wall are as crystal clear as the bracelets on the bride.

And to top it off, look into the round mirror on the far wall— the whole scene is reflected backward in miniature, showing the loving couple and two mysterious visitors. Is it the concerned parents? The minister? Van Eyck himself at his easel? Or has the artist painted you, the home viewer, into the scene?

The surface detail is extraordinary, but the painting lacks true Renaissance depth. The tiny room looks unnaturally narrow, cramped, and claustrophobic.

In medieval times (this was painted only a generation after *The Wilton Diptych*), everyone could read the hidden meaning of certain symbols—the chandelier with its one lit candle (love), the fruit on the windowsill (fertility), the dangling whisk broom (the bride's domestic responsibilities), and the terrier (Fido—fidelity).

By the way, she may not be pregnant. The fashion of the day was to wear a pillow to look pregnant in hopes you'd soon get that

way. At least, that's what they told their parents.
• *Return to Room 55, turn left into Room 57, then turn right into Room 58.*

THE ITALIAN RENAISSANCE (1400–1550)

The Renaissance—or "rebirth" of the culture of ancient Greece and Rome—was a cultural boom that changed people's thinking about every aspect of life. In politics, it meant democracy. In religion, it meant a move away from Church dominance and toward the assertion of man (humanism) and a more personal faith. Science and secular learning were revived after centuries of superstition and ignorance. In architecture, it was a return to the balanced columns and domes of Greece and Rome.

In painting, the Renaissance meant realism. Artists rediscovered the beauty of nature and the human body. With pictures of beautiful people in harmonious, 3-D surroundings, they expressed the optimism and confidence of this new age.

Botticelli—*Venus and Mars* (c. 1485)
Mars takes a break from war, succumbing to the delights of love (Venus), while impish satyrs play innocently with the discarded tools of death. In the early spring of the Renaissance, there was an optimistic mood in the air, the feeling that enlightened Man could solve all problems, narrowing the gap between mortals and the Greek gods. Artists felt free to use the pagan Greek gods as symbols of human traits, virtues, and vices. Venus has sapped man's medieval stiffness, and the Renaissance is coming.
• *Continue to Room 59.*

Crivelli—*The Annunciation with Saint Emidius* (1486)
Mary, in green, is visited by the dove of the Holy Ghost, who beams down from the distant heavens in a shaft of light.

Like Van Eyck's wedding, this is a brilliant collection of realistic details. Notice the hanging rug, the peacock, the architectural minutiae that lead you way, way back, then bam—you have a giant pickle in your face.

It combines meticulous detail with Italian spaciousness. The floor tiles and building bricks recede into the distance. We're sucked right in, accelerating through the alleyway, under the arch, and off into space. The Holy Ghost spans the entire distance, connecting heavenly background with earthly foreground. Crivelli creates an Escher-esque labyrinth of rooms and walkways that we want to walk through, around, and into—or is that just a male thing?

Renaissance Italians were interested in—even obsessed with—portraying 3-D space. Perhaps they focused their spiritual passion away from heaven and toward the physical world. With such restless energy, they needed lots of elbow room. Space, the final frontier.

• *Just two rooms ahead is the Leonardo in Room 51, where we started.*

The High Renaissance (1500)

With the "Big Three" of the High Renaissance—Leonardo, Michelangelo, and Raphael—painters had finally conquered realism. But these three Florence-trained artists weren't content just to copy nature, cranking out photographs-on-canvas. Like Renaissance architects (which they also were), they carefully composed their figures on the canvas, "building" them into geometrical patterns that reflected the balance and order they saw in nature.

• *In Room 51, enter the small, dark cave behind Leonardo's* Virgin of the Rocks.

Leonardo da Vinci—*Virgin and Child with St. John the Baptist and St. Anne* (c. 1499–1500)

At first glance, this chalk drawing, or cartoon, looks like a simple snapshot of two loving moms and two playful kids. The two children play—oblivious to the violent deaths they'll both suffer—beneath their mothers' Mona Lisa smiles.

But follow the eyes: Shadowy-eyed Anne turns toward Mary,

who looks tenderly down to Jesus, who blesses John, who gazes back dreamily. As your eyes follow theirs, you're led back to the literal and psychological center of the composition—Jesus—the alpha and omega. Without resorting to heavy-handed medieval symbolism, Leonardo drives home a theological concept in a natural, human way. Leonardo the perfectionist rarely finished paintings. This sketch—pieced together from two separate

---

Painting: From Tempera to Tubes

The technology of painting has evolved over the centuries.

1400s: Artists used tempera (pigments dissolved in egg yolk) on wood.

1500s: Still painting on wood, artists mainly used oil (pigments dissolved in vegetable oil, such as linseed, walnut, or poppy).

1600s: Artists applied oil paints to canvases stretched across wooden frames.

1850: Paints in convenient, collapsible tubes are invented, making open-air painting feasible.

The Frames: Although some frames are original, having been chosen by the artist, most are selected by museum curators. Some are old frames from another painting, some are Victorian-era reproductions in wood, and some are recent reproductions made of a composition substance to look like gilded wood.

---

papers (see the line down the middle)—gives us an inside peek at his genius.

• *Cross to the main building (the West Wing) and enter the large Room 9. We'll return to these big, colorful canvases, but first, turn right into Room 8. (Note: The following two paintings may currently be displayed in Room 2.)*

Michelangelo—*Entombment,* unfinished (c. 1500–1501)

Michelangelo, the greatest sculptor ever, proves it here in this "painted sculpture" of the crucified Jesus being carried to the tomb. Like a chiseled Greek god, the musclehead in red ripples beneath his clothes. Christ's naked body, shocking to the medieval Church, was completely acceptable in the Renaissance world, where classical nudes were admired as an expression of the divine.

Renaissance balance and symmetry reign. Christ is the center of the composition, flanked by two equally leaning people who support his body with strips of cloth. They, in turn, are flanked by two more.

Where Leonardo gave us expressive faces, Michelangelo lets the bodies do the talking. The two supporters strain to hold up Christ's body, and in their tension we, too, feel the great weight and tragedy of their dead god. Michelangelo expresses the divine through the human form.

Raphael—*Pope Julius II* (1511)

The new worldliness of the Renaissance even reached the Church. Pope Julius II, who was more a swaggering conquistador than a pious pope, set out to rebuild Rome in Renaissance style, hiring Michelangelo to paint the ceiling of the Vatican's Sistine Chapel.

Raphael gives a behind-the-scenes look at this complex man. On the one hand, the pope is an imposing pyramid of power, with a velvet shawl, silk shirt, and fancy rings boasting of wealth and success. But at the same time, he's a bent and broken man, his throne backed into a corner, with an expression that seems to say, "Is this all there is?"

In fact, the great era of Florence and Rome was coming to an end. With Raphael's death in 1520, the Renaissance shifted to Venice.

• *Return to the long Room 9.*

Venetian Renaissance (1510–1600)

Big change. The canvases are bigger, the colors brighter. Madonnas and saints are being replaced by goddesses and heroes. And there are nudes—not Michelangelo's lumps of noble, knotted muscle, but smooth-skinned, sexy, golden centerfolds.

Venice got wealthy by trading with the luxurious and exotic East. Its happy-go-lucky art style shows a taste for the finer things in life.

Titian—*Bacchus and Ariadne* (1523)

Bacchus, the god of wine, leaps from his leopard-drawn chariot, his red cape blowing behind him, to cheer up Ariadne (far left), who has been jilted by her lover. Bacchus' motley entourage rattles cymbals, bangs on tambourines, and literally shakes a leg.

Man and animal mingle in this pre-Christian orgy, with leopards, a snake, a dog, and the severed head and leg of an ass ready for the barbecue. Man and animal also literally "mix" in the satyrs—part man, part goat. The fat, sleepy guy in the background has had too much.

Titian (see his "Ticianus" signature on the gold vase, lower left) uses a pyramid composition to balance an otherwise chaotic scene. Follow Ariadne's gaze up to the peak of Bacchus' flowing cape, then down along the snake handler's spine to the lower-right corner. In addition, he balances the picture with harmonious colors—blue sky on the left, green trees on the right, while the two main figures stand out with loud splotches of red.

Tintoretto—*The Origin of the Milky Way* (c. 1575)

In another classical myth, the god Jupiter places his illegitimate son, baby Hercules, at his wife's breast. Juno says, "Wait a minute. That's not my baby!" Her milk spurts upward, becoming the Milky Way.

Tintoretto places us right up in the clouds, among the gods, who swirl around at every angle. Jupiter appears to be flying almost right at us. An X composition unites it all—Juno slants one way while Jupiter slants the other.

• *Exit Room 9 at the far end and turn left into Room 16 for Dutch art.*

Northern Protestant Art (1600–1700)

We switch from CinemaScope to a tiny TV—smaller canvases, subdued colors, everyday scenes, and not even a bare shoulder.

Money shapes art. While Italy had wealthy aristocrats and the powerful Catholic Church to purchase art, the North's patrons were middle-class, hardworking, Protestant merchants. They wanted simple, cheap, no-nonsense pictures to decorate their homes and offices. Greek gods and Virgin Marys were out, hometown folks and hometown places were in—portraits, landscapes, still lifes, and slice-of-life scenes. Painted with great attention to detail, this is art meant not to wow or preach at you, but to be enjoyed and lingered over. Sightsee.

Vermeer—*A Young Woman Standing at a Virginal* (c. 1670)

Inside a simple Dutch home, a prim virgin plays an early piano called a "virginal." We've surprised her and she pauses to look up at us.

Vermeer, by framing off such a small world to look at—from the blue chair in the foreground to the wall in back—forces us to appreciate the tiniest details, the beauty of everyday things. We can meditate on the tiles lining the floor, the subtle shades of the white wall, and the pale, dif-

fused light that seeps in from the window. Amid straight lines and rectangles, the woman's billowing dress adds a soft touch. The painting of a nude cupid on the back wall only strengthens this virgin's purity.

• *In Room 17, you'll find...*

A Peepshow

Look through the holes at the ends of this ingenious device to make the painting of a house interior come to three-dimensional life. Compare the twisted curves of the painting with the illusion it creates and appreciate the painstaking work of dedicated artists.

• *Zigzag—right, left, right, left—through Rooms 15, 18, and 24 to Room 23.*

Rembrandt—*Belshazzar's Feast* (c. 1635)

The wicked king has been feasting with God's sacred dinnerware when the meal is interrupted. Belshazzar turns to see the hand of God, burning an ominous message into the wall that Belshazzar's number is up. As he turns, he knocks over a goblet of wine. We see the jewels and riches of his decadent life.

Rembrandt captures the scene at the most ironic moment. Belshazzar is about to be ruined. We know it, his guests know it, and, judging by the look on his face, he's coming to the same conclusion.

Rembrandt's flair for the dramatic is accentuated by the strong contrast between light and dark. Most of his canvases are a rich, dark brown, with a few crucial details highlighted by a bright light.

Rembrandt—*Self-Portrait* (1669)

Rembrandt throws the light of truth on...himself. This craggy self-portrait was done the year he died, at age 63. Contrast it with one done three decades earlier (hanging nearby). Rembrandt, the greatest Dutch painter, started out as the successful, wealthy young genius of the art world. But he refused to crank out commercial works. Rembrandt painted things that he believed in but no one would invest in— family members, down-to-earth Bible scenes, and self-portraits like these.

Here, Rembrandt surveys the wreckage of his independent life. He was bankrupt, his mistress had just died, and he had also buried several of his children. We see a disillusioned, well-worn, but proud old genius.

• *Backtrack through several rooms to the long Room 29, with mint-green wallpaper.*

BAROQUE (1600–1700)

Rubens

This room holds big, colorful, emotional works by Peter Paul Rubens and others from Catholic Flanders (Belgium). While Protestant and democratic Europe painted simple scenes, Catholic and aristocratic countries turned to the style called Baroque. Baroque art took what was flashy in Venetian art and made it flashier, gaudy and made it gaudier, dramatic and made it shocking.

Rubens painted anything that would raise your pulse—battles, miracles, hunts, and, especially, fleshy women with dimples on all four cheeks. *The Judgment of Paris,* for instance, is little more than an excuse for a study of the female nude, showing front, back, and profile all on one canvas.

• *Exit Room 29 at the far end. To the left, in Room 31, you'll see the large canvas of...*

Van Dyck—*Charles I on Horseback* (c. 1637–1638)

King Charles sits on a huge horse, accentuating his power. The horse's small head makes sure that little Charles isn't dwarfed. Charles ruled firmly as a Catholic king in a Protestant country until England's Civil War (1648), when his genteel head was separated from his refined body by Cromwell and company.

Kings and bishops used the grandiose Baroque style to impress the masses with their power. Van Dyck's portrait style set the tone for all the stuffy, boring portraits of British aristocrats who wished to be portrayed as sophisticated gentlemen—whether they were or not.

• *For the complete opposite of a stuffy portrait, backpedal into Room 30 for...*

Velázquez—*The Rokeby Venus* (c. 1647–1651)

Like a Venetian centerfold, she lounges diagonally across the canvas, admiring herself, with flaring red, white, and gray fabrics to highlight her rosy-white skin and inflame our passion. Horny Spanish kings loved Titian-esque nudes, despite that country's strict Inquisition. This work by the king's personal court painter is the first (and, for over a century, the only) Spanish nude. About the only  concession to Spanish modesty is the false reflection in the mirror—if it really showed what the angle should show, Velázquez would have needed two mirrors…and a new job.

• *Turning your left cheek to hers, tango into Room 32.*

Michelangelo Merisi de da Caravaggio— The Supper at Emmaus (1601)

After Jesus was crucified, he rose from the dead and appeared without warning to some of his followers. Jesus just wants a quiet meal, but the man in green, suddenly realizing who he's eating with, is about to jump out of his chair in shock. To the right, a man spreads his hands in amazement, bridging the distance between Christ and us by sticking his hand in our face.

Baroque took reality and exaggerated it. Most artists amplified the prettiness, but Caravaggio exaggerated the grittiness, using real, ugly, unhaloed people in Bible scenes. Caravaggio's paintings look like a wet dog smells. Reality.

We've come a long way since the first medieval altarpieces that wrapped holy people in gold foil. From the torn shirts to the five o'clock shadows, from the blemished apples to the uneven part in Jesus' hair, we are witnessing a very human miracle.

• *Leave the Caravaggio Room at the far end, under the sign reading "East Wing, painting from 1700–1900," and enter Room 33.*

FRENCH ROCOCO (1700–1800)

As Europe's political and economic center shifted from Italy to France, Louis XIV's court at Versailles became its cultural hub. Every aristocrat spoke French, dressed French, and bought French paintings. The Rococo art of Louis' successors was as frilly, sensual, and suggestive as the decadent French court. We see their rosy-cheeked portraits and their fantasies: lords and ladies at play in classical gardens where mortals and gods cavort together.

• *One of the finest examples is the tiny…*

Boucher—*Pan and Syrinx* (1739-1759)

Curious Pan seeks a threesome, but Syrinx eventually changes to reeds, leaving him all wet.

Rococo art is like a Rubens that got shrunk in the wash—smaller, lighter pastel colors, frillier, and more delicate than the Baroque style. Same dimples, though.

• *Enter Room 34.*

BRITISH (1800–1850)

Constable—*The Hay Wain* (1821)

The more reserved British were more comfortable cavorting with nature than with the lofty gods. Come-as-you-are poets like Wordsworth found the same ecstasy just being outside.

John Constable set up his easel out-of-doors, painstakingly capturing the simple majesty of billowing clouds, billowing trees, and everyday rural life. Even British portraits (by Thomas Gainsborough and others) placed refined lords and ladies amid idealized greenery.

This simple style—believe it or not—was considered shocking in its day. The rough, thick, earth-toned paint and crude country settings scandalized art-lovers used to the highfalutin, prettified sheen of Baroque and Rococo.

• *Take a hike and enjoy the English-country-garden ambience of this room.*

Turner—*The Fighting Téméraire* (before 1839)

Constable's landscape was about to be paved over by the Industrial Revolution. Soon, machines began to replace humans, factories belched smoke over Constable's hay cart, and cloud-gazers had to punch the clock. Romantics tried to resist it, lauding the forces of nature and natural human emotions in the face of technological "progress." But alas, here a modern steamboat symbolically drags a famous but obsolete sailing battleship off into the sunset to be destroyed.

Turner's messy, colorful style gives us our first glimpse into the modern art world—he influenced the Impressionists. Turner takes an ordinary scene (like Constable), captures the play of light with messy paints (like Impressionists), and charges it with mystery (like, wow).

• *Enter Room 41.*

Paul Delaroche—*The Execution of Lady Jane Grey* (1833)

The teenage queen's nine-day reign has reached its curfew. This simple girl, manipulated into power politics by cunning advisors, is now sent to the execution site in the Tower of London. As her

friends swoon with grief, she's blindfolded and forced to kneel at the block. Legend has it that the confused, humiliated girl was left kneeling on the scaffold. She crawled around, groping for the chopping block, crying out, "Where is it? What am I supposed to do?" The executioner in scarlet

looks on with as much compassion as he can muster.

Britain's distinct contribution to art history is this Pre-Raphaelite style, showing medieval scenes in luminous realism with a mood of understated tragedy.

• *Exit Room 41, pass the door that leads downstairs to the café and WC, and enter Room 43. The Impressionist paintings are scattered throughout Rooms 43–46.*

IMPRESSIONISM AND BEYOND (1850–1910)

For 500 years, a great artist was someone who could paint the real world with perfect accuracy. Then along came the camera and, click, the artist was replaced by a machine. But unemployed artists refused to go the way of *The Fighting Téméraire.*

They couldn't match the camera for painstaking detail, but they could match it—even beat it—in capturing color, the fleeting moment, the candid pose, the play of light and shadow, the quick impression a scene makes on you. A new breed of artists burst out of the stuffy confines of the studio. They donned scarves and berets and set up their canvases in farmers' fields or carried their notebooks into a crowded café, dashing off quick sketches in order to catch a momentary…impression.

• *Start with the misty Monet train station.*

Monet—*Gare St. Lazare* (1877)

Claude Monet, the father of Impressionism, was more interested in the play of light off his subject than the subject itself. He uses smudges of white and gray paint to capture how sun filters through the glass roof of the train station and is refiltered through the clouds of steam.

Monet—*The Water-Lily Pond* (1916–1899)

We've traveled from medieval spirituality to Renaissance realism to Baroque elegance and Impressionist colors.  Before you spill out into the 21st-century hubbub of busy London, relax for a second in Monet's garden at Giverny, near Paris. Monet planned an artificial garden, rechanneled a stream, built a bridge, and planted these water lilies—a living work of art, a small section of order and calm in a hectic world.

Manet—*The Waitress (Corner of a Café-Concert, 1878–1880)*

Imagine how mundane (and therefore shocking) Manet's quick "impression" of this café must have been to a public that was raised on Greek gods, luscious nudes, and glowing Madonnas.

Renoir—*Boating on the Seine* (1879–1880)

It's a nice scene of boats on sun-dappled water. Now move in close. The "scene" breaks up into almost random patches of bright colors. The "blue" water is actually separate brushstrokes of blue, green, pink, purple, gray, white, etc. The rower's hat is a blob of green, white, and blue. Up close, it looks like a mess, but when you back up to a proper distance, voilà! It shimmers. This kind of rough, coarse brushwork (where you can actually see the brush strokes) is one of the telltale signs of Impressionism. Renoir was not trying to paint the water itself, but the reflection of sky, shore, and boats off its surface.

• *In Room 44, you'll see…*

Seurat—*Bathers at Asnières* (1883–1884)

Viewed from about 15 feet away, this is a bright sunny scene of people lounging on a riverbank. Up close it's a mess of dots, showing the Impressionist color technique taken to its logical extreme. The "green" grass is a shag rug of green, yellow, red, brown, purple, and white brush strokes. The boy's "red" cap is a collage of red, yellow, and blue.

Seurat has "built" the scene dot by dot, like a newspaper photo, using small points of different, bright colors. Only at a distance do the individual brushstrokes blend together. Impressionism is all about color. Even people's shadows are not dingy black, but warm blues, greens, and purples.

• *In Room 45…*

Van Gogh—*Sunflowers* (1888)

In military terms, van Gogh was the point man of his culture. He went ahead of his cohorts, explored the unknown, and caught a bullet young. He added emotion to Impressionism, infusing his love of life even into inanimate objects. These sunflowers, painted with characteristic swirling brush-strokes, shimmer and writhe in either agony or ecstasy—depending on your own mood.

Van Gogh painted these during his stay in southern France, a time of frenzied creativity, when he himself hovered between agony and ecstasy, bliss and madness. A year later, he shot himself.

In his day, van Gogh was a penniless nobody, selling only one painting in his whole career. Fairly recently, a *Sunflowers* (he did a half dozen versions) sold for $40 million (a salary of about $2,500 a day for 45 years), and it's not even his highest-priced painting. Hmm.

Cézanne—*Bathers* (*Les Grandes Baigneuses,* c. 1900–1906)

These bathers are arranged in strict triangles à la Leonardo—the five nudes on the left form one triangle, the seated nude on the right forms another, and even the background trees and clouds are triangular patterns of paint.

Cézanne uses the Impressionist technique of building a figure with dabs of paint (though his "dabs" are often larger-sized "cube" shapes) to make solid, 3-D geometrical figures in the style of the Renaissance. In the process, his cube shapes helped inspire a radical new art style—Cube-ism—bringing art into the 20th century.

BRITISH LIBRARY

The British Empire built its greatest monuments out of paper. It's with literature that England has made her lasting contribution to history and the arts. These national archives of Britain include more than 12 million books, 180 miles of shelving, and the deepest basement in London. But everything that matters for your visit is in one delightful room labeled Treasures. We'll concentrate on a handful of documents—literary and historical—that changed the course of history. Start with the top stops (described in this tour), then stray according to your interests.

ORIENTATION

Cost: Free.

Hours: Mon–Fri 9:30–18:00 (until 20:00 on Tue), Sat 9:30–17:00, Sun 11:00–17:00.

Getting There: Take the Tube to King's Cross. Leaving the station, turn right and walk a block to 96 Euston Road.

Information: Tel. 020/7412-7000, www.bl.uk.

Tours: One-hour general building tours are usually offered on Mon, Wed, and Fri–Sun at 15:00, Sat at 10:30, and Sun at 11:30 (£5; to confirm schedule and to reserve, tel. 020/7412-7332). A £3.50 audioguide giving a 45-minute tour of the Treasures is available at the information desk (photo ID and £20 deposit required).

Length of This Tour: One hour.

Cloakroom: Free. Lockers require £1 coin deposit (no large bags).

No-no's: No photography, smoking, or chewing gum.

Cuisine Art: A great cafeteria/restaurant that serves good hot meals is upstairs above the ground-floor café,which is next to a vast and fun pull-out stamp collection. The 50-foot-tall wall of 65,000 books within the cafés was given to the people by King George IV in 1823. This high-tech bookshelf is behind glass and has movable lifts.

Starring: Magna Carta, Bibles, Shakespeare, English Lit 101, and the Beatles.

THE TOUR BEGINS

Entering the library courtyard, you'll see a big statue of a naked Isaac Newton bending forward with a compass to measure the universe. The statue symbolizes the library's purpose: to gather all knowledge and promote our endless search for truth.

Stepping inside, you'll see the information desk and café. The cloakroom and WC are down a short staircase to the right. The reading rooms upstairs are not open to the public. Our tour is in the tiny but exciting area to the left, under the sign marked Exhibitions. While this zone has three sections, 90 percent of the thrills are contained in the room marked Treasures—and that's what we'll tour.

The priceless literary and historical treasures of the collection are in this one carefully designed and well-lit room. The Turning the Pages computer room (where you can electronically leaf through several rare manuscripts) is next door. Down a few steps you'll find the Pearson Gallery, with temporary exhibits usually requiring an admission charge.

❶ Maps

Navigate the wall of historic maps from left to right. "A Medieval Map of Britain," from 1250, puts medieval man in an unusual position—looking down on his homeland from 50 miles in the air. "Charting the Seas," from c. 1325, shows a well-defined west coast of Europe as European sailors ventured cautiously out of the Mediterranean. By 1564, you could plan your next trip to Britain with the map of "Mercator's Britain." "The End of a Tradition" (1688) has the world well-mapped, except that the United States has a Miami Beach perspective: Florida plus a lot of unexplored interior inhabited by strange beasts.

❷ Bibles

My favorite excuse for not learning a foreign language is: "If English was good enough for Jesus Christ, it's good enough for me!" I don't know what that has to do with anything, but obviously Jesus didn't speak English—nor did Moses or Isaiah or Paul or any other Bible authors or characters. As a result, our present-day English Bible is not directly from the mouths and pens of these religious figures, but the fitful product of centuries of evolution and translation.

The Bible is not a single book; it's an anthology of books by many authors from different historical periods writing in different languages (usually Hebrew or Greek). So there are three things that editors must consider in compiling the most accurate Bible: (1) deciding which books actually belong, (2) finding the oldest and most accurate version of each book, and (3) translating it accurately.

Codex Sinaiticus (c. A.D. 350)

The oldest complete "Bible" in existence (along with one in the Vatican), this is one of the first attempts to collect various books together into one authoritative anthology. It's in Greek, the language in which most of the New Testament was written. The Old Testament portions are Greek translations from the original Hebrew. This particular Bible, and the nearby *Codex Alexandrinus* (A.D. 425), contain some books not included in most modern English Bibles. (Even today, Catholic Bibles contain books not found in Protestant Bibles.)

Gospel Fragments

These gospels (an account of the life of Jesus of Nazareth) are about as old as any in existence, but they weren't written until several generations after Jesus died. Today, Bible scholars pore diligently over every word in the New Testament, trying to separate Jesus' authentic words from those that seem to have been added later.

The King James Bible (1611)

This Bible is in the same language you speak, but try reading it. The strange letters and archaic words clearly show how quickly languages evolve.

Jesus spoke Aramaic, a form of Hebrew. His words were written down in Greek. Greek manuscripts were translated into Latin, the language of medieval monks and scholars. By 1400 there was still no English version of the Bible, though only a small percentage of the population understood Latin. A few brave reformers risked death to make translations into English and print them using Gutenberg's new invention. Within two centuries, English translations were both legal and popular.

British Library

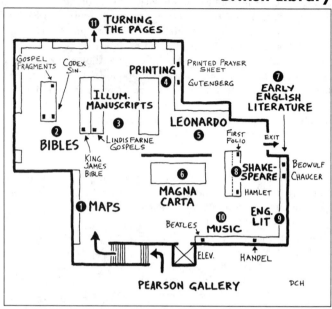

The King James version (done during his reign) has been the most widely used English translation. Fifty scholars worked for four years, borrowing heavily from previous translations, to produce the work. Its impact on the English language was enormous, making Elizabethan English something of the standard, even after all those *thee*s and *thou*s fell out of fashion in everyday speech.

Many of the most recent translations are both more accurate (based on better scholarship and original manuscripts) and more readable, using modern speech patterns. The late-20th-century debates over God's gender highlight the problems of translating old phrases to fit contemporary viewpoints.

❸ Lindisfarne Gospels (A.D. 698) and Illuminated Manuscripts

Throughout the Middle Ages, Bibles had to be reproduced by hand. This was a painstaking process, usually done by monks for a rich patron. This beautifully illustrated ("illuminated") collection of the four Gospels is the most magnificent of medieval British monk-uscripts. The text is in Latin, the language of scholars ever since the Roman Empire, but the illustrations—with elaborate tracery and interwoven decoration—mix Irish, classical, and even Byzantine forms. (Read an electronic copy in the adjacent Turning the Pages computer room.)

These Gospels are a reminder that Christianity almost didn't make it in Europe. After the fall of Rome (which had established Christianity as the official religion), much of Europe reverted to its pagan ways. This was the time of *Beowulf*, when people worshiped woodland spirits and terrible Teutonic gods. It took dedicated Irish missionaries 500 years to reestablish the faith on the Continent. Lindisfarne, an obscure monastery of Irish monks on an island off the east coast of England, was one of the few beacons of light after the fall of Rome, tending the embers of civilization through the long night of the Dark Ages.

Browse through more illuminated manuscripts (in the cases behind the Lindisfarne Gospels). This is some of the finest art from what we call the Dark Ages. The little intimate details offer a rare and fascinating peek into medieval life.

❹ Printing

Printing was invented by the Chinese (what wasn't?). The Printed Prayer Sheet (c. 618–907) was made seven centuries before the printing press was "invented" in Europe. A bodhisattva (an incarnation of Buddha) rides a lion, surrounded

by a prayer in Chinese characters. The faithful gained a blessing by saying the prayer, and so did the printer by reproducing it. Texts such as this were printed using wooden blocks carved with Chinese characters that were dipped into paint or ink.

The Gutenberg Bible (c. 1455)

It looks like just another monk-made Latin manuscript, but it was the first book printed in Europe using movable type. Printing is one of the most revolutionary inventions in history.

Johann Gutenberg (c. 1397–1468), a German silversmith, devised a convenient way to reproduce written materials quickly, neatly, and cheaply—by printing with movable type. You scratch each letter onto a separate metal block, then arrange them into words, ink them up, and press them onto paper. When one job was done you could reuse the same letters for a new one.

This simple idea had immediate and revolutionary consequences. Suddenly, the Bible was available for anyone to read, fueling the Protestant Reformation. Knowledge became cheap and accessible to a wide audience, not just the rich. Books became the mass medium of Europe, linking people by a common set of ideas.

❺ Leonardo da Vinci's Notebook

Books also spread secular knowledge. Renaissance men turned their attention away from heaven and toward the nuts and bolts of the material world around them. These pages from Leonardo's notebook show his powerful curiosity, his genius for invention, and his famous backward and inside-out handwriting, which makes sense only if you know Italian and have a mirror. Leonardo's restless mind ranged from how birds fly to mechanics to military fortifications to the "earthshine" reflecting onto the moon to an early helicopter.

One person's research inspired another's, and books allowed knowledge to accumulate. Galileo championed the counter-commonsense notion that the Earth spun around the sun, and Isaac Newton later perfected the mathematics of those moving bodies.

❻ Magna Carta (1215)

How did Britain, a tiny island with a few million people, come to rule a quarter of the world? Not by force, but by law. The Magna Carta was the basis for England's constitutional system of government. Though historians talk about "the" Magna Carta, there are several different versions of the document on display.

The Articles of the Barons: In 1215, England's barons rose in revolt against the slimy King John. After losing London, John was forced to negotiate. The barons presented him with this list of demands. John, whose rule was worthless without the support of the barons, had no choice but to affix his seal to it.

Magna Carta: A few days after John agreed to this original document, it was rewritten in legal form, and some 35 copies of this final version of the "Great Charter" were distributed around the kingdom.

This was a turning point in the history of government. Before, kings had ruled by God-given authority, above the laws of men. Now, for the first time, there were limits—in writing—on how a king could treat his subjects. More generally, it established the idea of "due process"— the notion that a government can't infringe on citizens' freedom without a legitimate legal reason. This small step became the basis for all constitutional governments, including yours.

So what did this radical piece of paper actually say? Not much, by today's standards. The specific demands had to do with things such as inheritance taxes, the king's duties to widows and orphans, and so on. It wasn't the specific articles that were important, but the simple fact that the king had to abide by them as law.

Around the corner there are many more historical documents in the library. The displays change frequently, but you may see letters by Queen Elizabeth I, Thomas More, Florence Nightingale, Gandhi, and others. But for now, let's trace the evolution of...

❼ Early English Literature

Four out of every five English words have been borrowed from other languages. The English language, like English culture (and London today), is a mix derived from foreign invaders. Some of the historic ingredients that make this cultural stew:

1. The original Celtic tribesmen
2. Latin-speaking Romans (A.D. 1–500)
3. Germanic tribes called Angles and Saxons (making English a Germanic language and naming the island "Angle-land"—England)
4. Vikings from Denmark (A.D. 800)
5. French-speaking Normans under William the Conqueror (1066–1250).

Beowulf (c. 1000)

This Anglo-Saxon epic poem, written in Old English, the early version of our language, almost makes the hieroglyphics on the Rosetta Stone look easy. The manuscript here is from A.D. 1000, although the story itself dates to about 750. This is the only existing medieval manuscript of this first English literary masterpiece.

In this epic story, the young hero Beowulf defeats two half-human monsters threatening the kingdom. Beowulf symbolizes England's emergence from the chaos and barbarism of the Dark Ages.

The Canterbury Tales (c. 1410)

Six hundred years later, England was Christian, but it was hardly the pious, predictable, Sunday-school world we might imagine. Geoffrey Chaucer's bawdy collection of stories, told by pilgrims on their way to Canterbury, gives us the full range of life's experiences—happy, sad, silly, sexy, pious. (Late in life, Chaucer wrote an apology for those works of his "that tend toward sin.")

While most serious literature of the time was written in scholarly Latin, the stories in *The Canterbury Tales* were written in Middle English, the language that developed after the French invasion (1066) added a Norman twist to Old English.

❽ Shakespeare (1564–1616)

William Shakespeare is the greatest author in any language. Period. He expanded and helped define modern English. In one fell swoop, he made the language of everyday people as important as Latin. In the process, he gave us phrases like "one fell swoop" that we quote without knowing it's Shakespeare.

Perhaps as important was his insight into humanity. With his stock of great characters—Hamlet, Othello, Macbeth, Falstaff, Lear, Romeo, Juliet—he probed the psychology of human beings 300 years before Freud. Even today, his characters strike a familiar chord.

Shakespeare in Collaboration

Shakespeare co-wrote a play titled *The Booke of Sir Thomas More.* Some scholars have wondered if maybe Shakespeare had help on other plays as well. After all, they reasoned, how could a journeyman actor, with little education, have written so many masterpieces? Modern scholars, though, unanimously agree that Shakespeare did indeed write the plays ascribed to him. This particular manuscript is believed to be in Shakespeare's own handwriting. The crossed-out lines indicate that even geniuses need editing.

The "Good" and "Bad" Quarto of *Hamlet*

Shakespeare wrote his plays to be performed, not read. He published a few, but as his reputation grew, unauthorized "bootleg" versions also began to circulate. Some of these were written out by actors who were trying (with faulty memories) to re-create plays they had appeared in years before. Here are two different versions of *Hamlet:* "good" and "bad."

The Shakespeare First Folio (1623)

It wasn't until seven years after his death that this complete collection of Shakespeare's plays came out. The editors were friends and fellow actors.

The engraving of Shakespeare on the title page is one of only two portraits done during his lifetime. Is this what he really looked like? No one knows. The best answer probably comes from his friend and fellow poet Ben Jonson in the introduction on the facing page. Jonson concludes, "Reader, look not on his picture, but his book."

❾ Other Greats in English Literature

The rest of the "*Beowulf*/Chaucer wall" is a greatest-hits sampling of British literature featuring works that have enlightened and brightened our lives for centuries. The displays rotate frequently, but there's always a tasty selection of famous works from Dickens to Austen to Kipling to Woolf to Joyce. Often on display is the original *Alice in Wonderland* by Lewis Carroll. Carroll (whose real name was Charles L. Dodgson) was a stutterer, which made him uncomfortable around everyone but children. For them he created a fantasy world where grown-up rules and logic were turned upside down.

⑩ Music

The Beatles

Future generations will have to judge whether this musical quartet ranks with artists such as Dickens and Keats, but no one can deny their historical significance. The Beatles burst onto the scene in the early 1960s to unheard-of popularity. With their long hair and loud music, they brought counterculture and revolutionary ideas to the middle class, affecting the values of a whole generation. Touring the globe, they served as a link between young people everywhere. Look for photos of John Lennon, Paul McCartney, George Harrison, and Ringo Starr before and after their fame.

Most interesting are the manuscripts of song lyrics written by Lennon and McCartney, the two guiding lights of the group. "I Wanna Hold Your Hand" was the song that launched them to superstardom. "A Hard Day's Night" was the title song of a film capturing their hectic touring schedule. Some call "A Ticket to Ride" the first heavy-metal song. In "Here, There, and Everywhere," notice the changes Paul made searching for just the right rhyme. "Yesterday," by Paul, was recorded with guitar and voice backed by a string quartet—a touch of sophistication by producer George Martin. Also, glance at the rambling, depressed, cynical, but humorous letter by a young John Lennon. Is that a self-portrait at the bottom?

Handel's *Messiah* (1741) and other Music Manuscripts

Kind of an anticlimax after the Fab Four, I know, but here are manuscripts by Mozart, Beethoven, Schubert, and others. George Frideric Handel's famous oratorio, the *Messiah,* was written in a flash of inspiration—three hours of music in 24 days. Here are the final bars of its most famous tune. Hallelujah.

⑪ Turning the Pages—Virtual-Reality Room

For a chance to page through a few of the most precious books in the collection, drop by the Turning the Pages room. Touch a computer screen and let your fingers do the walking.

WESTMINSTER ABBEY

Westminster Abbey is the greatest church in the English-speaking world. England's kings and queens have been crowned and buried here since 1066. The histories of Westminster Abbey and England are almost the same. A thousand years of English history—3,000 tombs, the remains of 29 kings and queens, and hundreds of memorials to poets, politicians, and warriors—lie within its stained-glass splendor and under its stone slabs.

ORIENTATION

Cost: £6. Praying is free, thank God, but you must inform the marshal at the door of your purpose. Or, for a free peek inside (without seeing all the historic tombs) and a quiet sit in the nave, you can tell a guard at the west end (where the tourists exit) that you'd like to pay your respects to Britain's Unknown Soldier, and he will let you slip in.

Hours: Mon–Fri 9:30–16:45, Wed also 18:00–19:45, Sat 9:30–14:45, last admission 60 minutes before closing, closed Sun to sightseers but open for services. The main entrance, on the Big Ben side, often has a sizable line; visit early or late to avoid tourist hordes. Mid-mornings are most crowded. On weekdays after 15:00 it's less crowded; come then and stay for the 17:00 evensong (see below).

Getting There: Near Big Ben and Houses of Parliament (Tube:

Westminster or St. James' Park).

Information: To confirm the times of guided tours, concerts, and services, tel. 020/7222-7110. Since special events and services can shut out sightseers, it's wise to call ahead simply to confirm the abbey is open. For more information and concert listings, see www.westminster-abbey.org.

Music: Evensong, a stirring experience in a nearly empty church, is on Mon, Tue, Thu, and Fri at 17:00, Sat and Sun at 15:00. Free organ recitals are held Sun at 17:45 (30 min, look for posted signs with schedules).

Tours: Vergers, the church equivalent of docents, give entertaining guided tours for £3 (up to 6/day, 90 min). Tour themes are the historic church, the personalities buried here, and the great coronations. Informative audioguide tours cost £2 (available weekdays until 15:00, Sat until 13:00, pick up at the information desk at the north door). Many prefer the audioguide to the vergers' tour because it is self-paced. Both live and audioguide tours include entry to the small museums by the cloister (otherwise £1).

Length of This Tour: 90 minutes.

Photography: Photos are prohibited.

Cuisine Art: Find reasonably priced, cafeteria-style lunches in the basement of Methodist Central Hall, across the street from the west entrance of the abbey.

Starring: Edwards, Elizabeths, Henrys, Annes, Richards, Marys, and poets.

THE TOUR BEGINS

You'll have no choice but to follow the steady flow of tourists circling clockwise through the church—in through the north entrance, behind the altar, into Poets' Corner in the south transept, detouring through the cloisters, and, finally, back out through the west end of the nave. It's all one-way, and the crowds can be a real crush. Here are the abbey's top 10 (plus one) stops:

• *Walk straight in, pick up the map flier that locates the most illustrious tombs, and belly up to the barricade in the center.*

❶ North Transept

Look down the long and narrow center aisle of the church. Lined with the praying hands of the Gothic arches, glowing with light from the stained glass, it's clear that this is more than a museum. With saints in stained glass, heroes in carved stone, and the bodies of England's greatest under the floor stones, Westminster Abbey is the religious heart of England.

You're standing at the center of a cross-shaped church. The main altar (with cross and candlesticks) sits on the platform up the

Westminster Abbey

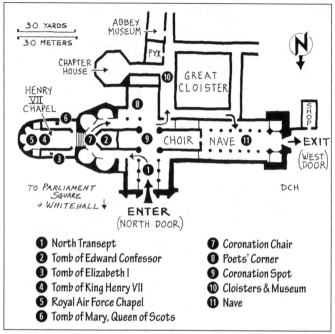

- ❶ North Transept
- ❷ Tomb of Edward Confessor
- ❸ Tomb of Elizabeth I
- ❹ Tomb of King Henry VII
- ❺ Royal Air Force Chapel
- ❻ Tomb of Mary, Queen of Scots
- ❼ Coronation Chair
- ❽ Poets' Corner
- ❾ Coronation Spot
- ❿ Cloisters & Museum
- ⓫ Nave

five stairs in front of you. To the right stretches the long, high-ceilinged nave. Nestled in the nave is the elaborately carved wooden seating of the choir (or "quire"), where monks once held intimate services and where, today, the Abbey boys' choir sings the evensong at 17:00.

The abbey was built in 1065. Its name, Westminster, means Church in the West (west of St. Paul's Cathedral). For the next 250 years, the abbey was redone and remodeled to become essentially the church you see today, notwithstanding an extensive resurfacing in the 19th century. Thankfully, later architects—ignoring building trends of their generation—honored the vision of the original planner, and the building was completed in one relatively harmonious style.

The abbey's 10-story nave is the tallest in England. The chandeliers, 10 feet tall, look small in comparison (16 were given to the abbey by the Guinness family).

The north transept (through which you entered) is nicknamed "Statesmen's Corner" and specializes in famous prime ministers. Find the rival prime ministers, proud William Gladstone and goateed Benjamin Disraeli, who presided over England's peak of power under Queen Victoria.

• Now turn left and follow the crowd. Walk under Robert ("Bob") Peel, the prime minister whose policemen were nicknamed "bobbies," and stroll *a few yards into the land of dead kings and queens. Stop at the wooden staircase on your right.*

❷ Tomb of Edward the Confessor

The holiest part of the church is the raised area behind the altar (where the wooden staircase leads—sorry, no tourist access). Step back and peek over the dark coffin of Edward I to see the green-and-gold wedding-cake tomb of King Edward the Confessor—the man who built Westminster Abbey.

God had told pious Edward to visit St. Peter's Basilica in Rome. But with Normans thinking conquest, it was too dangerous for him to leave England. Instead, he built this grand church and dedicated it to St. Peter. It was finished just in time to bury Edward and to crown his foreign successor, William the Conqueror, in 1066. After Edward's death, people prayed at his tomb and, after getting fine results, canonized him. This elevated, central tomb—which lost some of its luster when Henry VIII melted down the gold coffin-case—is surrounded by the tombs of eight kings and queens.

• *Continue on. At the top of the stone staircase, veer left into the private burial chapel of Queen Elizabeth I.*

❸ Tomb of Queen Elizabeth I and Mary I

Although there's only one effigy on the tomb (Elizabeth's), there are two queens buried beneath it, both daughters of Henry VIII (by different mothers). Bloody Mary—meek, pious, sickly, and Catholic—enforced Catholicism during her short reign (1553–1558) by burning "heretics" at the stake.

Elizabeth—strong, clever, "virginal," and Protestant—steered England on an Anglican course. She holds a royal orb symbolizing that she's queen of the whole globe. When 26-year-old Elizabeth was crowned in the abbey, her right to rule was questioned (especially by her Catholic subjects) because she was the bastard seed of Henry VIII's unsanctioned marriage to Anne Boleyn. But Elizabeth's long reign (1559–1603) was one of the greatest in English history, a time when England ruled the seas and Shakespeare explored human emotions. When she died, thousands turned out for the funeral in the abbey. Elizabeth's face, modeled after her death mask, is considered a very accurate take on this hook-nosed, imperious, virgin queen.

The two half-sisters disliked each other in life—Mary even had Elizabeth locked up in the Tower of London. Now they lie side by side for eternity—with a prayer for Christians of all persuasions to live peacefully together.

• *Continue into the ornate, flag-draped room behind the main altar.*

❹ Chapel of King Henry VII (a.k.a. the Lady Chapel)

The light from the stained-glass windows, the colorful banners overhead, and the elaborate tracery in stone, wood, and glass give this room the festive air of a medieval tournament. The prestigious

Knights of Bath meet here, under the magnificent ceiling studded with gold pendants. The ceiling—of carved stone, not plaster (1519)—is the finest English Perpendicular Gothic and fan vaulting you'll see (unless you're going to King's College Chapel in Cambridge). The ceiling was sculpted on the floor in pieces, then jigsaw-puzzled into place. It capped the Gothic period and signaled the vitality of the coming Renaissance.

The knights sit in the wooden stalls with their coats of arms on the back, churches on their heads, their banner flying above, and the graves of dozens of kings beneath their feet. When the queen worships here, she sits in the southwest corner chair under the carved wooden throne with the lion crown.

Behind the small altar is an iron cage housing tombs of the old warrior Henry VII of Lancaster and his wife, Elizabeth of York. Their love and marriage finally settled the Wars of the Roses between the two clans. The combined red-and-white rose symbol decorates the top band of the ironwork. Henry VII, the first Tudor king, was the father of Henry VIII and the grandfather of Elizabeth I. This exuberant chapel heralds a new optimistic, postwar era as England prepares to step onto the world stage.

• *At the far end of the chapel, stand at the banister in front of the modern set of stained-glass windows.*

❺ Royal Air Force Chapel

Saints in robes and halos mingle with pilots in parachutes and bomber jackets in this tribute to WWII flyers who earned their angel wings in the Battle of Britain (July–Oct, 1940). Hitler's air force ruled the skies in the early days of the war, bombing at will, threatening to snuff Britain out without a fight. But while determined Londoners hunkered down underground, British pilots in their Spitfires took advantage of a new invention—radar—to get the jump on the more powerful Luftwaffe. These were the fighters about whom Churchill said, "Never…was so much owed by so many to so few."

The abbey survived the Battle and the Blitz, but this window did not. As a memorial, a bit of bomb damage has been left—the little glassed-over hole in the wall below the windows in the lower left-hand corner. The book of remembrances lists each of the 1,497 airmen (including one American) who died in the Battle of Britain.

You're standing on the grave of Oliver Cromwell, leader of the rebel forces in England's Civil War. Or rather, Cromwell was buried here from 1658 to 1661. Then his corpse was exhumed, hanged, drawn, quartered, and decapitated, and the head displayed on a stake as a warning to anarchists.

• *Exit the Chapel of Henry VII. Turn left into a side chapel with the tomb (the central one of three in the chapel) of…*

❻ Mary, Queen of Scots

Historians get dewy-eyed over the fate of Mary, Queen of Scots (1542–1587). The beautiful, French-educated queen was held under house arrest for 19 years by Queen Elizabeth I, who considered her a threat to her sovereignty. Elizabeth got wind of a plot to assassinate her, suspected Mary was behind it, and had her beheaded. When Elizabeth—the "Virgin Queen"—died heirless, Mary's son James I became king of England. James buried his mom here (with her head sewn back on) in the abbey's most sumptuous tomb.

• *Exit Mary's chapel. Ahead of you, at the foot of the stairs, is the Coronation Chair. Behind the chair, again, is the tomb of the church's founder, Edward the Confessor.*

❼ Coronation Chair

The gold-painted wooden chair waits here—with its back to the high altar—for the next coronation. For every English coronation since 1308 (except two), it's been moved to its spot before the high altar to receive the royal buttocks. The chair's legs rest on lions, England's symbol. The space below the chair originally held a big rock from Scotland called the Stone of Scone (skoon), symbolizing Scotland's unity with England's king. Recently, however, Britain gave Scotland more sovereignty, its own parliament, and the stone. Scotland has agreed to loan the stone to Britain for future coronations.

• *Continue on. Turn left into the south transept. You're in Poets' Corner.*

❽ Poets' Corner

England's greatest artistic contributions are in the written word. Here lie buried the masters of arguably the world's most complex and expressive language. (Many writers are honored with plaques and monuments; relatively few are actually buried here.)

• *Start with Chaucer, buried in the wall under the blue windows. The plaques on the floor before Chaucer are gravestones and memorials to other literary greats.*

Geoffrey Chaucer (c. 1343–1400) is often considered the father of English literature. Chaucer's *Canterbury Tales* told of earthy people speaking everyday English. He was the first great writer buried here (thanks to his job as a Westminster clerk). Later, it became a tradition to bury other writers here, and Poets' Corner was built around his tomb. The blue windows have blank panels awaiting the names of future poets.

Lord Byron, the great lover of women and adventure: "Though the night was made for loving,/And the day returns too soon,/Yet we'll go no more a roving/By the light of the moon."

Dylan Thomas, alcoholic master of modernism, with a Romantic's heart: "Oh as I was young and easy in the mercy of his means,/Time held me green and dying/Though I sang in my chains like the sea."

W. H. Auden: "May I, composed like them/Of Eros and of dust/Beleaguered by the same/Negation and despair/Show an affirming flame."

Lewis Carroll, creator of *Alice in Wonderland:* "'Twas brillig, and the slithy toves/Did gyre and gimble in the wabe…"

T. S. Eliot, the dry voice of modern society: "This is the way the world ends/Not with a bang but a whimper."

Alfred, Lord Tennyson, conscience of the Victorian Age: "'Tis better to have loved and lost/Than never to have loved at all."

Robert Browning: "Oh, to be in England/Now that April's there."

• *Farther out in the south transept, you'll find…*

William Shakespeare: Although he's not buried here, this greatest of English writers is honored by a fine statue that stands near the end of the transept, overlooking the others: "All the world's a stage/And all the men and women merely players./They have their exits and their entrances/And one man in his time plays many parts."

George Handel: High on the wall opposite Shakespeare is the man famous for composing the *Messiah* oratorio: "Hallelujah, hallelujah, hallelujah." The statue's features are modeled on Handel's death mask. Musicians can read the vocal score in his hands for "I Know That My Redeemer Liveth." His actual tomb is on the floor next to…

Charles Dickens, whose serialized novels brought literature to the masses: "It was the best of times, it was the worst of times."

On the floor near Shakespeare, you'll also find the tombs of Samuel Johnson (who wrote the first English dictionary) and the great English actor Laurence Olivier. (Olivier disdained the "Method" style of experiencing intense emotions in order to portray them. When co-star Dustin Hoffman stayed up all night in order to appear haggard for a scene, Olivier said, "My dear boy, why don't you simply try acting?")

And finally, near the center of the transept, find the small white floor plaque of Thomas Parr (marked "THO: PARR"). Check the dates of his life (1483–1635) and do the math. In his (reputed) 152 years, he served 10 sovereigns and was a contemporary of Columbus, Henry VIII, Elizabeth I, Shakespeare, and Galileo.

• *Walk to the center of the church in front of the high altar.*

❾ The Coronation Spot

This is where nearly every English coronation since 1066 has taken place. Imagine the day when Prince William becomes king:

The nobles in robes and powdered wigs look on from the carved wooden stalls of the choir. The Archbishop of Canterbury stands at the high altar (table with candlesticks, up five steps). The coronation chair is placed before the altar on the round, brown pavement stone representing the earth. Surrounding the whole area are temporary bleachers for 8,000 VIPs, going halfway up the rose windows of each transept, creating a "theater."

Long silver trumpets hung with banners sound a fanfare as the monarch-to-be enters the church. The congregation sings, "I will go into the house of the Lord," as William parades slowly down the nave and up the steps to the altar. After a church service, he sits in the chair, facing the altar, where the crown jewels are placed. William is annointed with holy oil, then receives a ceremonial sword, ring, and cup. The royal scepter is placed in his hands, and— dut, dutta dah—the archbishop lowers the Crown of St. Edward the Confessor onto his royal head. Finally, King William stands up, descends the steps, and is presented to the people. As cannons roar throughout the city, the people cry, "God save the king!"

Royalty are also given funerals here. Princess Diana's coffin lay here before her funeral service. She was then buried on her family estate. The "Queen Mum" (mother of Elizabeth II) had her funeral here, and this is also where Prince Andrew married Sarah Ferguson.

• *Exit the church (temporarily) at the south door, which leads to...*

❿ Cloisters and Museum

The buildings that adjoin the church housed the monks. (The church is known as the "abbey" because it was the headquarters of the Benedictine order—until Henry VIII kicked them out in 1540.) Cloistered courtyards gave them a place to meditate on God's creations.

Look back at the church exterior and meditate on the flying buttresses—the stone bridges that push in on the church walls—that allowed Gothic architects to build so high.

Historians should pay £1 extra to cover admission to three more rooms (covered by audioguide or live tour). The Chapter House, where the monks had daily meetings, features fine architecture with faded but well-described medieval art. The tiny Pyx Chamber has an exhibit about the King's Treasury. The Abbey Museum, formerly the monks' lounge with a cozy fireplace and snacks, now has fascinating exhibits on royal coronations, funerals, abbey history, and a close-up look at medieval stained glass. See replicas of the Crown Jewels used for coronation practice. And look into the impressively realistic eyes of Elizabeth I, Charles II, Henry VII and others, part of a compelling series of wax-and-wood statues that, for three centuries, graced royal coffins during funeral processions.

• *Go back into the church for the last stop.*

⑪ Nave

On the floor near the west entrance of the abbey is the flower-lined Tomb of the Unknown Warrior, one ordinary WWI soldier buried in soil from France with lettering made from melted-down weapons from that war. Think about that million-man army from the Empire and Commonwealth and all those who gave their lives. Hanging on a column next to the tomb is the U.S. Congressional Medal of Honor, presented to England's WWI dead by General Pershing in 1921. Closer to the door is a memorial to the hero of World War II, Winston Churchill.

Near the choir screen is so-called "Scientists' Corner," with memorials to Isaac Newton, Michael Faraday, Charles Darwin, and others. When you leave the church through the west doors, turn around and look up over the doorway to find a statue (fifth from the left) of a 20th-century American martyr in the cause of freedom, Martin Luther King, Jr.

But first, find the stained-glass window of St. Edward the Confessor (third bay from the left on the north side, marked "S: Edwardus rex...") with crown, scepter, and ring, and thank him for the abbey.

Look down the nave, filled with the remains of the people who made Britain great—saints, royalty, poets, musicians, scientists, soldiers, politicians. Now step back outside into a city filled with the same kind of poets, saints, and heroes.

PARIS

Paris—the City of Light—has been a beacon of culture for centuries. It represents the finest and most beautiful products of our civilization—art, fashion, food, literature, and escargot forks. Stroll past ancient beauties in the Louvre and orbit *Venus de Milo*. Step into a sun-dappled Impressionist painting at the Orsay Museum. Climb Notre-Dame and rub shoulders with the gargoyles. Stand in awe of the size, grandeur, and opulence of the palace at Versailles. Gazing at the wonders of this city, even presidents and dictators become mere tourists.

Come prepared to celebrate, rather than judge, the cultural differences, and you'll capture the romance and joie de vivre that Paris exudes.

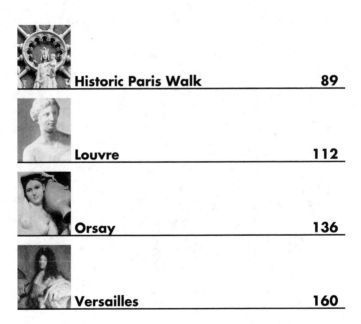

Historic Paris Walk   **89**

Louvre   **112**

Orsay   **136**

Versailles   **160**

Paris Sights

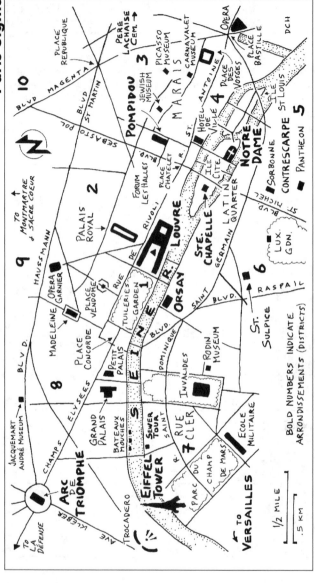

HISTORIC PARIS WALK

From Notre-Dame to Sainte-Chapelle

Paris has been the capital of Europe for centuries. We'll start where it did, on Ile de la Cité, with a foray onto the Left Bank, on a walk that laces together 80 generations of history: from Celtic fishing village to Roman city, bustling medieval capital, birthplace of the Revolution, bohemian haunt of the 1920s café scene, and the working world of modern Paris. Allow four hours to do justice to this three-mile walk.

ORIENTATION

Many sights that charge admission are covered by the Paris museum pass, which for many is a great time and money saver (€18 for one day, €36 for three days, and €54 for five days, sold at participating sights). The Archeological Crypt is a convenient place to buy your pass.

Notre-Dame: Free, church open daily 8:00–18:45; treasury–€2.50 (not covered by museum pass), daily 9:30–17:30; Sunday Mass at 8:00, 8:45, 10:00 (Gregorian), 11:30 (international), 12:30, and 18:30. Check the leaflet with the church schedule (at booth inside entrance). Organ performances are usually on Sat at 16:30. Free English tours, normally Wed and Thu at 12:00 and Sat at 14:30. The tower climb takes 400 steps and €5.50—worth it for the gargoyle's-eye view of the cathedral, Seine, and city (April–Sept daily 9:30–19:30, Oct–March daily 10:00–18:00, last entry 45 min before closing, covered by museum pass but no bypass line for passholders; to avoid crowds in peak

Historic Paris Walk

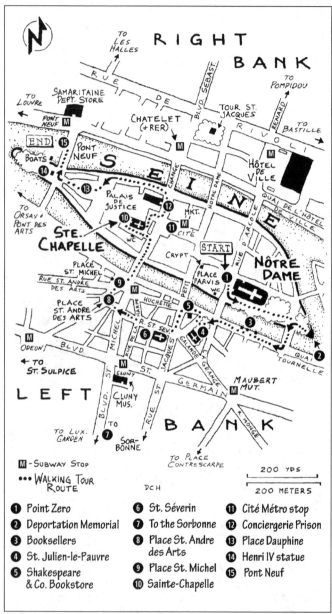

M – Subway Stop

••• Walking Tour Route

DCH

200 YDS

200 METERS

1 Point Zero

2 Deportation Memorial

3 Booksellers

4 St. Julien-le-Pauvre

5 Shakespeare & Co. Bookstore

6 St. Séverin

7 To the Sorbonne

8 Place St. Andre des Arts

9 Place St. Michel

10 Sainte-Chapelle

11 Cité Métro stop

12 Conciergerie Prison

13 Place Dauphine

14 Henri IV statue

15 Pont Neuf

season, arrive before 10:00 or after 18:00).

Paris Archeological Crypt: €3.50, covered by museum pass, Tue–Sun 10:00–18:00, closed Mon, entry 100 yards in front of the cathedral.

Deportation Memorial: Free, April–Sept daily 10:00–12:00 & 14:00–19:00, Oct–March daily 10:00–12:00 & 14:00–17:00.

Sainte-Chapelle and Conciergerie: €5.50 each, €8 combo-ticket, both covered by museum pass, daily 9:30–18:00, Mo: Cité, tel. 01 44 07 12 38.

THE TOUR BEGINS

Start at Notre-Dame Cathedral on the island in the River Seine, the physical and historic bull's-eye of your Paris map (closest Métro stops are Cité, Hôtel de Ville, and St. Michel, each requiring a short walk).

• *On the square in front of the cathedral, stand far enough back to take in the whole facade. Look at the circular window in the center.*

NOTRE-DAME

For centuries, the main figure in the Christian "pantheon" has been Mary, the mother of Jesus. Catholics petition her in times of trouble to gain comfort and to ask her to convince God to be compassionate with them. The church is dedicated to "Our Lady" (Notre-Dame), and there she is, cradling God, right in the heart of the facade, surrounded by the halo of the rose window. Though the church is massive and imposing, it has always stood for the grace and compassion of Mary, the "mother of God."

Imagine the faith of the people who built this. They broke

ground in 1163 with the hope that someday their great-great-great-great-great-great grand-children might attend the dedication Mass two centuries later in 1345. Look up the 200-foot-tall bell towers and imagine a tiny medieval community mustering the money and energy to build this. Master masons supervised, but the people did much

Paris Through History

250 B.C.	Small fishing village of the Parisii, a Celtic tribe.
52 B.C.	Julius Caesar conquers the Parisii capital of Lutetia (near Paris), and the Romans replace it with a new capital on the Left Bank.
A.D. 497	Rome falls to the Germanic Franks. King Clovis (482–511) converts to Christianity and makes Paris his capital.
885–886	Paris gets wasted in siege by Viking Norsemen (Normans).
1163	Notre-Dame cornerstone laid.
c. 1250	Paris is a bustling commercial city with a university and new construction such as Sainte-Chapelle and Notre-Dame.
c. 1600	King Henry IV beautifies Paris with buildings, roads, bridges, and squares.
c. 1700	Louis XIV makes Versailles his capital while Parisians grumble.
1789	Paris is the heart of France's Revolution, which condemns thousands to the guillotine.
1804	Napoleon Bonaparte crowns himself emperor in a ceremony at Notre-Dame.
1830 & 1848	Parisians take to the streets again in revolutions, fighting the return of royalty.
c. 1860	Napoleon's nephew, Napoleon III, builds Paris' wide boulevards.
1889	The centennial of the Revolution is celebrated with the Eiffel Tower. Paris enjoys wealth and middle-class prosperity in the belle époque (beautiful age).
1920s	After the draining Great War, Paris is a cheap place to live, attracting expatriates like Ernest Hemingway.
1940–44	Occupied Paris spends the war years under gray skies and gray Nazi uniforms.
Today	You arrive in Paris to make history.

of the grunt work themselves for free—hauling the huge stones from distant quarries, digging a 30-foot-deep trench to lay the foundations, and treading like rats on a wheel designed to lift the stones up, one by one. This kind of backbreaking, arduous manual labor created the real hunchbacks of Notre-Dame.

• *"Walk this way" toward the cathedral, and view it from the bronze plaque on the ground (30 yards from the central doorway) marked...*

Point Zero

You're standing at the center of France, the point from which all distances are measured. It was also the center of Paris 2,300 years ago, when the Parisii tribe fished here where the east-west river crossed a north-south road. The Romans conquered the Parisii and built their Temple of Jupiter where Notre-Dame is today (52 B.C.). When Rome fell, the Germanic Franks sealed their victory by replacing the temple with the Christian church of St. Etienne in the 6th century. See the outlines of the former church in the pavement (in smaller gray stones), showing where walls and columns were, angling out from Notre-Dame to Point Zero.

The grand equestrian statue (to your right, as you face the church) is of Charlemagne ("Charles the Great," 742–814), King of the Franks, whose reign marked the birth of modern France. He briefly united Europe and was crowned the first "Holy Roman Emperor" in 800, but after his death the kingdom was divided into what would become modern France and Germany. (Maybe even greater than Charles are the nearby pay toilets—the cleanest you'll find in downtown Paris.)

Before renovation 150 years ago, this square was much smaller, a characteristic medieval shambles facing a rundown church, surrounded by winding streets and higgledy-piggledy buildings. (Yellow bricks in the pavement show the medieval street plan and even identify some of the buildings.) The church's huge bell towers rose above this tangle of smaller buildings, inspiring Victor Hugo's story of a deformed bell-ringer who could look down on all of Paris.

Looking two-thirds of the way up Notre-Dame's left tower, those with binoculars or good eyes can find Paris' most photographed gargoyle. Propped on his elbows on the balcony rail, he looks down on all the tourists in line.

• *Much of Paris' history is right under your feet. Some may consider visiting it in the...*

Archaeological Crypt

Two thousand years of dirt and debris have raised the city's altitude. In the Crypt museum (entrance 100 yards in front of Notre-Dame's entrance), you can see cellars and foundations from many layers of Paris: a Roman building with central heating; a wall that didn't keep the Franks out; the main medieval road that once led grandly up the square to Notre-Dame; even (wow) a 19th-century sewer.

• *Now turn your attention to the church facade. Look at the left doorway and, to the left of the door, find the statue with his head in his hands.*

Notre-Dame Facade
St. Denis

When Christianity began making converts in Roman Paris, the

Notre-Dame Facade

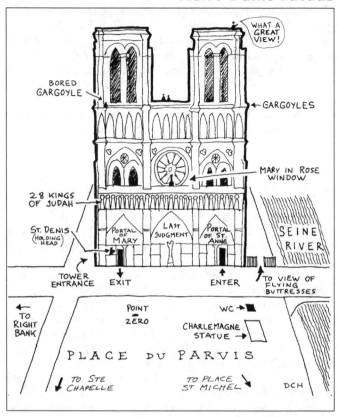

bishop of Paris (St. Denis) was beheaded. But those early Christians were hard to keep down. St. Denis got up, tucked his head under his arm, headed north, paused at a fountain to wash it off, and continued until he found just the right place to meet his maker. The Parisians were convinced by this miracle, Christianity gained

ground, and a church soon replaced the pagan temple.

• *Above the central doorway, you'll find scenes from the Last Judgment.*

Central Portal

It's the end of the world, and Christ sits on the throne of judgment (just under the arches, holding both hands up). Below him, an angel and a demon weigh souls in the balance; the demon cheats by pressing down. The good people stand to the left, gazing up to heaven.

The naughty ones to the right are
chained up and led off to a six-hour tour
of the Louvre on a hot day. Notice the
crazy, sculpted demons to the right, at
the base of the arch. Find the flaming
cauldron with the sinner diving into it
headfirst. The lower panel shows
Judgment Day, as angels with trumpets
remind worshipers that all social classes
will be judged—clergy, nobility, army,
and peasants. Below that, Jesus stands

between the 12 apostles—each barefoot and with their ID symbol
(such as Peter with his keys).
• *Above the arches is a row of 28 statues, known as...*

The Kings of Judah

In the days of the French Revolution (1789–1799), these Biblical
kings were mistaken for the hated French kings, and Notre-Dame
represented the oppressive Catholic hierarchy. The citizens stormed
the church, crying, "Off with their heads!" Plop, they lopped off the
crowned heads of these kings with glee, creating a row of St. Denises
that wasn't repaired for decades.

But the story doesn't end there. A schoolteacher who lived
nearby collected the heads and buried them in his backyard for safe-
keeping. There they slept until 1977, when they were accidentally
unearthed. Today you can stare into the eyes of the original kings in
the Cluny Museum, a few blocks away.
• *Enter the church and find a spot where you can view the long, high central aisle. (Be careful: Pickpockets attend church here religiously.)*

Notre-Dame Interior
Nave

Remove your metaphorical hat and become a simple bareheaded
peasant, entering the dim medieval light of the church. Take a
minute to let your pupils dilate, then take in the subtle, mysterious
light show God beams through the stained-glass windows. Follow
the slender columns up 10 stories to the praying-hands arches of the
ceiling and contemplate the heavens. Let's say it's dedication day for
this great stone wonder. The priest intones the words of the Mass
that echo through the hall: *"Terribilis est locus iste"*—"This place is
terribilis," meaning awe-inspiring or even terrifying. It's a huge, dark,
earthly cavern lit with an unearthly light.

This is Gothic. Taller and filled with light, this was a major
improvement over the earlier Romanesque style. Gothic architects
needed only a few structural columns, topped by pointed arches that
crisscross the columns to support the weight of the roof. This let

them build higher than ever, freeing up the walls for windows.

Notre-Dame is designed in the shape of a cross, with the altar placed where the crossbeam intersects. The church can hold up to 10,000 faithful.

• *Walk up to the main altar.*

Altar

This marks the spot where Mass is said and the bread and wine of Communion are blessed and distributed. In olden days, there were no chairs. This was the holy spot for Romans, Christians…and even atheists. When the Revolutionaries stormed the church, they gutted it and turned it into a "Temple of Reason." A woman dressed up like the Statue of Liberty held court at the altar as a symbol of the divinity of Man. France today, while nominally Catholic, remains aloof from Vatican dogmatism. Instead of traditional wooden confessional booths, notice the open, glass-walled room (right aisle) where modern sinners seek counseling as much as forgiveness.

Right Transept

A statue of Joan of Arc (*Jeanne d'Arc*, 1412–1431), dressed in armor and praying, honors the French teenager who rallied the French soldiers to try to drive English invaders from Paris, before being burned at the stake for claiming to hear heavenly voices. Almost immediately, Parisians rallied to condemn Joan's execution, and finally, in 1909, here in Notre-Dame, the former "witch" was beatified.

Join the statue in gazing up to the blue and purple rose-shaped window with teeny green Mary and baby Jesus in the center. It's the only one of the three with its original medieval glass.

A large painting shows portly Thomas Aquinas (1225–1274) teaching while his students drink from the fountain of knowledge. This Italian monk did undergrad and master's work at the multicultural University of Paris, then taught there for several years while writing his theological works. His "scholasticism" used Aristotle's logic to examine the Christian universe, aiming to fuse faith and reason.

The Rest of the Church

Just past the altar are the walls of the choir, where more intimate services can be held in this spacious building. Surrounding the choir are chapels, each dedicated to a particular saint. The faithful can pause at their favorite, light a candle as an offering, and meditate in the cool light of the stained glass. (The nearby treasury, containing lavish robes and golden reliquaries, lacks English explanations and probably isn't worth the €2.50 entry fee.)

Behind the altar, you'll see a fine 17th-century *pietà* flanked by two kneeling kings: Louis XIII and Louis XIV.

• *Amble around the ambulatory, spill back outside, and make a U-turn left. Walk to the back end of the church along the riverside.*

Notre-Dame Side View

Along the side of the church, you'll notice the flying buttresses. These 50-foot stone "beams" that stick out of the church were the key to the complex architecture of Gothic. The pointed arches we saw inside caused the weight of the roof to push outward rather than downward. The "flying" buttresses support the roof by pushing back inward. Gothic architects were masters at playing architectural forces against each other to build loftier and loftier churches, with walls opened up to stained-glass windows.

Picture Quasimodo limping around along the railed balcony at the base of the roof among the gargoyles. These grotesque beasts sticking out from pillars and buttresses represent souls caught between heaven and earth. They also function as rain spouts (from the same French root as "gargle") when there are no evil spirits to battle.

The neo-Gothic 300-foot spire is a product of the 1860 reconstruction of the dilapidated old church. Victor Hugo's book *The Hunchback of Notre-Dame* (1831) inspired a young architecture student named Eugène-Emmanuel Viollet-le-Duc to dedicate his career to a major renovation in Gothic style. Find Viollet-le-Duc himself at the base of the spire among the green apostles and evangelists (visible from the back end of the church). The apostles look outward, blessing the city, while the architect (at top) looks up the spire, marveling at his fine work.

• *Behind Notre-Dame, cross the street and enter the iron gate into the park at the tip of the island.*

Deportation Memorial (Mémorial de la Déportation)

This memorial to the 200,000 French victims of the Nazi concentration camps (1940–1945) draws you into their experience. France was quickly overrun by Nazi Germany, and Paris spent the war years under Nazi occupation. Jews and dissidents were rounded up and deported—many never returned.

As you descend the steps, the city around you disappears. Surrounded by walls, you have become a prisoner. Your only freedom is your view of the sky and the tiny glimpse of the river below. Enter the dark, single-file chamber up ahead. Inside, the circular plaque in the floor reads, "They went into the earth and they did not return."

The hallway stretching in front of you is lined with 200,000 lighted crystals, one for each French citizen who died. Flickering at the far end is the eternal flame of hope. The tomb of the unknown deportee lies at your feet. Above, the inscription reads, "Dedicated to the living memory of the 200,000 French deportees sleeping in the night and the fog, exterminated in the Nazi concentration camps." The side rooms are filled with triangles—reminiscent of the identification patches inmates were forced to wear—each bearing the name of a concentration camp. Above the exit as you leave is the message you'll find at all Nazi sites: "Forgive, but never forget."

Ile St. Louis

Back on street level, look across the river to the Ile St. Louis. If the Ile de la Cité is a tug laden with the history of Paris, it's towing this classy little residential dinghy laden only with high-rent apartments, boutiques, characteristic restaurants, and famous sorbet shops.

This island wasn't developed until much later (17th century) than the Ile de la Cité. What was a swampy mess is now harmonious Parisian architecture and one of Paris' most exclusive neighborhoods. Its uppity residents complain that the local ice cream shop—Berthillon—draws crowds until late into the night (31 rue St. Louis-en-l'Ile).

• *From the tip of Ile de la Cité, cross the bridge to the Left Bank and turn right. Walk along the river, toward the front end of Notre-Dame. Stairs detour down to the riverbank if you need a place to picnic. This side view of the church from across the river is one of Europe's great sights.*

LEFT BANK (RIVE GAUCHE)

The Left Bank of the Seine—"left" if you were floating downstream—still has many of the twisting lanes and narrow buildings of  medieval times. The Right Bank is more modern and business-oriented, with wide boulevards and stressed Parisians in suits. Here along the riverbank, the "big business" is secondhand books, displayed in the green metal stalls on the parapet. These literary entrepreneurs pride themselves on their easygoing business style. With flexible hours and virtually no overhead, they run their businesses as they have since medieval times.

• *When you reach the bridge (pont au Double) that crosses over in front of Notre-Dame, veer to the left across the street to a small park (square Viviani) where you'll find the small rough-stone church of St. Julien-le-Pauvre. You'll pass Paris' oldest inhabitant—an acacia tree nicknamed Robinier after the guy who planted it in 1602—that may once have shaded the Sun King.*

Medieval Paris (1000–1400)

Picture Paris in 1250, when the church of St. Julien-le-Pauvre was still new. Notre-Dame was nearly done (so they thought), Sainte-Chapelle had just opened, the University was expanding human knowledge, and Paris was fast becoming a prosperous industrial and commercial center. The area around the church gives you some of the medieval feel. A half-timbered house stands to the right of the entrance. Many buildings in medieval times were built like this, with a wooden frame filled in with a plaster of mud, straw, and dung. Back then, the humble "half-timbered" structure would have been hidden by a veneer of upscale stucco.

Looking along nearby rue Galande, you'll see a few old houses leaning every which way. (La Guillotine Pub at #52 sports an authentic guillotine from 1792 on its wall.) In medieval days, people were piled on top of each other, building at all angles, as they scrambled for this prime real estate near the main commercial artery of the day—the Seine. The smell of fish competed with the smell of neighbors in this knot of humanity.

Narrow dirt (or mud) streets sloped from here down into the mucky Seine, until modern quays and embankments cleaned that up.

• *Return to the river and turn left on rue de la Bûcherie. At #37, drop into the…*

Shakespeare and Company Bookstore

In addition to hosting butchers and fishmongers, the Left Bank has been home to scholars, philosophers, and poets since medieval times. This funky bookstore—a reincarnation of  the original shop from the 1920s—has picked up the literary torch. Sylvia Beach, an American with a passion for free thinking, opened Shakespeare and Company for the post-WWI Lost Generation who came to Paris to find themselves. American writers flocked here for the cheap rents, fleeing the uptight, Prohibition-era United States. Beach's bookstore was famous as a meeting place

of Paris' literary expatriate elite. Ernest Hemingway borrowed books from here regularly. James Joyce struggled to find a publisher for his now-classic novel *Ulysses*—until Sylvia Beach published it. George Bernard Shaw, Gertrude Stein, and Ezra Pound also got their English fix here.

Today, the bookstore carries on that literary tradition. Struggling writers are given free accommodations upstairs in tiny rooms with views of Notre-Dame. Downstairs, travelers enjoy a great selection of used English books. Pick up the *Paris Voice* newspaper and say hi to owner George and his daughter…Sylvia.

Notice the green water fountain (1900) in front of the bookstore, one of the many in Paris donated by the English philanthropist Sir Richard Wallace. The hooks below the carytids once held metal mugs for drinking the water.

• *Continue to the rue du Petit-Pont (which becomes rue St. Jacques). This busy north-south boulevard was the Romans' busiest boulevard 2,000 years ago, with chariots racing in and out of the city. (Romaniacs can see remains from the 3rd-century baths, along with a fine medieval collection, at the nearby Cluny Museum, 4 blocks away; €7 entry, €5.50 on Sun, free first Sun of month, covered by museum pass, Wed–Mon 9:15–17:45, closed Tue, near corner of boulevards St. Michel and St. Germain.)*

Walking away from the river for one block, turn right at the Gothic church of St. Séverin and walk into the Latin Quarter.

St. Séverin

Don't ask me why, but it took a century longer to build this church than Notre-Dame. This is flamboyant, or "flame-like," Gothic, and you can see the short, prickly spires meant to make this building flicker in the eyes of the faithful. The church gives us a close-up look at gargoyles. This weird, winged species of

flying mammal, now extinct, used to swoop down on unwary peasants, occasionally carrying off small children in their beaks. Today, they're most impressive in thunderstorms, when they vomit rain.

• *At #22 rue St. Séverin, you'll find the skinniest house in Paris, two windows wide. Rue St. Séverin leads right through…*

The Latin Quarter

While it may look more like the Greek Quarter today (cheap gyros sandwiches abound), this area is the Latin Quarter, named for the language you'd have heard on these streets if you walked them in the Middle Ages. The University of Paris (founded 1215), one of the leading educational institutions of medieval Europe, was (and still is) nearby.

A thousand years ago, the "crude" or vernacular local languages were sophisticated enough to communicate basic human needs, but if you wanted to get philosophical, the language of choice was Latin. The educated elite of medieval Europe was a class that transcended nations and borders. From Sicily to Sweden, they spoke and corresponded in Latin. Now the most Latin thing about this area is the beat you may hear coming from some of the subterranean jazz clubs.

Along rue St. Séverin, you can still see the shadow of the medieval sewer system. The street slopes into a central channel of bricks. In the days before plumbing and toilets, when people still went to the river or neighborhood wells for their water, flushing meant throwing it out the window. At certain times of day, maids on the fourth floor would holler, *"Garde de l'eau!"* ("Look out for the water!") and heave it into the streets, where it would eventually wash down into the Seine.

As you wander, remember that before Napoleon III commissioned Baron Haussmann to modernize the city with grand boulevards (19th century), Paris was just like this—a medieval tangle. The ethnic feel of this area is nothing new—it's been a melting pot and university district for almost 800 years.

Boulevard St. Michel

Busy boulevard St. Michel (or "boul' Miche") is famous as the main artery for Paris' café and arts scene, culminating a block away (to the left), where it intersects boulevard St. Germain. Although nowadays you're more likely to find pantyhose at 30 percent off, there are still many cafés, boutiques, and bohemian haunts nearby.

The Sorbonne—the University of Paris' humanities department—is also close, if you want to make a detour. (Turn left on boulevard St. Michel and walk two blocks south. Gaze at the dome from the place de la Sorbonne courtyard or, when school is in session, poke your head into some of the buildings. The entrance at 17 rue de la Sorbonne can sell you an overpriced guidebook.) Originally founded as a theological school, the Sorbonne began attracting more students and famous professors—such as St. Thomas Aquinas and Peter Abélard—as its prestige grew. By the time the school expanded to include other subjects, it had a reputation for bold, new ideas. Nonconformity is a tradition here, and Paris remains a world center for new intellectual trends.

• *Cross boulevard St. Michel. Just ahead is...*

Place St. André-des-Arts

This tree-filled square is lined with cafés. In Paris, most serious thinking goes on in cafés. For centuries, these have been social watering holes, where you can get a warm place to sit and stimulating conversation for the price of a cup of coffee. Every great French writer—from Voltaire and Jean-Jacques Rousseau to Jean-Paul Sartre and Jacques Derrida—had a favorite haunt.

Paris honors its writers. If you visit the Panthéon—a few blocks up boulevard St. Michel and to the left—you will find French writers (Voltaire, Victor Hugo, Emile Zola, and Rousseau), inventors (Louis Braille), and scientists (including Marie and Pierre Curie) buried in a setting usually reserved for warriors and politicians.

• *Adjoining this square is the triangular place St. Michel, with a Métro stop and a statue of St. Michael killing a devil. Note: If you were to continue west along rue St. André-des-Arts, you'd find more Left Bank action.*

Place St. Michel

You're standing at the traditional core of the Left Bank's artsy, liberal, hippie, bohemian district of poets, philosophers, and winos. Nearby, you'll find international eateries, far-out bookshops, street singers, pale girls in black berets, jazz clubs, and—these days— tourists. Small cinemas show avant-garde films, almost always in the *version originale* (v.o.). For colorful wandering and café-sitting, afternoons and evenings are best. In the morning, it feels sleepy. The Latin Quarter stays up late and sleeps in.

In less commercial times, place St. Michel was a gathering point for the city's malcontents and misfits. In 1830, 1848, and again in 1871, the citizens took the streets from the government troops, set up barricades *Les Miz*–style, and fought against royalist oppression. In World War II, the locals rose up against their Nazi oppressors (read the plaques under the dragons at the foot of the St. Michel fountain).

And in the spring of 1968, a time of social upheaval all over the world, young students battled riot batons and tear gas, took over the square, and declared it an independent state. Factory workers followed their call to arms and went on strike, toppling the de Gaulle government and forcing change. Eventually, the students were pacified, the university was reformed, and the Latin Quarter's original cobblestones were replaced with pavement, so future scholars could never again use the streets as weapons.

• *From place St. Michel, look across the river and find the spire of the Sainte-Chapelle church, with its weathervane angel nearby. Cross the river on pont St. Michel and continue north along the boulevard du Palais. On your left, you'll see the doorway to the Sainte-Chapelle. You'll need to pass through a metal detector to get into the Sainte-Chapelle complex. Once past security, restrooms are ahead on the left. The line into the church may be long. (Museum passholders can go directly in.)*

Enter the humble ground floor (pick up an English info flier and check the concert schedule if you're interested).

SAINTE-CHAPELLE

Sainte-Chapelle, the triumph of Gothic church architecture, is a cathedral of glass like no other. It was built in 1248 for King Louis IX (the only French king who is now a saint) to house the supposed Crown of Thorns. Its architectural harmony is due to the fact that it was completed under the direction of one architect and in only five years—unheard of in Gothic times. Recall that Notre-Dame took over 200 years.

The exterior is ugly. But those fat buttresses are all the support needed to hold up the roof, opening up the walls for stained glass. Inside the layout clearly shows an *ancien régime* approach to worship. The low-ceilinged basement was for staff and more common folks—worshiping under a sky filled with painted fleurs-de-lis, a symbol of the king. Royal Christians worshiped upstairs. The paint job, a 19th-century restoration, helps you imagine how grand this small, painted, jeweled chapel was. (Imagine Notre-Dame painted like this....)

It takes 13 tourists to build a Gothic church: six columns, six buttresses, and one steeple.

• *Climb the spiral staircase to the Haute Chapelle. Leave the rough stone of the earth and step into the light.*

The Stained Glass

Fiat lux. "Let there be light." From the first page of the Bible, it's clear—light is divine. Light shines through stained glass like God's grace shining down to earth, and Gothic architects used their new technology to turn dark stone buildings into lanterns of light. For me, the glory of Gothic shines brighter here than in any other church.

Sainte-Chapelle

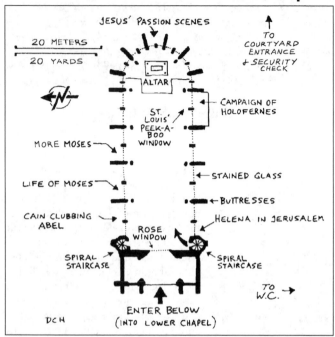

JESUS' PASSION SCENES

TO COURTYARD ENTRANCE & SECURITY CHECK

20 METERS
20 YARDS

N

ALTAR

CAMPAIGN OF HOLOFERNES

ST. LOUIS' PEEK-A-BOO WINDOW

MORE MOSES

LIFE OF MOSES

STAINED GLASS

CAIN CLUBBING ABEL

BUTTRESSES

HELENA IN JERUSALEM

ROSE WINDOW

SPIRAL STAIRCASE

SPIRAL STAIRCASE

TO W.C. →

DCH

ENTER BELOW
(INTO LOWER CHAPEL)

There are 15 separate panels of stained glass, with more than 1,100 different scenes, mostly from the Bible. These cover the entire Christian history of the world, from the Creation in Genesis (first window on the left, as you face the altar), to the coming of Christ (over the altar), to the end of the world (the round "rose"-shaped window at the rear of the church). Each individual scene is interesting, and the whole effect is overwhelming.

• *Working clockwise from the entrance, here are some scenes worth a look. (Note: The sun lights up different windows at different times of day. Overcast days give the most even light. On bright, sunny days, some sections are glorious while others look like a sheet of lead.)*

Genesis—Cain clubbing Abel (first window on left—always dark

because of a building butted up against it): On the bottom level in the third circle from left, God creates the round earth and holds it up. On the next level up, we see glimpses of naked Adam and Eve. On the third level (far right circle), Cain, in red, clubs his brother Abel, creating murder.

Stained Glass Supreme

Craftsmen made glass—which is, essentially, melted sand—using this recipe:

- Melt one part sand with two parts wood ash.
- Mix in rusty metals to get different colors—iron makes red, cobalt makes blue, copper green, manganese purple, cadmium yellow.
- Blow glass into a cylinder shape, cut lengthwise, and lay flat.
- Cut into pieces with an iron tool, or by heating and cooling a select spot to make it crack.
- Fit pieces together to form a figure, using strips of lead to hold in place.
- Place masterpiece so high on a wall that no one can read it.

Life of Moses (second window, the bottom row of diamond panels): The first panel shows baby Moses in a basket, placed by his sister in the squiggly brown river. Next, he's found by the pharaoh's daughter. Then, he grows up. And finally, he's a man, a prince of Egypt on his royal throne.

More Moses (third window, in middle and upper sections): You'll see various scenes of Moses, the guy with the bright yellow horns—the result of a medieval mistranslation of the Hebrew word for "rays of light," or halo.

Jesus' Passion Scenes (over the altar): These scenes from Jesus' arrest and crucifixion were the backdrop for the Crown of Thorns, which originally was displayed on the altar. Stand far enough back to look through the canopy to find Jesus in yellow shorts carrying his cross. A little below that, see Jesus being whipped (left) and—the key scene in this relic chapel—Jesus in purple being fitted with the painful Crown of Thorns (right). Finally (as high as you can see), Jesus on the cross is speared by a soldier.

Campaign of Holofernes: On the bottom row are four scenes of colorful knights. The second circle from the left is a battle scene (the campaign of Holofernes), showing three soldiers with swords slaughtering three men. The background is blue. The men have different-colored clothes—red, blue, green, mauve, and white. Notice some of the details. You can see the folds in the robes, the hair, and facial features. Look at the victim in the center—his head splotched with blood. Details like the folds in the robes (see the victim in white, lower left) came either by scratching on

the glass or by baking on paint. It was a painstaking process of finding just the right colors, fitting them together to make a scene…and then multiplying by 1,100.

Helena in Jerusalem (first window on the right wall): This window tells the story of how Christ's Crown of Thorns found its way from Jerusalem to Constantinople to this chapel. Start in the lower left corner, where the Roman emperor Constantine (in blue, on his throne) waves goodbye to his Christian mom, Helena. She arrives at the gate of Jerusalem (next panel to the right). Her men (in the two-part medallion above Jerusalem) dig through ruins and find Christ's (tiny) cross and other relics. She returns to Constantinople with a stash of holy relics, including the Crown of Thorns. Nine hundred years later, French Crusader knights (the next double medallion above) invade the Holy Land and visit Constantinople. Finally, King Louis IX, dressed in blue (in the panel up one and to the right of the last one) returns to France with the sacred relic.

Rose Window (above entrance): It's Judgment Day, with a tiny Christ in the center of the chaos and miracles. This window is 200 years newer then the rest, from the Flamboyant period. Facing west and the sunset, it's best late in the day.

If you can't read much into the individual windows, you're not alone. (For some tutoring, a little book with color photos is on sale downstairs with the postcards.)

Altar

The altar was raised up high (notice the staircase for the priest) to better display the relic around which this chapel was built—the Crown of Thorns. This was the crown put on Jesus when the Romans were torturing and humiliating him before his execution. King Louis IX, convinced he'd found the real McCoy, paid three times as much money for the thorns as was spent on this entire chapel. Today, the supposed Crown of Thorns is kept in the Notre-Dame Treasury (and shown only on Fridays during Lent).

Notice the little private viewing window in the right wall, near the altar. Louis was both saintly and shy. He liked to be able to go to church without dealing with the rigors of public royal life. Here he could worship still dressed in his jammies.

Lay your camera on the

ground and shoot the ceiling. Those pure and simple ribs growing out of the slender columns are the essence of Gothic structure.

• *Exit Sainte-Chapelle. Back outside, as you walk around the church exterior, look down to see the foundation and notice how much Paris has risen in the 750 years since the Sainte-Chapelle was built.*

Palais de Justice

You're in a huge complex of buildings that has housed the local government since ancient Roman times. It was the site of the original Gothic palace of the early kings of France. The only surviving medieval parts are Sainte-Chapelle and the Conciergerie prison.

Most of the site is now covered by the giant Palais de Justice, built in 1776, home of France's supreme court. The motto *Liberté, Egalité,*

Paris' Palais de Justice in 1650, with Sainte-Chapelle, the Conciergerie, and Pont Neuf (then 30 years old) in the background.

Fraternité over the doors is a reminder that this was also the headquarters of the Revolutionary government. Here, they doled out justice, condemning many to imprisonment in the Conciergerie downstairs or to the guillotine.

• *Now pass through the big iron gate to the noisy boulevard du Palais. Cross the street to the wide pedestrian-only rue de Lutèce.*

Cité "Metropolitain" Stop

Of the 141 original early-20th-century subway entrances, this is one of only a few survivors—now preserved as a national art treasure. (New York's Museum of Modern Art even exhibits one.) It marks Paris at its peak in 1900—on the cutting edge of modernism but with an eye to beauty. The curvy, plantlike ironwork is a textbook example of Art Nouveau, the style that rebelled against the erector-set squareness of the Industrial Age. In Paris, only the stations at Abbesses and Porte Dauphine survive with their canopies.

The flower and plant market on place Louis Lépine is a pleasant detour. On Sundays, this square is all aflutter with a busy bird market. And across the way is the Prefecture de Police, where Inspector Clouseau of *Pink Panther* fame used to work, and where the local resistance fighters took the first building from the Nazis in August of 1944, leading to the Allied liberation of Paris a week later.

Sainte-Chapelle Area

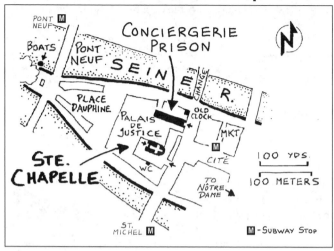

• *Pause here to admire the view. Sainte-Chapelle is a pearl in an ugly architectural oyster. To the right of the Palais de Justice is the Conciergerie, with its entrance on boulevard du Palais. Though pretty barren inside, the Conciergerie echoes with history and is free with the museum pass.*

Conciergerie

Positioned next to the courthouse, the Conciergerie was the gloomy prison famous as the last stop for 2,780 victims of the guillotine, including France's last queen, Marie-Antoinette. Before then, kings had used the building to torture and execute failed assassins. (One of its towers along the river was called "the babbler," named for the painful sounds that leaked from it.) When the Revolution (1789) toppled the king, the building kept its same function, but without torture. The progressive Revolutionaries proudly unveiled a modern and more humane way to execute people—the guillotine.

Inside, pick up a free map and breeze through. See the spacious, low-ceilinged Hall of Men-at-Arms (Room 2) with four large fireplaces, used as a staff cafeteria in medieval times. This big room gives a feel for the grandeur of the Great Hall (upstairs, not open to visitors) where the Revolutionary tribunals grilled scared prisoners on their political correctness. The raised area at the far end of the room (Room 4, today's bookstore) was notorious as the walkway of the executioner, who was known affectionately as "Monsieur de Paris." The Prisoners' Gallery (Room 5) is a hall where the condemned milled about, waiting for the open-air cart (tumbrel) to pull up outside to carry them to the guillotine on place de la Concorde.

Upstairs in the Audio-Visual Room (top of the stairs), a video recreates prison life. Lining the walls are lists of the 2,780 citizens condemned to death by the guillotine. In alphabetical order, find: Georges Danton (prominent revolutionary who was later condemned for being insufficiently liberal, a nasty crime), Charlotte Corday (a noblewoman who snuck into the bathroom of the revolutionary writer, Jean-Paul Marat, and stabbed him while he bathed), Anne-Elizabeth Capet (whose crime was being "sister of the tyrant"), Louis XVI ("called Capet: last king of France"), Marie-Antoinette, and—oh the irony—Maximilien de Robespierre, the head of the Revolution, the man who sent so many to the guillotine and who was eventually toppled, humiliated, imprisoned here, and beheaded.

Also upstairs, you'll walk by some reconstructed cells showing how the poor slept on straw while the wealthy got a cot.

Back downstairs, you wind up in the re-creation of Marie-Antoinette's Cell (Room 12), on the actual site of her original cell, though the building's layout has seen some changes. This was where the Queen spent her last days—separated from her 10-year-old son, and now widowed, because the King had already been executed. Mannequins and period furniture set the scene. The guard stands modestly behind a screen while the queen psyches herself up with a crucifix. In the glass display case, see her actual crucifix, napkin, and small water pitcher. On October 16, 1793, the queen walked the corridor, stepped onto the cart, and was slowly carried to place de la Concorde, where she had a date with "Monsieur de Paris."

• *Back outside, turn left on boulevard du Palais and head toward the river (north). On the corner is the city's oldest public clock. The mechanism of the present clock is from 1334, and even though the case is Baroque, it keeps on ticking.*

Turn left onto quai de l'Horloge and walk west along the river, past the round medieval tower called "the babbler." The bridge up ahead is the pont Neuf, where we'll end this walk. At the first corner, veer left into a sleepy triangular square called place Dauphine.

Place Dauphine

It's amazing to find such coziness in the heart of Paris. This city of two million is still a city of neighborhoods, a collection of villages. The French Supreme Court building looms behind like a giant marble gavel. Enjoy the village-Paris feeling in the park. You may see lawyers on their lunch break playing *boules*.

Boules

Each player starts with three iron balls, with the object of getting them close to the target, a small wooden ball called a *cochonnet*. The first player tosses the *cochonnet* about 30 feet, then throws the first of his iron balls near the target. The next player takes a turn. As soon as a player's ball is closest, it's the other guy's turn. Once all balls have been thrown, the score is tallied—the player with the closest ball gets one point for each ball closer to the target than his opponent's. The loser gets zero. Games are generally to 15 points.

A regulation *boules* field is 10-by-43 feet, but the game is played everywhere—just scratch a throwing circle in the sand, toss the *cochonnet,* and you're off. Strategists can try to knock the opponent's balls out of position, knock the *cochonnet* itself out of position, or guard their best ball with the other two.

• *Continue through place Dauphine. As you pop out the other end, you're face to face with a…*

Statue of Henry IV

Henry IV (1553–1610) is not as famous as his grandson, Louis XIV, but Henry helped make Paris what it is today—a European capital of elegant buildings and quiet squares. He built the place Dauphine (behind you), the pont Neuf (to the right), residences (to the left, down rue Dauphine), the Louvre's long Grand Gallery, and the tree-filled square Vert-Galant (directly behind the statue, on the tip of the island). The square is one of Paris' make-out spots; its name comes from Henry's own nickname, the Green Knight, as Henry was a notorious ladies' man. The park is a great place to relax, dangling your legs over the concrete prow of this boat-shaped island.

• *From the statue, turn right onto the old bridge. Walk to the little nook halfway across.*

Pont Neuf

The pont Neuf, or "new bridge," is Paris' oldest standing bridge (built 1578–1607). Its 12 arches span the widest part of the river. Unlike other bridges, this one never had houses or buildings growing on it. The turrets were originally for vendors and street entertainers. In the days of Henry IV, who promised his peasants "a chicken in every pot every Sunday," this would have been a lively scene. From the bridge, look downstream (west) to see the next bridge, the pedestrian-only pont des Arts. Ahead on the Right Bank is the long Louvre Museum. Beyond that on the Left Bank is the Orsay. And what's that tall black tower in the distance?

The Seine

Our walk ends where Paris began—on the Seine River. From Dijon to the English Channel, the Seine meanders 500 miles, cutting through the center of Paris. The river is shallow and slow within the city, but still dangerous enough to require steep stone embankments (built 1910) to prevent occasional floods. You'll see tourist boats and commercial barges that carry 20 percent of Paris' transported goods. And on the banks, sportsmen today cast into the waters once fished by Paris' original Celtic inhabitants.

• *We're done. You can take a boat tour that leaves from near the base of pont Neuf on the island side (Vedettes du Pont-Neuf, €9, departs hourly on the hour, twice hourly after dark, has live guide with explanations in French and English) or catch the Métro to anywhere in Paris (the nearest Métro stop is Pont Neuf, across the bridge on the Right Bank).*

LOUVRE

(Musée du Louvre)

Paris walks you through world history in three world-class museums—the Louvre (ancient world to 1850), the Orsay (1850–1914, including Impressionism), and the Pompidou (20th century to today). Start your "art-yssey" at the Louvre. With more than 30,000 works of art, the Louvre is a full inventory of Western civilization. To cover it all in one visit is in-Seine. Let's focus on the Louvre's specialties— Greek sculpture, Italian painting, and French painting.

We'll see "Venuses" through history, from scrawny Stone Age fertility goddesses to the curvy *Venus de Milo*, from the wind-blown *Winged Victory of Samothrace* to placid medieval Madonnas, from *Mona Lisa* to the symbol of modern democracy. We'll consider how each generation defines beauty differently and gain insight into long-ago civilizations by admiring the things they found beautiful.

In addition—for those with a little more time—we can visit some impressive chunks of stone from the "Cradle of Civilization," modern-day Iraq.

ORIENTATION

Cost: €8.50, €6 after 18:00 on Mon and Wed, free on first Sun of month and for those under 18, covered by museum pass. Tickets good all day; reentry allowed.

The Louvre—A Bird's Eye View

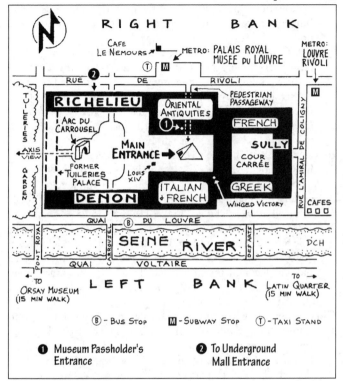

Hours: Wed–Mon 9:00–18:00, closed Tue. All wings open Wed until 21:45. On Mon, only the Denon wing is open until 21:45 (but it contains the biggies—*Mona Lisa* and *Venus de Milo*, etc.) and sometimes part of the Sully and Richelieu (Egyptian and Oriental antiquities) wings. Galleries start shutting down 30 minutes early. The last entry is 45 minutes before closing. Crowds are worst on Sun, Mon, Wed, and mornings.

Getting There: The Métro stop Palais Royal-Musée du Louvre is closer to the entrance than the stop called Louvre-Rivoli. From the Palais Royal-Musée du Louvre stop, you can stay underground to enter the Louvre, or exit above ground if you want to enter the Louvre through the pyramid (more details below). There's a taxi stand on rue de Rivoli next to the Palais Royal-Musée du Louvre Métro station.

Getting In: There is no grander entry than through the main entrance at the pyramid in the central courtyard, but metal detectors (not ticket-buying lines) create a long line at times. There are several ways to avoid the line:

Museum passholders can use the group entrance in the pedestrian passageway between the pyramid and rue de Rivoli (under the arches, a few steps north of the pyramid, find the uniformed guard at the entrance, with the escalator down).

Otherwise, you can enter the Louvre from its (usually less-crowded) underground entrance, accessed through the "Carrousel du Louvre" shopping mall. Enter the mall at 99 rue de Rivoli (the door with the red awning, daily 8:30–23:00) or directly from the Métro stop Palais Royal-Musée du Louvre (stepping off the train, exit to the left, following signs to Carrousel du Louvre-Musée du Louvre).

Information: Pick up the free *Louvre Handbook* in English at the information desk under the pyramid as you enter. Tel. 01 40 20 51 51, recorded info tel. 01 40 20 53 17, www.louvre.fr.

Tours: The 90-minute English-language tours leave three times daily except Sun (normally at 11:00, 14:00, and 15:45, €3 plus your entry ticket, tour tel. 01 40 20 52 63). Digital audioguides (available for €5 at entries to the three wings, at top of escalators) give you a directory of about 130 masterpieces, allowing you to dial a rather dull commentary on included works as you stumble upon them. I prefer the free, self-guided tour described below.

Length of This Tour: Two hours.

Checkrooms: Located under the escalators. They will accept no cameras or any valuables in your bag. The coat check, which can have a torturously slow line (worst early in the morning and late afternoon), does not take bags. The baggage check (which doesn't take coats that are not stuffed into bags) is separate from the coat check and generally has almost no line.

Photography: Photography without a flash is allowed.

Cuisine Art: The underground shopping mall has a dizzying assortment of good-value, smoke-free eateries (up the escalator near the inverted pyramid). You'll also find a post office, handy TI, SNCF train office, glittering boutiques, and the Palais Royal-Musée du Louvre Métro entrance. Stairs at the far end take you right into the Tuileries Garden, a perfect antidote to the stuffy, crowded rooms of the Louvre. For a fine but more expensive light lunch than the Louvre's eateries, cross rue de Rivoli to the venerable Café le Nemours (open daily; leaving the Louvre, cross rue de Rivoli and veer left, 2 place Colette, adjacent to the Comédie Française).

Starring: *Venus de Milo, Winged Victory of Samothrace, Mona Lisa,* Raphael, Michelangelo, and the French painters.

THE TOUR BEGINS

The Louvre, the largest museum in the Western world, fills three wings in this immense U-shaped palace. The Richelieu wing (north side of Louvre) houses Oriental antiquities (covered in the second part of this tour), plus French, Dutch, and Northern art. The Sully wing (east side) has the extensive French painting and ancient Egypt collections.

For this part of the tour, we'll concentrate on the Louvre's Denon wing (south side), which houses many of the superstars: ancient Greek sculpture, Italian Renaissance painting, and French neoclassical and Romantic painting.

Expect changes. The sprawling Louvre is constantly in flux. If you can't find a particular work, ask a guard where it is. Point to the photo in your book and ask, *"Où est, s'il vous plaît?"* (it rhymes). And move quickly. Try to finish our once-over tour with enough energy left to browse.

• *Orient from underneath the glass pyramid. Pick up the free map at the information desk inside the pyramid, and look for signs to the three wings. Take escalator up one floor to the Denon wing. After showing your ticket, take the first left you can, follow signs to Antiquités Grecques, and climb a set of stairs to the brick-ceilinged Salle 1: La Grèce préclassique (salle = room). Enter prehistory.*

DENON WING—GREEK STATUES (3,000 B.C.–A.D. 1)

Pre-Classical Greece

These statues are noble but crude. The Greek Barbie dolls (3000 B.C.) are older than the pyramids, as old as writing itself. These pre-rational voodoo dolls whittle women down to their life-giving traits. Farther along, a woman *(Dame d'Auxerre)* pledges allegiance to stability. Another *(Core)* is essentially a column with breasts. A young, naked man *(Couros)* seems to have a gun to his back—his hands at his sides, facing front, with sketchy muscles and a mask-like face. "Don't move."

The early Greeks, who admired such statues, found stability more attractive than movement. Like their legendary hero, Odysseus, the Greek people had spent generations wandering, war-weary, and longing for the comforts of a secure home. The noble strength and

The Louvre—Pre-Classical Greece

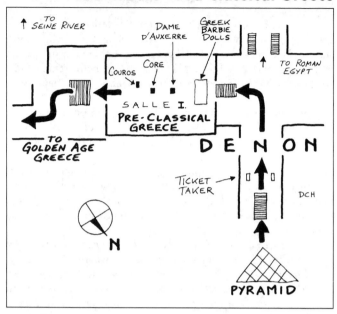

↑ TO
SEINE RIVER

DAME
D'AUXERRE

GREEK
BARBIE
DOLLS

COUROS

CORE

↑ TO ROMAN
EGYPT

SALLE I.
PRE-CLASSICAL
GREECE

TO
GOLDEN AGE
GREECE

D E N O N

TICKET
TAKER

DCH

N

PYRAMID

sturdiness of these works looked beautiful.

• *Exit Salle 1 at the far end and climb the stairs one flight. At the top, veer 10 o'clock left, where you'll soon see* Venus de Milo, *floating above a sea of worshiping tourists. It's been said that, among the warlike Greeks, this was the first statue to unilaterally disarm.*

Venus de Milo (Aphrodite, c. 100 B.C.)

The *Venus de Milo* (or goddess of love, from the Greek island of Melos) created a sensation when it was discovered in 1820. Europe was already in the grip of a classical fad, and this statue seemed to sum up all that ancient Greece stood for. The Greeks pictured their gods in human form (meaning humans are god-like), telling us they had an optimistic view of the human race. *Venus'* well-proportioned body embodies the balance and orderliness of the Greek universe.

Split *Venus* down the middle from nose to toes and see how the two halves balance each other. *Venus* rests on her right foot (called *contrapposto,* or "counterpoise"), then lifts her left leg, setting her whole body in motion. As the left leg rises, her right shoulder droops down. And as her

Greek Statues

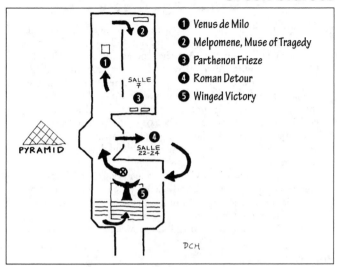

1 Venus de Milo

2 Melpomene, Muse of Tragedy

3 Parthenon Frieze

4 Roman Detour

5 Winged Victory

SALLE 7

SALLE 22-24

PYRAMID

DCH

knee points one way, her head turns the other. *Venus* is a harmonious balance of opposites, orbiting slowly around a vertical axis. The twisting pose gives a balanced S-curve to her body (especially noticeable from the back view) that the Greeks and succeeding generations found beautiful.

Other opposites balance as well, like the smooth skin of her upper half that sets off the rough-cut texture of her dress (size 14). She's actually made from two different pieces of stone plugged together at the hips (the seam is visible). The face is realistic and anatomically accurate, but it's also idealized, a goddess, too generic and too perfect. This isn't any particular woman, but Everywoman—all the idealized features that appealed to the Greeks.

Most "Greek" statues are actually later Roman copies. This is a rare Greek original. This "epitome of the Golden Age" was actually sculpted three centuries after the Golden Age, though in a retro-style.

What were her missing arms doing? Some say her right arm held her dress while her left arm was raised. Others say she was hugging a man statue or leaning on a column. I say she was picking her navel.

• *Orbit* Venus. *This statue is interesting and different from every angle. Remember the view from the back—we'll see it again later. Make your reentry to Earth behind her, with a U-turn to the right, doubling back down a room lined with Greek statues. Try to find even one that's not* contrapposto. *The large statue of* Melpomene, *holding the frowning mask of Tragedy, dominates the room. At the far end (in Salle 7, the Salle du Parthénon), you'll bump into two carved panels on the wall.*

Golden Age Greece

The great Greek cultural explosion that changed the course of history unfolded over 50 years (around 450 B.C.) in Athens, a Greek town smaller than Muncie, Indiana. Having united the Greeks to repel a Persian invasion, Athens rebuilt, with the Parthenon as the centerpiece of the city. The Greeks dominated the ancient world through brain, not brawn, and the art shows their love of rationality, order, and balance. The ideal Greek was well-rounded—an athlete and a bookworm, a lover and a philosopher, a carpenter who plays the piano, a warrior and a poet. In art, the balance between timeless stability and fleeting movement made beauty.

In a sense, we're all Greek. Democracy, mathematics, theater, philosophy, literature, and science were practically invented in ancient Greece. Most of the art that we'll see in the Louvre either came from Greece or was inspired by it.

Parthenon Frieze
(*Fragment de la Frise des Panathénées*, c. 440 B.C.)

These stone fragments once decorated the exterior of the greatest Athenian temple, the Parthenon, built at the peak of the Greek Golden Age. The right panel shows a centaur sexually harassing a woman. It tells the story of how these rude creatures crashed a party of humans. But the Greeks fought back and threw the brutes out, just as Athens (metaphorically) conquered its barbarian neighbors and became civilized.

The other relief shows the sacred procession of young girls who marched up the hill every four years with an embroidered veil for the 40-foot-high statue of Athena, the goddess of  wisdom. Though headless, the maidens speak volumes about Greek craftsmanship. Carved in only a couple inches of stone, they're amazingly realistic—more so than anything we saw in the pre-Classical period. They glide along horizontally (their belts and shoulders all in a line), while the folds of their dresses drape down vertically. The man in the center is relaxed, realistic, and *contrapposto*. Notice the veins in his arm. The maidens' pleated dresses make them look as stable as fluted columns, but their arms and legs step out naturally—the human form is emerging from the stone.

• *Make a lo-o-o-ng (50-step) loop behind the Parthenon Frieze panels, turning left into Salle 22, the Antiquités Romaines, for a ...*

Roman Detour
(Salles 22–24 and beyond)

Stroll among the Caesars and try to see the person behind the public persona. You might spot Augustus *(Auguste)*, the first emperor, and his wily wife, Livia *(Livie)*. Their son Tiberius *(Tibere)* was the Caesar that Jesus Christ "rendered unto." Curly-haired Domitia murdered her husband, Hadrian popularized the beard, Trajan ruled the Empire at its peak, Marcus Aurelius *(Marc Aurele)* presided stoically over Rome's slow fall. And you can't miss the many faces of the ubiquitous Emperor *Inconnu* ("unknown").

The pragmatic Romans (500 B.C.–A.D. 500) were great conquerors, but bad artists. One area in which the Romans excelled was realistic portrait busts, especially of their emperors, who were worshiped as gods on earth. Fortunately for us, the Romans also had a huge appetite for Greek statues and made countless copies. They took the Greek style and wrote it in capital letters, adding a veneer of sophistication to their homes, temples, baths, and government buildings.

The Roman rooms also contain sarcophagi and an impressive mosaic floor. Weary? Kick back and relax with the statues in the Etruscan Lounge (in Salle 18).

• *This Roman detour deposits you at the base of stairs leading up to the First Floor and the dramatic…*

Winged Victory of Samothrace
(Victoire de Samothrace, c. 190 B.C.)

This woman with wings, poised on the prow of a ship, once stood on a hilltop to commemorate a naval victory. Her clothes are windblown and sea-sprayed, clinging to her body close enough to win a wet T-shirt contest. (Notice the detail in the folds of her dress around the navel, curving down to her hips.) Originally, her right arm was stretched high, celebrating the victory like a Super Bowl champion, waving a "we're-number-one" finger.

This is the *Venus de Milo* gone Hellenistic, from the time after the culture of Athens was spread around the Mediterranean by Alexander the Great (c. 325 B.C.). As *Victory* strides forward, the wind blows her and her wings back. Her feet are firmly on the ground, but her wings (and missing arms) stretch upward. She is a pillar of vertical strength while the clothes curve and whip around her. These opposing forces create a feeling of great energy, making her the lightest two-ton piece of rock in captivity.

The earlier Golden Age Greeks might have considered this statue ugly. Her rippling excitement is a far cry from the dainty Parthenon maidens and the soft-focus beauty of *Venus*. And the statue's off-balance pose leaves you hanging, like an unfinished melody. But Hellenistic Greeks loved these cliff-hanging scenes of real-life humans struggling to make their mark.

In the glass case nearby is *Victory*'s open right hand with an outstretched finger, discovered in 1950, a century after the statue itself was unearthed. When the French discovered this was in Turkey, they negotiated with the Turkish government for the rights to it. Considering all the other ancient treasures the French had looted from Turkey in the past, the Turks thought it only appropriate to give France the finger.

• *Enter the octagonal room to the left as you face the* Winged Victory, *with Icarus bungee-jumping from the ceiling. Bench yourself under a window and look out toward the pyramid.*

View from the Octagonal Room— The Louvre as a Palace

The Louvre, the former royal palace, was built in stages over eight centuries. On your right (the eastern Sully wing) was the original medieval fortress. Next, another palace, the Tuileries, was built 500 yards to the west—in the now-open area past the pyramid and past the triumphal arch. Succeeding kings tried to connect these two palaces, each one adding another section onto the long, skinny north and south wings. Finally, in 1852, after three centuries of building, the two palaces were connected, creating a rectangular Louvre. Nineteen years later, the Tuileries Palace burned down during a riot, leaving the U-shaped Louvre we see today.

The glass pyramid was designed by the American architect I. M. Pei (1989). Many Parisians hated the pyramid, like they used to hate another new and controversial structure 100 years ago—the Eiffel Tower.

In the octagonal room, a plaque at the base of the dome explains that France's Revolutionary National Assembly (the same people who brought you the guillotine) founded this museum in 1793. What could be more logical? You behead the king, inherit his palace and art collection, open the doors to the masses, and, *Voilà!* You have Europe's first public museum.

• *The Italian collection ("Peintures Italiennes") is on the other side of the* Winged Victory. *Cross in front of the* Winged Victory *to the other side and pause (in Salle 1) at the two Botticelli fresco paintings on the wall to the left. These pure maidens, like colorized versions of the Parthenon frieze, give us a taste of how ancient Greece would be "reborn" in the Renaissance. But first, continue into the large Salle 3.*

THE MEDIEVAL WORLD (1200–1500)

Cimabue—*The Madonna of the Angels* (1280)

During the Age of Faith (1200s), most every church in Europe had a painting like this one. Mary was a cult figure—bigger than even the 20th-century Madonna—adored and prayed to by the faithful for bringing baby Jesus into the world. After the collapse of the Roman Empire (c. A.D. 500), medieval Europe was a poorer and more violent place, with the Christian Church being the only constant in troubled times.

Altarpieces like this followed the same formula: Somber iconic faces, stiff poses, elegant folds in the robes, and generic angels. Violating 3-D space, the angels at the "back" of Mary's throne are the same size as those holding the front. These holy figures are laid flat on a gold background like cardboard cutouts, existing in a golden never-never-land, as though the faithful couldn't imagine them as flesh-and-blood humans inhabiting our dark and sinful earth.

Giotto—*St. Francis of Assisi Receiving the Stigmata* (c. 1290–1295)

Francis of Assisi (c. 1181–1226), a wandering Italian monk of renowned goodness, kneels on a rocky Italian hillside, pondering the pain of Christ's torture and execution. Suddenly he looks up, startled, to see Christ himself, with six wings, hovering above. Christ shoots lasers from his wounds to burn marks on the hands, feet, and side of the empathetic monk. Francis went on to breathe the spirit of

the Renaissance into medieval Europe. His humble love of man and nature inspired artists like Giotto to portray real human beings with real emotions and living in a physical world of beauty.

Like a good filmmaker, Giotto (c. 1266–1337; JOT-toh) doesn't just *tell* us what happened, he *shows* us in present tense, freezing the scene at the most dramatic moment. Though the perspective is crude—Francis' hut is smaller than he is, and Christ is somehow shooting at Francis while facing us—Giotto gives a glimpse of the 3-D world of the coming Renaissance. He paints a foreground

(Francis), middle ground (his hut), and background (the hillside) to create the illusion of depth. Painting a 3-D world on a 2-D surface is tough, and after a millennium of Dark Ages, artists were rusty.

In the *predella* (the panel of paintings below the altarpiece), birds gather at Francis' feet to hear him talk about God. Giotto catches the late arrivals in mid-flight, an astonishing technical feat for an artist more than a century before the Renaissance. The simple gesture of Francis' companion speaks volumes about his amazement. Breaking the stiff, iconic mold for saints, Francis bends forward at the waist to talk to his fellow creatures, while the tree bends down symmetrically to catch a few words from the beloved hippie of Assisi.

• *The long Grand Gallery displays Italian Renaissance painting, some masterpieces, some not.*

The Grand Gallery

The Grand Gallery was built in the late 1500s to connect the old palace with the Tuileries Palace. From the doorway, look to the far end and consider this challenge: I hold the world's record for the Grand Gallery Heel-Toe-Fun-Walk-Tourist-Slalom, going end to end in one minute 58 seconds, two injured. Time yourself. Along the way, notice some of the...

Features of Italian Renaissance Painting

- **Religious:** Lots of Madonnas, children, martyrs, and saints.
- **Symmetrical:** The Madonnas are flanked by saints—two to the left, two to the right, and so on.
- **Realistic:** Real-life human features are especially obvious in the occasional portrait.
- **Three-Dimensional:** Every scene gets a spacious setting with a distant horizon.
- **Classical:** You'll see some Greek gods and classical nudes, but even Christian saints pose like Greek statues, and Mary is a Venus whose face and gestures embody all that was good in the Christian world.

Andrea Mantegna—*St. Sebastian* (c. 1480)

This isn't the patron saint of acupuncture. St. Sebastian was a Christian martyr, although here he looks more like a classical Greek

The Louvre—Grand Gallery

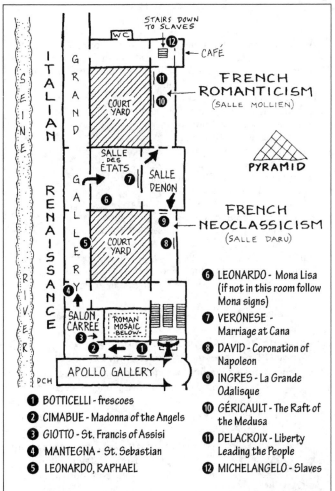

```
STAIRS DOWN
TO SLAVES
WC
⑫
← CAFÉ

FRENCH
ROMANTICISM
(SALLE MOLLIEN)
⑪
⑩

COURT YARD

SALLE DES ÉTATS
⑦  SALLE DENON

PYRAMID

⑥

⑨  FRENCH
NEOCLASSICISM
(SALLE DARU)

⑤  COURT YARD  ⑧

④

SALON CARRÉE
ROMAN MOSAIC BELOW
③
②  ←  ①

APOLLO GALLERY
DCH

ITALIAN

RENAISSANCE

SEINE RIVER

GRAND GALLERY
```

❶ BOTTICELLI - frescoes
❷ CIMABUE - Madonna of the Angels
❸ GIOTTO - St. Francis of Assisi
❹ MANTEGNA - St. Sebastian
❺ LEONARDO, RAPHAEL

❻ LEONARDO - Mona Lisa (if not in this room follow Mona signs)
❼ VERONESE - Marriage at Cana
❽ DAVID - Coronation of Napoleon
❾ INGRES - La Grande Odalisque
❿ GÉRICAULT - The Raft of the Medusa
⓫ DELACROIX - Liberty Leading the People
⓬ MICHELANGELO - Slaves

statue. Notice the *contrapposto* stance (all of his weight resting on one leg) and the Greek ruins scattered around him. His executioners look like ignorant medieval brutes bewildered by this enlightened Renaissance man. Italian artists were beginning to learn how to create human realism and earthly beauty on the canvas. Let the Renaissance begin.

• *Look for the following masterpieces by Leonardo and Raphael in the Grand Gallery.*

Italian Renaissance
(1400–1600)

A thousand years after Rome fell, plunging Europe into the Dark Ages, the Greek ideal of beauty was "reborn" in 15th-century Italy. The Renaissance—or "rebirth" of the culture of ancient Greece and Rome—was a cultural boom that changed people's thinking about every aspect of life. In politics, it meant democracy. In religion, it meant a move away from Church dominance and toward the assertion of man (humanism) and a more personal faith. Science and secular learning were revived after centuries of superstition and ignorance. In architecture, it was a return to the balanced columns and domes of Greece and Rome.

In painting, the Renaissance meant realism, and for the Italians, realism was spelled "3-D." Artists rediscovered the beauty of nature and the human body. With pictures of beautiful people in harmonious, 3-D surroundings, they expressed the optimism and confidence of this new age.

Leonardo da Vinci—*Virgin, Child, and St. Anne* (*La Vierge, l'Enfant Jésus, et Sainte-Anne,* c. 1510)

Three generations—grandmother, mother, and child—are arranged in a pyramid with Anne's face as the peak and the lamb as the lower-right corner. Within this balanced structure, Leonardo sets the figures in motion. Anne's legs are pointed to our left. (Is Anne *Mona?* Hmm.) Her daughter Mary, sitting on her lap, reaches to the right. Jesus looks at her playfully while turning away. The lamb pulls away from him. But even with all the twisting and turning, this is still a placid scene. It's as orderly as the geometrically perfect universe created by the Renaissance god.

There's a psychological kidney punch in this happy painting. Jesus, the picture of childish joy, is innocently playing with a lamb—the symbol of his inevitable sacrificial death.

The Louvre has the greatest collection of Leonardos in the world—all five of them. Look for the neighboring *Virgin of the Rocks* and his androgynous *John the Baptist.* Leonardo was the consummate Renaissance man. Musician, sculptor, engineer, scientist, and sometimes painter, he combined knowledge from all areas to create beauty. If he were alive today, he'd create a Unified Field Theory in physics—and set it to music.

Raphael—*La Belle Jardinière* (1507)

Raphael perfected the style Leonardo pioneered. This configuration of Madonna, Child, and John the Baptist is also a balanced pyramid with hazy grace and beauty. Mary is a mountain of maternal tenderness (the title translates as "The Beautiful Gardener"), as she eyes her son with a knowing look. Jesus looks up innocently, standing *contrapposto* like a chubby Greek statue.

With Raphael, the Greek ideal of beauty reborn in the Renaissance reached its peak. His work spawned so many imitators who cranked out sickly sweet, generic Madonnas that we often take him for granted. Don't. This is the real thing.

• *The* Mona Lisa (La Joconde) *is in the Salle des Etats, midway down the Grand Gallery. (If she's been moved elsewhere, you can't miss her. Just follow the signs and crowds.)*

Leonardo da Vinci—*Mona Lisa* (1503–1506)

Leonardo was already an old man when François I invited him to France. Determined to pack light, he took only a few paintings with him. One was a portrait of Lisa del Giocondo, the wife of a wealthy Florentine merchant. When Leonardo arrived, François immediately fell in love with the painting, making it the centerpiece of the small collection of Italian masterpieces that would, in three centuries, become the Louvre museum. He called it *La Joconde.* We know it as a contraction of the Italian for "my lady Lisa"—*Mona Lisa.*

Mona may disappoint you. She's smaller than you'd expect, darker, engulfed in a huge room, and hidden behind a glaring pane of glass. So, you ask, "Why all the hubbub?" Let's take a closer look. Like any lover, you've got to take her for what she is, not what you'd like her to be.

The famous smile attracts you first. Leonardo used a hazy technique called *sfumato,* blurring the edges of *Mona*'s mysterious smile. Try as you might, you can never quite see the corners of her mouth. Is she happy? Sad? Tender? Or is it a cynical supermodel's smirk? Every viewer reads it differently, projecting his own mood onto *Mona*'s enigmatic face. *Mona* is a Rorschach inkblot...so how are you feeling?

Now look past the smile and the eyes that really do follow you (most eyes in portraits do) to some of the subtle Renaissance elements that make this work work. The body is surprisingly massive and statue-like, a perfectly balanced pyramid turned at an angle so that we can see its mass. Her arm is resting lightly on the chair's armrest almost on the level of the frame itself, like she's sitting in a window looking out at us. The folds of her sleeves and her gently folded hands are remarkably realistic and relaxed. The typical Leonardo landscape shows distance by getting hazier and hazier.

The overall mood is one of balance and serenity, but there's also an element of mystery. Her smile and long-distance beauty are subtle and elusive, tempting but always just out of reach, like strands of a street singer's melody drifting through the Métro tunnel. *Mona* doesn't knock your socks off, but she winks at the patient viewer.

• *The huge canvas at the far end of the Salle des Etats is...*

Paolo Veronese—*The Marriage at Cana* (1562–1563)

Stand 10 steps away from this enormous canvas to where it just fills your field of vision, and suddenly...you're in a party! Help yourself to a glass of wine. This is the Renaissance love of beautiful things gone hog-wild. Venetian artists like Veronese painted the good life of rich, happy-go-lucky Venetian merchants.

In a spacious setting of Renaissance architecture, colorful lords and ladies decked out in their fanciest duds feast on a great spread of food and drink, while the musicians fuel the fires of good fun. Servants prepare and serve the food, jesters play, and animals roam. In the upper left, a dog and his master look on. A sturdy linebacker in yellow pours wine out of a jug (right foreground). The man in white samples some wine and thinks, "Hmm, not bad," while nearby a ferocious cat battles a lion. The wedding couple at the far left is almost forgotten.

Believe it or not, this is a religious work showing the wedding celebration where Jesus turned water into wine. And there's Jesus in the dead center of 130 frolicking figures, wondering if maybe wine coolers might not have been a better choice. With true Renaissance optimism, Venetians pictured Christ as a party animal, someone who loved the created world as much as they did.

Now, let's hear it for the band! On bass—the bad cat with the funny hat—Titian the Venetian! And joining him on viola—Crazy Veronese!

• *Exit behind* The Marriage at Cana *into the Salle Denon. The dramatic Romantic room is to your left, and the grand neoclassical room is to your right. They feature the most exciting French canvases in the Louvre. In the neoclassical room, kneel before the largest canvas in the Louvre.*

FRENCH PAINTING—NEOCLASSICAL (1780–1850)

Jacques-Louis David—*The Coronation of Napoleon* (1806–1807)

Napoleon holds aloft an imperial crown. This common-born son of immigrants is about to be crowned emperor of a "New Rome." He has just made his wife, Josephine, the empress, and she kneels at his feet. Seated behind Napoleon is the pope, who journeyed from Rome to place the imperial crown on his head. But Napoleon felt that no one was worthy of the task. At the last moment, he shrugged the pope aside, grabbed the crown, held it up for all to see…and crowned himself. The pope looks p.o.'d.

After the French people decapitated their king during the Revolution (1793), their fledgling democracy floundered in chaos. France was united by a charismatic, brilliant, temperamental upstart general who kept his feet on the ground, his eyes on the horizon, and his hand in his coat—Napoleon Bonaparte. Napoleon quickly conquered most of Europe and insisted on being made emperor (not merely king). The painter David (dah-veed) recorded the coronation for posterity.

The radiant woman in the gallery in the background center wasn't actually there. Napoleon's mother couldn't make it to see her boy become the most powerful man in Europe, but he had David paint her in anyway. (There's a key on the frame telling who's who in the picture.)

The traditional place of French coronations was the ultra-Gothic Notre-Dame cathedral. But Napoleon wanted a setting that would reflect the glories of Greece and the grandeur of Rome. So interior decorators erected stage sets of Greek columns and Roman arches to give the cathedral the architectural political correctness you see in this painting. (The *Pietà* statue on the right edge of the painting is still in Notre-Dame today.)

David was the new emperor's official painter

and propagandist, in charge of color-coordinating the costumes and flags for public ceremonies and spectacles. (Find his self-portrait with curly gray hair in the *Coronation*, way up in the second balcony, peeking around the tassel directly above Napoleon's crown.) His "neoclassical" style influenced French fashion. Take a look at his *Madame Juliet Récamier* portrait on the opposite wall, showing a modern Parisian woman in ancient garb and Pompeii hairstyle reclining on a Roman couch. Nearby paintings, such as *The Death of Socrates* and *The Oath of the Horatii (Le Serment des Horaces)*, are fine examples of neoclassicism, with Greek subjects, patriotic sentiment, and a clean, simple style.

• *As you double back toward the Romantic room, stop at...*

Jean-Auguste-Dominique Ingres— La Grande Odalisque (1819)

Take *Venus de Milo*, turn her around, lay her down, and stick a hash pipe next to her and you have the *Grande Odalisque*. OK, maybe you'd have to add a vertebra or two.

Using clean, polished, sculptural lines, Ingres (ang-gruh, with a soft "gruh") exaggerates the S-curve of a standing Greek nude. As in the *Venus de Milo*, rough folds of cloth set off her smooth skin. The face, too, has a touch of Venus' idealized features (or like Raphael's kindergarten teacher), taking nature and improving on it. Contrast the cool colors of this statue-like nude with Titian's golden girls. Ingres preserves *Venus'* backside for posterior—I mean, posterity.

• *Cross back through the Salle Denon and into a room gushing with...*

ROMANTICISM (1800–1850)

Théodore Géricault—The Raft of the Medusa (Le Radeau de la Méduse, 1819)

In the artistic war between hearts and minds, the heart style was known as Romanticism. Stressing motion and emotion, it was the flip side of cool, balanced neoclassicism, though they both flourished in the early 1800s.

What better setting for an emotional work than a shipwreck? Clinging to a raft is a tangle of bodies and lunatics sprawled over each other. The scene writhes with agitated, ominous motion—the ripple of muscles, churning clouds, and choppy seas. On the right is a deathly green corpse dangling overboard. The face of the man at left cradling a dead body says it all—the despair of spending weeks stranded in the middle of nowhere.

This painting was based on the actual sinking of the ship *Medusa* off the coast of Africa. The survivors floated in open seas on a raft, suffering hardship and hunger, even resorting to cannibalism—all the exotic elements for a painter determined to

shock the public and arouse its emotions. That painter was young Géricault (zhair-ee-ko). He'd honed his craft sketching dead bodies in the morgue and the twisted faces of lunatics in asylums, capturing the moment when all hope is lost.

But wait. There's a stir in the crowd. Someone has spotted something. The bodies rise up in a pyramid of hope culminating in a waving flag. They wave frantically, trying to catch the attention of the tiny ship on the horizon, their last desperate hope…which did finally save them. Géricault uses rippling movement and powerful colors to catch us up in the excitement. If art controls your heartbeat, this is a masterpiece.

Eugène Delacroix—*Liberty Leading the People* (*La Liberté Guidant le Peuple*, 1830)

The year is 1830. The Parisians have taken to the streets once again, *Les Miz* style, to fight royalist oppressors. There's a hard-bitten proletarian with a sword (far left), an intellectual with a top hat and a sawed-off shotgun, and even a little boy brandishing pistols.

Leading them on through the smoke and over the dead and dying is the figure of Liberty, a strong woman waving the French flag. Does this symbol of victory look familiar? It's the *Winged Victory*, wingless and topless.

To stir our emotions, Delacroix (del-ah-kwah) uses only three major colors—the red, white, and blue of the French flag. France is the symbol of modern democracy. The French weren't the first to adopt it (Americans were), nor are they the best working example of it, but they've had to work harder to achieve it than any other country. No sooner would they throw one king or dictator out than they'd get another. They're now working on their fifth republic.

This symbol of freedom is a fitting tribute to the Louvre, the first museum ever opened to the common rabble of humanity. The good things in life don't belong only to a small wealthy part of society, but to everyone. The motto of France is *Liberté, Egalité, Fraternité*—liberty, equality, and the brotherhood of all.

• *Exit the room at the far end (past a café) and go downstairs, where you'll bump into the bum of a large, twisting male nude looking like he's just waking up after a thousand-year nap.*

Michelangelo—*Slaves* (1513–1515)

These two statues by earth's greatest sculptor are a fitting end to this museum—works that bridge the ancient and modern worlds. Michelangelo, like his fellow Renaissance artists, learned from the Greeks. The perfect anatomy, twisting poses, and idealized faces look like they could have been done 2,000 years earlier.

The so-called *Dying Slave* (also called the Sleeping Slave, he looks like he should be stretched out on a sofa) twists listlessly against his T-shirt-like bonds, revealing his smooth skin. Compare the polished detail of the rippling, bulging left arm with the sketchy details of the face and neck. With Michelangelo, the body does the talking. This is probably the most sensual nude ever done by the master of the male body.

The *Rebellious Slave* fights against his bondage. His shoulders turn one way while his head and leg turn the other. He looks upward, straining to get free. He even seems to be trying to free himself from the rock he's made of. Michelangelo said that his purpose was to carve away the marble to reveal the figures God put inside. This slave shows the agony of that process and the ecstasy of the result.

• *These two may be slaves of the museum, but you are free to go. You could either escape the Louvre, or, if you're interested in ancient Middle Eastern art, head to the...*

RICHELIEU WING

Oriental Antiquities (Antiquités Orientales)

Saddam Hussein is only the latest iron-fisted, palace-building conqueror to fall in Iraq's long history, which stretches back to the dawn of civilization. Civilization began 6,000 years ago in Iraq, between the Tigris and Euphrates Rivers, in the area called the Fertile Crescent.

In the Louvre's Richelieu wing, you can sweep quickly through 2,000 years of Iraq's ancient history. See how each new civilization toppled the previous one—pulling down their statues, destroying their palaces, looting their cultural heritage, and replacing it with victory monuments of their own.

• *From under the pyramid, enter the Richelieu wing. Show your ticket, then take the first right. Go up one flight of stairs and one escalator to the ground floor* (Rez-de-Chaussée). *Enter Salle 1-a* (Mesopotamie archaïque) *and come face to face with fragments of the broken…*

Stela of the Vultures (Stele de victoire d'Eannatum, roi de Lagash, c. 2450 B.C.)

As old as the pyramids, this stela (ceremonial stone pillar) may be the oldest pictorial depiction of a historical event—the battle between the city of Lagash (100 miles north of modern Basra) and its arch-rival Umma.

Bearded King Eannatum waves the eagle flag of Lagash with one hand, while with the other he clubs a puny enemy soldier trapped in a battle net, making his enemies pledge allegiance to Lagash's gods.

Circle around to the flip side of the stela for the rest of the story, "reading" from top to bottom. Top level: A phalanx of helmeted soldiers advances behind their shields, trampling the enemy. They pile the corpses (right) while vultures swoop down from above to pluck the remains. Middle level: The king waves to the crowd from his chariot in the victory parade. Bottom level: They dig a mass grave while a priest gives thanks to the gods. A tethered ox is about to become a burnt sacrifice.

The inscription on the stela is in cuneiform, the world's first written language, invented by the Sumerians.

• *Enter Salle 1-b, with the blissful statue of…*

Ebih-Il, The Superintendent of Mari (c. 2400 B.C.)

Bald, bearded, blue-eyed Ebih-il (his name is inscribed on his shoulder) sits in his fleece skirt, folds his hands reverently across his chest and gazes rapturously at…Ishtar. Ebih-il was a priest in the goddess Ishtar's temple, and the statue is dedicated to her.

Ishtar was the chief goddess of many Middle Eastern peoples. As goddess of both Love and War, she was a favorite of horny soldiers. She was both a giver of life (this statue is dedicated "to Ishtar the virile") and, miraculously, a virgin. She was also a great hunter with bow and arrow and a great lover ("Her lips are sweet… her figure is beautiful, her eyes are brilliant… women and men adore her," sang the *Hymn to Ishtar,* c. 1600 B.C.).

Ebih-il adores her eternally with his eyes made of seashells and lapis lazuli. The smile on his face reflects the pleasure the goddess has just given him, perhaps through one of the sacred prostitutes who resided in Ishtar's Temple.

• *Go up the steps behind Ebih-Il into Salle 2, containing a dozen statues all of the same man, named…*

Just Enough Geography and History for this Tour

The northern half of Iraq is mountainous, the southern half is the delta of the Tigris and Euphrates rivers. Baghdad sits roughly in between north and south, along the Tigris. The Sumerians inhabited the south, the Assyrians the north, and the Akkadians and Babylonians the center, around Baghdad.

Here's a brief timeline:

3500–2400 B.C. Sumerian city-states flourish between the Tigris and Euphrates rivers. Sumerians invent writing.

2300 B.C. Akkadians invade Sumer.

1750 B.C. Hammurabi establishes first Babylonian empire.

710 B.C. Sargon II rules over a vast Assyrian-controlled empire, encompassing modern Iraq, Israel, Syria, and Egypt.

612 B.C. Babylonians revolt against the Assyrians and destroy the Assyrian capital of Nineveh (300 miles north of Baghdad), then built their own in Baghdad.

Gudea, Prince of Lagash (c. 2125–2110 B.C.)

Gudea (ruled 2141–2122 B.C.), in his wool stocking cap, folds his hands and prays to the gods to save them from invading barbarians. One of Sumeria's last great rulers, the peaceful and pious Gudea rebuilt temples (where these statues once stood) to thank the gods for their help.

• *Along the wall of Salle 2, find the rosy-colored...*

Stela of Naram-Sin (*Stele de victoire de Naram-Sin, roi d'Akkad,* c. 2230)

Sumeria was plundered (c. 2250) as the Akkadians became the new king of the mountain. Here, King Naram-Sin climbs up to the sunny heavens, crowned with the horned helmet of a god. His soldiers look up to admire him as he tramples his enemies. Next to him, a victim tries to remove a spear from his neck while another pleads to the conqueror for mercy.

• *Enter the large Salle 4, dominated by colossal winged bulls. First, direct your attention to the stela standing in the room.*

Law Codex of Hammurabi, King of Babylon (c. 1760 B.C.)

Hammurabi (ruled c. 1792–1750 B.C.) established the next great civilization, ruling as King of Babylon (50 miles south of modern

Baghdad). He established 282 laws, inscribed on this 8-foot black basalt stela, perhaps the first formal legal document, four centuries before the Ten Commandments.

At the top of the stela, Hammurabi (standing and wearing Gudea's hat of kingship) receives the scepter of judgment from the god of justice and the sun, who radiates flames from his shoulders. The inscription begins, "When Anu the Sublime...called me, Hammurabi, by name...I did right, and brought about the well-being of the oppressed."

Next come the laws, covering very specific situations, on everything from lying, theft, and trade to marriage and medical malpractice. Here's a sample:

   #1:   If any man ensnare another falsely, he shall be put to death.

   #57: If your sheep graze another man's land, you must repay 20 *gur* of grain.

   #129: If a couple is caught in adultery, they shall both be tied up and thrown in the water.

   #137: If you divorce your wife, you must pay alimony and child support.

   #218: A surgeon who bungles an operation shall have his hands cut off.

   #282: If a slave shall say, "You are not my master," the master can cut off his ear.

The most quoted laws—summing up the spirit of ancient Middle Eastern justice—are #196 ("If a man put out the eye of another man, his eye shall be put out") and #200 (a tooth for a tooth).

• *The other sculptures in Salle 4—including five winged bulls and many relief panels along the walls—are from the...*

Palace of Sargon II

The Assyrian king spared no expense on his palace (see various reconstructions on plaques in Salle 4). In Assyrian society, the palace and the king—not the temple and the gods—were the focus of life, and each ruler demonstrated his authority with large residences.

Sargon II actually built a whole new city for his palace, just north of the traditional capital of Nineveh (modern-day Mosul). He called it Dur Sharrukin ("Sargonburg"), and its dimensions were 4,000 cubits by—oh, excuse me—it covered about 150 acres (or about 150 football fields pieced together). The whole city was built on a raised, artificial mound, and the palace itself sat even higher, surrounded by walls, with courtyards, temples, the king's residence, and a wedding-cake-shaped temple (called a ziggurat) dedicated to the god Sin.

• *Start with the two biggest bulls, which support a (reconstructed) arch.*

The Assyrians

This Semitic people from the agriculturally-challenged hills of northern Iraq became traders and conquerors, not farmers. They conquered their southern neighbors and dominated the Middle East for 300 years (c. 900–600 B.C.).

Their strength came from a superb army (chariots, mounted cavalry, and seige engines), a policy of terrorism against enemies ("I tied their heads to tree trunks all around the city," reads a royal inscription), ethnic cleansing and mass deportations of the vanquished, and efficient administration (roads and express postal service). They have been called "The Romans of the East."

Winged Bulls (c. 710 B.C.)

These 30-ton, 14-foot alabaster bulls with human faces once guarded the entrance to the throne room of the Assyrian King Sargon II. A visitor to the palace back then could have looked over the bulls' heads and seen a 15-story ziggurat (a stepped-pyramid temple) towering overhead. The winged bulls were guardian spirits to keep out demons and intimidate liberals.

Between their legs is a cuneiform inscription: "I Sargon, King of the Universe, built palaces for my royal residence… I had winged bulls with human heads carved from great blocks of mountain stone, and I placed them at the doors facing the four winds as powerful divine guardians… My creation was worthy of great admiration."

• *We'll see a few relief panels from the palace, working counter-clockwise around the room. Start with the panel just to the left of the two big bulls.*

King Sargon II and a Dignitary (c. 710 B.C.)

Sargon II (ruled 721–705 B.C.), wearing a fez-like crown with a cone on the top and straps down the back, holds his staff and receives a foreign ambassador who's come to pay tribute. Sargon II controlled a vast empire, consisting of modern-day Iraq and extending westward to the Mediterranean and Egypt.

Before becoming emperor, Sargon II was a conquering general who invaded Israel (2 Kings 17:1-6). After a three year seige, he took Jerusalem and deported much of the population, inspiring the legends of the "Lost" Ten Tribes. The prophet Isaiah saw him as God's tool to punish the sinful Israelites, "to seize loot and snatch plunder, and to trample them down like mud in the streets" (Isaiah 10:6).

• *On the wall to the left of Sargon are four panels depicting…*

Transport of the Cedars of Lebanon
(Transport du bois de cèdre du Liban)

Boats carry the finest-quality logs for Sargon II's palace, crossing a wavy sea populated with fish, turtles, crabs, and mermen.

• *Continue counterclockwise around the room—past more big-winged animals, past the huge hero Gilgamesh crushing a lion—until you reach more relief panels. These depict...*

Scenes of Court Life

The brown, eroded gypsum panels we see were originally painted and varnished. The panels read like a comic strip, showing the king's men parading in to serve him.

First, bearded warriors sheath their swords and fold their hands reverently. A winged spirit prepares them to enter the king's presence by shaking a pine cone to anoint them with holy perfume. Next, servants hurry to the throne room with the king's dinner, while carrying his table, chair, and bowl. Other servants bring in horses and the king's chariots.

From Sargon to Saddam

Sargon II's great empire dissolved over the next few generations. When the Babylonians revolted and conquered their northern neighbors (612 B.C.), the whole Middle East applauded. As the Bible put it: "Nineveh is in ruins—who will mourn for her?...Everyone who hears the news claps his hands at your fall, for who has not felt your endless cruelty?" (Nahum 3:7, 19).

The new capital was Babylon (50 miles south of modern Baghdad), ruled by King Nebuchadnezzar, who conquered Judea (586 B.C., the Bible's "Babylonian Captivity") and built a palace with the Hanging Gardens, one of the Seven Wonders of the World.

Over the succeeding centuries, Babylon/Baghdad fell to Persians (539 B.C.), Greeks (Alexander the Great, 331 B.C.), Persians again (2nd-century B.C.), Arab Muslims (A.D. 634), Mongol hordes (Genghis Khan's grandson, 1258), Iranians (1502), Ottoman Turks (1535), British-controlled kings (1921), and military regimes (1958), the most recent headed by Saddam Hussein (1979).

In A.D. 2003, five thousand years of invasions, violence, and regime change finally came to an end when peace, prosperity, and democracy were established in Iraq by the United States of America under the benevolent guidance of George W. Bush.

ORSAY

(Musée d'Orsay)

The Orsay Museum houses French art of the 1800s (specifically 1848–1914), picking up where the Louvre leaves off. For us, that means Impressionism, the art of sun-dappled fields, bright colors, and crowded Parisian cafés. The Orsay houses the best general collection of Manet, Monet, Renoir, Degas, van Gogh, Cézanne, and Gauguin anywhere. If you like Impressionism, visit this museum. If you don't like Impressionism, visit this museum. I personally find it a more enjoyable and rewarding place than the Louvre. Sure, ya gotta see the *Mona Lisa* and *Venus de Milo,* but after you get your gottas out of the way, enjoy the Orsay.

ORIENTATION

The Orsay was recently renovated, so some paintings described in this tour may be moved to a new location. If you can't find a particular painting, ask a room guard or simply skip ahead.

Cost: €7; €5 after 16:15, on Sun, and for ages 18–25; free for youth under 18 and for anyone first Sun of month; covered by museum pass. Tickets are good all day. Museum passholders can enter to the left of the main entrance.

Hours: June 20–Sept 20 Tue–Sun 9:00–18:00, Sept 21–June 19 Tue–Sat 10:00–18:00, Sun 9:00–18:00, Thu until 21:45 all year, always closed Mon. Last entrance is 45 minutes before closing. The Impressionist galleries start closing at 17:15, frustrating unwary visitors. Note: The Orsay is crowded on Tue, when the Louvre is closed.

Getting There: It sits above the RER-C stop called Musée d'Orsay. The nearest Métro stop is Solférino, three blocks south of the Orsay. Bus #69 from the Marais and the rue Cler neighborhoods stops at the museum on the river side (quai Anatole France). From the Louvre, it's a lovely 15-minute walk through the Tuileries and across the river on the pedestrian bridge to the Orsay. A taxi stand is in front of the museum on quai Anatole France.

Information: The booth near the entrance gives free floor plans in English. Tel. 01 40 49 48 48, www.musee-orsay.fr.

Tours: Audioguides are €5. English-language guided tours usually run daily (except Sun) at 11:30 (90-min tours-€6). Tours in English focusing on the Impressionists are offered Tuesdays at 14:30 and Thursdays at 18:30 (sometimes also on other days, €6). I recommend the free, self-guided tour described below.

Length of This Tour: Two hours.

Photography: Photography without a flash is allowed.

Cuisine Art: The elegant second-floor restaurant has a pricey but fine buffet and salad bar. A simple fourth-floor café is sandwiched between the Impressionists.

Starring: Manet, Monet, Renoir, Degas, van Gogh, Cézanne, and Gauguin.

THE TOUR BEGINS

Gare d'Orsay: The Old Train Station

• *Pick up a free English map upon entering, buy your ticket, and check your bag. Belly up to the stone balustrade overlooking the main floor and orient yourself.*

Trains used to run right under our feet down the center of the gallery. This former train station, or *gare,* barely escaped the wrecking ball in the 1970s, when the French realized it'd be a great place to house their enormous collections of 19th-century art scattered throughout the city.

The main floor has early 19th-century art—as usual, Conservative on the right, Realism on the left. Upstairs (not visible from here) is the core of the collection—the Impressionist rooms; if you are pressed for time, go directly there (for directions, see page 143 after "Opéra Exhibit"). We'll start with the Conservatives and early rebels on the ground floor, then head upstairs to see how a few visionary young artists bucked the system and revolutionized the art world, paving the way for the 20th century. Finally, we'll end the tour with "the other Orsay" on the mezzanine level. Clear as Seine water? *Bien.*

Orsay—Ground Floor

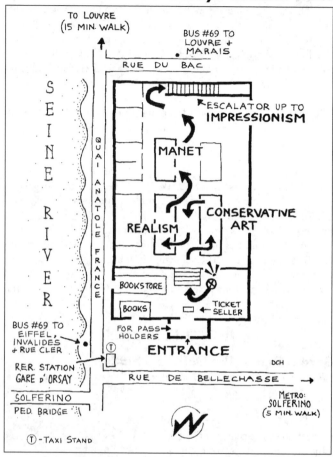

• *Walk down the steps to the main floor, a gallery filled with statues.*

CONSERVATIVE ART

Main Gallery Statues

No, this isn't ancient Greece. These statues are from the same era as the Theory of Relativity. It's the Conservative art of the French schools that was so popular throughout the 19th century. It was well-liked because it's beautiful. The balanced poses, perfect anatomy, sweet faces, curving lines, and gleaming white stone—all of this is very appealing. (I'll be bad-mouthing it later, but for now appreciate the exquisite craftsmanship of this "perfect" art.)

The Orsay's "19th Century"
(1848–1914)

Einstein and Geronimo. Abraham Lincoln and Karl Marx. The train, the bicycle, the horse and buggy, the automobile, and the balloon. Freud and Dickens. Darwin's *Origin of Species* and the Church's Immaculate Conception. Louis Pasteur and Billy the Kid. V. I. Lenin and Ty Cobb.

The 19th century was a mix of old and new side by side. Europe was entering the modern Industrial Age, with cities, factories, rapid transit, instant communication, and global networks. At the same time, it clung to the past with traditional, rural—almost medieval—attitudes and morals.

According to the Orsay, the "19th century" began in 1848 with the socialist and democratic revolutions (Marx's *Communist Manifesto*). It ended in 1914 with the pull of an assassin's trigger, which ignited World War I and ushered in the modern world. The museum shows art that is also both old and new, conservative and revolutionary.

• *Take your first right into the small Room 1, marked "Ingres." Look for a nude woman with a pitcher of water.*

Jean-Auguste-Dominique Ingres—*The Source* (*La Source,* 1856)

Let's start where the Louvre left off. Ingres (ang-gruh, with a soft "gruh"), who helped cap the Louvre collection, championed a neoclassical style. *The Source* is virtually a Greek statue on canvas. Like *Venus de Milo*, she's a balance of opposite motions—her hips tilt one way, her breasts the other; one arm goes up, the other down; the water falling from the pitcher matches the fluid curve of her body. Her skin is porcelain-smooth, painted with seamless brush strokes.

Ingres worked on this over the course of 35 years and considered it his "image of perfection." Famous in its day, *The Source* influenced many artists whose classical statues and paintings are in the Orsay gallery.

In this and the next few rooms, you'll see more of these visions of idealized beauty—nude women in languid poses, Greek myths, and so on. The "Romantics," like Eugène Delacroix, added bright

Conservative Art & Realism

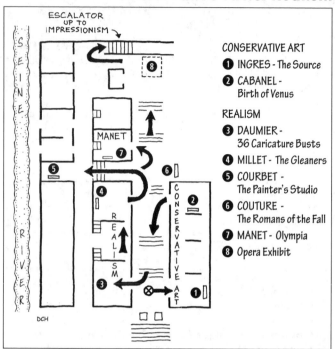

ESCALATOR UP TO IMPRESSIONISM

SEINE RIVER

MANET

REALISM

CONSERVATIVE ART

8

5

7

6

4

2

3

1

⊗

DCH

CONSERVATIVE ART
1. INGRES - The Source
2. CABANEL - Birth of Venus

REALISM
3. DAUMIER - 36 Caricature Busts
4. MILLET - The Gleaners
5. COURBET - The Painter's Studio
6. COUTURE - The Romans of the Fall
7. MANET - Olympia
8. Opera Exhibit

colors, movement, and emotion to the classical coolness of Ingres.
• *Walk uphill (quickly, this is background stuff) to the last room (Room 3), and find a pastel blue–green painting.*

Alexandre Cabanel—*The Birth of Venus* (*La Naissance de Vénus*, 1863)

Cabanel lays Ingres' *The Source* on her back. This goddess is a perfect fantasy, an orgasm of beauty. The Love Goddess stretches back seductively, recently birthed from the ephemeral foam of the wave. This is art of a pre-Freudian society, when sex was dirty and mysterious and had to be exalted into a more pure and divine form. The sex drive was channeled into an acute sense of beauty. French folk would literally swoon in ecstasy before these works of art.

The art world of Cabanel's day was dominated by two conservative institutions: The Academy (the state-funded art school) and the Salon, where works were exhibited to the buying public. The public loved Cabanel's Venus (and Napoleon III purchased it).

Get a feel for the ideal beauty and refined emotion of these Greek-style works. (Out in the gallery, you'll find a statue of another swooning Venus.) Go ahead, swoon. If it feels good, enjoy it. Now, take a mental cold shower, and let's cross over to the "wrong side of the tracks," to the art of the early rebels.

• *Exit Room 3 into the main gallery, turn left and head back toward the entrance, turning right into Room 4, marked "Daumier" (opposite the Ingres room).*

REALISM—EARLY REBELS

Honoré Daumier—*Celebrities of the Happy Medium* (*Célébrités du juste milieu,* 1832–1835)

This is a liberal's look at the stuffy bourgeois establishment that controlled the Academy and the Salon. In these 36 bustlets, Daumier, trained as a political cartoonist, exaggerates each subject's most distinct characteristic to capture with vicious precision the pomposity and self-righteousness of these self-appointed arbiters of taste. The labels next to the busts give the name of the person being caricatured, his title or job (most were members of the French parliament), and an insulting nickname (like "gross, fat, and satisfied" and Monsieur "Platehead"). Give a few nicknames yourself. Can you find Reagan, Clinton, Yeltsin, Thatcher, and Rumsfeld?

These people hated what you're about to see. Their prudish faces tightened as their fantasy world was shattered by the Realists.

• *Go uphill four steps and through a leafy room to the final room, #6.*

Jean-François Millet—*The Gleaners* (*Les Glaneuses,* 1867)

Millet (mee-yay) shows us three gleaners, the poor women who pick up the meager leavings after a field has already been harvested by the wealthy. Millet grew up on a humble farm. He didn't attend the Academy and despised the uppity Paris art scene.  Instead of idealized gods, goddesses, nymphs, and winged babies, he painted simple rural scenes. He was strongly affected by the socialist revolution of 1848, with its affirmation of the working class. Here he captures the innate dignity of these stocky, tanned women who work quietly in a large field for their small reward.

This is "Realism" in two senses. It's painted "realistically," unlike the prettified pastels of Cabanel's *Birth of Venus.* And it's the "real" world—not the fantasy world of Greek myth, but the harsh

life of the working poor.
• *Exit Room 6 into the main gallery, and make a U-turn to the left, climbing the steps to a large alcove with two huge canvases. On the left…*

Gustave Courbet—*The Painter's Studio* (*L'Atelier du Peintre,* 1855)

The Salon of 1855 rejected this dark-colored, sprawling, monumental painting of… "What's it about?" In an age when "Realist painter" was equated with "bomb-throwing Socialist," it took courage to buck the system. Dismissed by the so-called experts, Courbet (coor-bay) held his own one-man exhibit. He built a shed in the middle of Paris, defiantly hung his art out, and basically "mooned" the shocked public.

Courbet's painting takes us backstage, showing the gritty reality behind the creation of pretty pictures. We see Courbet himself in his studio, working diligently on a Realistic landscape, oblivious to the confusion around him. Milling around are ordinary citizens, not Greek heroes. The woman who looks on is not a nude Venus but a naked artists' model. And the little boy with an adoring look on his face? Perhaps it's Courbet's inner child admiring the artist who sticks to his guns, whether it's popular or not.
• *Return to the main gallery. Back across "the tracks," the huge canvas you see is…*

Thomas Couture—*The Romans of the Decadence* (*Les Romains de la Décadence,* 1847)

We see a fin de siècle (end-of-century) society that looks like it's packed in a big hot tub. It's stuffed with too much luxury, too much classical beauty, too much pleasure; it's wasted, burned-out, and in decay. The old, backward-looking order was about to be slapped in the face.

• *Continue up the gallery, then left into Room 14 ("Manet, Monet, Bazille, Renoir avant 1870"). Find the reclining nude.*

Edouard Manet—*Olympia* (1863)

"This brunette is thoroughly ugly. Her face is stupid, her skin cadaverous. All this clash of colors is stupefying." So wrote a critic when Edouard Manet's nude hung in the Salon. The public hated it, attacking Manet (man-ay) in print and literally attacking the canvas.

Think back on Cabanel's painting, *The Birth of Venus:* an idealized, pastel, Vaseline-on-the-lens beauty—soft-core pornography, the kind you see selling lingerie and perfume.

Manet's nude doesn't gloss over anything. The pose is classic, used by Titian, Goya, and countless others. But this is a Realist's take on the classics. The sharp outlines and harsh, contrasting colors are new and shocking. Her hand is a clamp, and her stare is shockingly defiant, with not a hint of the seductive, hey-sailor look of most nudes. This prostitute, ignoring the flowers sent by her last customer, looks out to us as if to say, "Next." Manet replaced soft-core porn with hard-core art.

Edouard Manet (1832–1883) had an upper-class upbringing and some formal art training, and he had been accepted by the Salon. He could have cranked out pretty nudes and been a successful painter. Instead, he surrounded himself with a group of young artists experimenting with new techniques. With his reputation and strong personality, he was their master, though he learned equally from them. Let the Impressionist revolution begin.

• *Continue to the far end of the gallery, where you'll walk on a glass floor over a model of Paris.*

Opéra Exhibit

Expand to 100 times your size and hover over this scale-model section of the city. In the center sits the 19th-century Opéra Garnier, with its green roof.

Nearby, you'll also see a cross-section model of the Opéra. You'd enter from the right end, buy your ticket in the foyer, then move into the entrance hall with its grand staircase, where you could see and be seen by *toute* Paris. At curtain time, you'd find your seat in the red and gold auditorium, topped by a glorious painted ceiling. (The current ceiling, done by Marc Chagall, is even more wonderful than the one in the model). Notice that the stage, with elaborate riggings to raise and lower scenery, is as big as the seating area. Nearby, there are models of set designs from some famous productions. These days, Parisians enjoy their Verdi and Gounod at the modern opera house at place de la Bastille.

• *Behind the Opéra model (go left around model), a covered escalator leads to the often-crowded Impressionist rooms. To take a break and read ahead, consider wandering to the quiet far-left corner of the ground floor, where you'll find a huge painting of a hot-air-balloonist's-eye view of pre–Eiffel Tower Paris (c. 1855).*

Ride the escalator to the top floor. Take your first left for a commanding view of the Orsay. The second left takes you past a bookshop and a giant "backwards" clock (with great city views) to the art, starting in Room 29. Now, let there be light.

Rooms 29–34: Impressionism—Manet, Degas, Monet, Renoir, and More

Light! Color! Vibrations! You don't hang an Impressionist canvas—you tether it. Impressionism features bright colors, easygoing open-air scenes, spontaneity, broad brushstrokes, and the play of light.

The Impressionists made their canvases shimmer by a simple but revolutionary technique. Let's say you mix red, yellow, and blue together; you'll get brown, right? But Impressionists didn't bother to mix them. They'd slap a thick brushstroke of yellow down, then a stroke of green next to it, then red next to that. Up close, all you see are the three messy strokes, but as you back up...*voilà!* Brown! The colors blend in the eye, at a distance. But while your eye is saying "bland old brown," your subconscious is shouting, "Red! Yellow! Blue! Yes!"

There are no lines in nature. Yet someone in the classical tradition (Ingres, for example) would draw an outline of his subject, then fill it in with color. But the Impressionists built a figure with dabs of paint...a snowman of color.

• *The Impressionist collection is scattered somewhat randomly through the next few rooms. Shadows dance and the displays mingle. You'll find nearly all of the following paintings, but exactly where they're hung is a lot like their brushwork...delightfully sloppy. (If you don't see a described painting, move on. It's either hanging farther down or it's on vacation.)*

Edouard Manet—*Luncheon on the Grass* (*Le Déjeuner sur l'Herbe,* 1863)

A shocked public looked at this and wondered: What are these

scantily clad women doing with these men? Or rather, what will they be doing after the last baguette is eaten? It wasn't the nudity but the presence of the men in ordinary clothes that suddenly made the nude look naked. Once again, the public judged the painting on moral terms rather than artistic ones.

A new revolutionary movement is budding: Impressionism. Notice the background: the messy brushwork of trees and leaves, the

Impressionism

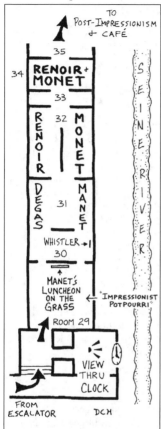

play of light on the pond, and the light that filters through the trees onto the woman who stoops in the haze. Also note the strong contrast of colors (white skin, black clothes, green grass), and the fact that this is a true out-of-doors painting, not a studio production.

• *Enter Room 30.*

James Abbott McNeill Whistler—*Portrait of the Artist's Mother (Portrait de la Mère de l'Auteur, 1871)*

Why so famous? I don't know either. Perhaps because it's by an American, and we see in his mother some of the monumental solidity of our own ancestral moms, who were made tough by pioneering the American wilderness.

Or perhaps because it was so starkly different in its day. In a roomful of golden goddesses, it'd stand out like a fish in a tree. The alternate title is *Arrangement in Gray and Black, No. 1* and the whole point is the subtle variations of dark shades softened by the rosy tint of her cheeks. Nevertheless, the critics kept waiting for it to come out in Colorization.

• *In Room 31, left side of the room, is work by…*

Edgar Degas—*The Dance Class (La Classe de Danse, c. 1873–1875)*

Clearly, Degas loved dance and the theater. (Catch his statue, *Tiny Dancer, 14 Years Old,* in the glass case.) The play of stage lights off his dancers, especially the halos of ballet skirts, is made to order for an

Impressionism

The camera threatened to make artists obsolete. Now a machine could capture a better likeness faster than you could say Etch-a-Sketch.

But true art is more than just painting reality. It gives us reality from the artist's point of view, with the artist's personal impressions of the scene. Impressions are often fleeting, so you have to work quickly.

The "Impressionist" painters rejected camera-like detail for a quick style more suited to capturing the passing moment. Feeling stifled by the rigid rules and stuffy atmosphere of the Academy, the Impressionists took as their motto, "out of the studio, into the open air." They grabbed their berets and scarves and took excursions to the country, where they set up their easels (and newly-invented tubes of premixed paint) on riverbanks and hillsides, or they sketched in cafés and dance halls. Gods, goddesses, nymphs, and fantasy scenes were out; common people and rural landscapes were in.

The quick style and everyday subjects were ridiculed and called childish by the "experts." Rejected by the Salon, the Impressionists staged their own exhibition in 1874. They brashly took their name from an insult thrown at them by a critic who laughed at one of Monet's "impressions" of a sunrise. During the next decade, they exhibited their own work independently. The public, opposed at first, was slowly drawn in by the simplicity, the color, and the vibrancy of Impressionist art.

Impressionist. In *The Dance Class,* bored, tired dancers scratch their backs restlessly at the end of a long rehearsal. And look at the bright green bow on the girl with her back to us. In the Impressionist style, Degas slopped green paint onto her dress and didn't even say, *"Excusez-moi."*

Edgar Degas (1834–1917, day-gah) was a rich kid from a family of bankers who got the best classical-style art training. Adoring Ingres' pure lines and cool colors, he painted in the Academic style. His work was exhibited in the Salon. He gained success and a good reputation, and then...he met the Impressionists.

Degas blends classical lines with Impressionist color, spontaneity, and everyday subjects from urban Paris. Degas loved the unposed "snapshot" effect, catching his models off guard. Dance students, women at work, and café scenes are seen from an odd angle that's not always ideal but makes the scene seem more real.

Edgar Degas—*In a Café, or The Glass of Absinthe* (*Au Café, dit L'Absinthe,* 1876)

Degas hung out with low-life Impressionists discussing art, love, and life in the cheap cafés and bars in Montmartre. Here, a weary lady of the evening meets morning with a last lonely coffin-nail drink in the glaring light of a four-in-the-morning café. The pale-green drink forming the center of the composition is that toxic substance, absinthe, that fueled many artists and burned out many more.

* *The next rooms (32–34) feature works by two Impressionist masters at their peak, Monet and Renoir. You're looking at the quintessence of Impressionism. (If you don't find a particular painting by Monet or Renoir, it may be hanging farther along, in Room 39.)*

Claude Monet—*The Cathedral of Rouen* (*La Cathédrale de Rouen,* 1893)

Claude Monet (1840–1926, mo-nay) is the father of Impressionism. He fully explored the possibilities of open-air painting and tried to faithfully reproduce nature's colors with bright blobs of paint.

Monet went to Rouen, rented a room across from the cathedral, set up his easel...and waited. He wanted to catch "a series of differing impressions" of the cathedral facade at various times of day and year. He often had several canvases going at once. In all, he did 30 paintings of the cathedral, and each is unique. The time-lapse series shows the sun passing slowly across the sky, creating different-colored light and shadows. The labels next to the art describe the conditions: in gray weather, in the morning, morning sun, full sunlight, etc.

As Monet zeroes in on the play of colors and light, the physical subject—the cathedral—is dissolving. It's only a rack upon which to hang the light and color. Later artists would boldly throw away the rack, leaving purely abstract modern art in its place.

Claude Monet—Paintings from Monet's Garden at Giverny

One of Monet's favorite places to paint was the garden he landscaped at his home in Giverny, west of Paris (and worth a visit if you like Monet more than you hate crowds). The Japanese bridge and the water lilies floating in the pond were his two favorite subjects. As Monet aged and his eyesight failed, he made bigger canvases of

smaller subjects. The final water lilies are monumental smudges of thick paint surrounded by paint-splotched clouds reflected on the surface of the pond.

You can see more Monet at the Marmottan Museum (€6.50, not covered by museum pass, Tue–Sun 10:00–18:00, closed Mon, 2 rue Louis Boilly, Mo: La Muette, follow brown museum signs six blocks down chaussée de la Muette through park to museum). His most famous water lilies are at L'Orangerie Museum (scheduled to reopen by 2005), in the Tuileries Garden.

Pierre-Auguste Renoir—*Dance at the Moulin de la Galette* (*Bal du Moulin de la Galette,* 1876)

On Sunday afternoons, working-class folk would dress up and head

for the fields on butte Montmartre (near Sacré-Cœur basilicas) to dance, drink, and eat little crêpes *(galettes)* till dark. Pierre-Auguste Renoir (1841–1919, ren-wah) liked to go there to paint the common Parisians living and loving in the afternoon sun. The sunlight filtering through the trees creates a kaleidoscope of colors, like the 19th-century equivalent of a mirror ball throwing darts of light onto the dancers.

He captures the dappled light with quick blobs of yellow, staining the ground, the men's jackets, and the sun-dappled straw hat (right of center). Smell the powder on the ladies' faces. The painting glows with bright colors. Even the shadows on the ground, which should be gray or black, are colored a warm blue. Like a photographer who uses a slow shutter speed to show motion, Renoir paints a waltzing blur.

Renoir's work is lighthearted, with light colors, almost pastels. He seems to be searching for an ideal, the pure beauty we saw on the ground floor. In later years, he used more and more red tones, as if trying for even more warmth.

Camille Pissarro, Alfred Sisley, and Others

We've neglected many of the founders of the Impressionist style. Browse around and discover your own favorites. Pissarro is one of mine. His grainy landscapes are more subtle and subdued than the flashy Monet and Renoir, but, as someone said, "He did for the earth what Monet did for the water."

• *Notice the skylight above you: These Impressionist rooms are appropriately lit by ever-changing natural light. Then carry on to Room 35.*

Post-Impressionism

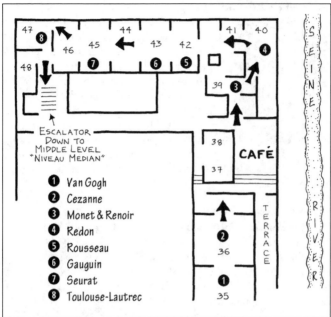

1 Van Gogh
2 Cezanne
3 Monet & Renoir
4 Redon
5 Rousseau
6 Gauguin
7 Seurat
8 Toulouse-Lautrec

POST-IMPRESSIONISM

Vincent van Gogh

Impressionists have been accused of being "light"-weights. The colorful style lends itself to bright country scenes, gardens, sunlight on the water, and happy crowds of simple people. It took a remarkable genius to add profound emotion to the Impressionist style.

Vincent van Gogh (1853–1890, van-hock by the Dutch and the snooty)—like Michelangelo, Beethoven, Rembrandt, Wayne Newton, and a select handful of others—put so much of himself into his work that art and life became one. In this room, you'll see both van Gogh's painting style and his life unfold.

Vincent van Gogh—*Peasant Woman Near the Hearth (Paysanne près de l'Âtre,* 1885)

Vincent was the son of a Dutch minister. He too felt a religious calling, and he spread the gospel among the poorest of the poor—peasants and miners in overcast Holland and Belgium. He painted these hardworking, dignified folks in a crude, dark style reflecting the oppressiveness of their lives…and the loneliness of his own as he roamed northern Europe in search of a calling.

Vincent Van Gogh—*Self-Portrait, Paris*
(*Portrait de l'Artiste,* 1887)

Encouraged by his art-dealer brother, van Gogh moves to Paris and, *voilà!* The color! He meets Monet, drinks with Paul Gauguin and Henri de Toulouse-Lautrec, and soaks up the Impressionist style. (See how he builds a bristling brown beard using thick strokes of red, yellow, and green side by side.)

At first, he paints like the others, but soon he develops his own style. By using thick, swirling brush strokes, he infuses life into even inanimate objects. Van Gogh's brush strokes curve and thrash like a garden hose pumped with wine.

Vincent van Gogh—*Midday*
(*La Méridienne,* 1890, based on a painting by Millet)

The social life of Paris becomes too much for the solitary van Gogh. He moves to the South of France. At first, in the glow of the bright spring sunshine, he has a period of incredible creativity and happiness, as he is overwhelmed by the bright colors, landscape vistas, and common people—an Impressionist's dream.

Vincent van Gogh—*Van Gogh's Room at Arles*
(*La Chambre de Van Gogh à Arles,* 1889)

But being alone in a strange country begins to wear on him. An ugly man, he finds it hard to get a date. The close-up perspective of this painting makes his tiny rented room look even more cramped. He invites his friend Gauguin to join him, but after two months together arguing passionately about art, nerves get raw. Van Gogh threatens Gauguin with a knife, which drives his friend back to Paris. In crazed despair, van Gogh mutilates his own ear.

The people of Arles realize they have a madman on their hands and convince van Gogh to seek help. He enters a mental hospital.

Vincent van Gogh—*The Church at Auvers-sur-Oise*
(*L'Eglise d'Auvers-sur-Oise,* 1890)

Van Gogh's paintings done in the peace of the mental hospital are more meditative—fewer bright landscapes, more closed-in scenes with deeper and almost surreal colors. The sky is cobalt blue and the church's windows are also blue, as if we're looking right through the building to an infinite sky. There's a road that leads from us to the church, then splits to go behind. A choice must be made. Which way?

Van Gogh, the preacher's son, saw painting as a calling, and he approached it with a spiritual intensity.

Vincent van Gogh—*Self-Portrait, St. Rémy* (1889)

Van Gogh wavered between happiness and madness. He despaired of ever being sane enough to continue painting.

This self-portrait shows a man engulfed in a confused background of brush strokes that swirl and rave, setting in motion the waves of the jacket. But in the midst of this rippling sea of mystery floats a still, detached island of a face with probing, questioning, yet wise eyes.

Do his troubled eyes know that only a few months on, he will take a pistol and put a bullet through his chest?

• *Vincent van Gone. Continue to room 36.*

Paul Cézanne—*Self-Portrait (Portrait de l'Artiste)*

Paul Cézanne (1839–1906, say-zahn) brought Impressionism into the 20th century. After the color of Monet, the warmth of Renoir, and van Gogh's passion, Cézanne's rather impersonal canvases can be difficult to appreciate. Bowls of fruit, landscapes, and a few portraits were Cézanne's passion. Because of his style (not the content), he is often called the first Modern painter.

Cézanne was virtually unknown and unappreciated in his lifetime. He worked alone, lived alone, and died alone, ignored by all but a few revolutionary young artists who understood his efforts. Cézanne's brush was a blunt instrument. With it, he'd bludgeon reality into submission, drag it across a canvas, and leave it there to dry. But Cézanne, the mediocre painter, was a great innovator. His work spoke for itself—which is good because, as you can see here, he had no mouth.

Paul Cézanne—Landscape (*Rochers près des Grottes au dessus de Château-Noir,* 1904)

Cézanne used chunks of green, tan, and blue paint as building blocks to construct this rocky brown cliff. Where the Impressionists built a figure out of a mosaic of individual brushstrokes, Cézanne used blocks of paint to give it a more solid, geometrical shape.

These chunks are like little "cubes." It's no coincidence that his experiments in reducing forms to their geometric basics influenced the...Cubists.

Paul Cézanne—*The Card Players* (*Les Joueurs de Cartes,* c. 1890–1895)

These aren't people. They're studies in color and pattern. The subject matter—two guys playing cards—is less important than the pleasingly balanced pattern they make on the canvas, two sloping forms framing a cylinder (a bottle) in the center. Later, abstract artists would focus solely on the shapes and colors.

The jacket of the player to the right is a patchwork of tans, greens, and browns. Even the "empty" space between the men—painted with fragmented chunks of color—is almost as tangible as they are. As one art scholar put it: "Cézanne confused intermingled forms and colors, achieving an extraordinarily luminous density in which lyricism is controlled by a rigorously constructed rhythm." Just what I said—chunks of color.

• *Exit to the café and consider a well-deserved break. From the café, continue ahead, walking under the large green beam, following signs saying "Impressionisme/Post-Impressionisme, 39–48." A hallway leads past WCs to Room 39, which often displays work by Monet and Renoir (and may include paintings covered earlier in this tour). Then continue into dark Room 40 in the right corner....*

Odilon Redon

Flip out the lights and step into Odilon Redon's mysterious world. If the Orsay's a zoo, this is the nocturnal house. Prowl around. This is wild, wild stuff. It's intense—imagine Richard Nixon on mushrooms playing sax.

If the Impressionists painted by sunlight, Odilon Redon (1840–1916) painted by moonlight. His pastels (protected by dim lighting) portray dream imagery and mythological archetypes. Classed as Symbolism, Redon's weird work later inspired the Surrealists.

• *Coming out of the darkness, pass into the gallery lined with metal columns containing the primitive art of Rousseau and Gauguin. Start in the first alcove to the left.*

PRIMITIVES

Henri Rousseau—*War*
(*La Guerre,* or *La Chevauchée de la Discorde,* 1894)

Some artists, rejecting the harried, scientific, and rational world, remembered a time before "isms," when works of art weren't scholarly "studies in form and color" but voodoo dolls full of mystery and magic power. They learned from the art of primitive tribes in Africa and the South Seas, trying to recreate a primal Garden of Eden of peace and wholeness. In doing so, they created another "ism": Primitivism.

Henri Rousseau (1844–1910), a man who painted like a child, was an amateur artist who palled around with all the great painters, but they never took his naive style of art seriously. Like a child's drawing of a nightmare, the images are primitive—flat and simple, with unreal colors—but the effect is both beautiful and terrifying. War, in the form of a woman with a sword, flies on horseback across the battlefield, leaving destruction in her wake: broken bare trees, burning clouds in the background, and heaps of corpses picked at by the birds.

• *Farther along this columned gallery, you'll find work by...*

Paul Gauguin—*Arearea,* or *Joyousness* (*Joyeusetés,* 1892)

Paul Gauguin (1848–1903, go-gan) got the travel bug early in childhood and grew up wanting to be a sailor. Instead, he became a stockbroker. In his spare time, he painted and was introduced to the Impressionist circle. He learned their bright clashing colors, but diverged from this path about the time van Gogh waved a knife in his face. At the age of 35, he got fed up with it all, quit his job, abandoned his wife (her stern portrait bust may be nearby) and family, and took refuge in his art. He traveled to the South Seas in search of the exotic, finally settling on Tahiti.

In Tahiti, Gauguin found his Garden of Eden. He simplified his life to the routine of eating, sleeping, and painting. He simplified his painting still more, to flat images with heavy black outlines filled in with bright, pure colors. He painted the native girls in their naked innocence (so different from Cabanel's seductive *Venus*). But this simple style had a deep undercurrent of symbolic meaning.

Arearea shows native women and a dog. In the "distance" (there's no attempt at traditional 3-D here), a procession goes by with a large pagan idol. What's the connection between the idol and the foreground figures, who are apparently unaware of it? In primitive societies, religion permeates life. Idols, dogs, and women are holy.

• *Farther along, find...*

Georges Seurat—*The Circus* (*Le Cirque*, 1891)

Pointillism brings Impressionism to its logical conclusion—little dabs of different colors placed side by side to blend in the viewer's eye. Using only red, yellow, blue, and green points of paint, Seurat (sur-rah) creates a mosaic of colors that shimmers at a distance, capturing the wonder of the dawn of electric lights.

• *In darkened Room 47 are pastels by...*

Henri de Toulouse-Lautrec— *The Clownesse Cha-U-Kao* (1895)

Henri de Toulouse-Lautrec (1864–1901) was the black sheep of a noble family. At age 15, he broke both legs, which left him a cripple. Shunned by his family, a freak to society, he felt more at home in the underworld of other outcasts—prostitutes, drunks, thieves, dancers, and actors. He painted the lowlife in the bars, cafés, dance halls, and brothels he frequented. Toulouse-Lautrec died young of alcoholism.

The Clownesse Cha-U-Kao is one of his fellow freaks, a fat lady clown who made her living by being laughed at. She slumps wearily after a performance, indifferent to the applause, and adjusts her dress to prepare for the curtain call.

Toulouse-Lautrec was a true *impression*-ist, catching his models in candid poses. He worked spontaneously, never correcting his mistakes, as you can see from the blotches on her dark skirt and the unintentional yellow sash that hangs down. Can you see a bit of Degas here, in the subject matter, snapshot pose, and colors?

Henri de Toulouse-Lautrec—*Jane Avril Dancing (Jane Avril dansant,* 1891)

Toulouse-Lautrec hung out at the Moulin Rouge dance hall in Montmartre. One of the most popular dancers was this slim, graceful, elegant, and melancholy woman who stood out above the rabble of the Moulin Rouge. Her legs keep dancing while her mind is far away. Toulouse-Lautrec the artist-ocrat might have identified with her noble face—sad and weary of the nightlife, but immersed in it.

• *You've seen the essential Orsay and are permitted to cut out (the exit is straight below you). But there's an "Other Orsay" I think you'll find entertaining.*

To reach the middle level ("niveau median"), go down three flights (escalator nearby), turn left, and cross to the other side of the gallery. Along the way, on the middle level, peek into Le Restaurant du Musée (enjoy a cup of coffee or tea and the €10 salad bar—available any time; if it's not on the menu, ask). This was part of the original hotel that adjoined the station (built in 1900, abandoned after 1939, condemned, and restored to the elegance you see today).

Now find the palatial Room 52, with mirrors and chandeliers, marked "Salle des Fêtes."

THE "OTHER" ORSAY—MIDDLE LEVEL

The beauty of the Orsay is that it combines all the art of the 1800s (1848–1914), both modern and classical, in one building. The classical art, so popular in its own day, has been maligned and was forgotten in the 20th century. It's time for a reassessment. Is it as gaudy and gawd-awful as we've been led to believe? From our 21st-century perspective, let's take a look at the opulent, fin de siècle, French high society and its luxurious art.

The Grand Ballroom *(Salle des Fêtes)*

This was one of France's poshest nightspots when the Orsay hotel was here. You can easily imagine gowned debutantes and white-gloved dandies waltzing the night away to the music of a chamber orchestra.

The "Other" Orsay

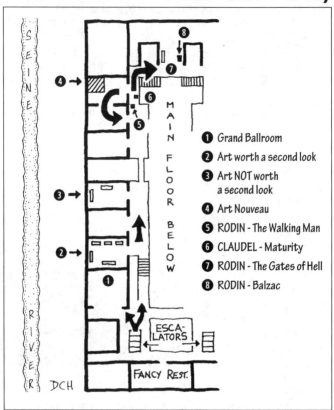

1. Grand Ballroom
2. Art worth a second look
3. Art NOT worth a second look
4. Art Nouveau
5. RODIN - The Walking Man
6. CLAUDEL - Maturity
7. RODIN - The Gates of Hell
8. RODIN - Balzac

Notice:

• The interior decorating: raspberry marble-ripple ice-cream columns, pastel-colored ceiling painting, gold work, mirrors, and leafy garlands of chandeliers.

• The statue *Bacchante Couchée* sprawled in the middle of the room. Familiar pose? If not, you flunk this tour.

• *La Nature,* a statue of a woman dressed in multi-colored marble.

• The statue *Aurore,* with her canopy of hair, hide-and-seek face, and silver-dollar nipples, looking like a shampoo ad.

• The large painting *The Birth of Venus (La Naissance de Vénus)* by William Bouguereau. Van Gogh once said: "If I painted like Bouguereau, I could hope to make money. The public will never change—they love only sweet things."

Is this stuff beautiful or merely gaudy? Divine or decadent?

• *Exit the Salles des Fêtes and turn left, then left again onto the mezzanine overlooking the main gallery. Head toward the far end. Enter the first room on the left (#55).*

Art Worth a Second Look

We've seen some great art; now let's see some not-so-great art—at least, that's what modern critics tell us. This is realistic art with a subconscious kick.

• *Working clockwise, you'll see...*

Cain

The world's first murderer, with the murder weapon still in his belt, is exiled with his family. Archaeologists had recently discovered a Neanderthal skull, so the artist makes the family part of a prehistoric hunter/gatherer tribe.

The Dream (Le Rêve)

Soldiers sleep, while visions of Gatling guns dance in their heads.

Payday (La Paye des Moissonneurs)

Peasants getting paid, painted by Leon L'Hermitte, called "the grandson of Courbet and Millet." The subtitle of the work should be, "Is this all there is to life?"

The Excommunication of Robert le Pieux

The bishops exit after performing the rite. The king and queen are stunned, the scepter dropped. The ritual candle has been snuffed out; it falls, fuming, echoing through the huge hall....Is this art or only cheap theatrics?

• *Continue down the mezzanine. Skip the next room, then go left into Room 59.*

Art Not Worth a Second Look

The Orsay's director said: "Certainly, we have bad paintings. But we have only the greatest bad paintings." And here they are.

Serenity

An idyll in the woods. Three nymphs with harps waft off to the right. These people are stoned on something.

The School of Plato (L'Ecole de Platon)

Subtitled "The Athens YMCA." A Christlike Plato surrounded by adoring, half-naked nubile youths gives new meaning to the term

"Platonic relationship."

Will the pendulum shift so that one day art like *The School of Plato* becomes the new, radical avant-garde style?

• *Return to the mezzanine and continue to the far end. Enter the last room on the left (#65) and head for the far corner, Room 66.*

ART NOUVEAU

Alexandre Charpentier—*Dining Room of Adrien Benard* (*Boiserie de la Salle à Mangé de la Propriété Benard*)

The Industrial Age brought factories, row houses, machines, train stations, geometrical precision—and ugliness. At the turn of the century, some artists reacted against the unrelieved geometry of harsh, pragmatic, iron-and-steel Eiffel Tower art with a "new art"—Art Nouveau. (Hmm. I think I had a driver's-ed teacher by that name.)

Like nature, which also abhors a straight line, Art Nouveau artists used the curves of flowers and vines as their pattern. They were convinced that "practical" didn't have to mean "ugly" as well. They turned everyday household objects into art.

This wood-paneled dining room, with its organic shapes, is one of the finest examples of the Art Nouveau style. Another is the curvy, wrought-iron work of some of Paris' early Métro entrances, built by the same man who commissioned this dining room for his home.

• *Browse through the Art Nouveau rooms to the left. You'll spill out back onto the mezzanine. Grab a seat in front of the Rodin statue of a man missing everything but his legs.*

Auguste Rodin—*The Walking Man* (*L'Homme Qui Marche*)

Like this statue, Auguste Rodin (1840–1917) had one foot in the past and one stepping into the future. Rodin combined classical solidity with Impressionist surfaces to become the greatest sculptor since Michelangelo.

This muscular, forcefully striding man could be a symbol of the Renaissance Man with his classical power. With no mouth or hands, he speaks with his body. Get close and look at the statue's surface. This rough, "unfinished" look reflects light like the rough Impressionist brushwork, making the statue come

alive, never quite at rest in the viewer's eye.

• *Near the far end of the mezzanine you'll see a small bronze couple* (L'Age Mur) *by Camille Claudel, a student of Rodin's.*

Camille Claudel—*Maturity* (*L'Age Mûr,* 1899–1903)

Camille Claudel, Rodin's student and mistress, may have portrayed their doomed love affair here. A young girl desperately reaches out to an older man, who is led away reluctantly by an older woman. The center of the composition is the empty space left when their hands separate. In real life, Rodin refused to leave his wife, and Camille (see her head sticking up from a block of marble nearby) ended up in an insane asylum.

Auguste Rodin—*The Gates of Hell* (*Porte de l'Enfer,* 1880–1917)

Rodin worked for decades on these doors depicting Dante's Hell, and they contain some of his greatest hits, small statues that he later executed in full size. Find *The Thinker* squatting above the doorway, contemplating Man's fate. And in the lower left is the same kneeling man eating his children *(Ugolin)* that you'll see in full size nearby. Rodin paid models to run, squat, leap, and spin around his studio however they wanted. When he saw an interesting pose, he'd yell, "freeze" (or "statue maker") and get out his sketch pad.

Auguste Rodin—*Honoré de Balzac* (1897)

The great French novelist is given a heroic, monumental ugliness. Wrapped in a long cloak, he thrusts his head out at a defiant angle, showing the strong individualism and egoism of the 19th-century Romantic movement. Balzac is proud and snooty—but his body forms a question mark, and underneath the twisted features we can see a touch of personal pain and self-doubt. This is hardly camera-eye realism—Balzac wasn't that grotesque—but it captures a personality that strikes us even if we don't know the man.

From this perch, look over the main floor at all the classical statues between you and the big clock and realize how far we've come—not in years but in style changes. Many of the statues below—beautiful, smooth, balanced, and idealized—were done at the same time as Rodin's powerful, haunting works. Rodin is a good place to end the tour. With a stable base of 19th-century stone, he launched art into the 20th century.

VERSAILLES

(Château de Versailles)

If you've ever wondered why your American passport has French writing in it, you'll find the answer at Versailles (vehr-"sigh"). The powerful court of Louis XIV at Versailles set the standard of culture for all of Europe, right up to modern times. Versailles was every king's dream palace. Today, if you're planning to visit just one palace in all of Europe, make it Versailles.

ORIENTATION

Cost: There are several different parts of the palace, each with a separate admission. The **State's Apartments** (our self-guided tour) is €7.50, covered by the museum pass; €5.50 after 15:30, under 18 free. The palace is also theoretically free for all teachers, professors, and architecture students. Guided tours cost extra (see "Touring Versailles from A to D" sidebar).

The **gardens** cost €3 (not covered by museum pass). But on summer weekends, when the fountains blast, the price shoots up to €5.50 (see "Fountain Spectacles," below).

Entering the **Grand and Petit Trianon Palaces** costs €5 together, €3 after 15:30 (both covered by museum pass).

If you don't have a Paris museum pass, consider getting the Versailles Pass, which covers your entrance, gives you priority access to everything (no lines), and includes an audioguide (€21, sold at Versailles train station, RER stations that serve Versailles, and at FNAC department stores).

Versailles

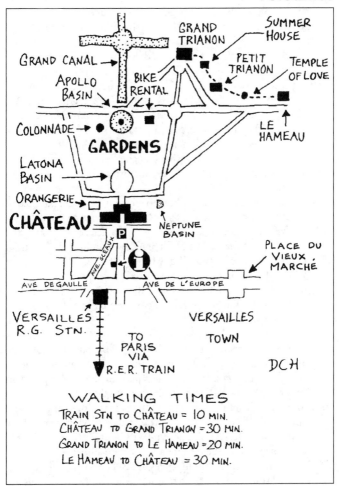

GRAND TRIANON

SUMMER HOUSE

GRAND CANAL →

PETIT TRIANON

TEMPLE OF LOVE

APOLLO BASIN

BIKE RENTAL

COLONNADE →

LE HAMEAU

GARDENS

LATONA BASIN

ORANGERIE

CHÂTEAU

Neptune BASIN

P

PLACE DU VIEUX MARCHÉ

AVE SCEAUX

AVE DE GAULLE

AVE DE L'EUROPE

VERSAILLES R.G. STN.

VERSAILLES TOWN

TO PARIS VIA R.E.R. TRAIN

DCH

WALKING TIMES
TRAIN STN TO CHÂTEAU = 10 MIN.
CHÂTEAU TO GRAND TRIANON = 30 MIN.
GRAND TRIANON TO LE HAMEAU = 20 MIN.
LE HAMEAU TO CHÂTEAU = 30 MIN.

Hours: The **palace** is open May–Sept Tue–Sun 9:00–18:30, Oct–April Tue–Sun 9:00–17:30, closed Mon (last entry 30 min before closing). The **Grand and Petit Trianon Palaces** are open daily April–Oct 12:00–18:00, Nov–March 12:00–17:00, closed Mon. The **garden** is open daily from 7:00 (8:00 in winter) to sunset (as late as 21:30 or as early as 17:30).

When to Go: In summer, Versailles is especially crowded around 10:00 and 13:00, and all day Tue and Sun. Remember, the crowds gave Marie-Antoinette a pain in the neck, too, so relax and let them eat cake. For fewer crowds, go early or late: Either arrive by 9:00 (when the palace opens, touring the palace first, then the gardens) or after 15:30 (you'll get a reduced entry ticket but you'll probably miss the last guided tours of the day, which generally depart at 15:00). If you arrive midday, see the gardens first and the palace later, at 15:00. The gardens and palace are great late. On my last visit, at 18:00 I was the only tourist in the Hall of Mirrors...even on a Tuesday.

Getting There: Take the **RER-C train** (€5 round-trip, 30 min one way) from any of these RER stops: Gare d'Austerlitz, St. Michel, Musée d'Orsay, Invalides, Pont de l'Alma, and Champ de Mars. Any train whose name starts with a V (e.g., "Vick") goes to Versailles; don't board other trains. Get off at the last stop (Versailles R.G. or "Rive Gauche"—not Versailles C.H., which is farther from the palace) and exit through the turnstiles by inserting your ticket.

To reach the château, turn right out of the station, then left at the first boulevard. It's a 10-minute walk to the palace.

When returning to Paris from Versailles, look through the windows past the turnstiles for the departure board. Any train leaving Versailles serves all downtown Paris RER stops on the C line (they're marked on the schedule as stopping at *"toutes les gares jusqu'à Austerlitz,"* meaning "all stations up to Austerlitz").

Taxis for the 30-minute ride between Versailles and Paris cost about €25.

To reach Versailles from Paris by car, get on the *périphérique* freeway that circles Paris and take the toll-free autoroute A-13 toward Rouen. Follow signs into Versailles, then look for *"château"* signs and park in the huge pay lot in front of the palace. The drive takes about 30 minutes one way.

Information: A helpful TI is just past the Sofitel Hôtel on your walk from the RER station to the palace (May–Sept daily 9:00–19:00, Oct–April daily 9:00–18:00, tel. 01 39 24 88 88, www.chateauversailles.fr). You'll also find information booths inside the château (at entrances A, B-2, and C) and, during peak season, kiosks scattered around the courtyard. The useful brochure "Versailles Orientation Guide" explains your sightseeing options.

Length of This Tour: Allow two hours for the palace and two for the gardens. Including two hours to cover your round-trip transit time, it's a six-hour day trip from Paris.

Baggage Check: Available at door A.

Cuisine Art: The cafeteria and WCs are next to the general entrance (door A). There's a sandwich kiosk and a decent restaurant at the canal in the garden.

You'll find restaurants on the street to the right of the parking lot (as you face the château). A handy McDonald's is immediately across from the train station (WC without crowds), and many restaurants line rue de Satory, midway between the train station and the palace.

Fountain Spectacles: Classical music fills the king's backyard, and the garden's fountains are in full squirt, July–Sept Sat and early April–early Oct Sun (schedule for both days: 11:00–12:00 & 15:30–17:00 & 17:20–17:30). On these "spray days," the gardens cost €5.50 (not covered by museum pass, ask for a map of fountains). Louis had his engineers literally reroute a river to fuel these fountains. Even by today's standards, they are impressive. Pick up the helpful brochure of the fountain show ("Les Grandes Eaux Musicales") at any information booth for a guide to the fountains. Also ask about the impressive *Les Fêtes de Nuit* nighttime spectacle (July–mid-Sept some Sat).

Starring: Louis XIV and the *ancien régime*.

THE TOUR BEGINS

• *Start outside the palace at the equestrian statue of Louis XIV.*

The Original Château and the Courtyard

The part of the palace directly behind the horse statue (the section

with the clock) is the original château, once a small hunting lodge where little Louis XIV spent his happiest boyhood years. The Sun King's private bedroom (the three arched windows beneath the clock), naturally, faced the rising sun. The palace and grounds are laid out on an east-west axis.

Once king, Louis XIV expanded the lodge, by attaching wings to create the present U-shape. Later, the long north and south wings were built. The total cost of the project has been estimated at half of France's entire GNP for one year.

Think how busy this courtyard must have been 300 years ago. There were as many as 5,000 nobles here at any one time, each with an entourage. They'd buzz from games to parties to amorous rendezvous in sedan-chair taxis. Servants ran about delivering secret messages and roast legs of lamb. Horse-drawn carriages arrived at the fancy gate with their finely dressed passengers, having driven up the broad boulevard that ran direct from Paris (the horse stables still line the boulevard). Incredible as it seems, both the grounds and most of the palace were public territory where even the lowliest peasant could come to gawk (so long as they followed a dress code). Then as now, there were hordes of tourists, pickpockets, palace workers, and men selling wind-up children's toys.

Touring Versailles from A to D

Versailles' highlights are the State Apartments (including the magnificent Hall of Mirrors) and the gardens, dotted with the Trianon Palaces—both covered on our self-guided tour. Versailles aficionados should spend extra time and money to see the lavish King's Private Apartments, the Opera House, and more, which can be visited only with an audioguide or live guide.

The price of any tour is added to the €7.50 entry fee to Versailles (entry covered by Paris museum pass, but tours are not). If you don't have a pass, keep your ticket as proof you've paid for admission, in case you decide to take a guided tour after you've wandered through the palace by yourself.

• *Stand in the courtyard to orient yourself to Versailles' entrances.*

Entrance A—State Apartments, Self-Guided Tour: To tour the palace on your own (by following my tour, below, or a €4 audioguide), join the line at entrance A if you need to pay admission. Those with a museum pass are allowed in through entrance B-2 without a wait. Enter the palace and take a one-way walk through the State Apartments from the King's Wing, through the Hall of Mirrors, and out via the Queen's and Nobles' Wing.

Entrance B-2: Museum passholders can avoid the line to buy tickets at Entrance A by using this entrance to get into the State Apartments.

Entrance C—King's Private Apartments: Using a dry but informative audioguide, tour Louis XIV's private bedroom, some other rooms, and the Hall of Mirrors.

Entrance D—Various Guided Tours: You can select a one-hour guided tour from a variety of themes, such as the daily life of a king or the lives of such lesser-known nobles as the well-coiffed Madame de Pompadour (€4, join first English tour available). Or consider the 90-minute tour (€6) of the King's Private Apartments (Louis XV, Louis XVI, and Marie-Antoinette) and

Versailles' Entrances

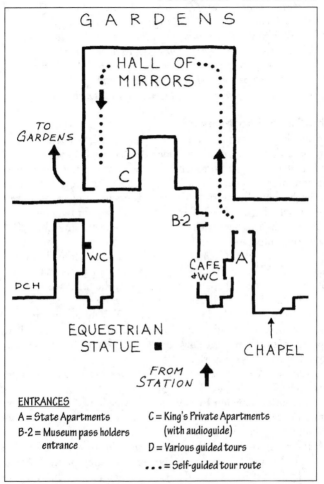

GARDENS

HALL OF MIRRORS

TO GARDENS

D

C

B-2

WC

DCH

CAFE &WC

A

EQUESTRIAN STATUE ■

CHAPEL

FROM STATION ↑

ENTRANCES

A = State Apartments
B-2 = Museum pass holders entrance

C = King's Private Apartments (with audioguide)
D = Various guided tours

• • • = Self-guided tour route

the chapel. This tour, which is the only way visitors can see the sumptuous Opera House, can be long depending on the quality of your guide.

For a live tour, make reservations immediately upon arrival, as tours can sell out by 13:00 (first tours generally begin at 10:00, last tours depart usually at 15:00 but as late as 16:00).

The Gardens: If you want to visit these first, go around the left side of the palace. The spacious gardens stretch for miles behind the palace and feature landscaped plots, statues, bubbling fountains, a Grand Canal, and several smaller palaces, interesting both outside and in.

• *You'll see signs marking the various entrances (A, B, B-2, C, and D) into the U-shaped palace. For this tour of the State Apartments, which covers the ceremonial center of the palace, start at Entrance A (if you need to pay admission) or Entrance B-2 (if you have a museum pass).*

You'll be directed, first, through the 21 rooms of the history museum, with paintings on the background of Versailles and its kings.

Our tour starts upstairs, in the room that overlooks the lavish Royal Chapel with its pipe organ. (Note: As you jostle through the crowded corridors of the palace, pickpockets will be working the tourist crowds.)

The State Apartments

Royal Chapel: Every morning at 10:00, the organist and musicians struck up the music, these big golden doors opened, and Louis XIV and his family walked through to attend Mass. While Louis XIV sat here on the upper level and looked down on the golden altar, the lowly nobles below knelt with their backs to the altar and looked up—worshiping Louis worshiping God. Important religious ceremonies took place here, including the marriage of young Louis XVI to Marie-Antoinette.

In the vast pagan "temple" that is Versailles, built to glorify one man, Louis XIV, this Royal Chapel is a paltry tip of the hat to that "other" god—the Christian one. It's virtually the first, last, and only hint of Christianity you'll see in the entire complex. Versailles celebrates Man, not God, by raising Louis XIV to almost godlike status, the personification of all good human qualities. In a way, Versailles is the last great flowering of Renaissance humanism and revival of the classical world.

• *Take a map flier and enter the next room, a large space with a fireplace and a colorful painting on the ceiling.*

Hercules Drawing Room: Pleasure ruled. The main suppers, balls, and receptions were held in this room. Picture elegant party-goers in fine silks, wigs, rouge, lipstick, and fake moles (and that's just the men), as they dance to the strains of a string quartet.

On the wall opposite the fireplace is an appropriate painting showing Christ in the middle of a Venetian party. The work by Paolo Veronese, a gift from the Republic of Venice, was one of Louis XIV's favorites, so they decorated the room around it. (Stand by the fireplace for the full effect: The room's columns, arches, and frieze match the height and style of Veronese's painted architecture, which makes the painting an extension of the room.)

The ceiling painting of Hercules being crowned a god gives the room its name. Hercules (with his club) hurries up to heaven on a chariot, late for his wedding to the king of the gods' daughter. Louis XIV built the room for his own daughter's wedding reception in the style of the day—pure Baroque. As you wander, the palace feels bare, but remember that entire industries were created to furnish and decorate the place with carpets, mirrors, furniture, and tapestries.

• *From here on, it's a one-way tour—getting lost is not allowed. Follow the crowds into the small green room with a goddess in pink on the ceiling. The names of the rooms generally come from the paintings on the ceilings.*

The King's Wing

Cornucopia Room: If the party in the Hercules Room got too intense, you could always step in here for some refreshments. Silver trays were loaded up with liqueurs, exotic stimulants (coffee), juice, chocolates, and, on really special occasions, three-bean salad.

The ceiling painting shows the cornucopia of riches poured down on invited guests. Around the edges of the ceiling are painted versions of the king's actual dinnerware and treasures. The two black chests-of-drawers are from Louis' furniture collection (most of it was lost in the Revolution). They rest on heavy bases and are heavily ornamented—the so-called "Louis XIV style."

Louis himself might be here. He was a gracious host who enjoyed letting his hair down at night. If he took a liking to you, he might sneak you through those doors there (in the middle of the wall) and into his own private study, where he'd show off his collection of dishes, medals, jewels, or…the *Mona Lisa*, which hung on his wall.

The paintings on the walls are of Louis XIV's heirs. He reigned more than 70 years and outlived three of them, finally leaving the crown to his pink-cheeked, five-year-old great-grandson, Louis XV (on the right).

Venus Room: Love ruled at Versailles. In this room, couples would cavort beneath the Greek goddess of love (on the ceiling), who sends down a canopy of golden garlands to ensnare mortals in delicious *amour*. Notice how a painted garland goes "out" the bottom of the central painting, becomes a golden garland held by a satyr, transforms into a gilded wood garland, and then turns back to a painting again. Baroque artists loved to mix their media to fool the eye. Another illusion is in the paintings at both ends of the room—the painted columns match the room's real ones and so extend this grand room into mythical courtyards.

Don't let the statue of a confident Louis XIV as a Roman emperor fool you. He started out as a poor little rich kid with a chip on his shoulder. His father died before Louis was old enough to rule, and, during the regency period, the French Parliament treated little Louis and his mother like trash. They were virtual prisoners, humiliated in their home (the Royal Palace of the Louvre in Paris) and getting by with bland meals, hand-me-down leotards, and pointed shoes. Once Louis XIV attained power and wealth, there was one topic you never discussed in his presence—poverty. Maybe Versailles was his way of saying, "Living well is the best revenge."

Kings and Queens and Guillotines

• *You could read this on the train ride to Versailles. Relax, the palace is the last stop.*

Come the Revolution, when they line us up and make us stick out our hands, will you have enough calluses to keep them from shooting you? A grim thought, but Versailles raises questions like that. It's the symbol of the *ancien régime,* a time when society was divided into rulers and the ruled, when you were born to be rich or to be poor. To some it's the pinnacle of civilization, to others the sign of a civilization in decay. Either way, it remains one of Europe's most impressive sights.

Versailles was the residence of the king and seat of France's government for a hundred years. Louis XIV (reigned 1643–1715) moved out of the Louvre in Paris, the previous royal residence, and built an elaborate palace in the forests and swamps of Versailles, 10 miles west. The reasons for the move were partly personal—Louis XIV loved the outdoors and disliked the sniping environs of stuffy Paris—and partly political.

Louis XIV was creating the first modern, centralized state. At Versailles, he consolidated Paris' scattered ministries so that he could personally control policy. More important, he invited to Versailles all of France's nobles, so that he could control them. Living a life of almost enforced idleness, the "domesticated" aristocracy couldn't interfere with the way Louis ran things. With 18 million people

united under one king (England had only 5.5 million), a booming economy, and a powerful military, France was Europe's number-one power.

Around 1700, Versailles was the cultural heartbeat of Europe, and French culture was at its zenith. Throughout Europe, when you said "the king," you were referring to the French king…Louis XIV. Every king wanted a palace like Versailles. Everyone learned French. French taste in clothes, hairstyles, table manners, theater, music, art, and kissing

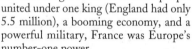

Diana Room: Here in the billiards room, Louis and his men played on a table that stood in the center of the room, while ladies sat surrounding them on Persian-carpet cushions and music wafted in from the next room. Louis was a good pool player, a sore loser, and a king—he rarely lost.

The famous bust of Louis by Giovanni Lorenzo Bernini (in the center) shows a

spread across the Continent. That cultural dominance has continued, to some extent, right up to this century.

Louis XIV

At the center of all this was Europe's greatest king. He was a true Renaissance man, a century after the Renaissance: athletic, good-looking, a musician, dancer, horseman, statesman, art-lover, lover. For all his grandeur, he was one of history's most polite and approachable kings, a good listener who could put even commoners at ease in his presence.

Louis XIV called himself the Sun King because he gave life and warmth to all that he touched. He was also thought of as Apollo, the Greek god of the sun. Versailles became the personal temple of this god on earth, decorated with statues and symbols of Apollo, the sun, and Louis XIV himself.

Louis XIV was a hands-on king who personally ran affairs of state. All decisions were made by him. Nobles, who in other countries were the center of power, became virtual slaves dependent on Louis XIV's generosity. For 70 years, he was the perfect embodiment of the absolute monarch. He summed it up best himself with his famous rhyme—*"L'état, c'est moi!"* (lay-tah say-mwah): "The state, that's me!"

Another Louis or Two to Remember

Three kings lived in Versailles during its century of glory. Louis XIV built it and established French dominance. Louis XV, his great-grandson (Louis XIV reigned for 72 years), carried on the tradition and policies, but without the Sun King's flair. During Louis XV's reign (1715–1774), France's power abroad was weakening, and there were rumblings of rebellion from within.

France's monarchy was crumbling, and the time was ripe for a strong leader to reestablish the old feudal order. They didn't get one. Instead, they got Louis XVI (ruled 1774–1792), a shy, meek book-worm, the kind of guy who lost sleep over Revolutionary graffiti...because it was misspelled. Louis XVI married a sweet girl from the Austrian royal family, Marie-Antoinette, and together they retreated into the idyllic gardens of Versailles while Revolutionary fires smoldered.

handsome, dashing, 27-year-old playboy-king. His gaze is steady amid his windblown cloak and hair. Young Louis loved life. He hunted animals by day (notice Diana the Huntress on the ceiling) and chased beautiful women at night.

Games were actually an important part of Louis' political strategy, known as "the domestication of the nobility." By distracting the nobles with the pleasures of courtly life, he was free to run the government his way. Billiards, dancing, and concerts were popular, but the biggest distraction was gambling, usually a card game similar to blackjack. Louis lent money to the losers, making them even more indebted to him. The good life was an addiction, and Louis kept the medicine cabinet well-stocked.

As you move into the next room, notice the fat walls that hid thin servants, who were to be at their master's constant call—but out of sight when not needed.

Mars Room: Decorated with a military flair, this was the room for Louis' Swiss bodyguards. On the ceiling, there's Mars, the Greek god of war, in a chariot pulled by wolves. The bronze cupids in the corners are escalating from love arrows to heavier artillery.

Out the window are sculpted gardens in the style of a traditional Italian villa—landscaped symmetrically, with trimmed hedges and cone-shaped trees lining walkways that lead to fountains.

Mercury Room: Louis' life was a work of art, and Versailles was the display case. Everything he did was a public event designed to show his subjects how it should be done. This room served as Louis' official (not actual) bedroom, where the Sun King would ritually rise each morning to warm his subjects.

From a canopied bed (like this 18th-century one), Louis would get up, dress, and take a seat for morning prayer. Meanwhile, the nobles stand behind a balustrade, in awe of his piety, nobility, and clean socks. At breakfast, they murmur with delight as he deftly decapitates his boiled egg with a knife. And when Louis went to bed at night, the dukes and barons would fight over who got to hold the candle while he slipped into his royal jammies. Bedtime, wake-up, and meals were all public rituals.

The clock dates from Louis' time. When the cocks crowed at the top of the hour and the temple doors opened, guess who popped out?

Apollo Room: This was the grand throne room. Louis held court from a 10-foot-tall, silver-canopied throne on a raised platform placed in the center of the room. (Notice the metal rings in the ceiling that once supported the canopy.)

Everything in here reminds us that Louis XIV was not just any ruler, but the Sun King, who lit the whole world with his presence. On the ceiling, the sun god Apollo drives his chariot, dragging the sun across the heavens to warm the four corners of the world (counterclockwise from above the exit door): 1) Europe, with a sword; 2) Asia, with a lion; 3) Africa, with an elephant; and 4) good old America, an Indian maiden with a crocodile. Notice the ceiling's beautifully gilded frame and Goldfinger maidens.

The famous portrait by Hyacinthe Rigaud over the fireplace gives a more human look at Louis XIV. He's shown in a dancer's pose, displaying the legs that made him one of the all-time dancing fools of king-ery. At night, they often held parties in this room, actually dancing around the throne.

Louis XIV (who was 63 when this was painted) had more than 300 wigs like this one, and he changed them many times a day. This fashion first started when his hairline began to recede, then sprouted all over Europe, and even to the American colonies in the time of George Washington.

Louis XIV may have been treated like a god, but he was not an overly arrogant man. His subjects adored him because he was a symbol of everything a man could be, the fullest expression of the Renaissance Man. Compare the portrait of Louis XIV with the one across the room of his last successor, Louis XVI—same arrogant pose, but without the inner confidence to keep his head on his shoulders.

The War Room: "Louis Quatorze was addicted to wars…" and France's success made other countries jealous and nervous. At the base of the ceiling, we see Germany (with the double eagle), Holland (with its ships), and Spain (with a red flag and roaring lion) ganging up on Louis XIV. But Lady France (center of ceiling), protected by the shield of Louis XIV, hurls thunderbolts down to defeat them. The stucco relief on the wall shows Louis XIV on horseback, triumphing over his fallen enemies.

Versailles was good propaganda. It showed the rest of the world how rich and powerful France was. One look at this eye-saturating view of the gardens sent visitors reeling. But Louis XIV's greatest triumph may be the next room, the one that everybody wrote home about.

The Hall of Mirrors: No one had ever seen anything like this hall when it was opened. Mirrors were still a great luxury at the time, and the number and size of these monsters were astounding. The hall is nearly 250 feet long. There are 17 arched mirrors, matched by 17 windows reflecting that breathtaking view of the gardens. Lining the hall are 24 gilded candelabras, eight busts of Roman emperors, and eight classical-style statues (seven of them ancient). The ceiling decoration chronicles Louis' military accomplishments, topped off by Louis himself in the central panel (with cupids playing cards at his divine feet), doing what he did best—triumphing. Originally, two huge carpets mirrored the action on the ceiling.

Imagine this place lit by the flames of thousands of candles, filled with ambassadors, nobles, and guests dressed in silks and powdered wigs. At the far end of the room sits the king, on the canopied throne moved temporarily from the Apollo Room. Servants glide by with silver trays of hors d'ouevres and an orchestra fuels the festivities. The mirrors reflect an age when beautiful people loved to look at themselves. It was no longer a sin to be proud of good looks or fine clothes, or to enjoy the good things in life: laughing, dancing, eating, drinking, flirting, and watching the sun set into the distant canal.

From the center of the hall, you can fully appreciate the epic scale of Versailles. The huge palace (by architect Louis Le Vau), the fantasy interior (by Charles Le Brun), and the endless gardens (by André Le Nôtre) made Versailles *le* best. In 1871, after the Prussians defeated the French, Otto von Bismarck declared the establishment of the German Empire in this room. And in 1919, here in the Hall of Mirrors, Germany and the Allies signed the Treaty of Versailles, ending World War I (and, some say, starting World War II).

• *Enter the small Peace Room.*

The Peace Room: By the end of Louis XIV's long life, he was tired of fighting. In this sequel to the War Room, peace is granted to Germany, Holland, and Spain as cupids play with the discarded cannons, armor, and swords.

The oval painting above the fireplace shows 19-year-old Louis XV bestowing an olive branch on Europe. Beside him is his wife, Marie, from Poland, cradling their baby twin daughters.

The Peace Room marks the beginning of the queen's half of the palace. On Sundays, the queen held chamber-music concerts here for family and friends (notice the gilded music motifs).

• *Enter the first room of the Queen's Wing, with its canopied bed.*

The Queen's and Nobles' Wing

The Queen's Bedchamber: It was here that the queen rendezvoused with her husband. Two queens died here. This is where 19 princes were born. The chandelier is where two of them were conceived. Just kidding.

True, Louis XIV was not the most faithful husband. There was no attempt to hide the fact that the Sun King warmed more than one bed, for he was above the rules of mere mortals. Adultery became acceptable—even fashionable—in court circles. The secret-looking door on the left side of the bed was for Louis' late-night liaisons—it led straight to his rooms.

Some of Louis XIV's mistresses became more famous and powerful than his rather quiet queen, but he was faithful to the show of

The King's Vegetable Garden
(Le Potager du Roi)

When Louis XIV demanded fresh asparagus in the middle of winter, he got it, thanks to his vegetable garden. Located a few blocks from the château, the 22-acre garden—still productive—is open to visitors. Stroll through symmetrically laid-out plots planted with vegetables both ordinary and exotic, among thousands of fruit trees. The garden is surrounded by walls and sunk below street level to create its own microclimate. Overseeing the central fountain is a statue of the agronomist Jean de la Quintinie, who wowed Louis XIV's court with Versailles-sized produce. Even today, the garden sprouts 20 tons of vegetables and 50 tons of fruit a year, which you can buy in season (€4.50 on weekdays, €6.50 on weekends, April–Oct daily 10:00–18:00, 10 rue du Maréchal Joffre).

marriage and had genuine affection for his wife. Their private apartments were connected, and Louis XIV made a point of sleeping with the queen as often as possible, regardless of whose tiara he tickled earlier in the evening.

This room looks like it did in the days of the last queen, Marie-Antoinette, who substantially redecorated the entire wing. That's her bust over the fireplace, and the double eagle of her native Austria in the corners. The big chest to the left of the bed held her jewels.

The queen's canopied bed is a reconstruction. The bed, chair, and wall coverings switched with the seasons. This was the cheery summer pattern.

Drawing Room of the Nobles: The queen's circle of friends met here, seated on the stools. Discussions ranged from politics to gossip, food to literature, fashion to philosophy. The Versailles kings considered themselves enlightened monarchs who promoted the arts and new ideas. Folks like Voltaire—a political radical—and the playwright Molière participated in the Versailles court. Ironically, these discussions planted the seeds of liberal thought that would grow into the Revolution.

Queen's Antechamber: The royal family dined here publicly, while servants and nobles fluttered around them, admired their table manners, and laughed at the king's jokes like courtly Paul Shaffers. A typical dinner consisted of four different soups, two whole birds stuffed with truffles, mutton, ham slices, fruit, pastries, compotes, and preserves.

The central portrait is of luxury-loving, "Let-them-eat-cake" Marie-Antoinette, who became a symbol of decadence to the peasants. The portrait at the far end is a public-relations attempt to soften her image, by showing her with three of her children.

Queen's Guard Room: On October 6, 1789, a mob of revolutionaries—appalled by their queen's taste in wallpaper—stormed the palace. They were fed up with the ruling class leading a life of luxury in the countryside while they were starving in the grimy streets of Paris.

The king and queen locked themselves in. Some of the revolutionaries gained access to this upper floor. They burst into this room where Marie-Antoinette was hiding, overcame her bodyguards, and dragged her and her husband off. (Some claim that, as they carried her away, she sang "Louis, Louis, oh-oh...we gotta go now.")

The enraged peasants then proceeded to ransack the place, as revenge for the years of poverty and oppression they'd suffered. Marie-Antoinette and Louis XVI were later taken to the place de la Concorde in Paris, where they knelt under the guillotine and were made a foot shorter at the top.

Did the king and queen deserve it? Were the revolutionaries destroying civilization or clearing the decks for a new and better one? Was Versailles a symbol of progress or decadence?

Coronation Room: No sooner did they throw out a king than they got an emperor. The Revolution established democracy, but it was shaky in a country that wasn't used to it. In the midst of the confusion, the upstart general Napoleon Bonaparte took control and soon held dictatorial powers. This room captures the glory of the Napoleon years, when he conquered most of Europe. In the huge canvas on the left-hand wall, we see him crowning himself emperor of a new, revived "Roman" Empire. (While also painted by the master, Jacques-Louis David, this is a lesser-quality version of the famous one hanging in the Louvre.)

Turn and face the windows to see the portrait (between the windows) of a dashing, young, charismatic Napoleon in 1796, when he was just a general in command of the Revolution's army in Italy. Compare this with the adjacent portrait from 10 years later—looking less like a revolutionary and more like a Louis. Above the young Napoleon is a portrait of Josephine, his wife and France's empress. In David's *Distribution of Eagles* (opposite the *Coronation*), the victorious general (in imperial garb) passes out emblems of victory to his loyal troops. In *The Battle of Aboukir* (opposite the window), Joachim Murat—Napoleon's general and brother-in-law—looks bored as he slashes through a tangle of dark-skinned warriors. His horse, though, has a look of "What are we doing in this mob? Let's get out of here!" Let's.

• *The exit staircase puts you outside on the left (south) side of the palace, where you enter the gardens.*

The Gardens—Controlling Nature

Louis was a divine-right ruler. One way he proved it was by controlling nature like a god. These lavish grounds, elaborately planned out, pruned, and decorated, showed everyone that Louis was in total command.

• *Buy your ticket (not covered by museum pass) and enter the gardens, then turn left toward the stone railing about 70 yards away. You'll pass through flowers and cookie-cutter patterns of shrubs and green cones. Stand at the railing overlooking the courtyard below and the Louis-made lake in the distance.*

The Orangerie: The warmth from the Sun King was so great that he could even grow orange trees in chilly France. Louis XIV had a thousand of these to amaze his visitors. In winter, they were kept in the greenhouses (beneath your feet) that surround the court-

yard. On sunny days, they were wheeled out in their silver planters and scattered around the grounds.

• *From the stone railing, turn about-face and walk to the back side of the palace, with two large pools of water. Sit on the top stair and look away from the palace.*

View down the Royal Drive: This, to me, is the most stunning spot in all of Versailles. In one direction, the palace. Stretching out in the other direction, the endless grounds. Versailles was laid out along an eight-mile axis that included the grounds, the palace, and the town of Versailles itself, one of the first instances of urban planning since Roman times and a model for future capitals such as Washington, D.C. and Brasilia.

Looking down the Royal Drive (also known as "The Green Carpet"), you see the round Apollo fountain far in the distance. Just beyond that is the Grand Canal. The groves on either side of the Royal Drive were planted with trees from all over, laid out in an elaborate grid and dotted with statues and fountains. Of the original 1,500 fountains, 300 remain.

Looking back at the palace, you can see the Hall of Mirrors—it's the middle story, with the arched windows.

• *Stroll down the steps to get a good look at the frogs and lizards that fill the round Latona Basin.*

The Latona Basin: Absolutely everything in the garden has a

Getting Around the Gardens

It's a 30-minute hike from the palace, down to the canal, past the two Trianon palaces to the Hamlet—our self-guided tour. The fast-looking, slow-moving tram for tired tourists leaves from behind the château (north side) and serves the Grand Canal and the Trianon palaces; you can hop on and off as you like (€5, 4/hr, 4 stops but not the Hamlet, commentary is nearly worthless). A horse carriage also departs from the north side of the palace. You can rent bikes near the Grand Canal (1 hr–€6).

symbolic meaning. The theme of Versailles is Apollo, the god of the sun, associated with Louis XIV. This round fountain tells the story of the birth of Apollo and his sister, Diana. On top of the fountain are Apollo and Diana as little kids with their mother, Latona (they're facing toward the Apollo fountain). Latona, an unwed mother, was insulted by the local peasants. She called on the king of the gods, Zeus (the children's father), to avenge the insult. Zeus swooped down and turned all the peasants into the frogs and lizards that ring the fountain.

• *As you walk down past the basin toward the Royal Drive, you'll pass by "ancient" statues done by 17th-century French sculptors. The Colonnade is hidden in the woods on the left-hand side of the Royal Drive, about three-fourths of the way to the Apollo Basin.*

The Colonnade: Versailles had no prestigious ancient ruins, so the king built his own. This prefab Roman ruin is a 100-foot circle of 64 marble columns supporting arches. Beneath the arches are small birdbath fountains. Nobles would picnic in the shade to the tunes of a string quartet and pretend that they were the enlightened citizens of the ancient world.

The Apollo Basin: The fountains of Versailles were its most famous attraction, a marvel of both art and engineering. This one was the centerpiece, showing the sun god—Louis XIV—in his sunny chariot, as he starts his journey across the sky. The horses are half-submerged, giving the impression, when the fountains play, of the sun rising out of the mists of dawn. Most of the fountains were only turned on when the king walked by, but this one played constantly for the benefit of those watching from the palace.

All the fountains are gravity-powered. They work on the same principle as blocking a hose with your finger to make it squirt. Underground streams (pumped into Versailles by Seine River pressure) feed into smaller pipes at the fountains, which shoot the water high into the air.

Looking back at the palace from here, realize that the distance you just walked is only a fraction of this vast complex of buildings, gardens, and waterways. Be glad you don't have to mow the lawn.

The Grand Canal: Why visit Venice when you can just build your own? In an era before virtual reality, this was the next best thing to an actual trip. Couples in gondolas would pole along the waters accompanied by barges with orchestras playing "O Sole Mio." The canal is actually cross-shaped, this being the long arm, one mile from end to end. Of course, this too is a man-made body of water with no function other than to please. Originally, actual gondoliers, imported with their boats from Venice, lived in a little settlement next to the canal.

The Trianon Area—Retreat from Reality

Versailles began as an escape from the pressures of kingship. In a short time, the palace was as busy as Paris ever was. Louis XIV needed an escape from his escape and built a smaller palace out in the tulies. Later, his successors retreated still farther into the garden and built a fantasy world of simple pleasures from which to ignore the real world, which was crumbling all around them.

• *You can rent a bike or catch the pokey tourist train, but the walk is half the fun. It's about a 30-minute walk from here to the end of the tour, plus another 30 minutes to walk back to the palace.*

Grand Trianon: This was the king's private residence away from the main palace. Louis usually spent a couple of nights a week here, but the two later Louises spent more and more time retreating. While the main palace of Versailles was a screen separating French reality from the royal utopia, the Trianon palaces were engulfed in the royals' fantasy world and therefore favored.

The facade of this one-story building is a charming combination of pink, yellow, and white, a cheery contrast to the imposing Baroque facade of the main palace. Ahead you can see the gardens through the columns. The king's apartments were to the left of the columns.

The flower gardens were changed daily for the king's pleasure—for new color combinations and new "nasal cocktails."

Walk around the palace (to the right), if you'd like, for a view of the gardens and rear facade.

• *Facing the front, do an about-face. The Summer House is not down the driveway but about 180 yards away, along the smaller pathway at about 10 o'clock.*

Summer House of the French Garden: This small white building with four rooms fanning out from the center was one more step away from the modern world. Here, the queen spent summer evenings with family and a few friends, listening to music or playing parlor games. All avenues of *la douceur de vivre*—"the sweetness of living"—were explored. To the left are the buildings of the Ménagerie, where cows, goats, chickens, and ducks were bred.

• *Continue frolicking along the path until you run into the...*

Petit Trianon: Louis XV developed an interest in botany. He wanted to spend more time near the French Gardens, but the Summer House just wasn't big enough. He built the Petit Trianon (the "small" Trianon), a masterpiece of neoclassical architecture. This gray, cubical building has four distinct facades, each a perfect and harmonious combination of Greek-style columns, windows, and railings. Walk around it and find your favorite.

Louis XVI's wife, Marie-Antoinette, made this her home base. Despite her bad public reputation, Marie-Antoinette was a sweet girl from Vienna who never quite fit in with the fast, sophisticated crowd at Versailles. Here at the Petit Trianon, she could get away and re-create the simple home life she remembered from her childhood. On the lawn outside, she installed a merry-go-round.

• *Five minutes more will bring you to the...*

Temple of Love: A circle of 12 marble Corinthian columns supporting a dome decorates a path where lovers would stroll. Underneath, there's a statue of Cupid making a bow (to shoot arrows of love) out of the club of Hercules. It's a delightful monument to a society whose rich could afford that ultimate luxury, romantic love. When the Revolution came, I bet they wished they'd kept the club.

• *And finally, you'll reach...*

The Hamlet (Le Hameau): Marie-Antoinette longed for the simple life of a peasant. Not the hard labor of real peasants—who sweated and starved around her—but the fairy-tale world of simple country pleasures. She built this complex of 12 buildings as her own private village.

This was an actual working farm with a dairy, a water mill, and domestic animals. The harvest was served at Marie-Antoinette's table. Marie-Antoinette didn't do much work herself, but she "supervised," dressed in a plain white muslin dress and a straw hat.

The Queen's House is the main building, actually two buildings connected by a wooden gallery. Like any typical peasant farmhouse, it had a billiard room, library, elegant dining hall, and two living rooms.

Nearby was the small theater. Here, Marie-Antoinette and her friends acted out plays, far from the rude intrusions of the real world...

• *The real world and the main palace are a 30-minute walk to the southeast. Along the way, stop at the Neptune Basin near the palace, an impressive miniature lake with fountains, and indulge your own favorite fantasy.*

AMSTERDAM

Often called the "Venice of the North," Amsterdam has more canals than Venice, as much art, and about as many tourists. Take a walk through the heart of town, observing how the modern world of bankers, buskers, and pot-smokers bustles along within the confines of a 17th-century city. Catch the optimistic spirit of the Golden Age in the Rijksmuseum's colorful slice-of-life paintings. Get lost in the swirling brushstrokes of a troubled genius at the Van Gogh Museum. Reflect on young Anne Frank, whose fate matched that of tens of thousands of Amsterdam's citizens during the Nazi occupation. Take it all in, then pause to watch the sunset—at 10 p.m.—and see the Golden Age reflected in a quiet canal.

Amsterdam City Walk   **181**

Rijksmuseum   **199**

Van Gogh Museum   **216**

Anne Frank House   **227**

Amsterdam Sights

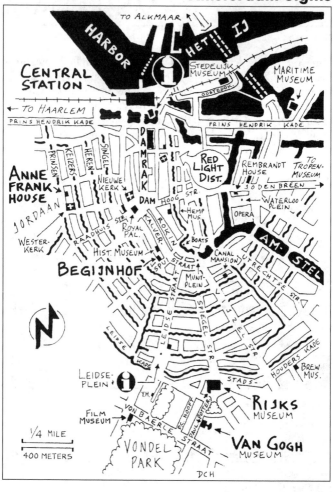

AMSTERDAM CITY WALK

From the Train Station to the Rijksmuseum

Amsterdam today looks much as it did in its Golden Age, the 1600s. It's a retired sea captain of a city, still in love with life, with a broad outlook and a salty story to tell.

Take a Dutch-sampler walk from one end of the old center to the other, tasting all that Amsterdam has to offer along the way. It's your best single stroll through Dutch clichés, democratic squares, businesses, afternoon happy-hour hangouts, and, yes, Amsterdam's 800-year history.

ORIENTATION

Route Overview: The walk starts at the central-as-can-be train station. You'll walk about three miles, heading down Damrak to Dam Square, continuing south down Kalverstraat to the Mint Tower, then wafting through the Bloemenmarkt (flower market), before continuing south to Leidseplein and jogging left to the Rijksmuseum. To return to Centraal Station, catch tram #2 or #5 from the southwest corner of the Rijksmuseum.

Tips: Find public toilets at fast-food places (€0.25) and near the entrance to the Amsterdam History Museum. Beware of silent transport—trams and bikes. Stay off the tram tracks and bike paths, and yield to bell-ringing bikers.

Length of This Tour: Allow three hours for this walk.

Nieuwe Kerk: Fee if exhibition scheduled, Mon–Sat 10:00–18:00, Sun 13:00–18:00, Dam Square, tel. 020/638-6909, www.nieuwekerk.nl.

Amsterdam Diamond Center: Free, daily 9:30–18:00, shorter hours off-season, Rokin 1, tel. 020/624-5787.

De Papegaai Catholic Church: Free, daily 10:00–16:00, on Kalverstraat.

Amsterdam History Museum: €6, Mon–Fri 10:00–17:00, Sat–Sun 11:00–17:00, Kalverstraat 92, tel. 020/523-1822.

Begijnhof: Free, daily 10:00–17:00, on Begijnensteeg lane, just off Kalverstraat between #130 and #132.

House of Hajenius: Free, Rokin 92, tel. 020/623-7494, www.hajenius.com.

When Nature Calls: Free, daily 10:00–22:00, Keizersgracht 508, www.whennaturecalls.nl.

Delft Shop: Free, Prinsengracht 440, tel. 020/627-8299.

Rijksmuseum: €9, free if under 18, daily 10:00–17:00, tel. 020/674-7000, www.rijksmuseum.nl.

Van Gogh Museum: €9, €2 if under 18, daily 10:00–18:00, Paulus Potterstraat 7, tel. 020/570-5200, www.vangoghmuseum.nl.

THE TOUR BEGINS

Centraal Station

Here, where today's train travelers enter the city, sailors of yore disembarked from seagoing ships to be met by street musicians, pickpockets, hotel-runners, and ladies carrying red lanterns. When the

station was built at the former harbor mouth, Amsterdam lost some of its harbor feel, but it's still a bustling port of entry.

Centraal Station, with warm red brick and prickly spires, is the first of several neo-Gothic buildings we'll see from the late 1800s, built during Amsterdam's economic revival. One of the towers has a clock dial; the other tower's dial is a weathervane. Watch the hand twitch as the wind gusts.

As you emerge from the train station, the city spreads out before you in a series of concentric canals. Ahead of you stretches the street called Damrak, leading south to Dam Square, a half-mile away. To the left of Damrak is the city's old *(oude)* side, to the right is the new *(nieuwe)*.

The big church towering above the old side (at about 10 o'clock) is St. Nicholas Church, built in the 1880s when Catholics—after two centuries of oppression—were finally free to worship in public. The church marks the beginning of the Red Light District. The city's biggest bike garage, a multistoried wonder, is on your

Amsterdam City Walk

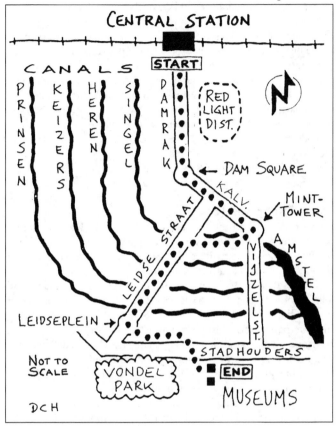

CENTRAL STATION

START

CANALS
PRINSEN
KEIZERS
HEREN
SINGEL
DAMRAK

RED LIGHT DIST.

N

← DAM SQUARE

KALV.

MINT-TOWER

LEIDSE STRAAT

VIJZELST.

AMSTEL

LEIDSEPLEIN →

NOT TO SCALE

VONDEL PARK

STADHOUDERS

END

MUSEUMS

DCH

right in front of the Ibis Hotel. If you'd like to make this "walk" a much faster "roll," there's a handy bike-rental place in the station (MacBike, daily 9:00–17:45, across from bike garage, Stationsplein 33, online reservations possible, tel. 020/625-3845, www.macbike.nl).
• *We'll basically walk south from here to the Rijksmuseum. The art museum and the station—designed by the same architect—stand like bookends holding the old town together. Follow the crowds south on Damrak, walking along the right side of the street.*

Damrak

Stroll past every Dutch cliché at the tourist shops: wooden shoes, plastic tulips, Heineken fridge magnets, and windmill saltshakers. Listen to a hand-cranked barrel organ. Order French fries (called *Vlaamse frites,* or Flemish fries, since they were invented in the Low Countries) and dip them in mayonnaise, not ketchup. Eating international cuisine (Indonesian *rijsttafel*, Argentine steaks, Middle Eastern *shoarma*, pronounced SHWAHR-mah) is like going local in cosmopolitan Amsterdam. And you'll find the city's most notorious commodity displayed disease-free at the Amsterdam sex museum.

The street was once a riverbed, where the Amstel River flowed north into the IJ (eye) River behind today's train station. Both rivers then emptied into a vast inlet of the North Sea (the Zuiderzee), making Amsterdam a major seaport. Today, the Amstel is channeled into canals, its former mouth has been covered by Centraal Station, the North Sea inlet has been diked off to make an inland lake, and 100,000 ships a year reach the open waters by sailing west through the North Sea Canal.

• *The long brick building with the square clock tower, along the left side of Damrak, is the...*

Stock Exchange (Beurs)

Built of nine million bricks on 4,880 tree trunks hammered into the marshy soil, the Beurs van Berlage (named for an early-20th-century Amsterdam architect with vision) stands as a symbol of the city's long tradition as a trading town.

Back when "stock" meant whatever could be loaded and unloaded onto a boat, Amsterdamers gathered to trade. Soon, rather than trading goats, chickens, and kegs of beer, they were exchanging slips of paper and "futures" at one of the world's first stock exchanges. Traders needed money-changers, who needed bankers, who made money by lending money...and Amsterdam of the 1600s became one of the world's first great capitalist cities, loaning money to free-spending kings, dukes, and bishops.

This impressive building, built in 1903 in a geometric, minimal, no frills style, is one of the world's first "modern" (i.e., 20th-century-style) buildings, emphasizing function over looks. In 1984, the stock exchange moved next door (see the stock-exchange readout) to the Euronext complex—a joint attempt by France, Belgium, and the Netherlands to compete with the power of Britain's stock exchange. The old Beurs building now hosts concerts and a museum for temporary exhibits.

Amsterdam still thrives as the center of Dutch businesses such as Heineken, Shell Oil, Philips Electronics, KLM Airlines, and Unilever. Amsterdamers have always had a reputation for putting business above ideological differences, staying neutral while trading with both sides.

• *Damrak opens into...*

Dam Square

The city got its start right here, around 1250, when fishermen in this marshy delta settled along the built-up banks of the Amstel River.

Amsterdam City Walk—First Half

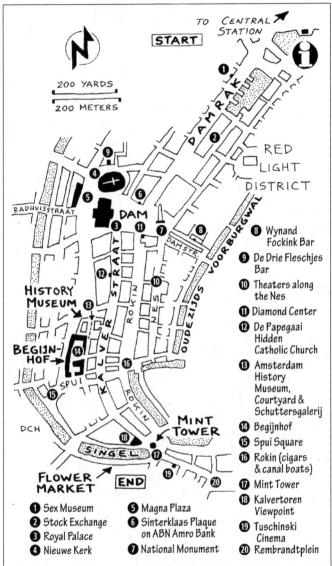

START

TO CENTRAL STATION

DAMRAK

RED LIGHT DISTRICT

RADHVISSTRAAT

DAM

HISTORY MUSEUM

BEGIJN-HOF

SPUI

DCH

VOORBURGWAL

DAM STR.

OUDEZIJDS

KALVER STRAAT

ROKIN

NES

MINT TOWER

SINGEL

FLOWER MARKET

END

200 YARDS

200 METERS

❶ Sex Museum
❷ Stock Exchange
❸ Royal Palace
❹ Nieuwe Kerk
❺ Magna Plaza
❻ Sinterklaas Plaque on ABN Amro Bank
❼ National Monument

❽ Wynand Fockink Bar
❾ De Drie Fleschjes Bar
❿ Theaters along the Nes
⓫ Diamond Center
⓬ De Papegaai Hidden Catholic Church
⓭ Amsterdam History Museum, Courtyard & Schuttersgalerij
⓮ Begijnhof
⓯ Spui Square
⓰ Rokin (cigars & canal boats)
⓱ Mint Tower
⓲ Kalvertoren Viewpoint
⓳ Tuschinski Cinema
⓴ Rembrandtplein

They blocked the river with a *damme*, and created a small village called "Amstel-damme." Soon the fishermen were trading with German riverboats traveling downstream and with seafaring boats from Stockholm, Hamburg, and London. Dam Square was the center of it all.

The dam on the Amstel divided the *damrak* (meaning "outer harbor"—for sea traffic) from the *rokin* ("inner harbor"—for river traffic). Land trade routes converged here as well, and a customs house stood here. Today the Damrak and Rokin (roh-KEEN) are major roads and the city's palace and major department stores face the  square, where mimes, jugglers, and human statues mingle with locals and tourists. This is the historic heart of the city. As the symbolic center of the Netherlands, it's where political demonstrations begin and end.

Pan the square clockwise to see the following: the Royal Palace (the large domed building on the west side), the Nieuwe Kerk (New Church), an ABN Amro bank, Damrak, the proud old De Bijenkorf ("The Beehive") department store, the Krasnapolsky Hotel, the white phallic obelisk of the National Monument, the Rokin, touristy Madame Tussaud's, and the entrance to pedestrian-only Kalverstraat.

Royal Palace

The name is misleading, since Amsterdam is one of the cradles of modern democracy. For centuries, this was the Town Hall of a  self-governing community that prided itself on its independence and thumbed its nose at royalty. The current building, built in 1652, is appropriately classical (like the democratic Greeks), with a triangular pediment featuring—fittingly for Amsterdam—denizens of the sea cavorting with Neptune (with his green copper trident).

After the city was conquered by the French, Napoleon imposed a monarchy on Holland, making his brother Louis the king of the Netherlands (1808). Louis used the city hall as his "royal palace," giving it the current name. When Napoleon was defeated, the victorious powers dictated that the Netherlands remain a monarchy, under a noble Dutch family called the House of Orange. If the current Queen Beatrix is in town, this is, technically, her residence (her permanent home is in the Royal Palace at The Hague). Amsterdam is the nominal capital of the Netherlands, but all governing activity is at The Hague (a city 30 miles southwest).

Nieuwe Kerk

In 1980 Queen Beatrix said "I do" in the Nieuwe Kerk, where the Netherlands' monarchs are crowned, wed, and buried. The "new" church is 600 years old (newer than the 700-year-old "old" church in the Red Light District). The sundial above the entrance once served as the city's official timepiece.

The church's bare, spacious, well-lit interior (often occupied by temporary art exhibits) looks quite different from the Baroque-encrusted churches found in the rest of Europe. In 1566 clear-eyed Protestant extremists throughout Holland marched into Catholic churches (like this once was), lopped off the heads of holy statues, stripped gold-leaf angels from the walls, urinated on Virgin Marys, and shattered stained-glass windows in a wave of anti-Catholic vandalism.

This Iconoclasm (icon-breaking) of 1566 started an 80-year war against Spain and the Hapsburgs, leading finally to Dutch independence in 1648. Catholic churches like this one were converted to the new dominant religion, Calvinist Protestantism (today's Dutch Reformed Church). From then on, Dutch churches downplayed the "graven images" and "idols" of ornate religious art.

The Nieuwe Kerk is now the symbolic religious center of the Netherlands. When Beatrix dies or retires, her son, Crown Prince Willem Alexander, will parade to the center of the church, sit in front of the golden choir screen, and—with TV lights glaring and flashbulbs popping—be crowned the next sovereign.

• *Looking between the Royal Palace and the Nieuwe Kerk, you'll see the fanciful brick facade of the Magna Plaza shopping center. Back in Dam Square, on the wall of the ABN Amro bank, find the colorful little stone plaque of...*

Sinterklaas—St. Nicholas

Jolly old St. Nicholas (Nicolaas in Dutch) is the patron saint of seafarers (see the three men in a tub) and of Amsterdam, and is also the model for Sinterklaas—the guy we call Santa Claus. Every year in late November, Holland's Santa Claus arrives by boat near Centraal Station (from his legendary home in Spain), rides a white horse up Damrak with his black servant, Peter, and arrives triumphant in this square while thousands of kids cheer.

December 5, the feast day of St. Nicholas, is when the Dutch exchange presents and Sinterklaas leaves goodies in good kids' wooden shoes. (Smart kids maximize capacity by putting out big boots.) Many Dutch celebrate Christmas on December 25, as well.

Around the corner in Damrak, the bank has an ATM and a chip-loader *(Oplaadpunt)*. The ATM is familiar, but what's that small keypad next to it? It's for loading up the Dutch cash card—an attempt to eliminate the need for small change. With the keypad,

City on a Sandbar

Amsterdam is built upon millions of wooden pilings. The city was founded on unstable mud, which sits on stable sand. In the Middle Ages, buildings were made of wood, which rests lightly and easily on mud. But devastating fires repeatedly wiped out entire neighborhoods, so stone became the building material of choice. Stone is fire-resistant but was too heavy for a mud foundation. For more support, pilings were driven 30 feet through the mud and into the sand. The Royal Palace sits upon 13,000 such pilings—still solid after 350 years. (The wood survives fine if kept wet and out of the air.) Since World War II, concrete rather than wood has been used for the pilings, with foundations driven 60 feet deep through the first layer of sand, through more mud, and into a second layer of sand. And today's biggest buildings have foundations sinking as much as 120 feet deep.

the Dutch transfer money from their accounts onto a card with a computer chip. Then they can make purchases at stores by inserting the card into a pay-point, the way Americans buy gas from the pump.

National Monument

The obelisk, which depicts a crucified Christ, men in chains, and howling dogs, was built in 1956 as a WWII memorial. Now it's considered a monument for peace.

The Nazis occupied Holland from 1940 to 1945. They deported 100,000 Amsterdam Jews, driving many—including young Anne Frank and her family—into hiding. Near the end of the war, the "Hunger Winter" of 1944–1945 killed thousands and forced many to survive on tulip bulbs. Today, Dutch people in their 70s—whose growth-spurt years coincided with the Hunger Winter—are easy to identify because they are uniformly short.

Circling the Square

You're at the center of Amsterdam. To the east a few blocks is the top of the Red Light District. Amsterdam is the world capital of experimental theater, and several edgy theaters line the street called the Nes (stretching south from Hotel Krasnapolsky).

Office workers do afternoon happy-hours at crowded bars that stock *jenevers* and liqueurs in wooden kegs. De Drie Fleschjes, a particularly casual pub, is tucked right behind the Nieuwe Kerk. The more upscale Wynand Fockink (100 yards down the alley along the right side of Hotel Krasnapolsky) serves fruit brandies produced in its adjoining distillery (which you can visit). Though the brew is bottled and distributed all over Holland, what you get here in the home-office bar is some of the best Fockink liqueur in the world.

At the Amsterdam Diamond Center (where Rokin street meets Dam Square), see cutters and jewelry-setters handling diamonds, plus some small educational displays and fake versions of big, famous stones. Since the 1500s, the city has been one of the world's diamond capitals. Eighty percent of industrial diamonds (for making drills and such) pass through here, as do many cut and polished jewels, like the Koh-i-Nohr diamond.

• *From Dam Square, head south on...*

Kalverstraat

This pedestrian-only street is lined with many familiar franchise stores and record shops. (If you're on a bike, you must dismount and walk it.) This has been a shopping street for centuries and today is notorious among locals as the place for cheesy, crass materialism. For smaller and more elegant stores, try  the adjacent district called De Negen Straatjes ("The Nine Little Streets"), where 190 shops mingle by the canals (about four blocks west of Kalverstraat).

• *About 120 yards along (across from the McDonald's), pop into...*

De Papegaai Hidden Catholic Church (Petrus en Paulus Kerk)

This Catholic church (daily 10:00–16:00), while not exactly hidden (you found it), keeps a low profile even now that Catholicism has been legalized in Amsterdam. In the late 1500s, with Protestants fighting Catholics and the Dutch fighting Spanish invaders, Amsterdam tried to stay neutral, doing business with all parties. Finally in 1578, Protestant extremists (following the teachings of Reformer John Calvin) took political control of the city. They expelled Catholic leaders and bishops, outlawed the religion, and allied Amsterdam with anti-Spanish forces in an action known to historians as The Alteration.

For the next two centuries, Amsterdam's Catholics were driven underground. Catholicism was illegal but tolerated, as long as it was not practiced in public, but in humble, unadvertised places like this, and for personal use only.

Today the church, which asks for a mere "15 minutes for God" *(een kwartier voor God)*, stands as a metaphor for how marginal religion has always been in highly commercial and secular Amsterdam.
• *Farther along (about 75 yards) at #92, where Kalverstraat crosses Wijde Kapel Steeg, look to the right at an archway leading to the...*

Courtyard of the Amsterdam History Museum

On the arch is Amsterdam's coat of arms—a red shield with three Xs and a crown. Not a reference to the city's sex trade, the X-shaped crosses (which appear everywhere in the city) represent the crucifixion of St. Andrew, the patron saint of fishermen, and symbolize heroism, determination, and mercy. The crown dates to 1489, when Maximilian I (the Low Countries' first Hapsburg ruler and later Holy Roman Emperor) paid off a big loan from city bankers and, as thanks for the cash, gave the city permission to use his prestigious trademark, the Hapsburg crown, atop its shield. The relief above the door (see photo), dated 1581, shows boys around a dove, reminding all who pass that this was an orphanage and asking for charity. Go inside.

The pleasant David and Goliath café (with a shady courtyard) is watched over by a giant statue of Goliath and a knee-high David (from 1650). In the courtyard are the lockers for the orphan's uniforms and a pay toilet.
• *The courtyard leads to another courtyard with the best city history museum in town, the Amsterdam History Museum (Mon–Fri 10:00–17:00, Sat–Sun 11:00–17:00). Between the two courtyards (on the left) is a free glassed-in passageway lined with paintings, called the...*

Civic Guard Gallery (Schuttersgalerij)

In these group portraits from Amsterdam's Golden Age (early 1600s), look into the eyes of the frank, dignified men (and occasionally women) with ruffs and lace collars who made Amsterdam the most prosperous city in Europe, sending trading ships to distant colonies and pocketing interest from loans. The weapons they carry are mostly symbolic, since these "Civic Guards" who once protected the town (fighting the Spanish) had become more like fraternal organizations of business bigwigs.

Many paintings look the same in this highly stylized genre. The company often sits in two rows. Someone holds the company

flag. The captain wields a traditional pike (a long axe-like
weapon topped with a spearhead-
shaped tip). His lieutenant holds
a partisan (pike with a sword-like
tip). Others wield hatchet-headed
halberds.

Everyone looks straight out,
and every face is lit perfectly. Each
paid for his own portrait and wanted it right. It took masters like
Rembrandt and Frans Hals to take the starch out of the collars and
compose more natural scenes.

• *The gallery offers a shortcut to the Begijnhof, 75 yards farther south. But
if the gallery is closed, backtrack to Kalverstraat, continue south, then turn
right on Begijnensteeg. This leads to the entrance of the walled courtyard
(daily 10:00–17:00) called the...*

Begijnhof

This quiet courtyard (gutturally: buh-HHHINE-hof) lined with
houses around a church, has sheltered women since 1346. In early
times, rich women gave up their wealth to live in Christian poverty
here as part of the lay order called Beguines. Poor women and
widows lived here as well, spinning wool and making lace to earn
their keep.

In 1578, when Catholicism was outlawed, the Dutch Reformed

Church (and the city) took over
many Catholic charities—such as
this place. Many Dutch women,
widowed by the hazards of overseas
trade, found a retirement home
here. The last Beguine died in 1971,
but the Begijnhof still provides sub-
sidized housing to single women in
need (mostly Catholic seniors and
students). The Begijnhof is just one
of about 75 *hofjes* (housing projects surrounding courtyards) that dot
Amsterdam.

Begin the Beguine visit at the
statue of one of these charitable sisters. She faces the wooden house
(houten huys) at #34. The city's oldest,
it dates from 1477. Originally the
whole city was built of wood. To the
left of the house is a display of carved
gable stones that once adorned house
fronts and served as street numbers

(and still do at #19 and #26, the former Mother Superior's house). Inside the covered passageway at the south end of the square (near the oldest house) find images of things forbidden in this all-female enclave—roosters (male), dogs (dirty), and male humans over age three (dangerous).

The brick-faced **English Church** (Engelse Kerk, from 1420) was the Beguine church until 1607, when it became Anglican. The Pilgrims (strict Protestants), fleeing persecution in England, stopped here in tolerant Amsterdam and prayed in this church before the *Mayflower* carried them to religious freedom at Plymouth Rock in America. (It remains a welcoming place, with English services on Sundays at 10:30.)

The "hidden" **Catholic Church** faces the English Church (enter through a low-profile doorway). Amsterdam's oppressed 17th-century Catholics, who refused to worship as Protestants, must have eagerly awaited the day when, in the 19th century, they were legally allowed to say Mass. Step inside.

Today, Holland is still divided religiously, but without the bitterness. Roughly a third is Catholic, a third Protestant...and a third list themselves as "unchurched."

• *From the Begijnhof, backtrack to busy Kalverstraat, then turn right, continuing south. Pause at the busy intersection with Spui Straat and get oriented.*

Spui and the Rokin

To the right down Spui Straat is the square called **Spui** (shpow, rhymes with "cow"). Lined with cafés and bars, it's one of the city's more popular spots for nightlife and sunny-afternoon people-watching.

A half-block to the left is the busy street called **Rokin** (ro-KEEN). A statue of Queen Wilhelmina (1860–1962) on the Rokin shows her riding daintily sidesaddle. In real life, she was the iron-willed inspiration for Dutch Resistance against the Nazis. The present Queen Beatrix is Wilhelmina's granddaughter.

Canal cruises depart from the Rondvaart Kooij dock (€6.50, daily 10:00–20:00, 2/hr, more frequent in summer).

The **House of Hajenius,** at Rokin 92, is a temple of cigars, a "paradise for the connoisseur" showing "175 years of tradition and good taste." To enter this sumptuous Art Nouveau building with its painted leather ceilings is to step back into 1910. The brown-capped canisters are for smelling fine pipe tobacco. Take a whiff. The personal humidifiers (read the explanation) allow locals to call in an order and have their cigars waiting for them in just the right humidity. Upstairs in back is a small, free museum (Rokin 92, www.hajenius.com).

• *Continue up Kalverstraat toward the...*

Mint Tower (Munttoren)

The tower, which marks the limit of the medieval walled city, served as one of the original gates (the steeple was added later, in 1620). The city walls were girdled by a moat—the Singelgracht. Until about 1500, the area beyond here was nothing but marshy fields and a few farms on reclaimed land.

On the way to the Mint Tower, you'll pass department stores with cafeterias. At the end of Kalverstraat, the Vroom & Dreesman department store is one of Holland's oldest chains. Inside, La Place is a sprawling self-service cafeteria—handy for a quick and healthy lunch. Across the street, the Kalvertoren shopping complex offers a top-floor viewpoint and café (venture into the glass atrium and slide up in the wild elevator).

From the busy intersection at Muntplein, look left (at about 10 o'clock) down Reguliersbreestraat. A long block east of here (where you see trees) is Rembrandtplein, another major center for nightlife. Halfway down the block (past the massive easyInternetcafé—daily 9:00–22:00, Reguliersbreestraat 33), the twin green domes mark the exotic Tuschinski Theater, where you can see modern movies in a sumptuous Art Deco setting. Sit inside and stare at the ever-changing ceiling, imagining this place during the Roaring '20s.

• *Just past the Mint Tower, turn right and walk west along the south bank of the Singelgracht, which is lined with the greenhouse shops of the...*

Flower Market (Bloemenmarkt)

Cut flowers, plants, bulbs, seeds, and garden supplies attest to Holland's reputation for growing flowers. Tulips, imported from Turkey in the 1600s, grew well in the sandy soil of the dunes and reclaimed land. By the 1630s the country was in the grip of a full-blown tulip mania, when a single bulb sold for as much as a house, and fortunes were

Amsterdam City Walk—Second Half

200 YARDS

200 METERS

㉑ Flower Market
㉒ Koningsplein
㉓ Metz & Co.
㉔ Smartshop
㉕ Delft Shop
㉖ Stadsschouwburg
㉗ AUB box office

㉘ Melkweg
㉙ Restaurant Row
㉚ Bulldog Café
㉛ Max Euweplein
㉜ Paradiso
㉝ Rijksmuseum
㉞ Trams #2 & #5

won and lost. Finally, in 1637, the market plummeted, and the tulip became just one of many beauties in the country's flower arsenal. Today Holland is a major exporter of flowers. Certain seeds are certified and OK to bring back into the United States (merchants have the details).

• *The long Flower Market ends at the next bridge, where you'll see a square named...*

Koningsplein

Choke down a raw or pickled herring—the commodity that first put Amsterdam on the trading map—with locals who flock to this popular outdoor herring stand. (*Hollandse nieuwe* means the herring are in season.)

• *From Koningsplein, we'll turn left, heading straight to Leidseplein. At first the street southward is just labeled Koningsplein (Scheltema, Amsterdam's leading bookstore, is at Koningsplein 20), but it soon becomes...*

Leidsestraat

Between here and Leidseplein you'll cross several grand canals, following a street lined with fashion and tourist shops, and crowded with shoppers, tourists, bicycles, and trams. Trams must wait their turn to share a single track as the street narrows.

The once-grand, now-frumpy Metz & Co. department store (where Leidsestraat crosses Herengracht) offers a rare above-the-rooftops panorama of the city from its sixth-floor café.

Looking left down Herengracht, you'll see the "Golden Curve" of the canal, lined with grand, classical-style gables.

• *Past the posh stores of Laura Ashley, DKNY, and Lush, find a humble establishment where Leidsestraat crosses the Keizersgracht.*

When Nature Calls Smartshop

"Smartshops" like this one are clean, well-lighted, fully professional retail outlets that sell powerful drugs, many of which are illegal in America. Their "natural" drugs include harmless nutrition boosters (royal jelly), harmful but familiar tobacco, herbal versions of popular dance-club drugs (herbal Ecstasy), and powerful psychoactive plants (psilocybin mushrooms). The big item: marijuana seeds.

Prices are clearly marked, with brief descriptions of the drugs, their ingredients, and effects. The knowledgeable salespeople can give more information on their "100 percent natural products that play with the human senses."

Still, my fellow Americans, *caveat emptor!* We've grown used to thinking, "If it's legal, it must be safe. (If it's not, I'll sue.)"

While perfectly legal and aboveboard, some of these substances can cause powerful, often unpleasant reactions. Even if you've smoked marijuana (itself a potent mind-alterer), use caution with less familiar drugs (Keizersgracht 508, daily 10:00–22:00, www.whennaturecalls.nl).

• *Where Leidsestraat crosses the Prinsengracht, just over the bridge on the right, you'll find...*

The Delft Shop (Prinsengracht 440)

The distinctive blue-and-white design characterizes glazed ceramics made in Delft (30 miles southwest of here). Dutch traders learned the technique from the Chinese of the Ming dynasty, and many pieces have an oriental look. The doodads with arms branching off a trunk are popular "flower pagodas," vases for displaying tulips.

• *Leidsestraat empties into the square called...*

Leidseplein

Filled with outdoor tables under trees, ringed with cafés, theaters, and nightclubs, bustling with tourists, diners, trams, mimes, and fire-eaters, and lit by sun- or lantern-light, Leidseplein is the city's liveliest square.

Do a 360-degree spin: Leidseplein's south side is bordered by the city's main serious theater, the **Stadsschouwburg,** which dates back to the 17th-century Golden Age (present building from 1890). To the right, down a lane behind the big theater, stands the **Melkweg** (Milky Way), the once-revolutionary, now-institutional entertainment complex housing all things youth-oriented under one roof (Lijnbaansgracht 234a); step into the lobby or check out posters plastered on walls to find out who's playing tonight. On Leidseplein's west side is the Boom Chicago nightclub theater (at #12), presenting English-language spoofs of politics, Amsterdam, and tourists. The neighborhood beyond Haagen Dazs and Burger King is the **Restaurant Row,** featuring countless Thai, Brazilian, Indian, Italian, Indonesian, and even a few Dutch eateries. Next, on the east end of Leidseplein, is the **Bulldog Café and Coffeeshop,** the flagship of several café/bar/coffeeshops in town with that name. (Notice the sign above the door: It once housed the police bureau). A small green-and-white decal in the window indicates that it's a city-licensed "coffeeshop," where marijuana is sold and smoked legally.

• *From Leidseplein, turn left and head along the taxi rank down the broad, busy, tram-filled boulevard called Kleine-Gartman Plantsoen, which becomes Weteringschans. At the triangular garden filled with iguanas, cross the street and pass under a row of tall, gray, Greek-style columns, entering...*

Max Euweplein

The Latin inscription above the colonnade—*Homo Sapiens non urinat in ventum*—means "Don't pee into the wind." Pass between the columns and through a passageway to reach a pleasant interior courtyard of cafés and a large chessboard with knee-high kings. (Dutchman Max Euwe was a world chess champion.) The square gives you access to the Casino, and just over the small bridge is the entrance to **Vondelpark.**

• *Return to Weteringschans street. Continue 80 yards east to a squat red-brick building called...*

Paradiso

Back when rock-and-roll was a religion, this former church staged intimate concerts by big-name acts such as the Rolling Stones. In the late 1960s, when city fathers were trying hard to tolerate hordes of young pot-smokers, this building was redecorated with psychedelic colors and opened up as the first place where marijuana could be smoked—not legally yet, but it was tolerated. Today the club hosts live bands and DJs and sells marijuana legally (for current shows, see www.paradiso.nl).

• *Continue down Weteringschans to the first bridge, where you'll see the Rijksmuseum across the canal.*

The Rijksmuseum and Beyond

The best visual chronicle of the Golden Age is found in the Rijksmuseum's portraits and slice-of-life scenes. For a tour of the Rembrandts, Vermeers, and others, see the Rijksmuseum Tour, page 199.

On this walk, we've seen landmarks built during the city's late-19th-century revival: Centraal Station, the Stadsschouwburg, and now the Rijksmuseum. They're all similar, with red brick and

Canals

Amsterdam's canals tamed the flow of the Amstel River, creating pockets of dry land to build on. The city's 100 canals are about three meters deep, crossed by some 1,200 bridges, fringed with 100,000 Dutch elm and lime trees, and bedecked with 2,500 houseboats. A system of locks (back near Centraal Station) controls the flow outward to (eventually) the North Sea and the flow inward to the Amstel River. The locks are opened periodically to flush out the system.

It is amazing how quiet and peaceful this big city of more than 700,000 can be. Some of the boats in the canals look pretty funky by day, but Amsterdam is an unpretentious, anti-status city. When the sun goes down and the lights come on, people cruise the sparkling canals with an on-board hibachi and a bottle of wine, and even scows can become chick magnets.

Gothic-style motifs (clock towers, steeples, prickly spires, and stained glass). Petrus Cuypers (1827–1921), who designed the train station and the Rijksmuseum, was extremely influential. Mainly a builder of Catholic churches, he made the Rijksmuseum, with its stained-glass windows, a temple to art.

Behind the Rijksmuseum is the always entertaining Museumplein and the Van Gogh Museum (see tour on page 216). The Heineken Brewery museum is a half-mile east of the Rijks on Stadhouderskade (€7.50 for self-guided hour-long tour, must be over age 18, Tue–Sun 10:00–18:00, last entry 17:00, closed Mon, Stadhouderskade 78).

To return to Centraal Station (or to nearly anyplace along this walk), catch tram #2 or #5 from the southwest corner of the Rijks. Trams #6, #7, and #10 (catch them on Weteringschans) can take you farther south, east, or west. Or walk north on Nieuwe Spiegel Straat, which leads (with a little detour) back to the Mint Tower.

RIJKSMUSEUM

At the Rijksmuseum ("Rijks" sounds like "hikes"), Holland's Golden Age shines with the best collection anywhere of the Dutch masters—from Vermeer's quiet domestic scenes to Steen's raucous family meals to Hals' snapshot portraits to Rembrandt's moody brilliance.

During the Golden Age (1600s), secular art dominated. With no local church or royalty to commission big canvases in the Protestant Dutch republic, artists had to find different patrons—the upper-middle-class businessmen who fueled Holland's capitalist economy. Artists painted their portraits and decorated their homes with pretty still-lifes and nonpreachy slice-of-life art.

The main core of the Rijksmuseum is closed until 2008 for a massive renovation. Thankfully, the most famous masterpieces—nearly everything on the typical tourist's hit list—are on display in the Philips Wing (southwest corner of the Rijks, the part of the building nearest the Van Gogh Museum).

ORIENTATION

Cost: €9; free under age 18; tickets good all day.

Hours: Daily 10:00–17:00, sometimes 9:00–21:00, closed only on Jan 1.

Getting There: The entrance to the Philips Wing is on Hobbemastraat, opposite the Van Gogh Museum. From the train station,

The Golden Age
(1600s)

Who bought this art? Look around at the Rijksmuseum's many portraits and you'll see—ordinary middle-class people, merchants, and traders. Even in their Sunday best, you can see that these are hardworking, businesslike, friendly, simple people (with a penchant for ruffled lace collars).

Dutch fishermen sold their surplus catch in distant areas of Europe, importing goods from these far lands. In time, fishermen became traders, and by 1600, Holland's merchant fleets ruled the waves with colonies as far away as India, Indonesia, and America (New York was originally "New Amsterdam"). The Dutch slave trade—selling Africans to Americans—generated a lot of profit for luxuries such as the art you're looking at. Back home, these traders were financed by shrewd Amsterdam businessmen on the new frontiers of capitalism.

Look around again. Is there even one crucifixion? One saint? One Madonna? OK, maybe one. But this is people art, not church art. In most countries, Catholic bishops and rich kings supported the arts. But the Republic of the Netherlands, recently free of Spanish rule and Vatican domination, was independent, democratic, and largely Protestant, with no taste for saints and Madonnas.

Instead, Dutch burghers bought portraits of themselves, and pretty, unpreachy, unpretentious works for their homes. Even poor people bought smaller canvases by "no-name" artists designed to fit the budgets and lifestyles of this less-than-rich-and-famous crowd. We'll see examples of their four favorite subjects—still-lifes (of food and everyday objects), landscapes, portraits (often of groups), and scenes from everyday life.

catch tram #2 or #5. The trams stop on Hobbemastraat, right at the Philips Wing.

Information: The helpful information booth has free maps and a good "Tour of the Golden Age" brochure (€0.50). Tel. 020/674-7000, www.rijksmuseum.nl.

Tour: €3.50, audioguide tour covers many paintings with dial-a-number convenience and provides a blitz tour for those interested in a quick visit of the highlights.

Length of This Tour: 60 minutes.

Checkrooms: Leave your bag at the free checkrooms.

Photography: Permitted without a flash.

Cuisine Art: Vondelpark (picnic-perfect park with the delightful Café Vertigo, daily 11:00–24:00, beneath Film Museum at Vondelpark 3) and Leidseplein (a lively square with cafés) are

each a short walk away. For good pancakes, try the untouristy Le Soleil (€7, daily 10:00–18:00, Nieuwe Spiegelstraat 8).

Starring: Frans Hals, Johannes Vermeer, Jan Steen, and Rembrandt van Rijn.

THE TOUR BEGINS

• *Enter Room 1, dominated by the large, colorful painting of a group of men staring at you.*

DUTCH ART

Dutch art is meant to be enjoyed, not studied. It's straightforward, meat-and-potatoes art for the common man. The Dutch love the beauty of everyday things painted realistically and with exquisite detail. So set your cerebral cortex on Low and let this art pass straight from the eyes to the heart with minimal detours.

Rooms 1–5: Golden Age Treasures

Welcome to the Golden Age. Gaze into the eyes of the men who made Amsterdam the richest city on earth in the 1600s. Though shown in their military uniforms, these men were really captains of industry—shipbuilders, seamen, salesmen, spice-tasters, bankers, and venture capitalists—all part of the complex economic web that planned and financed overseas trade. Also in Room 1, find a big wooden model of a 74-gun Dutch man-of-war that escorted convoys of merchant ships loaded with wealth.

The five rooms on the ground floor display objects that bring

Museumplein

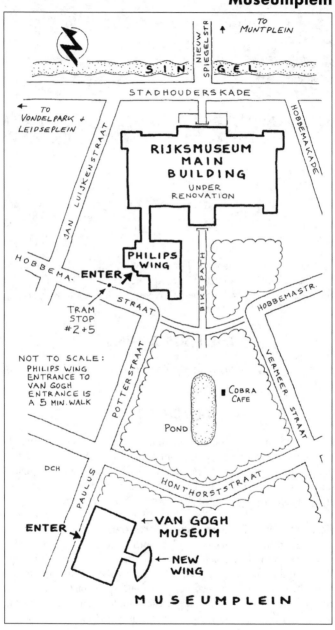

Holland's Golden Age to life, including weapons, dolls' houses, and precious objects (especially Delftware, inspired by Chinese porecelain). Soak up the ambience to prepare for the paintings that the Golden Age generation produced and enjoyed.

• *Head upstairs to Room 6.*

Room 6: New Genres

Rather than religious art, Dutch painters portrayed small-scale, down-home, happy subjects such as portraits, landscapes, still-lifes, and so-called "genre scenes" (snapshots of everday life).

Hendrick Avercamp (1585–1634)— *Winter Landscape with Ice Skaters*

The village stream has frozen over, and the people all come out to play. (Even today, tiny Holland's ice-skating teams routinely beat the superpowers.) In the center, a guy falls flat on his face. A couple makes out in the hay-tower silo. There's a "bad moon on the rise" in the broken-down outhouse at left, and another nearby. We see the scene from above (the horizon line is high), making it seem as if the fun goes on forever.

A song or a play is revealed to the audience at the writer's pace. But in a painting, we set the tempo, choosing where to look and how long to linger. Exercise your right to loiter. Avercamp, who was deaf and mute, presents a visual symphony of small little scenes. Just skate among these Dutch people—rich, poor, lovers hand in hand, kids, and moms—and appreciate the silent beauty of this intimate look at old Holland.

• *Enter Room 7.*

Frans Hals—*The Merry Drinker* (1627)

You're greeted by a jovial man in a black hat, capturing the earthy, exuberant spirit of the Golden Age. Notice the details—the happy red face of the man offering us a glass of wine, the sparkle in his eyes, the lacy collar, the decorative belt buckle, and so on.

Now move in closer. All these meticulous details are accomplished with a few quick, thick, and messy brushstrokes. The beard is a tangle of brown worms, the belt buckle a yellow blur. His hand is a study in smudges. Even the expressive face is done with a few well-chosen patches of color. Unlike the still-life scenes, this canvas is meant to be viewed from a distance where the colors and brush-strokes blend together.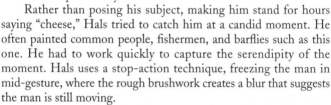

Frans Hals (c. 1580–1666) was the pre-mier Golden Age portrait painter. Merchants hired him the way we'd hire a wedding pho-tographer. With a few quick strokes, Hals captured not only the features but the personality.

Rather than posing his subject, making him stand for hours saying "cheese," Hals tried to catch him at a candid moment. He often painted common people, fishermen, and barflies such as this one. He had to work quickly to capture the serendipity of the moment. Hals uses a stop-action technique, freezing the man in mid-gesture, where the rough brushwork creates a blur that suggests the man is still moving.

Two centuries later the Impressionists learned from Hals' messy brushwork. In the Van Gogh Museum you'll see how van Gogh painted, say, a brown beard by using thick dabs of green, yellow, and red that blend at a distance to make brown.

Frans Hals (c. 1581–1666)—Wedding Portrait of Isaac Abrahamsz Massa and Beatrix van der Laen (1622)

This wedding portrait of a chubby, pleasant merchant and his bride sums up the story of the Golden Age. This overseas trader was away from home for years at a time on business. So Hals makes a special effort to point out his patron's commitment to marriage. Isaac pledges allegiance to his wife, putting his hand on his heart. Beatrix's wedding ring is prominently displayed, dead center between them (on her right-hand forefinger, Protestant style). The vine clinging to a tree is a symbol of man's support and woman's dependence. And in the distance at right, in the classical love garden, are other happy couples strolling arm in arm amid peacocks, a symbol of fertility.

In earlier times, marriage portraits put the man and wife in sep-arate canvases, staring out grimly. Hals' jolly couple reflects a societal shift from marriage as business partnership to an arrangement that's more friendly and intimate.

Hals didn't need symbolism to tell us that these two are pre-pared for their long-distance relationship—they seem relaxed together, but they each look at us directly, with a strong, individual identity. Good as gold, these are the type of people who propelled this soggy little country into its glorious Golden Age.

Shhh...Dutch Art

You can be sitting at home late one night and it's perfectly quiet. Not a sound, very peaceful. And then...the refrigerator motor turns off, and it's really quiet.

Dutch art is really quiet art. It silences our busy world so that every sound, every motion is noticed. You can hear cows tearing off grass 50 yards away.

Dutch art is still. It slows our fast-lane world so we notice the motion of birds. We notice how the cold night air makes the stars sharp. We notice that the undersides of leaves and of cats are always a lighter shade than the tops. Dutch art stills the world so we can hear our own heartbeat and reflect upon that most noble muscle that without thinking gives us life.

To see how subtle Dutch art is, realize that one of the museum's most exciting, dramatic, emotional, and extravagant Dutch paintings is probably *The Threatened Swan*. Quite a contrast to the rape scenes and visions of heaven of Italian Baroque from the same time period.

Various Still-Lifes (c. 1630)

Savor the fruits of Holland's rich overseas trade—lemons from the south, pitchers from Germany, and spices from Asia, including those most exotic of spices...salt and pepper. These carefully composed, photo-realistic still-lifes reflect the same sense of pride the Dutch have for their homes, cultivating them like gardens till they're immaculate, decorative, and well ordered.

Pick one. Get so close that the guard joins you. Linger over the little things: the pewterware, the seafood, the lemon peels, the rolls, and the glowing goblets that cast a warm reflection on the table-cloth. You'd swear you can see yourself reflected in the pewter vessels. At least you can see the faint reflections of the food and even of surrounding windows. The closer you get, the better it looks.

• *Enter Room 8.*

Rembrandt Van Rijn—Early Works

Rembrandt van Rijn (1606–1669) is the greatest Dutch painter. Whereas most painters specialized in one field—portraits, landscapes, still-lifes—Rembrandt excelled in them all.

Rembrandt—*Self-Portrait at an Early Age*

Here we see the young, small-town boy about to launch himself into whatever life has to offer. Rembrandt was a precocious kid. His father, a miller, insisted he be a lawyer. His mother hoped he'd be a preacher (look for a portrait of her reading the Bible, nearby). Rembrandt combined the secular and religious worlds by becoming an artist, someone who can hint at the spiritual by showing us the beauty of the created world.

He moved to Amsterdam and entered the highly competitive art world. Amsterdam was a booming town and, like today, a hip and cosmopolitan city. Rembrandt portrays himself at age 22 as being divided—half in light, half hidden by hair and shadows—open-eyed but wary of an uncertain future. As we'll see, Rembrandt's paintings are often light-and-dark, both in color and in subject, exploring the "darker" side of human experience.

Rembrandt—*Jeremiah Lamenting the Destruction of Jerusalem* (1630)

The Babylonians have sacked and burned Jerusalem. But Rembrandt leaves the pyrotechnics (in the murky background at left) to

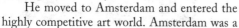

Spielberg and the big screen. Instead, he tells the story of Israel's destruction in the face of the prophet who predicted the disaster. Jeremiah slumps in defeat, deep in thought, confused and despondent, trying to understand why this evil had to happen. Rembrandt turns his floodlight of truth on the prophet's deeply lined forehead.

Rembrandt wasn't satisfied to crank out portraits of fat merchants in frilly bibs, no matter what they paid him. He wanted to experiment, trying new techniques and more probing subjects. Many of his paintings weren't commissioned and were never even intended for sale. His subjects could be brooding and melancholy, a bit dark for the public's taste. So was his technique.

You can recognize a Rembrandt canvas by his play of light and dark. Most of his paintings are a deep brown tone, with only a few

Rembrandt van Rijn
(1606-1669)

Rembrandt is the greatest Dutch painter, master of many styles, and perhaps history's finest painter of self-portraits. The son of a Leyden miller (who owned a waterwheel on the Rhine—"van Rijn"), he took Amsterdam by storm with his famous painting of *The Anatomy Lesson* (1632, currently in the Mauritshuis Museum in The Hague). The commissions poured in for official portraits, and he was soon wealthy and married (1634) to Saskia van Uylenburgh. They moved to an expensive home in the Jewish Quarter (today's Rembrandt House Museum), and decorated it with their collection of art and exotic furniture. His portraits were dutifully detailed, but other paintings explored strong contrasts of light and dark, with dramatic composition.

In 1642 Saskia died and his fortunes changed, as the public's taste shifted and commissions dried up. In 1649 he hired an 18-year-old model named Hendrickje Stoffels, and she soon moved in with him. Holland's war with England (1652–1654) devastated the art market, and Rembrandt's free-spending ways forced him to declare bankruptcy (1656)—the ultimate humiliation in success-oriented Amsterdam. He moved to more humble lodgings on Rozengracht Straat.

In his last years, his greatest works were his self-portraits, showing a tired, wrinkled man stoically enduring life's misfortunes. Rembrandt piled on layers of paint and glaze to capture increasingly subtle effects.

In 1668, his lone surviving child, Titus, died, and Rembrandt died the next year. His death effectively marks the end of the Dutch Golden Age.

---

bright spots glowing from the darkness. This allows Rembrandt to highlight the details he thinks are most important, and express moody emotions.

Light has a primal appeal to humans. (Dig deep into your DNA and remember the time when fire was not tamed. Light! In the middle of the night! This miracle separated us from our fellow animals.) Rembrandt strikes at that instinctive level.

Rembrandt—*Maria Trip* (1639)

This debutante daughter of a wealthy citizen is shy and reserved—maybe a bit awkward in her new dress and adult role, but still self-assured. When he chose to, Rembrandt could dash off a commissioned portrait like nobody's business. The details are immaculate—the lace and shiny satin, the pearls behind the veil, the subtle face and hands. Rembrandt gives us a person, and a personality.

Look at the red rings around her eyes, a detail a lesser painter would have airbrushed out. Rembrandt takes this feature unique to her and uses it as a setting for her luminous, jewel-like eyes. Without being prettified, she's beautiful.

Rembrandt—*A Young Woman,* or *The Portrait of Saskia* (1633)

It didn't take long for Amsterdam to recognize Rembrandt's great talent. Everyone wanted a portrait done by the young master. He became wealthy and famous. He fell in love with and married the rich, beautiful, and cultured Saskia. By all accounts, the two were enormously happy, entertaining friends, decorating their house with fine furniture, raising a family, and living the high life. In this wedding portrait thought to be of Saskia, the bride's face literally glows. A dash of white paint puts a sparkle in her eye. Barely 30 years old, Rembrandt was the most successful painter in Holland. He had it all.

Other "Rembrandts"

The Rijksmuseum displays real Rembrandts, paintings by others that look like his, portraits of Rembrandt by his students, and one or two "Rembrandts" that may not be his. A century ago, there were 1,000 so-called Rembrandt paintings in existence. Since then, a five-man panel of art scholars has declared most of those to be by someone else, winnowing the number of authentic Rembrandts to 300, with some 50 more that may one day be "audited" by the Internal Rembrandt Service. Most of the fakes are not out-and-out forgeries, but works by admirers of his distinctive style. Be careful the next time you plunk down $15 million for a "Rembrandt."

• *In Room 9, you'll find...*

Rembrandt's Later Works

Enjoying fame, wealth, and happiness, Rembrandt may have had it all, but not for long. His wife, Saskia, died. The commissions came more slowly. The money ran out. His mother died. One by one his sons died. He had to auction off his paintings and furniture to pay debts. He moved out of his fine house to a cheaper place. His bitter losses added a new wisdom to his work.

Rembrandt—*Isaac and Rebecca,* or *The Jewish Bride* (1667)

The man gently draws the woman toward him. She's comfortable enough with him to sink into thought, and she reaches up unconsciously to return the gentle touch. They're young but wizened.

This uncommissioned portrait (known as *The Jewish Bride,* though the subject is unknown) is a truly human look at the relationship between two people in love. They form a protective pyramid of love amid a gloomy background. The touching hands form the center of this somewhat sad but peaceful work. Van Gogh said, "Rembrandt alone has that tenderness—the heartbroken tenderness."

Rembrandt was a master of oil painting. In his later years, he rendered details with a messier, more Impressionistic style. The red-brown-gold of their clothes is a patchwork of oil laid on thick with a palette knife.

Rembrandt—*The Syndics of the Amsterdam Drapers' Guild (De Staalmeesters* 1662)

While commissions were more rare, Rembrandt could still paint an official group portrait better than anyone. In the painting made famous by Dutch Masters cigars, he catches the Drapers Guild in a natural but dignified pose (dignified at least until the guy on the left sits down in his friend's lap).

It's a business meeting, and they're all dressed in black with black hats—the standard power suit of the Golden Age. They gather around a table examining the company's books. Suddenly, someone walks in (us), and they look up. It's as natural as a snapshot, though X-rays show Rembrandt made many changes in posing them perfectly.

The figures are "framed" by the table beneath them and by the top of the wood paneling above their heads, making a three-part composition that brings this band of colleagues together. Even in this simple portrait we feel we can read the guild members' personalities in their faces. (If the table in the painting looks like it's sloping a bit unnaturally, lie on the floor to view it at Rembrandt's intended angle.)

Rembrandt—*The Denial of St. Peter* (1660)

Jesus has been arrested as a criminal. Here, his disciple Peter has followed him undercover to the prison to check on the proceedings. The young girl recognizes Peter and asks him, "Don't you know Jesus?" Peter, afraid of being arrested by the Romans, denies it.

She asks him again, and Peter must decide where his loyalties lie. With the Roman soldier who glares at him suspiciously from the left, not buying Peter's story at all? Or with his doomed master in the dark background on the right looking knowingly over his shoulder, understanding Peter's complicated situation? Peter's a bad liar. The confusion and self-doubt are written all over his face. That's his story and he's sticking to it.

The strong contrasts of light and dark heighten the drama of this psychologically tense scene. The soldier is a blotch of brown. Jesus is a distant shadowy figure, a lingering presence in Peter's conscience. The center of the picture is the light shining through the girl's translucent fingers, glowing like a lamp as she casts the light of truth on Peter. Peter's brokenhearted betrayal and sense of guilt could only have been portrayed by an older, wiser Rembrandt.

Rembrandt—*Self-Portrait as the Apostle Paul* (1661)

Rembrandt's many self-portraits show us the evolution of a great painter's style as well as the progress of a genius' life. For Rembrandt, the two were intertwined.

Compare this later self-portrait (he's 55 but looks 70) with the youthful, curious Rembrandt of age 22 we saw earlier. With lined forehead, bulbous nose, and messy hair, he peers out from under several coats of glazing, holding old, wrinkled pages. His look is...skeptical? Weary? Resigned to life's misfortunes? Or amused? (He's looking at us, but remember that a self-portrait is done staring into a mirror.)

This man has seen it all—success, love, money, fatherhood, loss, poverty, death. He took these experiences and wove them into his art. Rembrandt died poor and misunderstood, but he remained very much his own man to the end.

• *Enter Room 10.*

Johannes Vermeer (1632–1675)

Vermeer is the master of tranquility and stillness. He creates a clear and silent pool that is a world in itself. Most canvases show interiors of Dutch homes where Dutch women engage in everyday activities, lit by a side window.

Vermeer's father, an art dealer, had given Johannes a passion for painting. Late in the artist's career, with Holland fighting draining wars against England, the demand for art and luxuries went sour in the Netherlands, forcing Vermeer to downsize—he sold his big home, packed up his wife and 14 children, and moved in with his mother-in-law. He died two years later, and his works fell into centuries of obscurity.

The Rijksmuseum has the best collection of Vermeers in the world—all four of them. (There are only some 30 in captivity.) But each is a small jewel worth lingering over. Fans of Vermeer who want more could take the train to The Hague (Den Haag), where his *Girl with the Pearl Earring* and *View of Delft* hang in the Mauritshuis Museum.

Vermeer—*The Kitchen Maid* (c. 1658)

Shhh...you can practically hear the milk pouring into the bowl.

Vermeer brings out the beauty in everyday things. The subject is ordinary, a kitchen maid, but you could look for hours at the tiny details and rich color tones. These are everyday objects, but they glow in a diffused light: the crunchy crust, the hanging basket, even the rusty nail in the wall with its tiny shadow. Vermeer had a unique ability to create surface texture, to show how things feel when you touch them.

The maid is alive with Vermeer's distinctive yellow and blue—the colors of many traditional Dutch homes—against a white backdrop. She is content, solid, and sturdy, performing this simple task like it's the most important thing in the world. Her full arms are built with patches of reflected light. Vermeer squares off a little world in itself (framed by the table in the foreground, the wall in back, the window to the left, and the footstool at right), then fills this space with objects for our perusal.

Vermeer—*Woman Reading a Letter* (c. 1662–1663)

Vermeer's placid scenes often have an air of mystery. The woman is reading a letter. From whom? A lover? A father on a two-year business trip to Indonesia? Not even taking time to sit down, she reads it intently, with parted lips and a bowed head. It must be important. (She looks pregnant, adding to the mystery, but that may just be the cut of her clothes.)

Again, Vermeer has framed off a moment of everyday life. But within this small world are hints of a wider, wilder world. The light coming from the left is obviously from a large window, giving us a whiff of a much broader world outside. The map hangs prominently, reminding us of travel, perhaps where the letter is from.

Vermeer—*The Love Letter* (c. 1669–1670)

There's a similar theme here. The curtain parts, and we see through the doorway into a dollhouse world, then through the seascape on the back wall to the wide ocean. A woman is playing a lute when she's interrupted by a servant bringing a letter. The mysterious letter stops the music, intruding like a pebble dropped into the pool of Vermeer's quiet world. The floor tiles create a strong 3-D that sucks us in straight to the center of the painting—the woman's heart.

Vermeer—*View of Houses in Delft,* or *"The Little Street"* (c. 1658)

Vermeer was born in the picturesque town of Delft, grew up near its Market Square, and set a number of his paintings there. This may be the view from his front door.

In *The Little Street,* the details actually aren't very detailed—the cobblestone street doesn't have a single individual stone in it. But Vermeer shows the beautiful interplay of colored rectangles on the buildings. Our eyes move back and forth from shutter to gable to window...and then from front to back as we notice the woman deep in the alleyway.

• *Enter Room 11.*

Jan Steen (1626–1679)

Not everyone could afford a masterpiece, but even the poorer people wanted works of art for their own homes (like a landscape from Sears for over the sofa). Jan Steen, the Norman Rockwell of his day, painted humorous scenes from the lives of the lower classes. As a tavern owner, he observed society firsthand.

Ruffs

I cannot tell you why Dutch men and women of the Golden Age found these ruffled, fanlike collars attractive, but they were the rage here and elsewhere in Europe. Ruffled collars and sleeves

were first popular in Spain in the 1540s, but the style really took off with a marvelous discovery in 1565—starch. Within decades, Europe's wealthy merchant class was wearing nine-inch collars made from 18 yards of material.

The ruffs were detachable, made from a long, pleated strip of linen set into a neck (or wrist) band. You tied it in front with strings. Big ones required that you wear a wire frame underneath for support. There were various types—the "cartwheel" was the biggest, a "double ruff" had two layers of pleats, a "cabbage" was somewhat asymmetrical.

Ruffs required elaborate maintenance. You washed and starched the linen. While the cloth was still wet, hot metal pokers were inserted into the folds to form the characteristic figure-eight pattern. Ruffs were stored in special round boxes to hold their shape.

By 1630, Holland had come to its senses, and the fad faded.

Jan Steen—*The Feast of St. Nicholas*

It's Christmas time, and the kids have been given their gifts. A little girl got a doll. The mother says, "Let me see it," but the girl turns away playfully.

Everyone is happy except...the boy who's crying. His Christmas present is only a branch in his shoe—like coal in your stocking, the gift for bad boys. His sister gloats and passes it around. The kids laugh at him. But wait, it turns out the family is just playing a trick. In the background, the grandmother beckons to him saying, "Look, I have your real present in here." Out of the limelight but smack in the middle sits the father providing ballast to this family scene, and clearly enjoying his children's pleasure.

Steen has frozen the moment, sliced off a piece, and laid it on a canvas. He's told a story with a past, present, and future.

These are real people in a real scene.

Steen's fun art reminds us that museums aren't mausoleums.

Jan Steen—*The Merry Family* (1668)

This family—three generations living happily under one roof—is eating, drinking, and singing like there's no tomorrow. The broken

eggshells and scattered cookware symbolize waste and extravagance. The neglected proverb tacked to the fireplace reminds us that children will follow the footsteps of their parents. The father in this jolly scene is very drunk—ready to topple over—while in the foreground his mischievous daughter is feeding her brother wine straight from the flask. Mom and Grandma join the artist himself (playing the bagpipes) in a raucous singalong, but the child learning to smoke would rather follow dad's lead.

Golden Age Dutch families were notoriously lenient with their kids. Even today, the Dutch describe a raucous family as a "Jan Steen household."

• *Room 12 is dominated by…*

Rembrandt—*The Night Watch*

• *The best viewing spot is to the right of center—the angle Rembrandt had in mind when he designed it for its original location.*

This is Rembrandt's most famous—though not necessarily greatest—painting. Done in 1642 when he was 36, it was one of his most important commissions—a group portrait of a company of Amsterdam's civic guards to hang in their meeting hall.

It's an action shot. With flags waving and drums beating, the guardsmen (who, by the 1640s, were really only an honorary militia of rich bigwigs) spill into the street from under an arch in the back. It's all for one and one for all as they rush to the rescue of Amsterdam. The soldiers grab lances and load their muskets. In the center, the commander (in black, with a red sash) strides forward energetically with a hand gesture that seems to say, "What are we waiting for? Let's move out!" His lieutenant focuses on his every order.

Rembrandt caught the optimistic spirit of Holland in the 1600s. Their war of independence from Spain was heading to victory and their economy was booming. These guardsmen on the move epitomize the proud, independent, upwardly mobile Dutch.

Why is the *Night Watch* so famous? Compare it with other less famous group portraits, where every face is visible, and everyone is well lit, flat, and flashbulb-perfect. These people paid good money to have their mugs preserved for posterity, and they wanted it right up front. Other group portraits may be colorful, dignified, works by a master...but not quite masterpieces.

By contrast, Rembrandt rousted the Civic Guards off their fat duffs. By adding movement and depth to an otherwise static scene, he took posers and turned them into warriors. He turned a simple portrait into great art.

OK, some *Night Watch* scuttlebutt: First off, "Night Watch" is a misnomer. It's a daytime scene, but over the years, as the preserving varnish darkened and layers of dirt built up, the sun set on this painting and it got its popular title. When the painting was moved to a smaller room, the sides were lopped off (and the pieces lost), putting the two main characters in the center and causing the work to become more static than intended. During World War II, the painting was rolled up and hidden for five years. More recently, a madman attacked the painting, slicing the captain's legs (now repaired skillfully).

Night Watch, contrary to popular myth, was a smashing success in its day. However, there are elements in it that show why Rembrandt soon fell out of favor as a portrait painter. He seemed to spend as much time painting the dwarf and the mysterious glowing girl with a chicken (the very appropriate mascot of this "militia" of shopkeepers) as he did the faces of his employers.

Rembrandt's life darkened long before his *Night Watch* did. This work marks the peak of Rembrandt's popularity...and the beginning of his fall from grace. He continued to paint masterpieces. Free from the dictates of employers whose taste was in their mouths, he painted what he wanted, how he wanted it. Rembrandt goes beyond mere craftsmanship to probe into and draw life from the deepest wells of the human soul.

VAN GOGH MUSEUM

The Van Gogh Museum (we say "van GO," the Dutch say "van HOCK") is a cultural high even to those not into art. Located near the Rijksmuseum, the museum houses the 200 paintings owned by Vincent's younger brother, Theo. It's a user-friendly stroll through the work and life of one enigmatic man. If you like bright-colored landscapes in the Impressionist style, you'll like this museum. If you enjoy finding deeper meaning in works of art, you'll really love it. The mix of van Gogh's creative genius, his

tumultuous life, and the traveler's determination to connect to it makes this museum as much a walk with Vincent as with his art.

ORIENTATION

Cost: €7.25; €2.50 if under 18; free for those under 12 and for those with one ear.

Hours: Daily 10:00–18:00, closed only on Jan 1.

Crowd Control: There can be long lines to get into the crowded museum. But with three cashiers, the line moves quickly and the wait is rarely more than 15 minutes.

Getting There: It's behind the Rijksmuseum at Paulus Potterstraat 7. From Centraal Station, catch tram #2 or #5 to Hobbemastraat.

Information: At the information desk, pick up a free floor plan (containing a brief history of the artist's brief life). The bookstore is understandably popular, with several good "Vincent" guidebooks and lots of posters (with tubes). Tel. 020/570-5200, www.vangoghmuseum.nl.

Audioguide Tour: The €4 audioguide includes insightful commentaries about van Gogh's paintings, along with related quotations from Vincent himself.

Length of This Tour: One hour.

Checkroom: Free and mandatory.

Photography: No photos allowed.

Cuisine Art: The terrace cafeteria (soup, salads, sandwiches) is OK. You could also consider the Cobra café on Museumplein, the many cafés at Leidseplein (15-min walk to the northwest), or the picnic-friendly Vondelpark and Café Vertigo (Vondelpark 3).

THE TOUR BEGINS

Overview

The core of the museum and this entire tour is on the first floor (one flight up from the ground floor). The bookstore and cafeteria are on the ground floor. Also on the ground floor are paintings by artists who preceded and influenced van Gogh's generation. The second floor has a study area and more paintings (generally, van Gogh's smaller-scale works, including drawings). The third floor shows works by his friends and colleagues, from smooth-surfaced Academy art to Impressionists Claude Monet and Camille Pissarro to fellow post-Impressionists Paul Gauguin, Paul Cézanne, and Henri de Toulouse-Lautrec. These are painters who influenced and were influenced by van Gogh. The new wing (accessed from the ground floor by going down the escalator) showcases temporary exhibitions.

The paintings on the first floor are arranged chronologically, taking us through the changes in Vincent van Gogh's life and styles. The paintings are divided into five periods of Vincent's life—Netherlands, Paris, Arles, St. Rémy, and Auvers-sur-Oise—proceeding clockwise around the floor. (Although the busy curators frequently move the paintings around, they *usually* keep them within the same room, so look around.) Some background on Vincent's star-crossed life makes the museum even better, so I've included doses of biographical material for each painting.

• *Climb the stairs to the first floor. The first room (usually a temporary exhibit) introduces you to the artist.*

Vincent van Gogh (1853–1890)

"I am a man of passions..."

You can see Vincent van Gogh's canvases as a series of suicide notes—or as the record of a life full of beauty, too full of beauty. He attacked life with a passion, experiencing life's highs and lows more intensely than the average person. The beauty of the world

Van Gogh Museum—First Floor

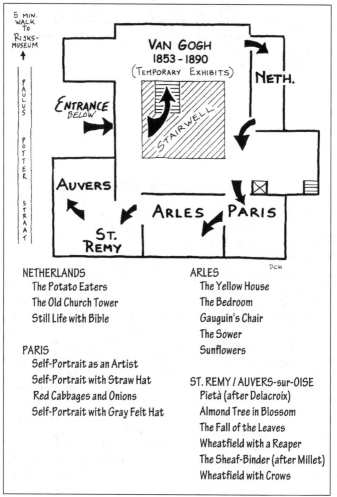

NETHERLANDS
  The Potato Eaters
  The Old Church Tower
  Still Life with Bible

PARIS
  Self-Portrait as an Artist
  Self-Portrait with Straw Hat
  Red Cabbages and Onions
  Self-Portrait with Gray Felt Hat

ARLES
  The Yellow House
  The Bedroom
  Gauguin's Chair
  The Sower
  Sunflowers

ST. REMY / AUVERS-sur-OISE
  Pietà (after Delacroix)
  Almond Tree in Blossom
  The Fall of the Leaves
  Wheatfield with a Reaper
  The Sheaf-Binder (after Millet)
  Wheatfield with Crows

overwhelmed him and its ugliness struck him as only another dimension of beauty. He tried to absorb all of life, good and bad, and channel it onto a canvas. The frustration of this overwhelming task drove him to madness. If all this is a bit overstated—and I guess it is—it's an attempt to show the emotional impact van Gogh's works have had on many people, myself included.

Vincent, a pastor's son from a small Dutch town, started working at age 16 as a clerk for an art dealership. But his two interests, art and religion, distracted him from his dreary work and, after several years, he was finally fired.

The next 10 years were a collage of dead ends as he traveled Northern Europe pursuing one path after another. He launched into each project with incredible energy, then became disillusioned and moved on to something else: teacher at a boarding school, assistant preacher, bookstore apprentice, preacher again, theology student, English student, literature student, art student. He bounced around England, France, Belgium, and the Netherlands. He fell in love but was rejected for someone more respectable. He quarreled with his family and was estranged. He lived with a prostitute and her daughter, offending the few friends he had. Finally, in his late 20s, worn out, flat broke, and in poor health, he returned to his family in Nuenen and made peace. He started to paint.

• *For his stark, early work, enter the next room.*

The Netherlands (1880–1885)— Poverty and Religion

These dark gray canvases show us the hard, plain existence of the people and town of Nuenen in the rural southern Netherlands. We

see simple buildings, bare or autumnal trees, and overcast skies, a world where it seems spring will never arrive. What warmth there is comes from the sturdy, gentle people themselves.

The style is crude—van Gogh couldn't draw very well, nor would he ever be a great technician. The paint is laid on thick, as though painted with Nuenen mud. The main subject is almost always dead center, with little or no

background, so there's a claustrophobic feeling. We are unable to see anything but the immediate surroundings.

The Potato Eaters (1885)

"Those that prefer to see the peasants in their Sunday-best may do as they like. I personally am convinced I get better results by painting them in their roughness.... If a peasant picture smells of bacon, smoke, potato steam—all right, that's healthy."

—Vincent van Gogh

In a dark, cramped room lit only by a dim lamp, poor workers help themselves to a steaming plate of potatoes. They've earned it. Vincent deliberately wanted the canvas to be potato-colored.

Vincent had dabbled as an artist during his wandering years, sketching things around him and taking a few art classes, but it wasn't until age 29 that he painted his first oil canvas. He soon threw himself into it with abandon.

He painted the poor working peasants. He worked as a lay minister among the poorest of the poor, peasants and miners. He joined them at work in the mines, taught their children, and even gave away his own few possessions to help them. The church authorities finally dismissed him for "excessive zeal," but he came away understanding the poor's harsh existence and the dignity with which they bore it.

The Old Church Tower at Nuenen (1885)

The crows circle above the local cemetery of Nuenen. Soon after his

father's death, Vincent, in poor health and depressed, moved briefly to Antwerp. He then decided to visit his brother Theo, an art dealer living in Paris, the art capital of the world. Theo's support—financial and emotional—allowed Vincent to spend the rest of his short life painting.

Still Life with Bible (1885)

"I have a terrible need of—shall I say the word?—religion. Then I go out and paint the stars."
   —Vincent van Gogh

A Bible and *Lust for Life*—these two books dominated van Gogh's life. In his art he tried to fuse his religious upbringing with his love of the world's beauty. He lusted after life with a religious fervor. The burned-out candle tells us of the recent death of his father. The Bible is open to Isaiah 53: "He was despised and rejected of men, a man of sorrows..."

Vincent moved from rural, religious, poor Holland to Paris, the City of Lights. Vincent van Gone.
• *Continue to the next room.*

Paris (March 1886–Feb 1888)—Impressionism

The sun begins to break through, lighting up everything he paints. His canvases are more colorful, and the landscapes more spacious, with plenty of open sky, giving a feeling of exhilaration after the closed, dark world of Nuenen.

In the cafés and bars of Paris' bohemian Montmartre district, Vincent met the revolutionary Impressionists. He roomed with Theo and became friends with other struggling young painters, such as Paul Gauguin and Henri de Toulouse-Lautrec. His health improved, he became more sociable, had an affair with an older woman, and was generally happy.

He signed up to study under a well-known classical teacher but quit after only a few classes. He couldn't afford to hire models, so he roamed the streets with sketch pad in hand and learned from his Impressionist friends.

The Impressionists emphasized getting out of the stuffy studio and setting up canvases outside on the street or in the countryside to paint the play of sunlight off the trees, buildings, and water.

As you see in this room, at first, Vincent copied from the Impressionist masters. He painted garden scenes like Claude Monet, café snapshots like Edgar Degas, "block prints" like the Japanese masters, and self-portraits...like nobody else.

Self-Portrait as an Artist (1888)

"I am now living with my brother Vincent, who is studying the art of painting with indefatigable zeal."
    —Theo van Gogh to a friend

Here, the budding young artist proudly displays his new palette full of bright new colors, trying his hand at the Impressionist technique of building a scene using dabs of different-colored paint. A whole new world of art—and life—opened up to him in Paris.

Self-Portrait with Straw Hat (1887)

"You wouldn't recognize Vincent, he has changed so much....The doctor says that he is now perfectly fit again. He is making tremendous strides with his work....He is also far livelier than he used to be and is popular with people."
    —Theo van Gogh to their mother

In Paris, Vincent learned the Impressionist painting technique. The shimmering effect comes from placing dabs of different colors side by side on the canvas. At a distance, the two colors blend in the eye of the viewer to become a third color. Here, Vincent uses separate strokes of blue, yellow, green, and red to create a brown beard—but a brown that throbs with excitement.

Still Lifes, such as Red Cabbages and Onions (1887)

Vincent quickly developed his own style—thicker paint, broad, swirling brush strokes, and brighter clashing colors that make even inanimate objects seem to pulsate with life.

The many different colors are supposed to blend together, but you'd have to back up to Belgium before these colors resolve into focus.

Self-Portrait with Gray Felt Hat (1887–1888)

"He has painted one or two portraits which have turned out well, but he insists on working for nothing. It is a pity that he shows no desire to earn some money because he could easily do so here. But you can't change people."
—Theo van Gogh to their mother

Despite his new sociability, Vincent never quite fit in with his Impressionist friends. As he developed into a good painter, he became anxious to strike out on his own. Also, he thought the social life of the big city was distracting him from serious work. In this painting, his face screams out from a swirling background of molecular activity. He wanted peace and quiet, a place where he could throw himself into his work completely. He headed for the sunny South of France.

• *Travel to the next room to reach...*

Arles (Feb 1888–May 1889)— Sunlight, Beauty, and Madness

Winter was just turning to spring when Vincent arrived in Arles near the French Riviera. After the dreary Paris winter, the colors of springtime overwhelmed him. The blossoming trees inspired him to paint canvas after canvas, drenched in sunlight.

The Yellow House, also called The Street (1888)

"It is my intention...to go temporarily to the South, where there is even more color, even more sun."
—Vincent van Gogh

Vincent rented this house with the green shutters. (He ate at the pink café next door.) Look at that blue sky! He painted in a frenzy, working feverishly to try and take it all in. For the next nine months, he produced an explosion of canvases, working very quickly when the

mood possessed him. His unique style evolved beyond the Impressionists'—thicker paint, stronger outlines, brighter colors (often applied right from the paint tube), and swirling brushwork that makes even inanimate objects pulse and vibrate with life.

Sunflowers (1889)

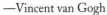

"The worse I get along with people the more I learn to have faith in Nature and concentrate on her."

—Vincent van Gogh

Vincent saw sunflowers as his signature subject, and he painted a half-dozen versions of them, each a study in intense yellow. If he signed the work (see the "V. G." on the vase), it means he was proud of it.

Even a simple work like *Sunflowers* bursts with life. Different people see different things in *Sunflowers*. Is it a happy painting, or is it a melancholy one? Take your own emotional temperature and see.

The Bedroom (1888)

"I am a man of passions, capable of and subject to doing more or less foolish things—which I happen to regret, more or less, afterwards."

—Vincent van Gogh

Vincent was alone, a Dutchman in Provence. And that had its downside. Vincent swung from flurries of ecstatic activity to bouts of great loneliness. Like anyone traveling alone he experienced those high highs and low lows. This narrow, trapezoid-shaped, single-room apartment (less than 200 square feet) must have seemed like a prison cell at times. (Psychologists point out that most everything in this painting comes in pairs—two chairs, two paintings, a double bed squeezed down to a single—indicating his desire for a mate. Hmm.)

He invited his friend Paul Gauguin to join him, envisioning a sort of artists' colony in Arles. He spent months preparing a room upstairs for Gauguin's arrival.

Gauguin's Chair (1888)

"Empty chairs—there are many of them, there will be even more, and sooner or later, there will be nothing but empty chairs."

—Vincent van Gogh

Gauguin arrived. At first they got along great, painting and carousing. But then things went bad. They clashed over art, life, and personalities. On Christmas Eve 1888, Vincent went ballistic. Enraged during an alcohol-fueled argument, he pulled out a knife and waved it in Gauguin's face. Gauguin took the hint and quickly left town. Vincent was horrified at himself. In a fit of remorse and madness, he mutilated his own ear and presented it to a prostitute.

The Sower (1888)

A dark, silhouetted figure sows seeds in the burning sun. It's late in the day. The heat from the sun, the source of all life, radiates out in

thick swirls of paint. The sower must be a hopeful man, because the field looks slanted and barren. Someday, he thinks, the seeds he's planting will grow into something great, like the tree that slashes diagonally across the scene—tough and craggy, but with small optimistic blossoms.

In his younger years, Vincent had worked in Belgium sowing the Christian gospel in a harsh environment (see Mark 4:1–9). Now in Arles, ignited by the sun, he cast his artistic seeds to the wind, hoping.

• *Continue into the next room.*

St. Rémy (May 1889–1890)— The Mental Hospital

The people of Arles realized they had a madman on their hands. A doctor diagnosed "acute mania with hallucinations," and the local vicar talked Vincent into admitting himself to a mental hospital. Vincent wrote to Theo, "Temporarily I wish to remain shut up, as much for my own peace of mind as for other people's."

In the mental hospital, Vincent continued to paint whenever he was well enough. He often couldn't go out, so he copied from books, making his own distinctive versions of works by Rembrandt, Delacroix, Millet, and others.

We see a change from bright, happy landscapes to more introspective subjects. The colors are less bright and more surreal, the brushwork even more furious. The strong outlines of figures are twisted and tortured.

Pietà, after Delacroix (1889)

It's evening after a thunderstorm. Jesus has been crucified, and the corpse lies at the mouth of a tomb. Mary, whipped by the cold wind, holds her empty arms out in despair and confusion. She is the tender mother who receives us all in death as though saying, "My child, you've been away so long—rest in my arms." Christ has a Vincent-esque red beard.

At first the peace and quiet of the asylum did Vincent good, and his health improved. Occasionally he was allowed outside to paint the gardens and landscapes. Meanwhile, the paintings he had sent to Theo began to attract attention in Paris for the first time. A woman in Brussels bought one of his canvases—the only painting he ever sold during his lifetime. Nowadays, a *Sunflowers* sells for $40 million.

The Garden of Saint Paul's Hospital, also called *The Fall of the Leaves* (1889)

"...a traveler going to a destination that does not exist..."
—Vincent van Gogh
The stark brown trees are blown by the wind. A solitary figure (Vincent?) winds along a narrow, snaky path as the wind blows leaves on him. The colors are surreal—blue, green, and red tree trunks with heavy black outlines. A road runs away from us, heading nowhere.

Wheatfield with a Reaper (1889)

"I have been working hard and fast in the last few days. This is how I try to express how desperately fast things pass in modern life."
—Vincent van Gogh

The harvest is here. The time is short. There's much work to be done. A lone reaper works uphill, scything through a swirling wheatfield, cutting slender paths of calm.

The Sheaf-Binder, after Millet (1889)

"I want to paint men and women with that something of the eternal which the halo used to symbolize..."
—Vincent van Gogh

Vincent's compassion for honest laborers remained constant since his work with Belgian miners. These sturdy folk with their curving bodies wrestle as one with their curving wheat. The world Vincent sees is charged from within by spiritual fires, twisting and turning, matter turning into energy and vice versa.

The fits of madness returned. During these spells, he lost all sense of his own actions. He couldn't paint, the one thing he felt driven to do. He wrote to Theo, "My surroundings here begin to weigh on me more than I can say—I need air. I feel overwhelmed by boredom and grief."

Auvers (May–July 1890)—Flying Away

"The bird looks through the bars at the overcast sky where a thunderstorm is gathering, and inwardly he rebels against his fate. 'I am caged, I am caged, and you tell me I have everything I need! Oh! I beg you, give me

liberty, that I may be a bird like other birds.' A certain idle man resembles this idle bird...."
—Vincent van Gogh

Branches of an Almond Tree in Blossom (1890)

Vincent moved north to Auvers, a small town near Paris where he could stay at a hotel under a doctor friend's supervision. On the way there, he visited Theo. Theo's wife had just had a baby, whom they named Vincent. Brother Vincent showed up with this painting under his arm as a birthday gift. Theo's wife later recalled, "I had expected a sick man, but here was a sturdy, broad-shouldered man with a healthy color, a smile on his face, and a very resolute appearance."

In his new surroundings he continued painting, averaging a

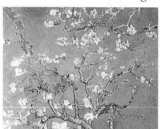

canvas a day, but was interrupted by spells that swung from boredom to madness. His letters to Theo were generally optimistic, but he worried that he'd soon succumb completely to insanity and never paint again. The final landscapes are walls of bright, thick paint.

Wheatfield with Crows (1890)

"This new attack...came on me in the fields, on a windy day, when I was busy painting."
—Vincent van Gogh

On July 27, 1890, Vincent left his hotel, walked out to a nearby field and put a bullet through his chest.

This is the last painting Vincent finished. We can try to search the wreckage of his life for the black box explaining what happened, but there's not much there. His life was sad and tragic, but the

record he left is one not of sadness but of beauty. Intense beauty.

The wind-blown wheatfield is a nest of restless energy. Scenes like this must have overwhelmed Vincent with their incredible beauty—too much, too fast with no release. The sky is stormy and dark blue, almost nighttime, barely lit by two suns boiling through the deep ocean of blue. The road starts nowhere, leads nowhere, disappearing into the burning wheatfield. Above all of this swirling beauty fly the crows, the dark ghosts that had hovered over his life since the cemetery in Nuenen.

ANNE FRANK HOUSE

On May 10, 1940, Germany's Luftwaffe began bombing Schiphol Airport, preparing to invade the Netherlands. The Dutch army fought back, and the Nazis responded by leveling Rotterdam. Within a week, the Netherlands surrendered, Queen Wilhelmina fled to Britain, and Nazi soldiers goose-stepped past the Westerkerk church and into Dam Square, where they draped huge swastikas on the Royal Palace. A five-year occupation began. The Netherlands had been neutral in World War I, and Amsterdam—progressive and modern but a bit naive—was in for a rude shock.

The Anne Frank House immerses you, in a very immediate way, in the struggles and pains of the war years. Walk through rooms where eight Amsterdam Jews hid for two years from Nazi persecution. Though they were eventually discovered, and seven of the eight died in concentration camps, their story has an uplifting twist—the diary of Anne Frank, preserving the human spirit that cannot be crushed.

ORIENTATION

Cost: €7.

Hours: April–Aug daily 9:00–21:00, Sept–March daily 9:00–19:00.

Crowd Control: Why do thousands endure hour-long daytime lines when they can walk right in by arriving after 18:00? Avoid crowds in summer by visiting after dinner.

Getting There: It's at Prinsengracht 267, near Westerkerk and about a 20-minute walk from Centraal Station. Or take tram

#13, #14, or #17 or bus #21, #170, #171, or #172 to the Westermarkt stop, about a block from the museum's entrance.

Information: The museum has excellent information in English—a pamphlet at the door and fine descriptions with quotes from the diary throughout. Use this chapter as background, then let the displays and videos tell more. Tel. 020/556-7100, www.annefrank.nl.

Length of This Tour: One hour.

THE TOUR BEGINS

Overview

We'll walk through the rooms where Anne Frank's family hid for 25 months. The front half of the building, facing the canal, remained the offices and warehouses of an operating business. The back half, where the Franks lived, was the Secret Annex, its entrance concealed by a bookcase.

• *Buy your ticket and enter the ground-floor exhibit.*

Models of the Secret Annex

Two models with dollhouse furniture help you envision life in the now-bare living quarters. Find the bookcase entrance, which leads to Anne's parents' room (with wood stove). Anne's room is next to it, with a blue bed, a brown sofa, a table-chair-bookcase ensemble, and photos on the wall. On the fourth floor was the living room and the van Pels' rooms. All told, eight people shared this tiny apartment.

• *After viewing the important five-minute video, go upstairs to the offices/warehouses of the front half of the building.*

First Floor: Offices

From these offices, Otto Frank ran a successful business called

Opekta, selling spices and pectin for making jelly. When the Nazis gained power in Germany in 1933, Otto had moved his family from Frankfurt to tolerant Amsterdam, hoping for a better life.

Photos and displays show Otto with some of his colleagues. During the Nazi occupation, while the Frank family hid in the back of the building, these brave people kept Otto's business running, while secretly bringing supplies to the Franks. Miep Gies, Otto's secretary, brought food every few days, while bookkeeper Victor Kugler cheered up Anne with the latest movie magazine.

• *Go upstairs to the...*

Second Floor: Warehouse

At first, the Nazi overlords were tolerant, even friendly, with the vanquished Dutch. But soon they imposed restrictions that affected one in ten Amsterdamers—that is, Jews. Jews had to wear yellow-star patches and register with the police. They were forbidden in movie theaters and on trams and even forbidden to ride bikes.

In February 1941, the Nazis started rounding up Jews, shipping them by train to "work camps," which, in reality, were transit stations on the way to death camps in the East. Outraged, the people of Amsterdam called a general strike that shut down the city for two days...but the Nazis responded with even harsher laws.

In July 1942, Anne's sister Margot got her **call-up notice** for a "work-force project." Otto handed over the keys to the business to his Aryan colleagues, sent a final postcard to relatives, gave the family cat to a neighbor, spread rumors they were fleeing to Switzerland, and prepared his family to "dive under" (*onderduik,* as it was called) into hiding.

Photos of *The People in Hiding* put faces on the eight people—all Jewish—who eventually inhabited the Secret Annex. First was the Frank family—Otto and Edith and their daughters, 13-year-old Anne and 16-year-old Margot. A week later, they were joined by the van Pels (called the "van Daans" in the *Diary*), with their teenage son, Peter. A few months later, Fritz Pfeffer (called "Mr. Dussel" in the *Diary*) was invited in.

• *At the back of the third floor warehouse is...*

The Bookcase Entrance

On a rainy Monday morning, July 6, 1942, the Frank family—wearing extra clothes to avoid carrying suspicious suitcases—breathed their last fresh air, took a long look at the Prinsengracht canal, and disappeared into the back part of the building, where they spent the next two years. Victor Kugler concealed the entrance to the annex with this swinging bookcase, stacked with business files.

Though not exactly a secret (since it's hard to hide an entire building), the annex was just one of thousands of back-houses *(achterhuis),* a common feature in Amsterdam, and the Nazis had no reason to suspect anything on the premises of the legitimate Opekta business.

• *Pass through the bookcase entrance into the Secret Annex into...*

Otto, Edith, and Margot's Room

The family carried on life as usual. Otto read Dickens' ***Sketches by Boz,*** Edith read from a **prayer book** in their native German, and the

Life in the Annex

By day, it's enforced silence, so no one can hear them in the offices. They whisper, tiptoe, and step around squeaky places in the floor. The windows are blacked out, so they can't even look outside. They read or study, and Anne writes in her diary.

At night and on weekends, when the offices close, one or two might sneak downstairs to listen to Winston Churchill's BBC broadcasts on the office radio. Everyone's spirits rise and sink with news of Allied victories and setbacks.

Anne's diaries make clear the tensions, petty quarrels, and domestic politics of eight people living under pressure. Mr. van Pels annoys Anne, but he gets along well with Margot. Anne never gets used to Mr. Pfeffer, who is literally invading her space. And, most of all, pubescent Anne is often striking sparks with her German mom (Anne's angriest comments about her mom were deleted from early editions).

Despite their hardships, the group feels guilty—they have shelter, while so many other Jews are rounded up and sent off.

As the war progresses, they endure long nights when the house shakes from Allied air raids, and Anne cuddles up in her dad's bed.

Boredom tinged with fear—Existentialist hell.

children continued their studies, with Margot taking **Latin lessons** by correspondence course. They avidly followed the course of the war by radio broadcasts and news from their helpers. As the tides of war slowly turned and it appeared they might one day be saved from the Nazis, Otto tracked the Allied advance on a **map** of Normandy.

The room is very small, even without the furniture. Imagine yourself and two fellow tourists confined here for two years....

Pencil lines on the wall track Margot's and Anne's heights, marking the point at which these growing lives were cut short.

Anne Frank's Room

Pan the room clockwise to see some of the young girl's idols in photos and clippings she pasted there herself: American actor Robert Stack, Queen Elizabeth II, matinee-idol Rudy Vallee, figure-skating actress Sonja Henie, and on the other wall, actress Greta Garbo, actor Ray Milland, Renaissance man Leonardo da Vinci, and actress Ginger Rogers.

Out the window (which had to be blacked out) is the back

courtyard—a chestnut tree and a few buildings. These things, along with the Westerkerk bell chiming every 15 minutes, represented the borders of Anne's "outside world."

Picture Anne at her small desk, writing in her diary.

In November 1942, they invited a Jewish neighbor to join them, and Anne was forced to share the tiny room. Fritz Pfeffer (known in the *Diary* as "Mr. Dussel") was a middle-aged dentist with whom Anne didn't get along. Pfeffer wrote a farewell letter to his non-Jewish fiancée, who continued to live nearby and receive news of him from Miep Gies without knowing his whereabouts.

The Bathroom

The eight inhabitants shared this bathroom. During the day, they didn't dare flush the toilet.

• *Ascend the steep staircase, silently, to the...*

Common Living Room

This was also the kitchen and dining room. Otto Frank was well-off, and early on the annex was well stocked with food. The **menu** for a special dinner lists soup, roast beef, salad, potatoes, rice, dessert, and coffee. Later, as war and German restrictions plunged Holland into poverty and famine, they survived on canned foods and dried kidney beans.

Miep Gies would dutifully take their shopping list, buy food for her "family" of eight, and lug it up secretly. Buying such large quantities in a coupon-rationed economy was highly suspicious, but she knew a sympathetic grocer (a block away in Leliegracht) who was part of a ring of Amsterdamers risking their lives to help "divers."

At night, the living room became sleeping quarters for Hermann and Auguste van Pels.

Peter van Pels' Room

On Peter's 16th birthday, he got a Monopoly-like board game as a present.

Initially, Anne was cool toward Peter, but after two years together, a courtship developed, and their flirtation culminated in a kiss.

The staircase (no visitor access) leads up to where they stored their food. Anne loved to steal away here for a bit of privacy. At night, they'd open a hatch to let in fresh air.

One hot August day, Otto was in this room helping Peter learn English, when they looked up to see a man with a gun. The hiding was over.

• *From here, we leave the Secret Annex, returning to the Opekta store-room and offices in the front house. As you work your way downstairs, you'll see a number of exhibits on the aftermath of this story.*

Front House: The Arrest, Deportation, and Auschwitz Exhibits

They went quietly. On August 4, 1944, a German policeman accompanied by three Dutch Nazis pulled up in a car, politely entered the Opekta office, and went straight to the bookcase entrance. No one knows who tipped them off. The police gave the surprised hiders time to pack. They demanded their valuables, and stuffed them into Anne's briefcase...after dumping her diaries onto the floor.

Taken in a van to Gestapo headquarters, the eight were processed in an efficient, bureaucratic manner, then placed on a train to Westerbork, a concentration camp northeast of the city (see their 3" x 5" **registration cards**).

From there, they were locked in a car on a normal passenger train and sent to Auschwitz (see the **transport list**), a Nazi extermination camp in Poland. On the platform at Auschwitz, they were "forcibly separated from each other" (as Otto later reported) and sent to different camps. Anne and Margot were sent to Bergen-Belsen.

Don't miss the **video** of one of Anne's former neighbors who, by chance, ended up at Bergen-Belsen with Anne. In English, she describes their reunion as they talked through a barbed wire fence shortly before Anne died. She says of Anne, "She didn't have any more tears."

Anne and Margot both died of typhus in March 1945, only weeks before the camp was liberated. Five of the other original eight were either gassed or died of disease. Only Otto survived.

The Franks' story was that of Holland's Jews. The seven who died were among 100,000 Dutch Jews (out of a total of 130,000) who did not survive the war. Of Anne's school class of 87 Jews, only 20 survived.

• *In the next room is an . . .*

Exhibit on the Diaries

See Anne's three diaries (and another notebook), and learn about how they were discovered and published after the war. Anne got the first diary as a birthday present when she turned 13, shortly before they went into hiding. She wrote it in the form of a letter to an imaginary friend named Kitty.

• *Go downstairs to view the . . .*

Videos and the Published Diaries

The video of Miep Gies describes how she found Anne's diaries in the Secret Annex after the arrest and gave them to Otto when he returned. Another video shows Otto's reaction. Though the annex's furniture had been ransacked during the arrest, afterward the rooms remained virtually untouched, and we see them today much as they were.

Otto decided to have the diaries published, and in 1947, *De Achterhuis (The Back-House)* appeared in Dutch, soon followed by many translations, a play, and a movie. While she was alive, Anne herself had recognized the uniqueness of her situation and had been in the process of revising her diaries, preparing them to one day be published.

• *Continue downstairs to the ground floor and enter the movie room.*

Neo-Nazi Video

The thinking that made the Holocaust possible survives. Even today, some groups promote the notion that the Holocaust never occurred and contend that stories like Anne Frank's are only a hoax. The people who run this museum offer a closing, interactive video about Neo-Nazism and racism today in hopes that the souvenir you'll take away from this visit is a heightened awareness of this evil, yet persistent, human trait.

VENICE

Venice is unique. Built on a hundred islands with wealth from trade with the East, its exotic-looking palaces are laced together by sun-speckled canals. The car-free streets suddenly make pedestrians feel safe and liberated.

St. Mark's Square is Venice's ballroom and playground mixed into one. Sip valpolicella wine at a café on the square as the orchestra plays "New York, New York." Visit the Basilica, with its golden mosaics glittering like the Byzantine heaven of centuries past. Echoes of a time when Venice was Europe's superpower still bounce down the grand halls of the Doge's Palace, wallpapered with Titians, Tintorettos, and Veroneses. In Venice, you'll see the seamy mystery, luxury, and decadence of this Most Serene Republic.

St. Mark's Square   **237**

St. Mark's Basilica   **246**

Doge's Palace   **262**

Venice Sights

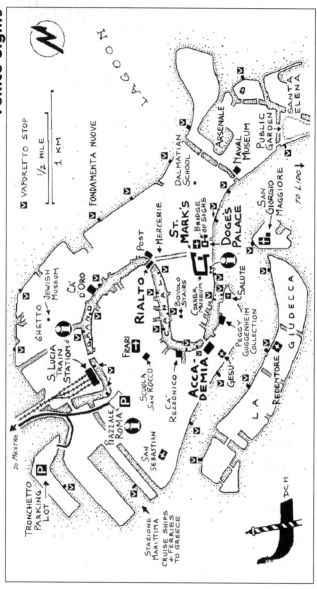

ST. MARK'S SQUARE

(Piazza San Marco)

Venice was once Europe's richest city, and the Piazza San Marco was its center. As middleman in the trade between Asia and Europe, Venice reaped wealth from both sides. In 1450, Venice had 180,000 citizens (far more than London) and a gross "national" product that exceeded that of entire countries.

The rich Venetians taught the rest of Europe the good life—silks, spices, and jewels from the East, crafts from northern Europe, good food and wine, fine architecture, music, theater, and laughter. Venice was a vibrant city full of painted palaces, glittering canals, and impressed visitors. Five centuries after its power began to decline, Venice is all of these still, with the added charm of romantic decay. In this tour we'll spend an hour in the heart of this Old World superpower.

ORIENTATION

Cost: If you ascend the Campanile bell tower, it'll cost you €6.

Hours: June–Sept daily 9:00–21:00, Oct–May 9:00–19:00.

Getting There: Signs all over town point to "San Marco"—both the square and the basilica, located where the Grand Canal spills out into the lagoon. Vaporetto stop: San Marco/Vallaresso.

Information: There are two tourist information offices. One TI is in the southwest corner of the Piazza; the other is along the water-front at the San Marco/Vallaresso vaporetto stop. In any given

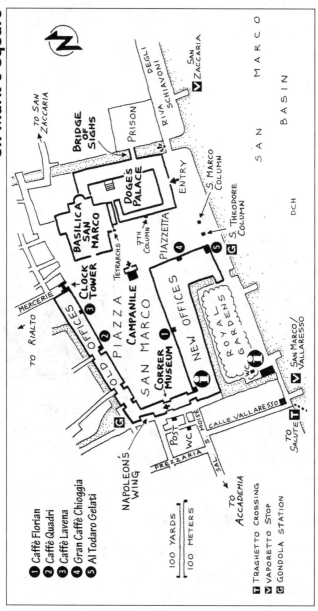

St. Mark's Square

1 Caffè Florian
2 Caffè Quadri
3 Caffè Lavena
4 Gran Caffè Chioggia
5 Al Todaro Gelati

■ TRAGHETTO CROSSING
✓ VAPORETTO STOP
G GONDOLA STATION

100 YARDS
100 METERS

year, expect a famous building to be covered with scaffolding. Restoration is an ongoing process.

Cuisine Art: Pricier cafés with live music are on St. Mark's Square. Cheaper bars are just off the square. The Correr Museum (far end of the square, opposite the basilica) has a quiet coffeeshop overlooking the crowded square.

Starring: Byzantine domes, Gothic arches, Renaissance arches...and the wonderful space they enclose.

• *For an overview of this grand square and the buildings that surround it, view it from the far end of the square (away from St. Mark's Basilica).*

THE TOUR BEGINS

The Piazza—Bride of the Sea

St. Mark's Basilica dominates the square with its Byzantine-style onion domes and glowing mosaics. Mark Twain said it looked like "a warty bug taking a meditative walk." To the right of the basilica is its 300-foot-tall bell tower, or Campanile. Between the basilica and the Campanile, you can

catch a glimpse of the pale pink Doge's Palace. Lining the square are the former government offices that administered the Venetian empire's vast network of trading outposts.

The square is big, but it feels intimate with its cafés and dueling orchestras. By day, it's great for people-watching and pigeon-chasing. By night, under lantern light, it transports you to another century, complete with its own romantic soundtrack. The Piazza draws Indians in saris, English nobles in blue blazers, and Nebraskans in shorts. Napoleon called the Piazza "the most beautiful drawing room in Europe." Napoleon himself added to the intimacy by building the final wing, opposite the basilica, that encloses the square.

For architecture buffs, here are three centuries of styles, bam, side by side, *uno-due-tre,* for easy comparison:

1) On the left side (as you face the basilica) are the "Old" offices, built in 1530 in solid, column-and-arch Renaissance style.

2) The "New" offices (on the right), from a century later, are a little heavier and more ornate, mixing arches, the three orders of columns from bottom to top—Doric, Ionic and Corinthian, and statues in the Baroque style.

3) Napoleon's wing is neoclassical—a return to simpler, more

austere classical columns and arches. Napoleon's architects tried to make his wing bridge the styles of the other two. But it turned out a little too high for one side and not enough for the other. Nice try.

Imagine this square full of water, with gondolas floating where people now sip cappuccinos. That happens every so often at very high tides *(acqua alta)*, a reminder that Venice and the sea are intertwined.

Venice became Europe's richest city from its trade with northern Europeans, Turkish Muslims, and Byzantine Christians. Here in St. Mark's Square, the exact center of this East–West axis, we see both the luxury and the mix of Eastern and Western influences.

• *The tourist information office is nearby, in the corner of Napoleon's Wing. With Venice's inconsistent opening hours, it's wise to confirm your sightseeing plans here. Behind you (southwest of the Piazza), you'll find the public WC, a post office, and the American Express office.*

Now approach the basilica. If it's hot and you're tired, grab a shady seat at the foot of the Campanile. Watch out for pigeon speckle.

St. Mark's Basilica—Exterior

The facade is a crazy mix of East and West. There are round Roman-style arches over the doorways, golden Byzantine mosaics, a roofline ringed with pointed French Gothic pinnacles, and Muslim-shaped onion domes (wood, covered with lead) on the roof. The brick-structure building is blanketed in marble from everywhere—columns from Alexandria, capitals from Sicily, and carvings from Constantinople. The columns flanking the doorways show the facade's variety—purple, green, gray, white, yellow, some speckled, some striped horizontally, some vertically, some fluted, all topped with a variety of different capitals.

What's amazing isn't so much the variety as the fact that the whole thing comes together in a bizarre sort of harmony. St. Mark's remains simply the most interesting church in Europe, a church that (paraphrasing Goethe) "can only be compared with itself."

For more on the basilica, inside and out, see St. Mark's Basilica Tour, page 246.

• *Facing the basilica, turn 90 degrees to the left to see...*

The Clock Tower

Two bronze Moors (African Muslims) stand atop the clock tower. (They only gained their ethnicity when the metal darkened over the centuries.) At the top of each hour they swing their giant clappers. The clock dial shows the 24 hours, the signs of the zodiac, and, in the blue center, the phases of the moon. Above the dial is the world's first digital clock, which changes every five minutes. The clock tower retains some of its original coloring of blue and gold, a reminder that, in centuries past, this city glowed with color. The tower is supposed to be open to the public in 2005.

An alert winged lion, the symbol of St. Mark and the city, looks down on the crowded square. He opens a book that reads "*Pax Tibi Marce*" or "Peace to you, Mark." As legend goes, these were the comforting words that an angel spoke to the stressed evangelist, assuring him he would find serenity during a stormy night that the saint spent here on the island. Eventually, St. Mark's body found its final resting place inside the basilica, and now his lion symbol is everywhere. (Find four in 20 seconds. Go.)

Venice's many lions express the city's various mood swings through history—triumphant after a naval victory, sad when a favorite son has died, hollow-eyed after a plague, smiling when the soccer team wins. The pair of lions squatting between the clock tower and basilica have probably been photographed being ridden by every Venetian child born since the dawn of cameras.

The Campanile

The original Campanile (camp-ah-NEE-lay), or bell tower, was a lighthouse and a marvel of 10th-century architecture until the 20th century (1902), when it toppled into the center of the Piazza. It had groaned ominously the night before, sending people scurrying from the cafés. The next morning...crash! The golden angel on top landed right at the basilica's front door, standing up.

The Campanile was rebuilt 10 years later complete with its golden angel, which always faces the breeze. You can ride a lift to the top for the best view of Venice. It's crowded at peak times, but well worth it.

Notice the tide gauges on the side of the bell tower. Since St. Mark's square is the first place in town to start flooding, it's an obvious place to take tidal measurements, although instruments like these can be found in several places around Venice. When Venice floods, the puddles appear first around round, white pavement stones like the one next to the Campanile. If the tide is mild, the water merely seeps up through the drains, but when there's a strong tide, it looks like someone's turned a faucet on down below as the water

Cafés on St. Mark's Square

Cafés line the square. All three café orchestras feature similar food, prices, and a three- or four-piece combo playing a selection of classical and pop hits, from Brahms to Besame Mucho. If you get just a drink, expect to pay about €15, including the cover charge. It's perfectly acceptable to nurse a cappuccino for an hour, since you're paying for the music with the cover charge.

Caffè Florian (on the right as you face the church) is the most famous Venetian café and one of the first places in Europe to serve coffee. It's been a popular spot for a discreet rendezvous in Venice since 1720. The orchestra plays a more classical repertoire than the other cafés. The outside tables are the main action, but do walk inside through the richly decorated, 18th-century rooms where Casanova, Lord Byron, Charles Dickens, and Woody Allen have all paid too much for a drink (reasonable prices at bar in back).

Caffè Quadri, exactly opposite the Florian, has an equally illustrous history of famous clientele, including Stendhal, Dumas, and Wagner. **Caffè Lavena,** near the Clock Tower, is newer and less prestigious.

Gran Caffè Chioggia, on the Piazzetta facing the Doge's Palace, charges slightly less, with one or two musicians playing cocktail jazz.

bubbles upwards and flows like a river to the lowest points in the square, and can cover it with a few inches of water in an hour or so. Check out the stone plaque showing the high water line from the disastrous floods of 1966.

• *The small square between the basilica and the water is...*

The Piazzetta

This "Little Square" is framed by the Doge's Palace on the left, the Library on the right, and the waterfront of the lagoon. In former days, the Piazzetta was closed off to the public for a few hours a day so that government officials and bigwigs could gather in the sun to strike shady deals.

The pale pink Doge's Palace is the epitome of the style known as "Venetian Gothic." Columns support traditional, pointed Gothic arches, but with a Venetian flair—they're curved to a point, ornamented with a trefoil (three-leaf clover), and topped with a round medallion of a quatrefoil (four-leaf clover). The pattern is

Venetian Gothic

$$\Lambda + \bigcap + \bigwedge + \clubsuit =$$

found on buildings all over Venice, but nowhere else in the world (except Las Vegas).

The two large 12th-century columns near the water were looted from Constantinople. Mark's winged lion sits on top of one. The lion's body (nearly 15 feet long) predates the wings, and is over 2,000 years old. The other column holds St. Theodore (battling a crocodile), the former patron saint who was replaced by Mark. I guess stabbing crocs in the back isn't classy enough for an upwardly mobile world power. These columns were used to execute criminals in hopes that the public could learn its lessons vicariously.

Venice was the "Bride of the Sea" because she was dependent on sea trading for her livelihood. This "marriage" was celebrated annually by the people. The doge, in full regalia, boarded a ritual boat (his Air Force One equivalent) here at the edge of the Piazzetta and sailed out into the lagoon. There a vow was made, and he dropped a jeweled ring into the water to seal the marriage. (I always think of that image whenever the café orchestras play the theme from *Titanic*.)

In the distance, on an island across the lagoon, is one of the grandest scenes in the city, the Church of San Giorgio Maggiore. With its four tall columns as the entryway, the church, designed by the late-Renaissance architect Palladio, influenced future government and bank buildings around the world.

Speaking of architects, I will: Sansovino. The Library (here in the Piazzetta), the Old Offices (in Piazza San Marco), and the delicate Loggetta (at the base of the Campanile) were all designed by Jacopo Sansovino. From the Piazzetta you can see all three of these at once. More than any single man, he made Piazza San Marco what it is, replacing the city's frilly, pointed-arch Venetian Gothic with the round-arch, sober Renaissance style.

The Tetrarchs and the Doge's Palace's Seventh Column

Where the basilica meets the Doge's Palace is the traditional entrance to the palace, decorated with four small Roman statues—the Tetrarchs. Legend says they're either the scared leaders of a divided Rome during its fall, or four brothers who poisoned each other over stolen treasure, with their loot ending up in Venice's coffers. Whatever the legend, these statues, made of purple porphyry marble, are very old, having guarded the doge's entrance since the city first rose from the mud.

The Doge's Palace's seventh column (the seventh from the water) tells a story of love, romance, and tragedy in its carved capital: 1) In the first scene (the carving facing the Piazzetta), a woman on a balcony is wooed by her lover, who says "Babe, I want *you!*" 2) She responds, "Why, little old *me?*" 3) They get married. 4) Kiss. 5) Hit the sack—pretty racy for 14th-century art. 6) Nine months later, guess what? 7) The baby takes its first steps. 8) And as was all too common in the 1300s...the child dies.

• *At the waterfront in the Piazzetta, turn left and walk (east) along the water. At the top of the first bridge, look inland at...*

The Bridge of Sighs

In the Doge's Palace (on your left), the government doled out justice. On your right are the prisons. (Don't let the palatial facade fool you. See the bars on the windows?) Prisoners sentenced in the palace crossed to the prisons by way of the covered bridge in front of you. From this bridge (according to romantic—and false—legend), they got their final view of sunny, joyous Venice before entering the black and dank prisons. They sighed.

Venice has been a major tourist center for four centuries. Anyone who ever came here has stood on this very spot, looking at the Bridge of Sighs. Lean on the railing leaned on by everyone from Casanova to Byron to Hemingway.

> *I stood in Venice, on the Bridge of Sighs,*
> *a palace and a prison on each hand.*
> *I saw, from out the wave, her structures rise,*
> *as from the stroke of the enchanter's wand.*
>
> *A thousand years their cloudy wings expand*
> *around me, and a dying glory smiles*
> *o'er the far times, when many a subject land*
> *looked to the Winged Lion's marble piles,*
> *where Venice sat in state, throned on her hundred isles!*
> —-from Lord Byron's *Childe Harold's Pilgrimage*

• *Sigh.*

ST. MARK'S BASILICA

(Basilica San Marco)

Among Europe's churches, St. Mark's is peerless. From the outside, it's a riot of domes, columns, and statues, completely unlike the towering Gothic churches of the North. Inside, the decor of mosaics, colored marbles, and oriental treasures is rarely seen elsewhere. Even the Christian symbolism is unfamiliar to Western eyes, done in the style of icons and even Islamic designs. Older than most of Europe's churches, it feels like a remnant of a lost world.

This is your best chance (outside of Istanbul or Ravenna) to glimpse a forgotten and somewhat mysterious part of the human story—Byzantium.

ORIENTATION

Cost: The church is free. There's a fee to see three museums inside: the Treasury (€2, includes informative audioguide—free for the asking), Golden Altarpiece (€1.50), and San Marco Museum (€3, enter from atrium either before or after you tour church).

Hours: The church is open Mon–Sat 9:45–16:30, Sun 14:00–16:00. The Treasury, Golden Altarpiece, and San Marco Museum are open Mon–Sat 9:45–16:00, Sun 9:45–15:30. The church is particularly beautiful when lit (unpredictable schedule, usually 11:30–12:00 Mon–Fri, all day Sat and Sun. To appreciate the gilded mosaic interior, this is worth attempting to see.

During peak times, the line can be very long (the only way to escape it is to go with a guided group; see "Tours," page 248). Much of the church interior is roped off for crowd-flow control. You just have to shuffle through on a one-way system. It's

St. Mark's Basilica

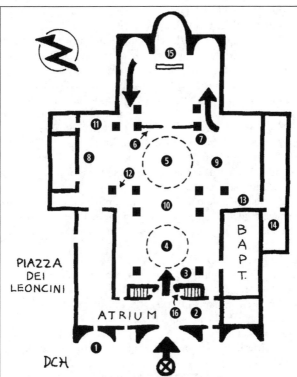

PIAZZA DEI LEONCINI

ATRIUM

DCH

ENTRANCE
FROM PIAZZA S. MARCO

1 Exterior—Mosaic of Mark's Relics
2 Atrium—Mosaic of Noah's Ark and the Great Flood
3 Nave—Mosaics and Greek Cross Floor Plan
4 Pentecost Mosaic
5 Central Dome—Ascension Mosaic
6 Rood Screen
7 Doge's Pulpit
8 Tree of Jesse Mosaic
9 Last Supper Mosaic
10 Crucifixion Mosaic
11 Nicopeia Icon
12 Rifle on Pillar
13 Discovery of Mark Mosaic
14 Treasury
15 Golden Altarpiece
16 Stairs up to Loggia: San Marco Museum & Bronze Horses

best to read this chapter before you go...or while standing in line (bring a small flashlight to illuminate the text).

Getting There: Signs throughout Venice point to "San Marco," meaning the square and the church. It's on St. Mark's Square (Piazza San Marco), near the end of the Grand Canal. Vaporetto stop: San Marco/Vallaresso.

Information: Tel. 041-522-5205. Guidebooks are sold in the bookstand in the basilica's atrium. There's a public pay WC just beyond the far end of the square or around the corner of the Piazzetta near Giardini Reali and the other St. Mark's TI. There's also one inside the San Marco Museum.

Bag Check: Free and mandatory for backpacks (small purses are fine), just around the corner to the left of the facade, two doors down Calle S. Basso at Ateno S. Basso.

Tours: See the schedule board in the atrium listing free English-language guided tours (schedules vary, but May–Oct generally Wed and Thu at 11:00, just show up at main door, tel. 041-270-2421).

Length of This Tour: One hour.

Dress Code: The strict dress code applies to everyone, even kids (no bare shoulders, shorts, or short skirts).

Cuisine Art: Pricier cafés offering live music are on St. Mark's Square; cheaper bars are just off the square.

Photography: Not allowed.

Starring: St. Mark, Byzantium, mosaics, and ancient bronze horses.

THE TOUR BEGINS

A complete visit to St. Mark's includes the church (free) plus three separate museums inside (with admission fees), all described in this chapter.

Exterior— Mosaic of Mark's Relics

St. Mark's Basilica is a treasure chest of booty looted during Venice's glory days. That's only appropriate for a church built on the bones of a stolen saint.

The **mosaic over the far left door** shows the theft that put Venice on the pilgrimage map. Two men (in the center, with crooked staffs) enter the church bearing a coffin with the body of St. Mark, who looks grumpy from the long voyage.

St. Mark's...Cathedral, Church, or Basilica?

All three are correct. The church is also a cathedral because it's the home church of the local bishop. It's a basilica because it's the home of a patriarch and because the meaning of 'basilica' evolved into an honorary title conferred on select churches by the pope. Coincidentally, it's also a basilica in the architectural sense. Its floor plan (if you ignore the transepts) has a central nave with flanking side aisles, a layout patterned after the ancient Roman law buildings called basilicas. The transepts turn the basilica plan into a cross—in this case, since it has four equal arms, a Greek cross.

St. Mark was the author of one of the four Bible books telling the story of Jesus' life (Matthew, Mark, Luke, and John). Seven centuries after his death, his holy body was in Muslim-occupied Alexandria, Egypt. In 828, two visiting merchants of Venice "rescued" the body from the "infidels," hid it in a pork barrel (which was unclean to Muslims) and spirited it away to Venice.

The merchants presented the body not to a pope or bishop, but to the doge (with white ermine collar, on the right) and his wife, the dogaressa (with entourage, on the left), giving instant status to Venice's budding secular state. They built a church here over Mark's bones, and made him the patron saint of the city. You'll see his symbol, the winged lion, all over Venice.

The original church burned down in 976. Today's structure was begun in 1063. The mosaic, from 1260, shows that the church hasn't changed much since then—you can see the onion domes and famous bronze horses on the balcony.

In subsequent centuries, the church was encrusted with materials looted from buildings throughout the Venetian empire. Their prize booty was the four bronze horses that adorn the balcony, stolen from Constantinople during the Fourth Crusades (these are copies; the originals are housed inside the church museum). The architectural style of St. Mark's has been called "Early Ransack."

• *Enter the atrium (entrance hall) of the basilica, past the guard who makes sure all who enter have covered legs and shoulders. The door is a sixth-century, bronze-paneled, Byzantine job. Immediately after entering the first door (crowd-flow permitting), peel off to the right and look overhead into an archway decorated with fine mosaics.*

Atrium—Mosaic of Noah's Ark and the Great Flood

St. Mark's famous mosaics, with their picture symbols, were easily understood in medieval times, even by illiterate masses. Today's literate masses have trouble reading them, so let's practice on these, some of the oldest (13th century), finest, and most accessible mosaics in the church.

If you turn around and face the door you just came through, to your left you'll see (on top of the arch) Noah and sons sawing logs to build an Ark. Below that are three scenes of Noah putting all species of animals into the Ark, two by two. (Who's at the head of the line? Lions.) Turning around and facing the church interior, you'll see the Flood in full force, drowning the wicked. Noah sends out a dove twice to see if there's any dry land to dock at. He finds it, leaves the Ark with a gorgeous rainbow overhead, and offers a sacrifice of thanks to God. Easy, huh?

• *Now that our medieval literacy rate has risen, rejoin the flow of people. Notice the entrance to the San Marco Museum ("Loggia dei Cavalli"), which you can visit later. Glance above the door at the golden mosaic of Mark who opens his arms to say, "Welcome to my church." Now climb seven steps, pass through the doorway, and enter the nave. Loiter somewhere just inside the door (crowd-flow permitting) and let your eyes adjust.*

The Nave—Mosaics and Greek Cross Floor Plan

The initial effect is dark and unimpressive (unless they've got the floodlights on). But as your pupils slowly unclench, you'll notice that the entire upper part is decorated in mosaic— 4,750 square yards (imagine paving a football field with contact lenses). These golden mosaics are in the Byzantine style, though many were designed by artists from the Italian Renaissance and later. The often-overlooked lower walls are covered with green, yellow, purple, and rose-colored marble slabs, cut to expose the grain, and laid out in geometric patterns. Even the floor is mosaic, mostly geometrical designs. It rolls like the sea. Venice is sinking and shifting, creating these cresting waves of stone.

The church is laid out with four equal arms, topped with domes, radiating out from the center to form a Greek Cross (+). Those familiar with Eastern Orthodox churches will find familiar elements in St. Mark's—a central floor plan, domes, mosaics, and iconic images of Mary and Christ as Pantocrator.

As your eyes adjust, the mosaics start to give off a "mystical,

Mosaics

St. Mark's mosaics are designs or pictures made with small cubes of colored stone or glass pressed into wet plaster. Ancient Romans paved floors, walls, and ceilings with them. When Rome "fell," the art form died out in the West, but was carried on by Byzantine craftsmen. They perfected the gold background effect by baking gold leaf into tiny cubes of glass called tiles *(tesserae)*. The uneven surfaces of the tiles give off a shimmering effect. The reflecting gold mosaics helped to light thick-walled, small-windowed, lantern-lit Byzantine churches, creating a golden glow that symbolized the divine light of heaven.

St. Mark's mosaics tell the entire Christian history from end to beginning. Entering the church, you're greeted with scenes from the end of the world (Apocalypse) and the Pentecost. As you approach the altar, you walk backward in time to the source, experiencing Jesus' Passion and crucifixion, his miraculous life, and continuing back to his birth and Old Testament predecessors. Over the altar at the far end of the church (and over the entrance door at the near end) are images of Christ—the beginning and the end, the alpha and omega of the Christian universe.

golden luminosity," the atmosphere of the Byzantine heaven. The air itself seems almost visible, like a cloud of incense. It's a subtle effect, one that grows on you as the filtered light changes. There are more beautiful, bigger, more overwhelming, and even holier churches, but none are as stately.

• *Find the chandelier near the entrance doorway (in the shape of a Greek Cross cathedral space station), and run your eyes up the support chain to the dome above.*

Pentecost Mosaic

In a golden heaven, the dove of the Holy Spirit shoots out a pinwheel of spiritual lasers, igniting tongues of fire on the heads of the 12 apostles below, giving them the ability to speak other languages without a Rick Steves Phrasebook. You'd think they'd be amazed, but their expressions are as solemn as...icons. One of the oldest mosaics in the church (c. 1125), it has distinct "Byzantine" features: A gold background, and apostles with halos, solemn faces, almond eyes, delicate blessing hands, and rumpled robes, all facing forward.

Byzantium

The Byzantine Empire was the eastern half of the ancient Roman Empire that *didn't* "fall" in A.D. 476. It remained Christian, Greek-speaking, and enlightened for another thousand years.

In A.D. 330, Constantine, the first Christian emperor, moved the Roman Empire's capital to the newly expanded city of Byzantium, which he humbly renamed Constantinople (modern Istanbul). With him went Rome's best and brightest. When the city of Rome decayed and fell, plunging western Europe into its "Dark Ages," Constantinople lived on as the greatest city in Europe.

Venice had strong ties with Byzantium from its earliest days. In the sixth century, Byzantine Emperor Justinian invaded northern Italy, briefly reuniting East and West, and making Ravenna his regional capital. In 800, Venetians asked the emperor in Constantinople to protect them from Charlemagne's marauding Franks.

Soon Venetian merchants were granted trading rights to Byzantine ports in the Adriatic and eastern Mediterranean. They traded raw materials from western Europe for luxury goods from the East.

When Muslim Turks threatened Christian Byzantium, the Venetians joined the Crusades, the series of military expeditions designed to "save" Jerusalem and Constantinople. Venetians grew rich renting ships to the Crusaders in exchange for money, favors, and booty.

During the Fourth Crusade (1202–1204), which went horribly awry, the Crusaders—led by the Venetian Doge Dandolo—sacked Constantinople, a fellow Christian city. This was, perhaps, the lowest point in Christian history, at least until the advent of TV evangelism. The Venetians carried home the bronze horses, the Pala d'Oro enamels, the Treasury's treasures, the Nicopeia icon, and much of the marble that now covers the (brick) church.

Venice rose while Byzantium faded. Then both civilizations nose-dived when Constantinople finally fell to the Turks in 1453 and Venice's monopoly on Eastern trade was broken.

Today, we find hints of Byzantium in the Eastern Orthodox Church, in mosaics and icons, and in the looted treasures shipped back to Venice.

This is art from a society still touchy about the Bible commandment against making "graven images" of holy things. Byzantium had recently emerged from two centuries of "Iconoclasm," where statues and paintings were broken and burned as sinful "false gods." The Byzantine style emphasizes otherworldliness rather than literal human detail. The poet W. B. Yeats stood here and described what he saw: "O sages standing in God's holy

Christ as Pantocrator

Most Eastern Orthodox churches have at least one mosaic or painting of Christ in a standard pose—as "Pantocrator," a Greek word meaning Ruler of All. St. Mark's features several Pantocrators, including the central dome, over the altar, and over the entrance door. The image, so familiar to Orthodox Christians, is a bit foreign to Protestants, Catholics, and secularists.

As King of the Universe, Christ sits (usually on a throne) facing directly out, with penetrating eyes. He wears a halo divided with a cross, worn only by the Trinity. In his left hand is a Bible, while his right hand blesses, with the fingers forming the Greek letters Chi and Rho, the first two letters of "Christos." The thumb touches the fingers, symbolizing how Christ unites both his divinity and his humanity. On either side of Christ's head are the Greek letters "IC XC," short for "IesuC XristoC."

fire as in the gold mosaic of a wall, come from the holy fire...and be the singing-masters of my soul."

• *Shuffle along with the crowds up to the central dome.*

Central Dome—Ascension Mosaic

Gape upwards to the very heart of the church. Christ, having lived his miraculous life and been crucified for man's sins, ascends into the starry sky riding on a rainbow. He raises his right hand and blesses the universe. This isn't the dead, crucified, mortal Jesus featured in most churches, but a powerful, resurrected god, the Ruler of All the Cosmos (Greek "Pantocrator").

Christ's blessing radiates out, rippling down to the ring of white-robed apostles below. They stand amid the trees of the Mount of Olives, waving goodbye as Christ ascends. Mary is with them, wearing blue with golden Greek crosses on each shoulder and looking ready to play patty-cake. From these saints, goodness descends to create the Virtues that ring the base of the dome between the windows. In Byzantine churches, the window-lit dome represented heaven, while the dark church below was earth—a microcosm of the hierarchical universe.

Beneath the dome at the four corners, the four Gospel writers ("Matev," "Marc," "Luca," and "Ioh") thoughtfully scribble down the heavenly events. This wisdom flows down like water from the symbolic Four Rivers below them, spreading through the church's four equal arms (the "four corners" of the world), and baptizing the congregation with God's love. The church building is a series of perfect circles within symmetrical squares—the cosmic order—with Christ in the center solemnly blessing us. God's in his heaven, saints are on earth, and all's right with the world.

Under the Ascension Dome—
The Church as Theater

Look around at the church's furniture and imagine a service here. The **rood screen** topped with 14 saints separates the congregation from the high altar, heightening the "mystery" of the Mass. The **pulpit on the right** was reserved for the Doge, who led prayers and made important announcements. Mosaics were visual aids for the priest, telling the whole story of Jesus, from his ancestors perched in the **Tree of Jesse** (in the north transept; facing the altar, turn 90-degrees left, and it's on the far (north) wall), to the **Last Supper** (in the arch leading to the south transept), to the **Crucifixion** (in the west arch).

The Crucifixion mosaic features a stick-figure Christ, emphasizing the symbolic solemnity of the moment, not its Mel Gibson gruesomeness. In fact, there aren't very many crucifixes at all in the church, giving it an Eastern Orthodox flavor. While Western Christianity focuses on the death of Jesus, to Orthodox believers, Christ's death is just the tragic Act I. Other scenes in the arch show the rest of the story, Christ's triumphant Resurrection and post-death miracles, leading to the climax, his Ascension (in the central dome).

The Venetian church service is a theatrical multimedia spectacle, combining words (prayers, Bible passages, Latin and Greek phrases), music (chants, a choir, organ, horns, and strings), costumes and props (priests' robes, golden reliquaries, candles, incense), set design (the mosaics, rood screen, Golden Altarpiece), and even stage direction (processionals through the crowd, priests' motions, standing, sitting, kneeling, crossing yourself). The symmetrical church is itself part of the set design. The Greek-cross floor plan symbolizes perfection, rather than the more common Latin cross of the crucifixion (emphasizing man's sinfulness). Coincidentally or not, the first modern opera—also a multimedia theatrical experience—was written by St. Mark's *maestro di capella*, Claudio Monteverdi (1567–1643).

North Transept

In the north transept (the arm of the church to the left of the altar), today's Venetians pray to a painted wooden icon of Mary and baby Jesus known as **Nicopeia**, or "Our Lady of Victory" (on the east wall of the north transept). Supposedly painted personally by the Evangelist Luke, it was once enamelled with bright paint and precious stones, and Mary was adorned with a crown and necklace of gold and jewels (now on display in the Treasury). This Madonna has helped Venice persevere through plagues, wars, and crucial soccer games. When Mary answers a prayer, grateful Venetians give her offerings, like the old **rifle** that hangs on a pillar (as you approach the north transept). A wife prayed to the Madonna for her husband's safe return from war with Austria in 1848. When he came home

The Legend (Mixed with a Little Truth) of Mark and Venice

Mark (died c. A.D. 68) was a Jewish-born Christian, and he may have actually met Jesus. (The Bible mentions a "Mark" and a "John Mark" that may be him.) He traveled with fellow convert Paul, eventually settling in Alexandria as the city's first Christian bishop. On a trip to Rome, Peter—Jesus' righthand man—asked him to write down the events of Jesus' life that became the Gospel of Mark.

During his travels, Mark stopped in the Lagoon (in Aquilea on the north coast), where he dreamed of a Latin-speaking angel who said, *"Pax tibi Marce, evangelista meus"* ("Peace to you, Mark, my evangelist"), promising him rest after death in the region. Back in Alexandria, Mark was attacked by an anti-Christian mob. They tied him with ropes and dragged his body through the streets until he died.

Eight centuries later, his body lay in an Alexandrian church about to be vandalized by Muslim fanatics. Two Venetian traders on a business trip saved the relics from desecration by hiding them in a barrel of pork—a meat considered unclean by Muslims—and quickly setting sail. The perilous voyage home was only completed after many more miracles. The doge received the body and, in 828, they built the first church of St. Mark's to house it. During construction of the current church (1094), Mark's relics were temporarily lost, and it took another miracle to find them, hidden inside a column. Today, Venetians celebrate Mark on the traditional date of his martyrdom, April 25.

The events of Mark's life are portrayed vividly in many frescoes throughout the Basilica. Unfortunately, most of them are either off-limits to tourists or in the dim reaches of the church. Enjoy them by buying a St. Mark's guidebook with photos.

alive, she gave his rifle to the Virgin in thanks.

• *In the south transept (to right of main altar), find the dim mosaic on the west wall.*

Discovery of Mark Mosaic

Not a Bible scene, this depicts the miraculous event that capped the construction of the present church.

It's 1094, the church is nearly complete (see the domes shown in cut-away fashion), and they're all set to re-inter Mark's bones under the new altar. There's just one problem: during the decades of construction, they forgot where they'd stored his body!

So (in the left half of the mosaic), all of Venice gathers inside the church to bow down and pray for help finding the bones. The Doge (from Latin "DUX") leads them. Soon after (the right half), the patriarch (far right) is inspired to look inside a hollow column where he finds the relics. Everyone turns and applauds, including the womenfolk (left side of scene) who stream in from the upper-floor galleries. The relics were soon placed under the altar in a ceremony that inaugurated the current structure.

The south transept also features horseshoe arches atop slender columns, giving the transept the exotic flavor of a Muslim mosque. The door under the rose window leads directly from the Doge's Palace. On important occasions, the doge entered the church through here, ascended the steps of his pulpit, and addressed the people.

ST. MARK'S THREE MUSEUMS

Inside the church are three sights, each requiring a separate admission. All are open Mon–Sat 9:45–16:00, Sun 9:45–15:30. None are must-sees, but they're your best chance (outside of Istanbul or Ravenna) to soak up Byzantine ambience.

Treasury (Tesoro)

• *The Treasury is in the south transept. Admission is €2 (includes audioguide when available—ask for it). The collection is housed in three tiny rooms.*

You'll see Byzantine chalices, silver reliquaries, monstrous monstrances (for displaying the Communion wafer), and icons done in gold, silver, enamels, gems and semiprecious stones. Some pieces represent the fruit of labor by different civilizations over a thousand-year period. For example, an ancient rock-crystal chalice made by the Romans might be decorated centuries later with Byzantine enamels, then finished still later with gold filigree by Venetian goldsmiths. This is marvelous handiwork, but all the more marvelous for having been done when western Europe was still rooting in the mud. Here are some highlights.

Entryway: The so-called "Throne of St. Mark," just as you enter, is one of the church's oldest Christian objects (around A.D. 550). Created when Europe was being overrun by pagan hordes (and early Venetians were hiding in the marshes), its sheer bulk and carved Tree of Life offered Christians an image of stability.

• *We'll tour the main room counterclockwise. But first, start at the glass case in the center of the room.*

Main Room: The glass case in the center of the room holds the most precious Byzantine objects. The hanging lamp with the protruding fish features fourth-century Roman rock crystal framed in 11th-century Byzantine metalwork. Just behind it, a purple bucket, carved with scenes of satyrs chasing nymphs, epitomizes the pagan world that was fading as Christianity triumphed. Also in the case are blue-and-gold lapis lazuli icons of the Crucifixion and of the

Archangel Michael featuring a Byzantine specialty—enamel work (more on that craft at the Golden Altarpiece). See various chalices (cups used for the bread and wine during Mass) made of onyx, agate, and rock crystal, and an incense burner shaped like a domed church.

Along the walls, find the following displays (working counterclockwise around the room): In a glass case, find several objects made by Muslims, Venice's other trading partner to the east. Next comes the Urn of Artaxerxes I (middle of the right wall), an Egyptian-made object that once held the ashes of the great Persian king who ruled 2,500 years ago (465–425 B.C.). The next glass case has bishops' robes and a 600-year-old crozier (ceremonial shepherd staff) still used today by the chief priest on holy days.

Next is the Ciborio di Anastasia (far left corner), a small marble canopy that once arched over the blessed communion wafer during Mass. The object may be a gift from "Anastasia," the name carved on it in Greek. She was a lady-in-waiting in the court of the emperor Justinian (483–565). Christian legend says she was so beautiful that Justinian (a married man) pursued her amorously, and she had to dress like a monk and flee to a desert monastery.

As you leave, notice the granite column that extends below current floor level—you can see how the floor has risen as things have settled in the last 1,000 years.

Relics/Sanctuary Room: Straight ahead, the glass case over the alabaster altar contains elaborate golden reliquaries holding relics of Jesus' Passion—his torture and execution. For example, the reliquary in the center (from 1125), showing Christ being whipped, holds a stone from the column he was tied to. You may scoff, but of all of Europe's "Pieces of the True Cross" and "Crown of Thorns," these have at least some claim of authenticity. Legend has it that Christ's possessions were gathered up in the fourth century by Constantine's mother and taken to Constantinople. During the Crusade heist of 1204, Venetians brought them here. They've been paraded through the city every Good Friday for 800 years.

Immediately to the left of the room's entrance is a reliquary with the bones of Doge Orseolo (976–978), who built the church that preceded the current structure, and of St. George, legendary dragon-slayer.

Golden Altarpiece (Pala d'Oro)

• *The Golden Altarpiece is located behind the main altar. The admission is €2.*

Under the stone canopy sits the high altar. Inside the altar is an urn (not visible) with the mortal remains of Mark, the Gospel writer. (Look through the grate of the altar to read, *"Corpus Divi Marci Evangelistae,"* or "Body of the Evangelist Mark".) Legend has it that while he was alive he visited Venice, where an angel promised him he could rest his weary bones when he died. Shhh.

As you shuffle along, notice the marble canopy's support columns carved with New Testament scenes in the 13th century. (On the right-hand pillar closest to the altarpiece, fourth row from the bottom: Is that a genie escaping from a bottle while someone tries to stuff him back in?)

The Golden Altarpiece is a stunning golden wall made of 250 blue-backed enamels with religious scenes, all set in a gold frame and studded with 15 hefty rubies, 300 emeralds, 1,500 pearls, and assorted sapphires, amethysts, and topaz. The Byzantine-made enamels (c. 1100) were part of the Venetians' plunder of 1204, subsequently pieced together by Byzantine craftsmen specifically for 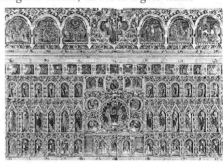 St. Mark's high altar. It's a bit much to take in all at once, but get up close and find several details you might recognize:

In the center, Jesus as Ruler of the Cosmos sits on a golden throne, with a halo of pearls and jewels. Like a good Byzantine Pantocrator, he dutifully faces forward and gives his blessing, while stealing a glance offstage at Mark ("Marcus") and the other saints.

Along the bottom row, Old Testament prophets show off the Bible books they've written. With halos, solemn faces, and elaborately creased robes, they epitomize the Byzantine icon style.

Follow Mark's story in the panels along the sides. In the bottom left panel, Mark meets Peter (seated) at the gates of Rome. It was Peter (legend has it) who gave Mark the eyewitness account of Jesus' life that Mark wrote down in his Gospel. Mark's story ends in the bottom right panel with the two Venetian merchants returning by ship, carrying his coffin here to be laid to rest.

Byzantium excelled in the art of *cloisonné* enameling. A piece of gold leaf is stamped with a design, then filled in with pools of enamel paint which are baked on. Look at a single saint to see the detail work: The gold background around the saint is the gold-leaf medallion that gets stamped. The golden folds in the robe are the raised edges of the impression. The different colors of the robe are different colored paints in the recessed areas, each color baked on in a separate firing. Some saints even have pearl crowns or jewel collars pinned on. This kind of craftsmanship—and the social infrastucture that could afford it—made Byzantium seem like an enchanted world during Europe's dim Middle Ages.

Once you've looked at some individual scenes, back up as far as this small room will let you and just let yourself be dazzled by the "whole picture"—this "mosaic" of Byzantine greatness. This magnificent altarpiece sits on a swivel (notice the mechanism at its base) and is swung around on festival Sundays so the entire congregation can enjoy it.

San Marco Museum (Museo di San Marco)— Bronze Horses, View of the Piazza, and More

• *This is the one sight certainly worth the admission price (€3), if only for the views of St. Mark's Square, the Piazzetta, and the interior of the church from above. The staircase up to the museum is in the atrium near the main entrance. The sign says "Loggia dei Cavalli, Museo." Once upstairs, belly up to the center of the stone balustrade to survey the interior.*

View of Church Interior: Take a closer look at the Pentecost Mosaic (first dome above you, described earlier). The unique design at the very top signifies the Trinity: throne (God), gospels (Christ), and dove (Holy Spirit). The couples below the ring of apostles are the people of the world (I can find Asia, Judea, and Cappadocia) who, despite their different languages, still understood the Spirit's message.

If you were a woman in medieval Venice, you'd enjoy this same close-up view, because in the Middle Ages, women did not worship on the floor level. They climbed the same stairs you just did and found a spot along the balconies at your feet. The church was divided into three realms—the balcony for women, the nave for men, and the altar for the priests. Back then the rood screen (the fence with the 15 figures on it) separated the priest from the public, and he officiated with his back to the people.

From here you can appreciate the mosaic—one of the finest in Italy—that covers the floor like a Persian carpet.

• *From here, the museum loops you to the far (altar) end of the church, then back to the bronze horses. Along the way, you'll see…*

Mosaic Fragments (Cassine): These mosaics once hung in the church, but when they became damaged or aesthetically old-fashioned, they were replaced by new and more fashionable mosaics. These few fragments avoided the garbage can. You'll see mosaics from the church's earliest days (and most "Byzantine" style, c. 1070) to the more recent (1700s) with realistic Renaissance detail.

The mosaics—made from small cubes of stone or colored glass pressed into wet clay—were assembled on the ground, then cemented onto the walls. Artists draw the pattern on paper, lay it on the wet clay, and slowly cut the paper away as they replace it with cubes. The first mosaic on your left as you enter shows a reproduction of a paper "cast" of a mosaic.

• *Continuing on, you'll see other artwork and catch glimpses of the interior of the church from the north transept. Descend the staircase to the next room, Sala Ongania (WCs to the right of entrance), with drawings and watercolors made for the works of the basilica. Around the corner is a large room filled with displays.*

Sala dei Banchetti: The ornate room is filled with religious objects, tapestries, carpets that once carpeted the church, Burano lace, music manuscripts, a doge's throne, and much more.

Try reading some music. The manuscripts date from the 16th century—before the age of treble and bass clefs. You'll see a C clef (which could slide along the staff to locate middle C). From this, you could chant notes in proper relationship to each other according to the rhythm indicated.

The most prestigious artwork is St. Mark's workaday altarpiece, the Pala Feriale, by Paolo Veneziano (1345). On ordinary workdays, these 14 scenes painted on wood covered the golden Pala d'Oro—seven saints above (including crucified Christ) and seven episodes in Mark's life below. The panel of the sailboat tells the story of the Venetian merchants' trip home with Mark's relics. A storm at sea billows their sails, ripples the flag, churns the waves, and scares the crew as the ship heads toward the rocks. But then Mark himself appears miraculously at the stern and calms the storm, bringing the ship (and his own body) safely to Venice. Paolo proudly signed his name (along the bottom) and the names of his two assistants, his sons Luca and Giovanni. The second half of the altarpiece (nearer to the exit of the room) is done in later Renaissance style by Maffeo Verona (1614).

• *Now double back through displays of stone fragments from the church, finally arriving at…*

The Bronze Horses (La Quadriga): Stepping lively in pairs

with smiles on their faces, they exude energy and exuberance. Art historians don't know how old they are—could be ancient Greece (4th century B.C.) or ancient Rome during its Fall (4th century A.D.). They look Greek Hellenistic (2nd century B.C.) to me, and Professor Carbon Fourteen says they're from around 175 B.C. Originally, the horses pulled a chariot *Ben Hur*-style. These bronze statues were not hammered and bent into shape by metalsmiths, but cast from clay molds, using the lost-wax technique. The bronze is high quality, with 97 percent copper. Originally gilded, they still have some streaks of gold. Long gone are the ruby pupils that gave the horses the original case of "red eye."

Megalomaniacs through the ages have coveted these horses not only for their artistic value but because they symbolize Apollo, the

Greco-Roman god of the sun...and of secular power. The doge spoke to his people standing between the horses when these graced the balcony atop the church's facade (where the copies, which you'll see next, stand today).

Their expressive faces seem to say, "Oh boy, Wilbur, have we done some travelin'." Legend says they were made in the time of Alexander the Great, then taken by Nero to Rome. Constantine brought them to his new capital in Constantinople to adorn the chariot racecourse. The Venetians then stole them from their fellow Christians during the looting of noble Constantinople and brought them to St. Mark's.

What goes around, comes around, and Napoleon came around and took the horses when he conquered Venice in 1797. They stood atop a triumphal arch in Paris until Napoleon's empire was "blown-aparte" and they were returned to their "rightful" home.

The horses were again removed from their spot when attacked by their most dangerous enemy yet—modern man. The threat of oxidation from pollution sent them galloping for cover inside the church.

• *The visit ends outside on the balcony overlooking St. Mark's Square.*

The Loggia and View of St. Mark's Square: You'll be drawn repeatedly to the viewpoint of the square, but remember to look at the facade to see how cleverly all the looted architectural elements blend together. Ramble among the statues of water-bearing slaves that serve as drain spouts. The horses are modern copies (note the 1978 date on their hoofs).

Be a doge and stand between the bronze horses overlooking St. Mark's Square. Under the gilded lion of St. Mark, in front of the four great evangelists (who once stood atop the columns), and flanked, like Apollo, by the four glorious horses, he inspired the Venetians in the square below to great things.

Admire the mesmerizing, commanding view of the center of this city, which so long ago was Europe's only superpower for centuries, and today is just a small town with a big history filled with tourists.

DOGE'S PALACE

(Palazzo Ducale)

Venice is a city of beautiful facades—palaces, churches, carnival masks—that can cover darker interiors of intrigue and decay. The Doge's Palace, with its frilly pink exterior, hides the fact that the "Most Serene Republic" (as it called itself—serene meaning stable) was far from serene in its heyday.

The Doge's Palace housed the fascinating government of this rich and powerful empire. It also served as the home for the Venetian ruler known as the doge (DOJE-eh), or duke. For four centuries (about 1150–1550), this was the most powerful half acre in Europe. The rest of Europe marveled at how Venice could govern itself without a dominant king, bishop, or tyrant. The doges wanted their palace to reflect the wealth and secular values of the Republic, impressing visitors and serving as a reminder that the Venetians were number one in Europe.

ORIENTATION

Cost: Covered by €11 Museum Card (valid for three months, one entry per card), which includes admission to the Correr Museum and two lesser museums at the Correr (National Archaeological Museum and the Monumental Rooms of the Marciana National Library). The pricier Museum Pass costs €15.50 and includes the above museums, plus Ca' Rezzonico, the museums on the neighboring islands, and more.

Doge's Palace Overview

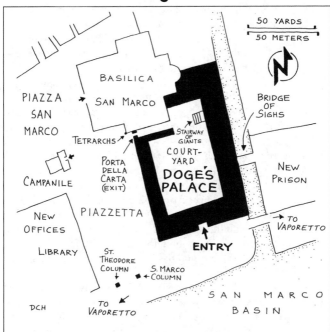

Hours: Daily April–Oct 9:00–19:00, Nov–March 9:00–17:00, last entry 60 minutes before closing.

Crowd Control: To avoid the long peak-season line at the Doge's Palace, you have several options (the first is best):

1. Buy your Museum Card at the Correr Museum (at far end of St. Mark's Square); then go directly to the turnstile of the Doge's Palace, skirting along to the right of the long line at the palace entrance.

2. If your visit falls between April and October, visit the palace around 17:00 when the line disappears (but note that the museum closes at 19:00 and the last entry is 18:00).

3. Book a guided "Secret Itineraries Tour;" see "Tours," below. The only (minor) drawback is that your palace entry fee does not include the Correr Museum.

Getting There: The palace is next to St. Mark's Basilica, on the lagoon waterfront, and just off St. Mark's Square. Vaporetto stop: San Marco/Vallaresso.

Information: There are some English descriptions. Guidebooks are on sale in the bookshop. Tel. 041-271-5911. WCs are in the courtyard near the palace exit and halfway up the stairs to balcony level.

Tours: High-tech palm-pilot audioguide tours are informative but dry (€5.50, 90 min, need ID or credit card for deposit). Pick it up after you pass through the turnstile after the ticket counter. (If you have a Museum Pass or Card, you'll need to go through the same turnstile as people buying their tickets at the palace—but you still don't have to wait in line.)

The fine "Secret Itineraries Tour," which follows the doge's footsteps through rooms not included in the general admission price, must be booked in advance (€12.50, at 9:55, 10:45, and 11:35 in English, 75 min, arrive 20 min early to check in, no need to wait in line, just *"scusi"* your way to the information desk in the room before the ticket counter). To make the reservation for the tour, call 041-291-5911 if you're reserving for visits on the same day or the day before, or call 041-520-9070 for visits several days in advance. After you pick up your tickets, go to the group meeting point in the courtyard to the left just after you pass through the turnstile. If you haven't booked ahead, you could try showing up at the information desk at 9:00 to get a spot on the 9:55 tour (and pass any wait time by going up the Campanile bell tower), but since tours are limited to 25, you are most likely to get a spot by reserving in advance. The cost includes admission only to the Doge's Palace (and allows you to bypass the long line). While the tour skips the main halls inside, it finishes inside the palace and you're welcome to visit the halls on your own. You cannot return to visit once you leave the palace.

Length of This Tour: 90 minutes.

Photography: Allowed without a flash.

Cuisine Art: Pricey cafeteria in Doge's Palace to the left of the bag check (behind grand staircase) accessed from the courtyard, expensive cafés on St. Mark's Square, cheaper bars/cafés off the square, and a handy canalside gelato shop on the Piazzetta (the small square with two big columns) across from the Doge's Palace.

Starring: Tintoretto and the doges.

THE TOUR BEGINS

Exterior—Venetian Gothic

"The Wedding Cake," "The Table Cloth," or "The Pink House" is also sometimes known as the Doge's Palace. The style is called Venetian Gothic—a fusion of Italian Gothic with a delicate Islamic flair. The columns originally had bases on the

bottoms, but these were covered over as the columns sank. If you compare this lacy, top-heavy structure with the massive fortress palaces of Florence, you realize the wisdom of building a city in the middle of the sea—you have no natural enemies except gravity. This unfortified palace in a city with no city wall was the doge's way of saying, "I am an elected and loved ruler. I do not fear my own people."

The palace was originally built in the 800s, but most of what we see came after 1300, as it was expanded to meet the needs of the empire. Each doge wanted to leave his mark on history with a new wing. But so much of the city's money was spent on the building that finally a law was passed levying an enormous fine on anyone who even mentioned any new building. That worked for a while, until one brave and wealthy doge proposed a new wing, paid his fine...and started building again.

• *Enter the Doge's Palace from along the waterfront. After you pass through the turnstile, ignore the signs and cross the square to stand at the foot of the grand staircase.*

The Courtyard and the Stairway of Giants (Scala dei Giganti)

Imagine yourself as a foreign dignitary on business to meet the doge. In the courtyard, you look up a grand staircase topped with two nearly nude statues of, I think, Moses and Paul Newman (more likely, Neptune and Mars, representing Venice's prowess at sea and at war). The doge and his aides would be waiting for you at the top, between the two statues and beneath the Winged Lion. No matter who you were—king, pope, or emperor—you'd have to hoof it up. The powerful doge would descend the stairs for no one.

Many doges were crowned here, between the two statues. The doge was something like an "elected king"—which makes sense only in the "dictatorial republic" that was Venice. Technically, he was just a noble selected by other nobles to carry out their laws and decisions. Many doges tried to extend their powers and rule more like divine-right kings. Many others just put on their funny hats and accepted their role as figurehead and ceremonial ribbon-cutter. Most were geezers, elected in their seventies, committed to preserving the Venetian traditions.

The palace is attached to the church, symbolically welding together church and state. You can see the ugly brick of both structures, the stern inner structure without its painted-lady veneer of marble. On this tour, we'll see the sometimes harsh inner structure of this outwardly serene Republic.

In the courtyard, you'll see a hodgepodge of architecture styles, as the palace was refurbished over the centuries. There are classical statues in Renaissance niches, shaded by Baroque awnings, topped by Flamboyant Gothic spires, and crusted with the Byzantine onion-domes of St. Mark's Basilica.

• *Cross back to near the entrance and follow the signs up the tourists' staircase to the first-floor balcony (Loggias) where you can look back down on the courtyard (but not the backside of Paul Newman). From here on, it's hard to get lost (though I've managed). It's a one-way system, so just follow the arrows.*

Midway along the balcony, you'll find a face in the wall, the...

Mouth of Truth

This fierce-looking androgyne opens his/her mouth, ready to swallow a piece of paper, hungry for gossip. Letterboxes like this (some with lions' heads) were scattered throughout the palace. Originally, anyone who had a complaint or suspicion about anyone else could accuse him anonymously *(Denontie Secrete)* by simply dropping a slip of paper in the mouth. This set the blades of justice turning inside the palace.

• *Towards Paul Newman is the entrance to the...*

Golden Staircase (Scala D'Oro)

The palace was propaganda, designed to impress visitors. This 24-karat gilded-ceiling staircase was something for them to write home about. As you ascend the stairs, look back at the floor below and marvel at its 3-D pattern.

• *Take the Golden Staircase to the first landing (Primo Piano Nobile), and turn right, which takes you up into the...*

Doge's Apartments (Appartamenti Ducale)

The dozen or so rooms on the first floor are where the doge actually lived. Wander around this once sumptuous, now sparse suite, admiring coffered wood ceilings, chandeliers, velvet-covered walls, and very little furniture, since doges were expected to bring their own. Despite his high office, the doge had to obey several rules that bound him to the city. He couldn't leave the palace unescorted, couldn't open official mail in private, and he and his family had to leave their own home and live in the Doge's Palace, poor guy.

In the large Room 6 (the Scudo, or "Shield" Room), ringed with maps, work clockwise around the room to trace local boy Marco Polo's (c. 1254–1325) eye-opening trip across Asia—from Italy to Greece (quite accurate maps) to Palestine, Arabia, and *Irac*. Finally, he arrived at the other side of the world. This last map (shown upside-down, with south on top) gives a glimpse at the Venetian worldview circa 1550. There's China, Taiwan *(Formosa)*, and Japan *(Giapan)*, while America is a nearby island with California and lots of *Terre Incognite*.

• *After browsing the dozen or so private rooms, continue up the Golden Staircase to the third floor, which was the "public" part of the palace. The first room at the top of the stairs is the...*

Square Room (Atrio Quadrato)

The ceiling painting, *Justice Presenting the Sword and Scales to Doge Girolamo Priuli* is by Tintoretto. (Stand at the top of the painting for the full 3-D effect.) It's a late-Renaissance masterpiece. So what? As you'll soon see, this palace is wallpapered with Titians, Tintorettos, and Veroneses. Many have the same theme you see here: a doge, in his ermine cape, gold-brocaded robe, and funny one-horned hat with earflaps, kneeling in the presence of saints, gods, or mythological figures.

• *Enter the next room.*

Room of the Four Doors (Sala delle Quattro Porte)

This was the central clearinghouse for all the goings-on in the palace. Visitors presented themselves here and were directed to their destination—the courts, councils, or doge himself.

The room was designed by Palladio, the architect who did the impressive Church of San Giorgio Maggiore, across the Grand Canal from St. Mark's Square. On the intricate stucco ceiling, notice the feet of the women dangling down below the edge (above the windows), extending the illusion.

On the wall next to the door you entered is a painting by (ho-hum) Titian, showing a **doge kneeling** with great piety before a woman embodying Faith holding the Cross of Jesus. Notice old Venice in the misty distance under the cross. This is one of many paintings you'll see of doges in uncharacteristically humble poses—paid for, of course, by the doges themselves.

G. B. Tiepolo's well-known ***Venice Receiving Neptune*** (now displayed on an easel but originally on the wall above the windows where they've put a copy;

you'll get closer to the painting as you progress through the museum) shows Venice as a woman—Venice is always a woman to artists—reclining in luxury, dressed in the ermine cape and pearl necklace of a doge's wife (dogaressa). Crude Neptune, enthralled by the First Lady's beauty, arrives bearing a seashell bulging with gold ducats. A bored Venice points and says, "Put it over there with the other stuff."

• *Enter the small room with the big fireplace and several paintings.*

Sala dell' Anticollegio

It took a big title or bribe to get in to see the doge. Once accepted for a visit, you would wait here before you entered, combing your hair, adjusting your robe, popping a breath mint, and preparing the gifts you'd brought. While you cooled your heels and warmed your hands at the elaborate fireplace, you might look at some of the paintings—among the finest in the palace, worthy of any museum in the world.

The Rape of Europa, by Paolo Veronese (on the wall opposite the fireplace), most likely shocked many small-town visitors with its risqué subject matter. Here Zeus, the king of the Greek gods, appears in the form of a bull with a foot fetish, seducing a beautiful earthling, while cupids spin playfully overhead. The Venetian Renaissance looked back to pagan Greek and Roman art, a big change from the saints and crucifixions of the Middle Ages. This painting doesn't portray the abduction as a medieval condemnation of sex and violence, but rather as a celebration in cheery pastel colors of the earthy, optimistic spirit of the Renaissance.

Tintoretto's ***Bacchus and Ariadne*** (to the left of the exit door) is another colorful display of Venice's sensual tastes. The god of wine seeks a threesome, offering a ring to the mortal Ariadne, who's being crowned with stars by Venus who turns slowly in zero gravity. The ring is the center of a spinning wheel of flesh, with the three arms like spokes.

But wait, the doge is ready for us. Let's go in.

• *Enter the next room and approach your imaginary doge.*

Sala del Collegio

Flanked by his cabinet of six advisers—one for each Venetian neighborhood—the doge would sit on the wood-paneled platform at the far end to receive ambassadors, who laid their gifts at his feet and pleaded their countries' cases. All official ceremonies, such as the ratification of treaties, were held here.

At other times, it was the "Oval Office" where the doge and his cabinet (the executive branch) met privately to discuss proposals to give the legislature, pull files from the cabinets (along the right wall) regarding business with Byzantium, or rehearse a meeting with the pope. The wooden benches around the sides (where they sat) are original. The clock on the wall is a backward-running 24-hour clock with Roman numerals and a sword for hands.

The ceiling is 24-karat gold, with paintings by Veronese. These are not frescoes (painting on wet plaster), like in the Sistine Chapel, but actual canvases painted here on the ground and then placed on the ceiling. Venice's humidity would have melted frescoes like so much mascara within years.

The T-shaped painting of the woman with the spider web (on the ceiling, opposite the big window) was the Venetian symbol of *Discussion.* You can imagine the webs of truth and lies woven in this room by the doge's nest of advisers.

In *Mars and Neptune with Campanile and Lion* (the ceiling painting near the entrance), Veronese presents four symbols of the Republic's strength—military, sea trade, city, and government (plus a cherub about to be circumcised by the Campanile).

• *Enter the large Senate Room.*

Senate Chamber *(Sala del Senato)*

While the doge presided from the stage, senators mounted the podium (middle of the wall with windows) to address their 120 colleagues. The legislators, chaired by the doge, debated and passed laws in this room.

Venice prided itself on its self-rule, independent of popes, kings, and tyrants, with most power placed in the hands of these annually-elected men. Which branch of government really ruled? All of them. It was an elaborate system of checks and balances to make sure no one rocked the boat, no one got too powerful, and the ship of state sailed smoothly ahead.

Tintoretto's large *Triumph of Venice* on the ceiling (central painting, best viewed from the top) shows the city in all its glory. Lady Venice is up in heaven with the Greek gods, while barbaric lesser nations swirl up to give her gifts and tribute. Do you get the feeling the Venetian aristocracy was proud of its city?

Executive and Legislative Rooms

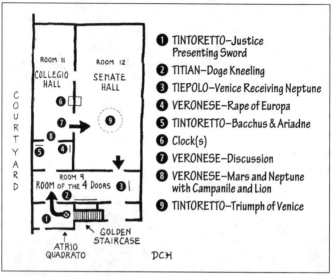

ROOM 11
COLLEGIO HALL

ROOM 12
SENATE HALL

COURTYARD

ROOM 9
ROOM OF THE 4 DOORS

GOLDEN STAIRCASE

ATRIO QUADRATO   DCH

① TINTORETTO–Justice Presenting Sword

② TITIAN–Doge Kneeling

③ TIEPOLO–Venice Receiving Neptune

④ VERONESE–Rape of Europa

⑤ TINTORETTO–Bacchus & Ariadne

⑥ Clock(s)

⑦ VERONESE–Discussion

⑧ VERONESE–Mars and Neptune with Campanile and Lion

⑨ TINTORETTO–Triumph of Venice

On the wall are two large clocks, one of which has the signs of the zodiac and phases of the moon. And there's one final oddity in this room, in case you hadn't noticed it yet. In one of the wall paintings (above the entry door), there's actually a doge...not kneeling.

• *Pass again through the Room of the Four Doors, then around the corner into the large hall with a semicircular platform at the far end.*

Hall of the Council of Ten
(Sala del Consiglio dei Dieci)

By the 1400s, Venice had a worldwide reputation for swift, harsh, and secret justice. The dreaded Council of Ten—10 judges, plus the doge and his six advisers—met here to dole out punishment to traitors, murderers, and "morals" violators. (Note the 17 wood panels where they presided.)

Slowly, they developed into a CIA-type unit with their own force of police officers, guards, spies, informers, and even assassins. They had their own budget and were accountable to no one, soon making them the de facto ruling body of the "Republic." It seemed no one was safe from the spying eye of the "Terrible Ten." You could be accused anonymously by a letter dropped into a "Mouth of

Judicial Rooms

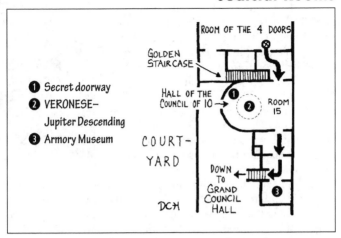

● Secret doorway
● VERONESE–
Jupiter Descending
● Armory Museum

ROOM OF THE 4 DOORS

GOLDEN STAIRCASE

HALL OF THE COUNCIL OF 10

COURT-YARD

ROOM 15

DOWN TO GRAND COUNCIL HALL

DCH

Truth," swept off the streets, tried, judged, and thrown into the dark dungeons in the palace for the rest of your life without so much as a Miranda warning.

It was in this room that the Council decided who lived, died, was decapitated, tortured, or merely thrown in jail. The small, hard-to-find door leading off the platform (the fifth panel to the right of center) leads through secret passages to the prisons and torture chambers.

The large, central, oval ceiling painting by Veronese (a copy of the original stolen by Napoleon and still in the Louvre) shows *Jupiter Descending from Heaven to Strike Down the Vices,* redundantly informing the accused that justice in Venice was swift and harsh. To the left of that, Juno showers Lady Venice with coins, crowns, and peace.

Though the dreaded Council of Ten was eventually disbanded, today their descendants enforce the dress code at St. Mark's Basilica.
• *Pass through the next room, then up the stairs to the Armory Museum.*

Armory Museum

The aesthetic of killing is beyond me, but I must admit I've never seen a better collection of halberds, falchions, ranseurs, targes, morions, and brigandines in my life. The weapons in these three rooms makes you realize the important role the military played in keeping the East–West trade lines open.

Room 1: In the glass case on the right, you'll see the suit of armor worn by the great Venetian mercenary general, Gattamelata (far right, on horseback), as well as "baby's first armor" (how soon they grow up). A full suit of armor could weigh 66 pounds. Before gunpowder, cross-bows (look up) were made still more lethal by turning a crank on the end to draw the bow with extra force.

Room 2: In the thick of battle, even horses needed a helmet. The hefty broadswords were brandished two-handed by the strongest and bravest soldiers who waded into enemy lines. Suspended from the ceiling is a large banner captured from the Turks at the Battle of Lepanto (1571).

Room 3: At the far end is a very, very early (17th-century) attempt at a 20-barrel machine gun. On the walls and weapons, the "C-X" insignia means that this was the private stash of the "Council of Ten."

Room 4: Squint out the window to see Palladio's San Giorgio Maggiore and, to the left in the distance, the tiny green dome at Venice's Lido (beach). To the right of the window, the glass case contains a tiny crossbow, some torture devices (including an effective-looking thumbscrew), the wooden "devil's box" (a clever item that could fire in four directions at once), and a nasty, two-holed chastity belt. These "iron breeches" were worn by the devoted wife of the Lord of Padua.

• *Exit the Armory Museum (enjoying a closer look at that early machine gun). Go downstairs, turn left, and pass through the long hall with a wood-beam ceiling. Now turn right and open your eyes as wide as you can...*

Hall of the Grand Council
(Sala del Maggiore Consiglio)

It took a room this size to contain the grandeur of the Most Serene Republic. This huge room (175 by 80 feet) could accommodate up to 2,600 people at one time. The doge presided from the raised dais, while the nobles, the backbone of the empire, filled the center and lined the long walls. Nobles were generally wealthy men over 25, but the title had less to do with money than with long bloodlines. In theory, the doge, the Senate, and the Council of Ten were all subordinate to the Grand Council of nobles that elected them.

On the wall over the doge's throne is Tintoretto's monsterpiece, *Paradise,* the largest oil painting in the world. At 190 square yards, it could be sliced up to wallpaper my entire apartment with enough left over for placemats.

Christ and Mary are at the top of heaven, surrounded by 500 saints

Hall of the Grand Council

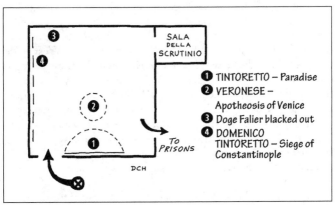

SALA
DELLA
SCRUTINIO

① TINTORETTO – Paradise

② VERONESE –
Apotheosis of Venice

③ Doge Falier blocked out

④ DOMENICO
TINTORETTO – Siege of
Constantinople

TO
PRISONS

DCH

who ripple out in concentric rings. Tintoretto worked on this in the last years of his long life. On the day it was finished, his daughter died. He got his brush out again and painted her as saint number 501. She's dead center with the blue skirt, hands clasped, getting sucked up to heaven. (At least that's what an Italian tour guide told me.)

Veronese's *The Apotheosis of Venice* (on the ceiling at the Tintoretto end; view it from the top) is a typically unsubtle work showing Lady Venice being crowned a goddess by an angel.

Ringing the hall are portraits, in chronological order, of the first 76 doges. The one at the far end that's blacked out is the notorious **Doge Marin Falier,** who opposed the will of the Grand Council in 1355. He was tried for treason, beheaded, and airbrushed from history.

Along the entire wall to the right of Paradise, **battle scenes** (by Tintoretto's son, Domenico) show Venice's greatest military—if not moral—victory, the conquest of the fellow-Christian city of Constantinople during the Fourth Crusade (1204). The mighty walls of Constantinople repelled every attack for nearly a thousand years. But the sneaky Venetians (in the *fifth painting*) circled around back

and attacked where the walls rose straight up from the water's edge. Skillful Venetian oarsmen cozied their galleys right up to the dock, allowing soldiers to scoot along crossbeams attached to the masts, to the top of the city walls. In the foreground, an archer cranks up his crossbow. The gates are opened, the Byzantine emperor parades out to surrender, and tiny Doge

Dandolo says, "Let's go in and steal some bronze horses."

But soon Venice would begin its long slide to historical oblivion. One by one the Turks gobbled up Venice's trading outposts. In the West the rest of Europe ganged up on Venice to reduce her power. By 1500, Portugal had broken Venice's East–West trade monopoly by finding a sea route to the East around Africa. To top it off, Venice suffered its greatest moral—if not military—victory in the draining Battle of Lepanto, 1571 (depicted in paintings in the adjoining Sala dello Scrutinio). Over the centuries, Venice remained a glorious city, but not the world power she once was. Finally, in 1797, the French general Napoleon marched into town shouting *"Liberté, Egalité, Fraternité."* The Most Serene Republic was finally conquered and the last doge was deposed in the name of modern democracy.

Out the windows (if they're open) is a fine view of the domes of the basilica, the palace courtyard below, and Paul Newman.

A newly elected doge was presented to the people of Venice from the balcony of the nearby Sala dello Scrutinio room that overlooks the Piazzetta. A noble would announce, "Here is your doge, if it pleases you." That was fine, until one time when the people weren't pleased. From then on they just said, "Here is your doge."

• *Consider reading about the prisons here in the Grand Council Hall, where there are more benches and fewer rats.*

Prisons

The palace had its own dungeons. In the privacy of his own home, a doge could oversee the sentencing, torturing, and jailing of political opponents. The most notorious cells were "the Wells" in the basement, so-called because they were deep, wet, and cramped.

By the 1500s, the Wells were full of political prisoners. New prisons were built across the canal to the east of the palace and connected with a covered bridge.

• *Exit the Grand Hall (squeezing through the door to the left of Tintoretto's monsterpiece) and pass through a series of rooms and once-secret passages, following signs for "Ponte dei Sospiri/Prigioni." Room 31 contains four fascinating paintings by Hieronymous Bosch (once hung in the Chamber of the Council of Ten), showing sinners tortured in hell by genetic mutants and Wizard-of-Oz monkeys. Then cross the covered Bridge of Sighs over the canal to the prisons. At the fork in the route, descend the stairs rather than continuing right into a cell or you'll miss the basement altogether and end up at the bookshop at the end of the palace visit.*

Medieval justice was harsh. The cells consisted of cold stone with heavily barred windows, a wooden plank for a bed, a shelf, and a bucket. (My question: What did they put on the shelf?) You can feel the cold dampness.

Circle the cells. Notice the carvings made by prisoners—from olden days up until 1930—on some of the stone windowsills of the cells, especially in the far corner of the building.

The Bridge of Sighs

According to romantic legend, criminals were tried and sentenced in the palace, then marched across the canal here to the dark prisons. On this bridge, they got their one last look at Venice. They gazed out at the sky, the water, and the beautiful buildings.

• *Cross back over the Bridge of Sighs, pausing to look through the marble-trellised windows at all of the tourists and the heavenly Church of San Giorgio Maggiore. Heave one last sigh and leave the palace.*

FLORENCE

As the home of the Renaissance and the birthplace of the modern world, Florence practiced the art of civilized living back when the rest of Europe was rural and crude. Democracy, science, and literature, as well as painting, sculpture, and architecture were all championed by the proud and energetic Florentines of the 1400s.

Today, Florence is geographically small but culturally rich, with more artistic masterpieces per square mile than anyplace else. Stroll the same pedestrian streets walked by Michelangelo, Leonardo, and Botticelli and climb the modern world's first dome, which still dominates the skyline. Size Michelangelo's *David* up from every angle. Study the works of Michelangelo's sculpting mentors in the Bargello. Then fall under the seductive sway of Botticelli's *Birth of Venus* at the Uffizi Gallery. Oh yes, and take a break now and then to drag your tongue slowly over the world's best gelato.

Renaissance Walk   **279**

Uffizi Gallery   **296**

Bargello   **316**

Florence Sights

RENAISSANCE WALK

From David to the Arno River

After centuries of labor, Florence gave birth to the Renaissance. We'll start with the Renaissance poster boy, Michelangelo's *David*. A short walk away are the Baptistery doors that opened the Renaissance and the dome that captured its soaring spirit. Finally, we'll reach Florence's political center, dotted with monuments of that proud time. Great and rich as this city is, it's easily covered on foot. Our walk through the top sights is less than a mile long, running from the Accademia (home of *David*), past the Duomo, and to the Arno River.

ORIENTATION

Accademia (Michelangelo's *David*): €6.50 (plus €3 reservation fee), Tue–Sun 8:15–18:50, 8:15–22:00 on holidays and maybe on summer Sat, closed Mon (last entry 45 min before closing, Via Ricasoli 60, tel. 055-238-8609). No photos or videos are allowed. The museum is most crowded on Sun, Tue, and the first thing in the morning. It's smart to reserve ahead; see page 282.

Duomo (cathedral): Free, Mon–Wed and Fri–Sat 10:00–17:00 (except first Sat of month 10:00–15:30), Thu 10:00–15:30, Sun 13:30–16:45. Tel. 055-230-2885.

Climbing the **dome** costs €6 (Mon–Fri 8:30–19:00, Sat 8:30–17:40 except first Sat of month 8:30–16:00, closed Sun; enter from outside church on south or river side, arrive by 8:30 to avoid a long wait in line).

Giotto's Tower: €6, daily 8:30–19:30, last entry 40 min before closing.

Baptistery: €3, interior open Mon–Sat 12:00–19:00, Sun 8:30–14:00. The famous bronze doors are on the outside so they're always "open" (viewable) and free. The original panels are in the Duomo Museum.

Getting There: The Accademia is a 15-minute walk from the train station or a 10-minute walk from the cathedral (head northeast on Via Ricasoli). Taxis are reasonable.

Information: The nearest TI is on Via Cavour, two blocks from the Accademia (pick up update of current museum hours). Two fine bookshops are across the street from the Accademia. WCs are in the Accademia basement and in cafés along the walk.

Length of This Tour: Three hours.

Photography: Photos are prohibited in the Accademia. In churches and other museums, photos without a flash are generally OK.

Cuisine Art: You'll find cafés, self-service cafeterias, bars, and gelato shops along the route. Many good eateries along this route are described in the Eating chapter.

Starring: Michelangelo, Brunelleschi, and Ghiberti.

THE TOUR BEGINS

The Duomo, the cathedral with the distinctive red dome, is the center of Florence and the orientation point for this walk. If you ever get lost, home's the dome.

We'll start at the Accademia (2.5 long blocks north of the Duomo), though you could easily start at the Duomo and visit the Accademia later.

• *Head to the Accademia. If there's a line, as you shuffle your way along, notice the perspective tricks on the walls of the ticket room.*

The Florentine Renaissance (1400–1550)

In the 13th and 14th centuries, Florence was a powerful center of banking, trading, and textile manufacturing. The resulting wealth fertilized the cultural soil. Then came the Black Plague in 1348. Nearly half of the population died, but the infrastructure remained strong, and the city rebuilt stronger than ever. Led by Florence's chief family, the art-crazy Medicis, and with the natural aggressive and creative spirit of the Florentines, it's no wonder the long-awaited Renaissance finally took root here.

The Renaissance—the "rebirth" of Greek and Roman culture that swept across Europe—started around 1400 and lasted about 150 years. In politics, the Renaissance meant democracy. In science, a renewed interest in exploring nature. The general mood was optimistic and "humanistic," with a confidence in the power of the individual.

Renaissance Walk Overview

In medieval times, poverty and ignorance had made life "nasty, brutish, and short" (for lack of a better cliché). The church was the people's opiate, and their lives were only a preparation for a happier time in heaven after leaving this miserable vale of tears.

Medieval art was the church's servant. The noblest art form was architecture—churches themselves—and other arts were considered most worthwhile if they embellished the house of God. Painting and sculpture were narrative and symbolic, to tell Bible stories to the devout and illiterate masses.

Make Reservations to Avoid Lines

Florence has a reservation system for its top five sights—Uffizi, Accademia, Bargello, Medici Chapels, and the Pitti Palace. Two of these sights always have long lines: the Accademia (Michelangelo's *David*) and the Uffizi (Renaissance paintings). To avoid long waits—up to two hours at the Uffizi—reserve by phone. Frankly, it's stupid not to.

While you can generally make a reservation a day in advance (upon arrival in Florence), you'll have a wider selection of entry times by calling a few days ahead. You dial 055-294-883 (busy signals common—be persistent, Mon–Fri 8:30–18:30, Sat 8:30–12:30, closed Sun), an English-speaking operator walks you through the process, and two minutes later you say *"grazie,"* with appointments (15-min entry window) and six-digit confirmation numbers for each of the top museums and galleries. The ticket phone number is often busy. If you call months in advance (during off-season) or request your hotel to make the appointment for you (when you confirm your hotel booking), you may save some frustration. Some booking agencies offer reservations online for a fee (such as www.weekendafirenze.it).

If you haven't booked ahead, you can make reservations for the top sights at the minor, less-crowded sights (such as the Museum of San Marco or Museum of Precious Stones). Clerks at the ticket booths at these sleepy sights can reserve and sell tickets to the major sights, often for admission the same day, allowing you to skip right past the dreary mob scene.

There is occasionally even a line at the Uffizi for those with reservations who are waiting to pick up tickets. If you have reservations, consider picking up your Uffizi ticket at a less-crowded sight (any ticket office can issue reserved tickets).

As prosperity rose in Florence, so did people's confidence in life and themselves. Middle-class craftsmen, merchants, and bankers felt they could control their own destinies, rather than being at the whim of nature. They found much in common with the ancient Greeks and Romans, who valued logic and reason above superstition and blind faith.

Renaissance art was a return to the realism and balance of Greek and Roman sculpture and architecture. Domes and round arches replaced Gothic spires and pointed arches. In painting and sculpture, Renaissance artists strove for realism. Merging art and science, they used mathematics, the laws of perspective, and direct observation of nature to paint the world on a flat surface.

This was not an anti-Christian movement, though it was a logical and scientific age. Artists saw themselves as an extension of God's creative powers. At times, the church even supported the

Renaissance and commissioned many of its greatest works. Raphael frescoed Plato and Aristotle on the walls of the Vatican. But for the first time in Europe since Roman times, we also find rich laymen who wanted art simply for art's sake.

After 1,000 years of waiting, the smoldering fires of Europe's classical heritage burst into flame in Florence.

The Accademia—Michelangelo's *David*

Start with the ultimate. When you look into the eyes of Michelangelo's *David,* you're looking into the eyes of Renaissance Man. This 14-foot-tall symbol of divine victory over evil represents a new century and a whole new Renaissance outlook. This is the age of Columbus and classicism, Galileo and Gutenberg, Luther and Leonardo—of Florence and the Renaissance.

In 1501 Michelangelo Buonarotti, age 26, a Florentine, was commissioned to carve a large-scale work for the Duomo. He was given a block of marble that other sculptors had rejected as too tall, shallow, and flawed to be of any value. But Michelangelo picked up his hammer and chisel, knocked a knot off what became *David*'s heart, and started to work.

The figure comes from a Bible story. The Israelites, God's chosen people, are surrounded by barbarian warriors led by a brutish giant named Goliath. The giant challenges the Israelites to send out someone to fight him. Everyone is afraid except one young shepherd boy—David. Armed only with a sling, which he throws over his shoulder, David cradles some stones in his other hand and heads out to face Goliath.

The statue captures David as he's sizing up his enemy. He stands relaxed but alert, leaning on one leg in a classical pose. In his powerful right hand, he fondles the stones he'll fling at the giant. His gaze is steady—searching with intense concentration, but also with extreme confidence. Michelangelo has caught the precise moment when David is saying to himself, "I can take this guy."

David is a symbol of Renaissance optimism. He's no brute but a civilized, thinking individual who can grapple with and overcome problems. He needs no armor, only his God-given body and wits. Look at his right hand, with the raised veins and strong, relaxed fingers. Many complained that it was too big and overdeveloped. But this is the hand of a man with the strength of God. No mere boy

More Michelangelo

If you're a fan of Earth's greatest sculptor, you won't leave Florence until there's a check next to each of these:
- Bargello Museum: several Michelangelo sculptures (see Bargello Tour on page 316).
- Duomo Museum: another moving Pietà.
- Medici Chapels: The Night and Day statues, plus others done for the Medici tomb (located at Church of San Lorenzo).
- Palazzo Vecchio: his "Victory" statue.
- Laurentian Library: Michelangelo designed the entrance staircase (located at Church of San Lorenzo).
- Uffizi: A rare Michelangelo painting (see Uffizi Gallery Tour on page 296).
- Michelangelo's House (Casa Buonarroti): A house on property Michelangelo once owned, at Via Ghibellina 70, containing some early works.
- Church of Santa Croce: Michelangelo's tomb.

could slay the giant. But David, powered by God, could...and did.

Originally, the statue was commissioned to go on top of the Duomo, but the people loved it so much they put it next to the Palazzo Vecchio on the main square, where a copy stands today. (If the relationship between the head and body seems a bit out of proportion, it's because Michelangelo designed it to be seen "correctly" from far below the rooftop of the church.) Note the crack in *David*'s left arm where it was broken off during a riot near the Palazzo Vecchio.

Florentines could identify with David. Like him, they considered themselves God-blessed underdogs fighting their city-state rivals. In a deeper sense, they were civilized Renaissance people slaying the ugly giant of medieval superstition, pessimism, and oppression.

• *Hang around a while. Eavesdrop on tour guides.* David *stands under a wonderful Renaissance-style dome. Lining the hall leading up to* David *are other statues by Michelangelo—his* Prisoners (Prigioni), St. Matthew, *and a* Pietà.

Prisoners

These unfinished figures seem to be fighting to free themselves from the stone. Michelangelo believed the sculptor was a tool of God, not creating but simply revealing the powerful and beautiful figures He put in the marble. Michelangelo's job was to chip away the excess, to reveal. He needed to be in tune with God's will, and whenever the spirit came upon him, Michelangelo worked in a frenzy, often for days on end without sleep.

The *Prisoners* give us a glimpse of this fitful process, showing the restless energy of someone possessed, struggling against the rock that binds him. Michelangelo was known to shout at his figures in frustration: "Speak!" You can still see the grooves from the chisel, and you can picture Michelangelo hacking away in a cloud of dust. Unlike most sculptors, who built a model and then marked up their block of marble to know where to chip, Michelangelo always worked freehand, starting from the front and working back. These figures emerge from the stone (as his colleague Vasari put it) "as though surfacing from a pool of water."

The *Prisoners* were designed for the never-completed tomb of Pope Julius II (who also commissioned the Sistine Chapel ceiling). Michelangelo may have abandoned them simply because the project itself petered out, but he may have deliberately left them unfinished. Having satisfied himself that he'd accomplished what he set out to do, and seeing no point in polishing them into their shiny, finished state, he went on to a new project.

As you study the *Prisoners,* notice Michelangelo's love and understanding of the human body. His greatest days were spent sketching the muscular, tanned, and sweating bodies of the workers in the Carrara marble quarries. Here, the prisoners' heads and faces are the least-developed part—they "speak" with their poses. Comparing these restless, claustrophobic *Prisoners* with the serene and confident *David* gives an idea of the sheer emotional range in Michelangelo's work.

Pietà (by Michelangelo or, more likely, by his followers)

In the unfinished *Pietà* (the threesome closest to *David*), they struggle to hold up the sagging body of Christ. Michelangelo emphasizes the heaviness of Jesus' dead body, driving home the point that this divine being suffered a very human death. Christ's massive arm is almost the size of his bent and broken legs. By stretching his body—if he stood up he'd be over seven feet tall—its weight is exaggerated.

• *Leaving the Accademia (possibly after a look at its paintings, including two Botticellis), turn left and walk toward the Duomo down Via Ricasoli. About halfway to the big church, turn right on Via dei Pucci. Directly ahead is the bustling San Lorenzo street market. Just before that (on the first corner) is the imposing Medici-Riccardi Palace.*

Medici Riccardi Palace

Renaissance Florence was ruled by the rich banking family, the Medici, who lived here. Studying this grand Florentine palace you'll notice fortified lower walls and elegance limited to the fancy upper stories. The Medici family may have been the local Rockefellers, but having self-made wealth rather than actual noble blood, they were always a bit defensive. The Greek motifs along the eaves highlight the palace's Renaissance roots. Back then, rather than having parking spots, grand buildings came with iron rings to tether your horse.

Teenage Michelangelo lived here, studying ancient sculpture from Lorenzo the Magnificent's collection. Later, he designed the so-called "kneeling windows" (windows flanked by scrolls), a style that turned up on buildings around the world.

The interior shows off a quintessential Florentine palazzo with a courtyard and a couple of impressive rooms, most notably the sumptuous little Chapel of the Magi (€4 palace entry, Thu–Tue 9:00–19:00, closed Wed). If your time is limited, save your energy for the biggies.

• *From the palace, head for the Duomo, down Via Martelli, with a possible detour to explore the San Lorenzo street market and, perhaps, the neighboring Medici Chapels (€6, daily 8:15–17:00 but closed the second and fourth Sun and the first, third, and fifth Mon of each month). The dome of the Duomo is best viewed just to the right of the facade on the corner of the pedestrian-only street.*

The Duomo—Florence's Cathedral

The dome of Florence's cathedral—visible from all over the city—inspired Florentines to do great things. The big but unremarkable church itself (nicknamed the Duomo) is Gothic, built in the Middle Ages by architects who left it unfinished.

Think of the confidence of the age: The Duomo was built with a big hole in its roof awaiting a dome. This was before the technology to span it with a dome was available. *No problema.* They knew that someone soon could handle the challenge. In the 1400s the architect Brunelleschi was called on to finish the job. Brunelleschi capped the church Roman-style—with a tall, self-supporting dome as grand as the ancient Pantheon, which he had studied.

He used a dome within a dome. First, he built the grand white skeletal ribs, which you can see, then filled them in with interlocking bricks in a herring-bone pattern. The dome grew upward igloo-style, supporting itself as it proceeded from the base. When they reached the top, Brunelleschi arched the ribs in and fixed them in place with

The Duomo

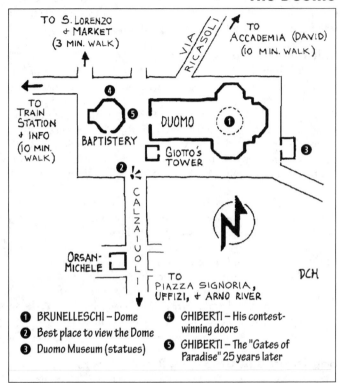

① BRUNELLESCHI – Dome	**④** GHIBERTI – His contest-winning doors
② Best place to view the Dome	**⑤** GHIBERTI – The "Gates of Paradise" 25 years later
③ Duomo Museum (statues)	

Map labels: TO S. LORENZO & MARKET (3 MIN. WALK); VIA RICASOLI; TO ACCADEMIA (DAVID) (10 MIN. WALK); TO TRAIN STATION & INFO (10 MIN. WALK); BAPTISTERY; DUOMO; GIOTTO'S TOWER; CALZAIUOLI; ORSAN-MICHELE; TO PIAZZA SIGNORIA, UFFIZI, & ARNO RIVER; DCH

the lantern. His dome, built in only 14 years, was the largest since Rome's Pantheon.

Brunelleschi's dome was the wonder of the age, the model for many domes to follow, from St. Peter's to the U.S. Capitol. People gave it the ultimate compliment, saying "not even the ancients could have done it." Michelangelo, setting out to construct the dome of St. Peter's, drew inspiration from the dome of Florence. He said, "I'll make its sister...bigger, but not more beautiful."

The church's facade looks old, but is actually neo-Gothic—only from 1870. Its "retro" look captures the feel of the original medieval

facade—green, white, and pink marble sheets that cover the brick construction; Gothic (pointed) arches; and three horizontal stories decorated with mosaics and statues. Still, the facade is generally ridiculed. (While one of this book's authors thinks it's the most beautiful church facade this side of heaven, the other one naively agrees with those who call it "the cathedral in pajamas.") The inside of the church is worth a walk only for its coolness and a look at how bare the terrible flood of 1966 left it.

Bell Tower ("Giotto's Tower")

You can climb the dome, but the bell tower (to the right of the facade) is easier, less crowded, and faster, and it rewards you with a view of the dome. Giotto, like any good Renaissance genius, wore several artistic hats. Considered the father of modern painting, he designed this 270-foot-tall bell tower for the Duomo two centuries before the age of Michelangelo. In his day, Giotto was called the ugliest man to ever walk the streets of Florence, but he left the city what, in our day, many call the most beautiful bell tower in all of Europe.

The bell tower served as a sculpture gallery for Renaissance artists—notice Donatello's four prophets on the side that faces out (west side). These are copies, but the originals are at the wonderful Duomo Museum, just behind the church. In the museum you'll also get a close-up look at Brunelleschi's wooden model of his dome, Ghiberti's doors (described below), and a late *Pietà* by Michelangelo.

• *The Baptistery is the small octagonal building in front of the church.*

Baptistery and Ghiberti's Bronze Doors

Florence's Baptistery is dear to the soul of the city. The locals, eager to link themselves to the classical past, believed (wrongly) that this was a Roman building. It *is* Florence's oldest building (11th century). Most festivals and parades either started or ended here. Go inside (for a modest €3 fee) for a fine example of pre-Renaissance mosaic art (1200s–1300s) in the Byzantine style.

The Last Judgment on the ceiling gives us a glimpse of the medieval worldview. Life was a preparation for the afterlife, when you would be judged good or bad, black or white, with no in-between. Christ, peaceful and reassuring, would bless you with heaven (on His right hand) or send you to hell (below Christ's double-jointed left hand, at the base of the ceiling) to be tortured by demons and gnashed between the teeth of monsters. This hellish scene looks like something right out of the *Inferno* by Dante...who was dipped into the baptismal waters right here.

The Baptistery's bronze doors bring us out of the Middle Ages and into the Renaissance. Florence had great civic spirit, with different guilds and merchant groups embellishing their city with great art. The city staged a competition in 1401 for the commission of the Baptistery's north doors (on the right side as you face the Baptistery with the Duomo at your back). All the greats entered, and 25-year-old Lorenzo Ghiberti won easily, beating out heavyweights such as Brunelleschi (who, having lost the Baptistery gig, was free to go to

Rome, study the Pantheon, and later design the Duomo's dome). The original entries of Brunelleschi and Ghiberti are in the Bargello, where you can judge them for yourself.

Later, in 1425, Ghiberti was given another commission, for the east doors (facing the church), and this time there was literally no contest. The bronze panels of these doors (the ones with the crowd of tourists looking on) added a whole new dimension to art—depth. Michelangelo said these doors were fit to be the gates of Paradise. (These panels are copies. The originals are in the nearby Duomo Museum.) Here we see how the Renaissance was a merging of art and science. Realism was in, and Renaissance artists used math, illusion, and dissection to get it.

In the "Jacob and Esau" panel (just above eye level on the left), receding arches, floor tiles, and banisters create a background for a realistic scene. The figures in the foreground stand and move like real people, telling the Bible story with human details. Amazingly, this spacious, three-dimensional scene is made from bronze only a few inches deep.

Ghiberti spent 27 years (1425–1452) working on these panels. That's him in the center of the door frame, atop the second row of panels—the head on the left with the shiny male-pattern baldness.

• *Facing the Duomo, turn right onto the pedestrian-only street that runs south from here toward the Arno River.*

Via dei Calzaiuoli

The pedestrian-only Via dei Calzaiuoli (kahlts-ay-WOH-lee) was part of the ancient Roman grid plan that became Florence. Throughout the city's history, this street has connected the religious center (where we are now) with the political center (where we're heading), a five-minute walk away. In the last decade, traffic jams have been replaced by potted plants, and this is a pleasant place to stroll, people-watch, window-shop, catch the drips on your gelato cone, and wonder why American cities can't become pedestrian-friendly.

Two blocks down, look right on Via degli Speziali to see a triumphal arch celebrating the unification of Italy. In ancient Roman times, the Piazza della Repubblica, where the arch stands, was the city center.

If you're in the mood for some of the world's best edible art, you're in the right place. Drop by one of several nearby ice-cream parlors for a cup of gelato. *Perchè no?* (Why not?) *Gelati* tips: *Artiginale, Nostra Produzione,* and *Produzione Propia* mean gelato is made on the premises. Also, gelato displayed in metal tins, rather than the normal white plastic, indicates it's likely to be homemade. A simple cone or cup will do; avoid fancy, rip-off €10 "tourist specials." Look at the price list, which usually shows pictures of scoops (one, two, or three) followed by the pertinent price.

Orsanmichele Church—Florence's Medieval Roots

The Orsanmichele Church (at the intersection with Via dei Tavolini) provides an interesting look at Florentine values. It's a combo church/granary. Originally this was an open loggia (covered porch) with a huge warehouse upstairs to store grain to feed the city during sieges. The arches of the loggia were artfully filled in (14th century) and the building gained a new purpose—as a church.

Circle the church. Each niche was filled with an important statue. In earlier Gothic times, statues were set deeply in the niches, simply embellishing the house of God. Here we see statues (as restless as man on the verge of the Renaissance) stepping out from the protection of the church.

Donatello's *St. George* (at northwest corner of church) is alert, perched on the edge of his niche, scanning the horizon for dragons, and announcing the new age with its new outlook. (The original statue is in the Bargello.) Compare this Renaissance-style *St. George* with Nanni's smaller-scale, deeply set, and less sophisticated *Four Saints* statue to its left.

Below some of the niches, you'll find the symbols of the various guilds and groups that paid for the art. The relief below the *Four Saints* is a good example. Art historians differ here. It was commissioned either by the guys who do the discount circumcisions or by the carpenters' and masons' guild.

Orsanmichele Church

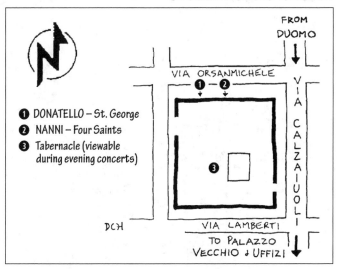

FROM DUOMO

VIA ORSANMICHELE

❶ — ❷

VIA CALZAIUOLI

❶ DONATELLO – St. George
❷ NANNI – Four Saints
❸ Tabernacle (viewable
   during evening concerts)

❸

DCH

VIA LAMBERTI

TO PALAZZO
VECCHIO ♩ UFFIZI

The entrance to the church is around back, one short block off Via del Calzaiuoli. Step inside and find the pillars with spouts in them (three feet off the ground) for delivering grain from the storage rooms upstairs. Stand before the Gothic tabernacle. Notice its medieval elegance, color, and disinterest in depth and realism. This is a wonderfully medieval scene—Florence in 1350. Remember the candlelit medieval atmosphere that surrounds this altarpiece as you view similar altarpieces out of context in the Uffizi Gallery.

• *Florence's best collection of sculpture, the Bargello (see page 316), is a few blocks east down Via del Tavolini. But let's continue down the mall 50 more yards, to the huge and historic square.*

Palazzo Vecchio—Florence's Political Center

The main civic center of Florence is dominated by the Palazzo Vecchio, the Uffizi Gallery, and the marble greatness of old Florence littering the cobbles. The square still vibrates with the echoes of Florence's past—executions, riots, and great celebrations. There's even Roman history—look for the chart showing the ancient city (on a waist-high, freestanding display to your right as you enter the square). Today, it's a tourist's world with pigeons, postcards, horse buggies, and tired hubbies. (And, if it would make your tired hubby happy, the ritzy Café Revoire—with the best view seats in town—is famous for its fancy desserts and hot chocolate.)

Before you towers the Palazzo Vecchio, the Medicis' palatial city hall—a fortress designed to contain riches and survive the many riots that went with local politics. The windows are just beyond the

Sights near Piazza della Signoria

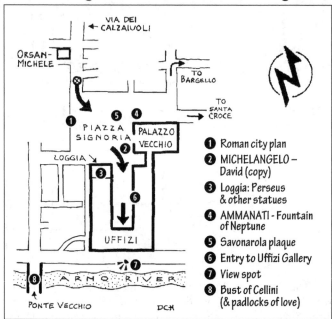

- **1** Roman city plan
- **2** MICHELANGELO – David (copy)
- **3** Loggia: Perseus & other statues
- **4** AMMANATI - Fountain of Neptune
- **5** Savonarola plaque
- **6** Entry to Uffizi Gallery
- **7** View spot
- **8** Bust of Cellini (& padlocks of love)

reach of angry stones, the tower was a handy lookout post, and justice was doled out sternly on this square. Michelangelo's *David* once stood (until 1873) where the replica stands today. The original *David,* damaged in a riot (when a bench thrown out of a palace window knocked its left arm off), was moved indoors for its protection.

While the palace interior is not worth touring on a short visit, be sure to step past the replica David through the front door into the Palazzo Vecchio's courtyard (free). This palace was Florence's civic center. You're surrounded by art for art's sake—a statue frivolously marking the courtyard's center, and ornate walls and columns. Such luxury was a big change 500 years ago. The squiggly, ornate wall painting is called *Grotteschi* (grotesques), inspired by the art that decorated the walls of ancient Roman villas being excavated at the time (c. 1500, named for "grotto" because the ancient villas were actually well below 15th-century Roman street level).

· *Back outside, check out the statue-filled loggia.*

The loggia, once a forum for public debate, was perfect for a city that prided itself on its democratic traditions. But later, when the Medicis figured good art was more desirable than free speech, it was turned into an outdoor sculpture gallery. Notice the squirming Florentine themes—conquest, dominance, rapes, and severed heads. The statues lining the back are Roman originals brought back to Florence by a Medici when he moved home after living in Rome. Two statues in the front deserve a closer look.

Benvenuto Cellini's *Perseus,* the Loggia's most noteworthy piece, shows the Greek hero who decapitated the snake-headed Medusa. They say Medusa was so ugly she turned humans who looked at her to stone—though one of this book's authors thinks she's kinda cute.

The Rape of the Sabines, with its a pulse-quickening rhythm of muscles, is Mannerist, from the restless period following the stately and confident Renaissance (c. 1560). The sculptor, Giambologna, proved his mastery of the medium by sculpting three entangled bodies from one piece of marble. The composition is best viewed from below in front. The relief panel below shows a wider view of the terrible scene. Note what looks like an IV tube on the arm of the horrified husband. It's an electrified wire that effectively keeps the pigeons away.

• *Cross the square to the big fountain of Neptune by Ammanati that Florentines (including Michelangelo) consider a huge waste of marble— though one of this book's authors…. Find the round bronze plaque in the cobbles 10 steps in front of the fountain.*

Savonarola

The Medici family was briefly thrown from power by an austere monk named Savonarola, who made Florence a constitutional republic. He organized huge rallies lit by roaring bonfires here on the square where he preached. While children sang hymns, the devout brought their rich "vanities" (such as paintings, musical instruments, and playing cards) and threw them into the flames.

But not everyone wanted a return to the medieval past. Encouraged by the pope, the Florentines fought back, and arrested Savonarola. For two days, they tortured him, trying unsuccessfully to persuade him to see their side of things. Finally, on the very spot where Savonarola's followers had built bonfires of vanities, the monk was burned. The bronze plaque, engraved in Italian ("*Qui dove…*"), reads: "Here, Girolamo Savonarola and his Dominican brothers were hanged and burned" in the year "MCCCCXCVIII" (1498).

• *Stay cool, we have 100 yards to go. Follow the gaze of the fake David into the courtyard of the two-toned horseshoe-shaped building…*

Uffizi Courtyard—The Renaissance Hall of Fame

The top floor of this building, known as the *uffizi* ("offices") during Medici days, is filled with the greatest collection of Florentine painting anywhere. It's one of Europe's top four or five galleries (see next chapter).

The Uffizi courtyard, filled with merchants and hustling young artists, is watched over by statues of the great figures of the Renaissance. Tourists zero in on the visual accomplishments of the Renaissance—not realizing that it was many-faceted. Let's pay tribute to the nonvisual Renaissance as well as we wander through Florence's Hall of Fame.

• *Stroll down the left side of the courtyard from Palazzo Vecchio to the river, noticing...*

1. **Lorenzo the Magnificent** was a great art patron and cunning power broker. Excelling in everything except modesty, he set the tone for the Renaissance.

2. **Giotto,** an architect (he holds the plan to the city's great bell tower—named for him), was the first great modern painter.

3. **Donatello,** the sculptor who served as a role model for Michelangelo, holds a hammer and chisel.

4. **Leonardo da Vinci** was a scientist, sculptor, musician, engineer...and not a bad painter either.

5. **Michelangelo** ponders the universe and/or stifles a belch.

6. **Dante,** with the laurel-leaf crown and lyre of a poet, says, "I am the father of the Italian language." He was the first Italian to write a popular work *(The Divine Comedy)* in non-Latin, using the Florentine dialect, which soon became "Italian" throughout the country.

7. The poet **Petrarch** wears laurel leaves from Greece, a robe from Rome, and a belt from Wal-Mart.

8. **Boccaccio** wrote *The Decameron,* stories told to pass the time during the 1348 Black Plague.

9. The devious-looking **Machiavelli** is hatching a plot—his book *The Prince* taught that the end justifies the means and paved the way for the slick and cunning "Machiavellian" politics of today.

10. **Amerigo Vespucci** (in the corner) was an explorer who gave his name to a fledgling New World.

11. **Galileo Galilei** (in the other corner) holds the humble telescope he used to spot the moons of Jupiter.

• *Finish our walk at the Arno River, overlooking the Ponte Vecchio.*

Ponte Vecchio

Before you is the Ponte Vecchio (Old Bridge). A bridge has spanned this narrowest part of the Arno since Roman times. While Rome "fell," Florence really didn't and remained a bustling trade center along the Arno. To get into the exclusive little park below, you'll need to join the Florence rowing club.

• *Finish by hiking to the center of the bridge.*

A fine bust of the great goldsmith, Cellini, graces the central point of the bridge. This statue is a reminder that, in the 1500s, the Medicis booted out the bridge's butchers and tanners and installed the gold- and silversmiths who still tempt visitors to this day. This is a very romantic spot late at night. In fact, hanging over the edge of the bridge (on either side of the Cellini bust) are piles of padlocks. Guys demonstrate the enduring quality of their love by ceremonially taking their girls here, locking a lock, and throwing the key into the Arno. (But what's with the combination lock?)

Notice the Medicis' protected and elevated passageway that led from the Palazzo Vecchio through the Uffizi, across the Ponte Vecchio, and up to the immense Pitti Palace, four blocks beyond the bridge.

During World War II, the local German commander was instructed to blow the bridge up. But even some Nazis appreciate history—he blew up the buildings at either end, leaving the bridge impassable but intact. *Grazie.*

UFFIZI GALLERY

(Galleria degli Uffizi)

In the Renaissance, Florentine artists rediscovered the beauty of the natural world. Medieval art had been symbolic, telling Bible stories. Realism didn't matter. But Renaissance people saw the beauty of God in nature and the human body. They used math and science to capture the natural world on canvas as realistically as possible.

The Uffizi Gallery (oo-FEEDZ-ee) has the greatest overall collection anywhere of Italian painting. We'll trace the rise of realism and savor the optimistic spirit that marked the Renaissance.

> *My eyes love things that are fair,*
> *and my soul for salvation cries.*
> *But neither will to Heaven rise*
> *unless the sight of Beauty lifts them there.*
> —Michelangelo

ORIENTATION

Cost: €9.50, plus €3 for optional but recommended reservation fee.

Hours: Tue–Sun 8:15–18:50, 8:15–22:00 on holidays and maybe summer Sat (last entry 45 min before closing), closed Mon.

Reservations: Avoid the two-hour peak-season midday wait by reserving ahead (see page 282). After you've booked your reservation, go to the Uffizi at your appointed time. Walk briskly past the 200-yard-long line—pondering the IQ of this gang—

Uffizi Gallery Overview

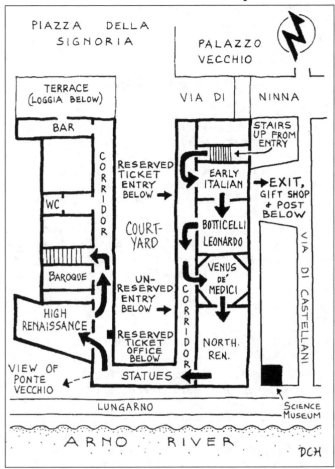

PIAZZA DELLA SIGNORIA

PALAZZO VECCHIO

TERRACE (LOGGIA BELOW)

BAR

VIA DI   NINNA

STAIRS UP FROM ENTRY

CORRIDOR

RESERVED TICKET ENTRY BELOW ➤

EARLY ITALIAN

➤EXIT, GIFT SHOP + POST BELOW

WC

COURT-YARD

BOTTICELLI LEONARDO

BAROQUE

VENUS DE' MEDICI

HIGH RENAISSANCE

UN-RESERVED ENTRY BELOW ➤

CORRIDOR

RESERVED TICKET OFFICE BELOW

NORTH. REN.

VIA DI CASTELLANI

VIEW OF PONTE VECCHIO ←

STATUES

LUNGARNO

SCIENCE MUSEUM

· A R N O   R I V E R ·

DCH

to the special entrance for those with reservations (labeled in English "Entrance for Reservations Only"), give your number, pay (cash only), and scoot right in.

Getting There: It's on the Arno River between Palazzo Vecchio and Ponte Vecchio, a 15-minute walk from the train station.

Information: You can buy cheap Uffizi guidebooks from street vendors. The Uffizi (www.arca.net/uffizi/) has a gift shop on the ground floor. The only WC is on the top floor, near the snack bar.

Length of This Tour: Two hours.

Cloakroom: At the start, far from the finish.

Photography: Cameras not allowed.

Cuisine Art: The simple café at the end of the gallery has salads, desserts, fruit cups, and a terrace with a Duomo/Palazzo Vecchio view. A cappuccino here is one of Europe's great $2 treats.

Starring: Botticelli, Venus, Raphael, Giotto, Titian, Leonardo, and Michelangelo.

THE TOUR BEGINS

The Ascent

• *Buy your ticket, then walk up the four long flights of the monumental staircase to the top floor. Your brain should be fully aerated from the hike up. Past the ticket-taker, look out the window.*

The U-ffizi is U-shaped, running around the courtyard. The entire collection is on this one floor, displayed chronologically. This left wing contains Florentine painting from medieval to Renaissance times. The right wing (which you can see across the courtyard) has art from the Roman and Venetian High Renaissance, works from the Baroque that followed, and a café terrace facing the Duomo. Connecting the two wings is a short corridor with sculpture. We'll concentrate on the Uffizi's forte, the Florentine section, then get a taste of the art it inspired.

• *Down the hall, enter the first door on the left and face Giotto's giant* Madonna and Child.

Medieval—When Art Was As Flat As The World (1200–1400)

Giotto (c. 1266–1337)—*Madonna and Child* (*Madonna col Bambino Gesu, Santi e Angeli*)

Mary and baby Jesus sit on a throne in a golden never-never land symbolizing heaven. It's as if medieval Christians couldn't imagine holy people inhabiting our dreary material world. It took Renaissance painters to bring Mary down to earth and give her human realism. For the Florentines, "realism" meant "three-dimen-

sional." In this room, pre-Renaissance paintings show the slow process of learning to paint a 3-D world on a 2-D surface.

Before concentrating on the Giotto, look at some others in the room. The **crucifixion** (on your right as you face the Giotto) was medieval 3-D—paint a crude two-dimensional work...then physically tilt the head forward. Nice try.

The three similar-looking Madonna-and-Bambinos in this room—all painted within a few decades of each other around the year 1300—show small baby steps in the march to realism. Duccio's (on the left as you face Giotto)

Giotto and Medieval Art

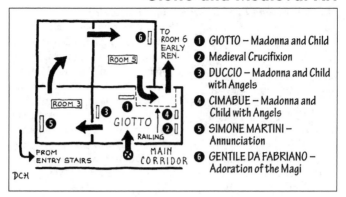

GIOTTO – Madonna and Child
Medieval Crucifixion
DUCCIO – Madonna and Child with Angels
CIMABUE – Madonna and Child with Angels
SIMONE MARTINI – Annunciation
GENTILE DA FABRIANO – Adoration of the Magi

is the most medieval and two-dimensional. There's no background. The angels are just stacked one on top of the other, floating in the golden atmosphere. Mary's throne is crudely drawn—the left side is at a three-quarters angle while the right is practically straight on. Mary herself is a wispy cardboard-cutout figure seemingly floating just above the throne.

On the opposite wall, **Cimabue**'s is an improvement. The large throne creates an illusion of depth. Mary's foot actually sticks out over the lip of the throne. Still, the angels are stacked like sardines, serving as a pair of heavenly bookends.

Giotto (JOT-oh) creates a space and fills it. Like a set designer, he builds a three-dimensional "stage"—the canopied throne—then peoples it with real beings. The throne has angels in front, prophets behind, and a canopy over the top, clearly defining the throne's three dimensions. The steps leading up to it lead from our space to Mary's, making the scene an extension of our world. But the real triumph here is Mary herself—big and monumental, like a Roman statue. Beneath her robe, she has a real live body—her knees and breasts stick out at us. This three-dimensionality was revolutionary in its day, a taste of the Renaissance a century before it began.

Giotto was one of the first "famous" artists. In the Middle Ages, artists were mostly unglamorous craftsmen, like carpenters or cable-TV repairmen. They cranked out generic art and could have signed their work with a bar code. But Giotto was recognized as a genius, a unique individual. He died in a plague that devastated Florence. If there had been no plague, would the Renaissance have started 100 years earlier?

• *Enter Room 3, to the left of Giotto.*

Simone Martini (c. 1285–1344)—*Annunciation (Annunciazione con i Santi Ansano e Giulitta)*

Simone Martini boils things down to the basic figures needed to get the message across: (1) The angel appears to sternly tell (2) Mary that she'll be the mother of Jesus. In the center is (3) a vase of lilies, a symbol of purity. Above is the (4) Holy Spirit as a dove about to descend on her. If the symbols aren't enough to get the message across, Simone Martini has spelled it right out for us in Latin: "*Ave Gratia Plena...*Hail, favored one, the Lord is with you." Mary doesn't look exactly pleased as punch.

This is not a three-dimensional work. The point was not to recreate reality but to teach religion, especially to the illiterate masses. This isn't a beautiful Mary or even a real Mary. She's a generic woman without distinctive features. We know she's pure—not from her face but only because of the halo and symbolic flowers. Before the Renaissance, artists didn't care about the beauty of individual people.

Simone Martini's *Annunciation* has medieval features you'll see in many of the paintings in the next few rooms: (1) religious subject, (2) gold background, (3) two-dimensionality, and (4) meticulous detail.
• *Pass through Room 4, full of golden altarpieces, stopping at the far end of Room 5.*

Gentile da Fabriano (c. 1370–1427)—*Adoration of the Magi (Adorazione dei Magi)*

Look at the incredible detail of the Three Kings' costumes, the fine horses, and the cow in the cave. The canvas is filled from top to bottom with realistic details—but it's far from realistic. While the Magi worship Jesus in the foreground, their return trip home dangles over their heads in the "background."

This is a textbook example of the International Gothic style popular with Europe's aristocrats in the early 1400s: well-dressed, elegant people in a colorful, design-oriented setting. The religious subject is just an excuse to paint secular luxuries like brocade-pattern clothes and jewelry. And the scene's background and foreground are compressed together to create an overall design that's pleasing to the eye.

Such exquisite detail work raises the question: Was Renaissance three-dimensionality truly an improvement over Gothic, or simply a different style?

• *Exit to your right and hang a U-turn left into Room 6.*

Early Renaissance (Mid-1400s)

Paolo Uccello (1397–1475)—*The Battle of San Romano* (*La Battaglia di S. Romano*)

In the 1400s, painters worked out the problems of painting realistically, using mathematics to create the illusion of three-dimensionality. This colorful battle scene is not so much a piece of art as an exercise in perspective. Paolo Uccello (oo-CHEL-loh) has challenged himself with every possible problem.

The broken lances at left set up a 3-D "grid" in which to place this crowded scene. The fallen horses and soldiers are experiments in

"foreshortening"—shortening the things that are farther away from us (which appear smaller) to create the illusion of distance. Some of the figures are definitely A-plus material, like the fallen gray horse in the center and the white horse at the far right walking away. But some are more like B-minus work—the kicking red horse's legs look like ham hocks at this angle, and the fallen soldier at far right would only be child-sized if he stood up.

And then there's the D-minus "Are-you-on-drugs?" work. The converging hedges in the background create a nice illusion of a distant hillside maybe 250 feet away. So what are those soldiers the size of the foreground figures doing there? And jumping the hedge, is that rabbit 40 feet tall?

Paolo Uccello almost literally went crazy trying to master the three dimensions (thank God he was born before Einstein discovered one more). Uccello got so wrapped up in it he kind of lost...perspective.

• *Enter Room 8.*

Fra Filippo Lippi (1406–1469)— *Madonna and Child with Two Angels* (*Madonna col Bambino e Due Angeli*)

Compare this Mary with the generic female in Martini's *Annunciation.* We don't need the wispy halo over her head to tell us she's holy—she radiates sweetness and light from her divine face. Heavenly beauty is expressed by a physically beautiful woman.

Fra (Brother) Lippi, an orphan raised as a

Early Renaissance

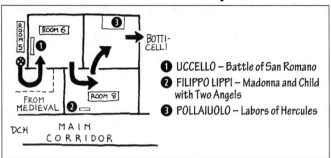

① UCCELLO – Battle of San Romano
② FILIPPO LIPPI – Madonna and Child with Two Angels
③ POLLAIUOLO – Labors of Hercules

monk, lived a less-than-monkish life. He lived with a nun who bore him two children. He spent his entire life searching for the perfect Virgin. Through his studio passed Florence's prettiest girls, many of whom decorate the walls here in this room.

Lippi painted idealized beauty, but his models were real flesh-and-blood human beings. You could look through all the thousands of paintings from the Middle Ages and not find anything so human as the mischievous face of one of Lippi's little angel boys.

• *Enter Room 9, with two small works by Pollaiuolo in the glass case between the windows.*

Antonio Pollaiuolo (c. 1431–1498)—*Labors of Hercules (Fatiche di Ercole)*

Hercules gets a workout in these two small panels showing the human form at odd angles. The poses are the wildest imaginable, to

show how each muscle twists and tightens. While Uccello worked on perspective, Pollaiuolo studied anatomy. In medieval times, dissection of corpses was a sin and a crime (the two were one then)—a desecration of the human body, which was the temple of God. But Pollaiuolo was willing to sell his soul to the devil for artistic knowledge. He dissected.

There's something funny about this room that I can't put my finger on...I've got it—no Madonnas. Not one.

We've seen how Early Renaissance artists worked to conquer reality. Now let's see the fruits of their work, the flowering of Florence's Renaissance.

• *Enter the large Botticelli room and take a seat.*

The Renaissance Blossoms

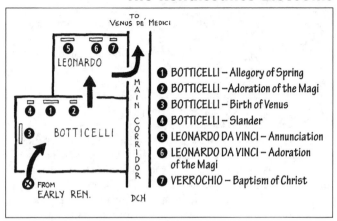

TO
VENUS DE' MEDICI

LEONARDO

BOTTICELLI

FROM
EARLY REN.

M A I N   C O R R I D O R

DCH

❶ BOTTICELLI – Allegory of Spring
❷ BOTTICELLI – Adoration of the Magi
❸ BOTTICELLI – Birth of Venus
❹ BOTTICELLI – Slander
❺ LEONARDO DA VINCI – Annunciation
❻ LEONARDO DA VINCI – Adoration of the Magi
❼ VERROCHIO – Baptism of Christ

Florence—The Renaissance Blossoms (1450–1500)

Florence in 1450 was in a firenz-y of activity. There was a can-do spirit of optimism in the air, led by prosperous merchants and bankers and a strong middle class. The government was reasonably democratic, and Florentines saw themselves as citizens of a strong republic like ancient Rome. Their civic pride showed in the public monuments and artworks they built. Man was leaving the protection of the church to stand on his own two feet.

Lorenzo de' Medici, head of the powerful Medici family, epitomized this new humanistic spirit. Strong, decisive, handsome, poetic, athletic, sensitive, charismatic, intelligent, brave, clean, and reverent, Lorenzo was a true Renaissance Man, deserving of the nickname he went by—"the Magnificent." He gathered Florence's best and brightest around him for evening wine and discussions of great ideas. One of this circle was the painter Botticelli (bot-i-CHEL-ee).

Sandro Botticelli (1444–1510)—*Allegory of Spring (Allegoria dell Primavera)*

It's springtime in a citrus grove. The winds of spring blow in (Mr. Blue at right), causing the woman on the right to sprout flowers from her lips as she morphs into Flora or Spring—who walks by, spreading flowers from her dress. At the left are Mercury and the Three Graces, dancing a delicate maypole dance. The Graces may be symbolic of the three forms of love—love of beauty, love of people, and sexual love, suggested by the raised intertwined fingers. (They forgot love of peanut butter on toast.) In the center stands Venus, the Greek goddess of love. Above her flies a blindfolded Cupid, happily shooting his arrows of love without worrying whom they'll hit.

Here is the Renaissance in its first bloom, its "spring-time" of innocence. Madonna is out, Venus is in. Adam and Eve hiding their nakedness are out, glorious flesh is in. This is a return to the pre-Christian pagan world of classical Greece, where things of the flesh are not sinful. But this is certainly no orgy—just fresh-faced innocence and playfulness.

Botticelli emphasizes pristine beauty over gritty realism. The lines of the bodies, especially of the Graces in their see-through nighties, have pleasing, S-like curves. The faces are idealized but have real human features. There's a look of thoughtfulness and even melancholy in the faces—as though everyone knows that the innocence of spring will not last forever.

• *Look at the next painting to the right.*

Botticelli—*Adoration of the Magi (Adorazione dei Magi)*

Here's the rat pack of confident young Florentines who reveled in the optimistic pagan spirit—even in a religious scene. Botticelli included himself among the adorers, looking vain in the yellow robe at far right. Lorenzo's the Magnificent-looking guy at the far left.

Botticelli—*Birth of Venus (Nascita di Venere)*

According to myth, Venus was born from the foam of a wave. Still only half awake, this fragile newborn beauty floats ashore on a clam shell, blown by the winds, where her maid waits to dress her. The pose is the same S-curve of classical statues (as we'll soon see). Botticelli's pastel colors make the world itself seem fresh and newly born.

This is the purest expression of Renaissance beauty. Venus' naked body is not sensual but innocent. Botticelli thought that phys-

ical beauty was a way of appreciating God. Remember Michelangelo's poem: souls will never ascend to Heaven "...until the sight of Beauty lifts them there."

Botticelli finds God in the details—Venus' wind-blown hair, the translucent skin, the maid's braided hair, the slight ripple of the wind's abs, and the flowers tumbling in the slowest of slow motions, suspended like musical notes, caught at the peak of their brief life.

Mr. and Mrs. Wind intertwine—notice her hands clasped around his body. Their hair, wings, and robes mingle like the wind. But what happened to those splayed toes?

• *"Venus on the Half-Shell" (as many tourists call this) is one of the masterpieces of Western art. Take some time with it. Then find the small canvas on the wall to the right, near La Primavera.*

Botticelli—*Slander (La Calumnia)*

The spring of Florence's Renaissance had to end. Lorenzo died young. The economy faltered. Into town rode the monk Savonarola, preaching medieval hellfire and damnation for those who embraced the "pagan" Renaissance spirit. "Down, down with all gold and decoration," he roared. "Down where the body is food for the worms." He presided over huge bonfires, where the people threw in their fine clothes, jewelry, pagan books...and paintings.

Slander spells the end of the Florentine Renaissance. The setting is classic Brunelleschian architecture, but look what's taking place beneath those stately arches. These aren't proud Renaissance Men and Women but a ragtag, medieval-looking bunch, a court of thieves in an abandoned hall of justice. The accusations fly and everyone is condemned. The naked man pleads for mercy but the hooded black figure, a symbol of his execution, turns away. The figure of Truth (naked Truth)—straight out of *The Birth of Venus*—looks up to heaven as if to ask, "What has happened to us?" The classical statues in their niches look on in disbelief.

Botticelli listened to Savonarola. He burned some of his own paintings and changed his tune. The last works of his life were darker, more somber, and pessimistic of humanity.

The German poet Heine said, "When they start by burning books, they'll end by burning people." Savonarola, after four short years of power, was burned on his own bonfire in the Piazza della Signoria, but by then the city was in shambles. The first flowering of the Renaissance was over.

• *Enter the next room.*

Leonardo da Vinci (1452–1519)—*Annunciation*

A scientist, architect, engineer, musician, and painter, Leonardo was a true Renaissance Man. He worked at his own pace rather than to please an employer, so he often left works unfinished. The two in this room aren't his best, but even a lesser Leonardo is enough to put a museum on the map, and they're definitely worth a look.

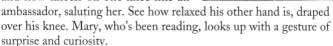

Gabriel has walked up to Mary and now kneels on one knee like an ambassador, saluting her. See how relaxed his other hand is, draped over his knee. Mary, who's been reading, looks up with a gesture of surprise and curiosity.

Leonardo constructs a beautifully landscaped "stage" and puts his characters in it. Look at the bricks on the right wall. If you extended lines from them, the lines would all converge at the center of the painting, the distant blue mountain. Same with the edge of the sarcophagus and the railing. Subconsciously, this subtle touch creates a feeling of balance, order, and spaciousness.

Think back to Simone Martini's *Annunciation* to realize how much more natural, relaxed, and realistic Leonardo's version is. He's taken a miraculous event—an angel appearing out of the blue—and presented it in a very human way.

Leonardo—*Adoration of the Magi*

Leonardo's human insight is even more apparent here, in this unfin-

ished work. The poor kings are amazed at the Christ child—even afraid of him. They scurry around like chimps around fire. This work is as agitated as the *Annunciation* is calm, giving us an idea of Leonardo's range. Leonardo was pioneering a new era of painting, showing not just the outer features but the inner personality.

The next painting to the right, *Baptism of Christ,* is by Verrochio, Leonardo's teacher. Legend has it that Leonardo painted the angel on the far left when he was only 14 years old. When Verrocchio saw that some kid had painted an angel better than he ever would...he hung up his brush for good.

Florence saw the first blossoming of the Renaissance. But when the cultural climate turned chilly, artists flew south to warmer climes. The Renaissance shifted to Rome.

• *Exit into the main corridor. Breathe. Sit. Admire the ceiling. Look out the window. See you in five.*

Back already? Now continue down the corridor and turn left into the octagonal Venus de' Medici room (they only allow 25 people in at a time). If you skip this because there's a line, you'll also be missing the next five rooms, which include works by Cranach, Dürer, Memling, Holbein, Giorgione, and others.

Classical Sculpture

If the Renaissance was the foundation of the modern world, the foundation of the Renaissance was classical sculpture. Sculptors, painters, and poets alike turned for inspiration to these ancient Greek and Roman works as the epitome of balance, 3-D, human anatomy, and beauty.

The *Venus de' Medici,* or *Medici Venus* (*Venere de' Medici*), ancient Greece

Is this pose familiar? Botticelli's *Birth of Venus* has the same position of the arms, the same S-curved body, and the same lifting of the right leg. A copy of this statue stood in Lorenzo the Magnificent's garden, where Botticelli used to hang out. This one is a Roman copy of the lost original by the great Greek sculptor Praxiteles. The *Medici Venus* is a balanced, harmonious, serene statue from Greece's "Golden Age," when balance was admired in every aspect of life.

Perhaps more than any other work of art, this statue has been the epitome of both ideal beauty and sexuality. In the 18th and 19th centuries, sex was "dirty," so the sex drive of cultured aristocrats was channeled into a love of pure beauty. Wealthy sons and daughters of Europe's aristocrats made the pilgrimage to the Uffizi to complete their classical education...where they swooned in ecstasy before the cold beauty of this goddess of love.

Louis XIV had a bronze copy made. Napoleon stole her away to Paris for himself. And in Philadelphia in the 1800s, a copy had to be kept under lock and key to prevent the innocent from catching the *Venere*-al disease. At first, it may be difficult for us to appreciate such passionate love of art, but if any generation knows the power of sex to sell something—be it art or underarm deodorant—it's ours.

The Other Statues

Venus de' Medici's male counterpart is on the right, facing Venus. *Apollino* (a.k.a. "Venus with a Penis") is also by the master of smooth, cool lines: Praxiteles.

The other works are later Greek (Hellenistic), when quiet balance was replaced by violent motion and emotion. *The Wrestlers* to

Classical Sculpture and Northern Renaissance

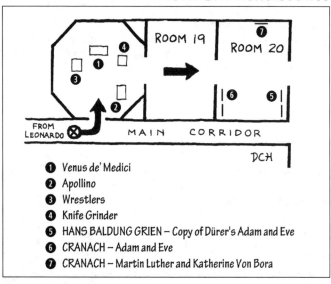

- ❶ Venus de' Medici
- ❷ Apollino
- ❸ Wrestlers
- ❹ Knife Grinder
- ❺ HANS BALDUNG GRIEN – Copy of Dürer's Adam and Eve
- ❻ CRANACH – Adam and Eve
- ❼ CRANACH – Martin Luther and Katherine Von Bora

the left of *Venus* is a study in anatomy and twisted limbs—like Pollaiuolo's paintings a thousand years later.

The drama of *The Knife Grinder* to the right of *Venus* stems from the off-stage action—he's sharpening the knife to flay a man alive.

• *Exit the octagonal room and pass through Room 19 into Room 20.*

Northern Renaissance

Hans Baldung Grien (c.1484–1545)— Copy of Dürer's *Adam and Eve*

The warm spirit of the Renaissance blew north into Germany. Albrecht Dürer (1471–1528), the famous German painter and engraver, traveled to Venice, where he fell in love with all things Italian. Returning home, he painted the First Couple in the Italian style—full-bodied, muscular (check out Adam's abs and Eve's knees), "carved" with strong shading, fresh-faced, and innocent in their earthly Paradise.

This copy by Hans Baldung Grien of Dürer's original (now in the Prado) was a training exercise.

Like many of Europe's artists—including Michelangelo and Raphael—Baldung Grien learned technique by studying Dürer's meticulous engravings, spread by the newly invented printing press.

Lucas Cranach (1472–1553)—*Adam and Eve*

Eve sashays forward, with heavy-lidded eyes, to offer the forbidden fruit. Adam stretches to display himself and his foliage to Eve. The two panels are linked by smoldering eye contact, as Man

and Woman awaken to their own nakedness. The Garden of Eden is about to be rocked by new ideas that are both liberating and troubling.

Though the German Lucas Cranach occasionally dabbled in the "Italian style," he chose to portray his Adam and Eve in the now-retro look of International Gothic.

They are slimmer than Dürer's, smoother, more S-shaped, elegant, graceful, shapely, and erotic, with the dainty pinkies of the refined aristocrats signing Cranach's paycheck.

Though life-sized, here Adam and Eve are not lifelike, not monumental, not full-bodied or muscular, and are not placed in a real-world landscape with distant perspectives. Even so, Cranach was very much a man of the Renaissance, a friend of Martin Luther, and a champion of humanism.

Cranach—*Martin Luther*

Martin Luther—German monk, fiery orator, and religious whistle-blower—sparked a century of European wars by speaking out against the Catholic Church.

Luther (1483–1546) lived a turbulent life. In early adulthood, the newly ordained priest suffered a severe personal crisis of faith, before finally emerging "born again." In 1517 he openly protested against church corruption and was excommunicated. Defying both the pope and the emperor, he lived on the run as an outlaw, watching as his ideas sparked peasant riots. He still found time to translate the New Testament from

Latin to modern German, write hymns such as "A Mighty Fortress," and spar with the humanist Erasmus and fellow-Reformer Zwingli.

Now 46 years old, Martin Luther is easing out of the fast lane. Recently married to an ex-nun, he has traded his monk's habit for street clothes, bought a house, had several kids...and has clearly been enjoying his wife's home cooking and home-brewed beer.

Cranach—*Katherine von Bora (Luther's wife)*

When "Katie" decided to leave her convent, the famous Martin Luther agreed to help find her a husband. She rejected his nominees, saying she'd marry no one...except Luther himself. In 1525 the 42-year-old ex-priest married the 26-year-old ex-nun "to please my father and annoy the pope." Martin turned his checkbook over to "my lord Katie," who also ran the family farm, raised their six children and 11 adopted orphans, and hosted Martin's circle of friends (including Cranach) at loud, chatty dinner parties.

• *Pass through the next couple of rooms, exiting to a great view of the Arno. Stroll through the sculpture wing.*

The Sculpture Wing

A hundred years ago, no one even looked at Botticelli—they came to the Uffizi to see the sculpture collection. And today, these 2,000-year-old Roman copies of 2,500-year-old Greek originals are hardly noticed.

• *There are benches at the other end of the wing with a superb view.*

View of the Arno

Enjoy Florence's best view of the Arno and Ponte Vecchio. You can also see the red-tiled roof of the Vasari Corridor, the "secret" passage connecting the Palazzo Vecchio, Uffizi, Ponte Vecchio, and Pitti

Palace on the other side of the river—a half-mile in all. This was a private walkway, wallpapered in great art, for the Medici family's commute from home to work.

As you appreciate the view (best at sunset), remember that it's this sort of pleasure that Renaissance painters wanted you

High Renaissance

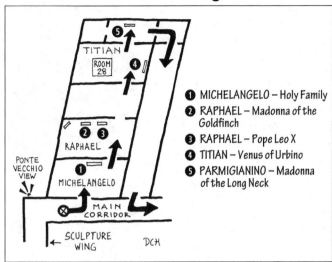

❶ MICHELANGELO – Holy Family

❷ RAPHAEL – Madonna of the Goldfinch

❸ RAPHAEL – Pope Leo X

❹ TITIAN – Venus of Urbino

❺ PARMIGIANINO – Madonna of the Long Neck

to get from their paintings. For them, a canvas was a window you looked through to see the wide world.

We're headed down the home stretch now. If your little U-feetsies are killing you and it feels like torture, remind yourself it's a pleasant torture and smile...like the statue next to you.

• *In the far corridor, turn left into the first room (#25) and grab a blast of cold from the air-conditioner vent on the floor to the left.*

High Renaissance—Michelangelo, Raphael, Titian (1500–1550)

Michelangelo Buonarroti (1475–1564)— *Holy Family (Sacra Famiglia)*

This is the only completed easel painting by the greatest sculptor in history. Florentine painters were sculptors with brushes. This shows it. Instead of a painting, it's more like three clusters of statues with some clothes painted on.

The main subject is the holy family—Mary, Joseph, and baby Jesus—and in the background are two groups of nudes looking like classical statues. The background represents the old pagan world, while Jesus in the foreground is the new age of Christianity. The figure of young John the Baptist at right is the link between the two.

This is a "peasant" Mary, with a plain face and sunburned arms. Michelangelo shows her from a very unflattering angle—we're looking up her nostrils. But Michelangelo himself was an ugly man, and he was among the first artists to recognize the beauty in everyday people.

Michelangelo was a Florentine—in fact he was like an adopted son of the Medicis, who recognized his talent—but much of his greatest work was done in Rome as part of the Pope's face-lift of the city. We can see here some of the techniques he used on the Sistine Chapel ceiling that revolutionized painting—monumental figures; dramatic angles (we're looking up Mary's nose); accentuated, rippling muscles; and bright, clashing colors (all the more apparent since both this work and the Sistine have been recently cleaned). These added an element of dramatic tension lacking in the graceful work of Leonardo and Botticelli.

Michelangelo painted this for Angelo Doni for 70 ducats. (Michelangelo designed but didn't carve the elaborate frame.) When the painting was delivered, Doni tried to talk Michelangelo down to 40. Proud Michelangelo took the painting away and would not sell it until the man finally agreed to pay double...140 ducats.

• *Enter Room 26.*

Raphael (Raffaello Sanzio, 1483–1520)— *Madonna of the Goldfinch (La Madonna del Cardellino)*

Raphael (roff-eye-ELL) brings Mary and Bambino down from heaven and into the real world of trees, water, and sky. He gives baby Jesus (right) and John the Baptist a realistic, human playfulness. It's a tender scene painted with warm colors and a hazy background that matches the golden skin of the children.

Raphael perfected his craft in Florence, following the graceful style of Leonardo. In typical Leonardo fashion, this group of Mary, John the Baptist, and Jesus is arranged in the shape of a pyramid, with Mary's head at the peak.

The two halves of the painting balance perfectly. Draw a line down the middle, through Mary's nose and down through her knee. John the Baptist on the left is balanced by Jesus on the right. Even the trees in the background balance each other, left and right. These things aren't immediately noticeable, but they help create the subconscious feelings of balance and order that reinforce the atmosphere of maternal security in this domestic scene—pure Renaissance.

Raphael—*Leo X and Cardinals (Leone X con i Cardinali)*

Raphael was called to Rome at the same time as Michelangelo,

Six Degrees of Leo X

This sophisticated, luxury-loving pope was at the center of an international, Renaissance world that spread across Europe. He crossed paths with many of the Renaissance Men of his generation. Based on the theory that any two people are linked by only "six degrees of separation," let's link Leo X with the actor Kevin Bacon:

- Leo X's father was Lorenzo the Magnificent, patron of Botticelli and Leonardo.
- When Leo X was age 13, his family took in 13-year-old Michelangelo.
- Michelangelo inspired Raphael, who was later hired by Leo X.
- Raphael exchanged masterpieces with fellow genius Albrecht Dürer, who was personally converted by Martin Luther (who was friends with Lucas Cranach), who was excommunicated by...Leo X.
- Leo X was portrayed in the movie *The Agony and the Ecstasy*, which starred Charlton Heston, who was in *Planet of the Apes* with Burgess Meredith, who was in *Rocky* with Sylvester Stallone...who ultimately connects with...Kevin Bacon.

working next door while Michelangelo did the Sistine ceiling. Raphael peeked in from time to time, learning from Michelangelo's monumental, dramatic figures. His later work is grittier and more realistic than the idealized, graceful, and "Leonardoesque" Madonna.

Pope Leo is big, like a Michelangelo statue. And Raphael captures some of the seamier side of Vatican life in the cardinals' eyes— shrewd, suspicious, and somewhat cynical. With Raphael, the photographic realism pursued by painters ever since Giotto was finally achieved.

The Florentine Renaissance ended in 1520 with the death of Raphael. Raphael (see his self-portrait to the left of the Madonna) is considered both the culmination and conclusion of the Renaissance. The realism, balance, and humanism we associate with the Renaissance are all found in Raphael's work. He combined the grace of Leonardo with the power of Michelangelo. With his death, the Renaissance shifted again— to Venice.

• *Pass through the next room and enter Room 28.*

Titian (Tiziano Vecelli, c. 1490–1576)—*Venus of Urbino (La Venere di Urbino)*

Compare this Venus with Botticelli's newly hatched Venus and you get a good idea of the difference between the Florentine and Venetian Renaissance. Botticelli's was pure, innocent, and otherworldly. Titian's should have a staple in her belly button. This isn't a Venus, it's a centerfold—with no purpose but to please the eye and other organs. While Botticelli's allegorical Venus is a message, this is a massage.

Titian and his fellow Venetians took the pagan spirit pioneered in Florence and carried it to its logical hedonistic conclusion. Using bright, rich colors, they captured the luxurious life of happy-go-lucky Venice.

While Raphael's *Madonna of the Goldfinch* was balanced with a figure on the left and one on the right, Titian balances his painting in a different way—with color. The canvas is split down the middle by the curtain. The left half is dark, the right half warmer. The two halves are connected by a diagonal slash of luminous gold—the nude woman. The girl in the background is trying to find her some clothes.

By the way, visitors from centuries past also panted in front of this Venus. The poet Byron called it *"the* Venus." With her sensual skin, hey-sailor look, and suggestively placed hand, she must have left them blithering idiots.

• *Find the n-n-n-next painting.*

Parmigianino (1503–1540)—*Madonna of the Long Neck (Madonna dal Collo Lungo)*

Raphael, Michelangelo, Leonardo, and Titian mastered reality. They

could place any scene onto a canvas with photographic accuracy. How could future artists top that?

"Mannerists" such as Parmigianino tried by going beyond realism, exaggerating it for effect. Using brighter colors and twisting poses (two techniques explored by Michelangelo), they created scenes more elegant and more exciting than real life.

By stretching the neck of his Madonna, Parmigianino (like the cheese) gives her an unnatural swanlike beauty. She has the same pose and position of hands as Botticelli's Venus and the *Venus de' Medici.* Her body forms an arcing S-curve—down her neck as far as her elbow, then back the other way along Jesus' body to her knee, then down to her foot. The baby Jesus seems to be blissfully gliding down this slippery slide of sheer beauty.

In the Uffizi, we've seen many images of female beauty: from ancient goddesses to medieval Madonnas to wicked Eves, from Botticelli's pristine nymphs to Michelangelo's peasant Mary, from Raphael's Madonna-and-baby to Titian's babe. Their physical beauty expresses different aspects of the human spirit.

• *Pass through several rooms, returning to the main corridor.*

The Rest of the Uffizi

As art moved into the Baroque period, artists took Renaissance realism and exaggerated it still more—more beauty, more emotion, or more drama. There's lots of great stuff in the following rooms, and I'd especially recommend the enormous canvases of Rubens, Rembrandt's *Self-Portrait,* and the shocking ultrarealism of Caravaggio's *Bacchus* and *Abraham Sacrificing Isaac.*

• *But first, head to the end of the corridor for a true aesthetic experience.*

The Little Cappuccin Monk (Cappuccino)

This drinkable art form, born in Italy, is now enjoyed all over the world. It's called *The Little Cappuccin Monk* because the coffee's frothy light-and-dark-brown foam looks like the two-toned cowls of the Cappuccin order. Drink it on the terrace in the shadow of the towering Palazzo Vecchio and argue the philosophy of Marx and Hegel—was the Renaissance an economic phenomenon or a spiritual one? *Salute.*

BARGELLO

(Museo Nazionale del Bargello)

The Renaissance began with sculpture. The great Florentine painters were "sculptors with brushes." The Bargello, which boasts the best collection of Florentine sculpture, takes you from the birth of this revolution of 3-D to the man who capped the Renaissance, Michelangelo. Along the way, see how each generation gave a different take on the subject of "David." It's a small, uncrowded museum and a pleasant break from the intensity of the rest of Florence.

ORIENTATION

Cost: €4 (higher if special exhibition is being held).

Hours: Daily 8:15–13:50 but closed the second and fourth Mon of each month. Last entry 40 minutes before closing.

Getting There: It's located at Via del Proconsolo 4, a three-minute walk northeast of the Uffizi. Facing the Palazzo Vecchio, go behind the Palazzo and turn left. Look for a rustic brick building with a spire that looks like a baby Palazzo Vecchio. If lost ask, "DOH-vay bar-JEL-oh?"

Information: Nothing in English. Tel. 055-238-8606.

Length of This Tour: One hour.

Photography: Cameras not allowed.

Cuisine Art: Inexpensive bars and cafés await in the surrounding streets.

Starring: Michelangelo, Donatello, Brunelleschi, Ghiberti, and four different *David*s.

THE TOUR BEGINS

Sculpture In Florence

• *Buy your ticket and take a seat in the courtyard.*

The Bargello, built in 1255, was an early Florence police station *(bargello)* and then a prison. The heavy fortifications tell us that politics in medieval Florence had its occupational hazards.

The Bargello, a three-story rectangular building, surrounds this cool and peaceful courtyard. The best statues are found in two rooms—one on the ground floor at the foot of the outdoor staircase and another one flight up, directly above it. We'll proceed logically in a chrono kind of way, from Donatello to Verrocchio to Michelangelo.

But first, meander around this courtyard and get a feel for sculpture in general and rocks in particular. Sculpture is a much more robust art form than painting. Think of the engineering problems in the sculpting process: quarrying and cutting the stone, transporting the block to the artist's studio, all the hours of chiseling chips away, then the painstaking process of sanding the final product by hand. A sculptor must be strong enough to gouge into the stone but delicate enough to groove out the smallest details. Think of Michelangelo's approach to sculpting—he wasn't creating a figure, he was liberating it from the rock that surrounded it.

If the Renaissance is humanism, then sculpture is the perfect medium to express it in. It shows the human form, standing alone, independent of church, state, or society, ready to create himself.

Finally, a viewing note. Every sculpture has an invisible "frame" around it—the stone block it was cut from. Visualizing this frame helps you find the center of the composition.

• *Climb the courtyard staircase to the next floor up and turn right into the large Donatello room. Pause at Donatello's painted bust of Niccolò da Uzzano.*

Donatello—*Niccolo da Uzzanò* (c. 1420)

Not an emperor, not a king, not a pope or prince, this is one of Florence's leading businessmen in a toga, portrayed in the style of an ancient Roman bust. In the 1400s, when Florence was inventing the Renaissance that all Europe would soon follow, there was an optimistic spirit of democracy that gloried in everyday people. With wrinkles, quizzical look, and bags under the eyes, Donatello has portrayed this man literally wart (left cheek) and all.

Donatello Room

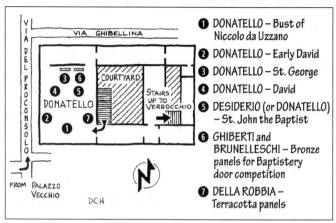

- ❶ DONATELLO – Bust of Niccolo da Uzzano
- ❷ DONATELLO – Early David
- ❸ DONATELLO – St. George
- ❹ DONATELLO – David
- ❺ DESIDERIO (or DONATELLO) – St. John the Baptist
- ❻ GHIBERTI and BRUNELLESCHI – Bronze panels for Baptistery door competition
- ❼ DELLA ROBBIA – Terracotta panels

Donatello—An early *David* (marble, 1408)

This is the first of several Davids we'll see in the Bargello. His dainty pose makes him a little unsteady on his feet. He's dressed like a medieval knight (fully clothed but showing some leg through the slit skirt). The generic face and blank, vacant eyes give him the look not of a real man but of an anonymous decoration on a church facade. At age 22, Donatello still had one foot in the old Gothic style. To tell the story of David, Donatello plants a huge rock right in the middle of Goliath's forehead.

• *At the far end of the room, St. George stands in a niche in the wall.*

Donatello—*St. George* (*S. Giorgio*, 1416)

The proud warrior has both feet planted firmly on the ground. He stands on the edge of his niche looking out alertly. He tenses his powerful right hand as he prepares to attack. George, the Christian slayer of dragons, was just the sort of righteous warrior that proud Renaissance Florentines could rally around in their struggles with nearby cities. Nearly a century later, Michelangelo's *David* replaced *George* as the unofficial symbol of Florence, but *David* was clearly inspired by *George*'s relaxed intensity and determination. (This is the original marble statue. A bronze version stands in its original niche at Orsanmichele Church.)

The relief panel below shows *George* doing what he's been pondering. To *George*'s right, the sketchy arches and trees create the illusion of a distant landscape. Donatello, who apprenticed in

Donatello
(1386–1466)

Donatello was the first great Renaissance genius, a model for Michelangelo and others. He mastered realism, creating the first truly lifelike statues of people since ancient times. Donatello's work is highly personal. Unlike the ancient Greeks—but like the ancient Romans—he often sculpted real people, not idealized versions of pretty gods and goddesses. Some of these people are downright ugly. In the true spirit of Renaissance humanism, Donatello appreciated the beauty of flesh-and-blood human beings.

    Donatello's personality was also a model for later artists. He was moody and irascible, purposely setting himself apart from others in order to concentrate on his sculpting. He developed the role of the "mad genius" that Michelangelo would later perfect.

Ghiberti's studio, is credited with teaching his master how to create 3-D illusions like this.

• *On the floor to your left, you'll find...*

Donatello—*David* (bronze, c. 1430)

He's naked. Donatello, who never married, sees David as a teenage boy wearing only a helmet, boots, and sword. The smooth-skinned warrior sways gracefully, poking his sword playfully at the severed head of the giant Goliath. His *contrapposto* stance is similar to Michelangelo's *David*, resting his weight on one leg in the classical style, but it gives him a feminine rather than masculine look. Gazing into his coy eyes and at his bulging belly is a very different experience from confronting Michelangelo's older and sturdier Renaissance Man.

    This *David* paved the way for Michelangelo's. Europe hadn't seen a free-standing male nude like this in a thousand years. In the Middle Ages, the human body was considered a dirty thing, a symbol of man's weakness, something to be covered up in shame. The church prohibited exhibitions of nudity like this one and certainly would never decorate a church with it. But in the Renaissance, a new class of rich and powerful merchants appeared that bought art for personal enjoyment. Reading Plato's *Symposium*, they saw the ideal of Beauty in the form of a young man. This particular statue stood in the courtyard of the Medicis' palace...where Michelangelo, practically an adopted son, grew up admiring it.

As we see the different *David*s in the Bargello, compare and contrast the artists' styles. How many ways can you slay a giant?

• St. John the Baptist, *done by Donatello or his student, is to the right of the boyish, naked* David.

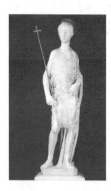

Desiderio da Settignano (or Donatello)—*St. John the Baptist (S. Giovanni Battista)*

John the Baptist was the wild-eyed, wildcat prophet who lived in the desert preaching, living on bugs 'n' honey, and baptizing Saviors of the World. Donatello, the mad prophet of the coming Renaissance, might have identified with this original eccentric.

• *On the wall next to* George, *you'll find some bronze relief panels. Don't look at the labels just yet.*

Ghiberti and Brunelleschi—*Baptistery Door Competition Entries* (two different relief panels, titled *Il Sacrificio di Abramo*)

Some would say these two panels are the first works of the Renaissance. These two versions of *Abraham Sacrificing Isaac* were finalists in the contest held in 1401 to decide who would do the bronze doors of the Baptistery. The contest sparked citywide excitement that evolved into the Renaissance spirit. Lorenzo Ghiberti won, and later did the doors known as the Gates of Paradise. Filippo Brunelleschi lost—fortunately for us—freeing him to design the Duomo's dome.

Both artists catch the crucial moment when Abraham, obeying God's orders, prepares to slaughter and burn his only son as a sacrifice. At the last moment, after Abraham passed this test of faith, an angel of God appears to stop the bloodshed.

Is one panel clearly better than the other? Composition: One is integrated and cohesive, the other a balanced knickknack shelf of

You be the judge. Here are the two finalists for the Baptistery door competition— Ghiberti's and Brunelleschi's. Which do you like best?

Ghiberti's, on the left, won.

segments. Human drama: One has bodies and faces that speak. The boy's body is a fine classical nude in itself, so real and vulnerable. Abraham's face is intense and ready to follow God's will. Perspective: An angel zooms in from out of nowhere to save the boy in the nick of time. Detail: One lamb's ram's wool is curlier than the other, one altar is more intricate.

It was obviously a tough call, but Ghiberti's was chosen, perhaps because his goldsmith training made him better suited for the technical end.

• *Along the walls, you'll find several colorful terra-cotta reliefs.*

Luca della Robbia—Terra-cotta Relief Panels

Mary and baby Jesus with accompanying angels look their most serene in these panels by the master of painted, glazed porcelain. Polished blue, white, green, and yellow, they have a gentle and feminine look that softens the rough masculine stone of this room. Luca was just one of a family of della Robbias that pioneered art in terra-cotta.

• *Exit the Donatello room through the same door you entered. Cross to the rooms on the other side of the courtyard. Take your first left, then turn right and climb the red-carpeted stairs to the next floor. At the top of the stairs, turn left, then left again. Verrocchio's* David *stands (when not out for restoration) in the center of the room.*

Verrocchio—*David* (c. 1470)

Andrea del Verrocchio (1435–1488) is best known as the teacher of Leonardo da Vinci, but he was also the premier sculptor of the generation between Donatello and Michelangelo. This saucy, impertinent *David* is younger and more masculine than Donatello's, but a far cry from Michelangelo's monumental version. He's definitely the shepherd "boy" described in the Bible. He leans on one leg, not with a firm, commanding stance but a nimble one (especially noticeable from behind). Compare the smug smile of the victor with Goliath's "Oh, have I got a headache" expression.

• *The doorway to your right leads to a room of glass cases filled with small statues. In the center of the room, you'll find...*

Pollaiuolo—*Hercules and Antaeus* (*Ercole e Anteo,* 1498)

Antaeus was invincible as long as he was in contact with the earth, his mother. So Hercules just picked him up like "The Rock" of the Renaissance and crushed him to death.

More than any early artist from this period, Antonio Pollaiuolo

studied the human body in motion. These figures are not dignified Renaissance Men. Yet, in this tangled pose of flailing arms and legs, there still is a Renaissance sense of balance—all the motion spins around the center of gravity where their bodies grind together.

• *In the nearby glass cases, you'll see small-scale, alternate versions of the Mercury that we'll soon see.*

The Rest of the Bargello

Before we lose elevation to visit the final room downstairs, browse around the upper floors. On this floor, you'll find ivories, jewelry, and terra-cotta Mary-baby-and-angel panels by other members of the della Robbia clan. The top floor has armor and medallions.

• *Now descend back to the courtyard on the ground floor. The final room we'll visit is through the door to your left at the bottom of the stairs.*

Lesser Michelangelos

Michelangelo—*Bacchus* (*Baccho*, c. 1497)

Bacchus, the god of wine and revelry, raises another cup to his lips, while his little companion goes straight for the grapes.

Maybe Michelangelo had a sense of humor after all. Compare this tipsy Greek god of wine with his sturdy, sober *David*, begun a few years later. *Bacchus* isn't nearly so muscular, so monumental...or so sure on his feet. Hope he's not driving. The pose, the smooth muscles, the beer belly and swaying hips look more like Donatello's boyish *David*.

This was Michelangelo's first major commission. He often vacillated between showing man as strong and noble, and as weak and perverse. This isn't the nobility of the classical world, but the decadent side of orgies and indulgence.

• *Just to the left, you'll find...*

Michelangelo—*Brutus* (*Bruto*, 1540)

Another example of the influence of Donatello is this so-ugly-he's-beautiful bust by Michelangelo. His rough intensity gives him the look of a man who has succeeded against all odds, a dignity and heroic quality that would be missing if he were too pretty.

The subject is Brutus, the Roman who, for the love of liberty, murdered his friend and dictator, Julius Caesar (*Et tu...?*).

Bargello—Ground Floor

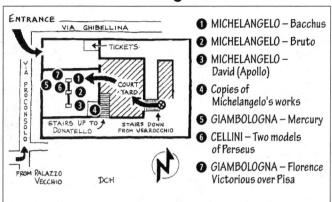

ENTRANCE
VIA GHIBELLINA
←TICKETS·
VIA PROCONSOLO
COURT·YARD·
STAIRS UP TO DONATELLO
STAIRS DOWN FROM VERROCCHIO
FROM PALAZZO VECCHIO
DCH

❶ MICHELANGELO – Bacchus

❷ MICHELANGELO – Bruto

❸ MICHELANGELO – David (Apollo)

❹ Copies of Michelangelo's works

❺ GIAMBOLOGNA – Mercury

❻ CELLINI – Two models of Perseus

❼ GIAMBOLOGNA – Florence Victorious over Pisa

Michelangelo could understand this man's dilemma. He himself was torn between his love of the democratic tradition of Florence and loyalty to his friends the Medicis, who had become dictators.

So he gives us two sides of a political assassin. The right profile (the front view) is heroic. But the hidden side, with the drooping mouth and squinting eye, makes him more cunning, sneering, and ominous.

Michelangelo—*David* (also known as *Apollo,* 1530–32)

This restless, twisting man is either David or Apollo (is he reaching

for a sling or a quiver?). As the last of the *David*s in the Bargello, it's a good time to think back on those we've seen: Donatello's generic warrior and girlish, gloating *David;* Verrocchio's boyish, impish version; and now this unfinished one by Michelangelo. Michelangelo certainly learned from these earlier versions, even copying certain elements, but what's truly amazing is that his famous *David* in the Accademia is so completely different from the others, so much larger than life in every way.

In the glass cases in the corner are small-scale copies of some of Michelangelo's most famous works. Back near the entrance there's a bust of Michelangelo by his fellow sculptor da Volterra, capturing Michelangelo's broken nose and brooding nature.

• *On the other side of the room...*

Giambologna—*Mercury*

Catch this statue while you can—he's got flowers waiting to be delivered. Despite all the bustle and motion, *Mercury* has a solid Renaissance core: the line of balance that runs straight up the center, from toes to hip to fingertip. He's caught in mid-stride. His top half leans forward, counterbalanced by his right leg in back, while the center of gravity rests firmly at the hip-bone. Down at the toes, notice the cupid practicing for the circus.

Cellini—*Models of Perseus (Perseo)*

The life-size statue of Perseus slaying Medusa, located in the open-air loggia next to Palazzo Vecchio, is cast bronze. Benvenuto Cellini started with these smaller models in wax and bronze to get the difficult process down. When it came time to cast the full-size work, everything was going fine...until he realized he didn't have enough metal! He ran around the studio, gathering up pewterware and throwing it in, narrowly avoiding a messterpiece.

Giambologna—*Florence Victorious over Pisa (Firenze Vittoriosa su Pisa)*

This shows the fierce Florentine chauvinism born in an era when Italy's cities struggled for economic and political dominance...and Florence won.

ROME

Two thousand years ago, the word Rome meant civilization itself. Today, Rome is Italy's political capital, the capital of Catholicism, and the center of the ancient world. It's littered with evocative remains. As you peel through its fascinating and jumbled layers, you'll find Rome's buildings, cats, laundry, traffic, and 2.6 million people endlessly entertaining. And then there are its magnificent sights.

Do the "Caesar Shuffle" through ancient Rome's Forum and Colosseum. Make meaningful eye contact with ancient emperors in the busts of the National Museum. Tour St. Peter's, the greatest church on earth, and scale Michelangelo's 328-foot-tall dome, the world's largest. Learn something about eternity by touring the huge Vatican Museum. End at the creation of the world—bright as the day it was painted—in the restored Sistine Chapel.

Colosseum   **327**

Roman Forum   **334**

National Museum of Rome   **347**

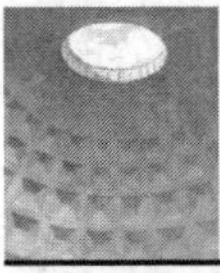

Pantheon   **360**

St. Peter's Basilica   **363**

Vatican Museum   **379**

Rome Sights

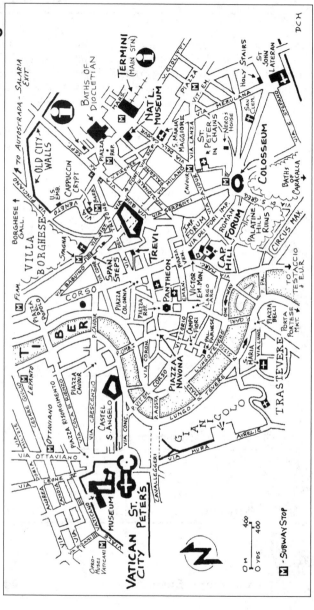

COLOSSEUM

(Colosseo)

Rome has many layers—modern, Baroque, Renaissance, Christian. But let's face it, "Rome" is Caesars, gladiators, chariots, centurions, *"Et tu, Brute,"* trumpet fanfares, and thumbs up or thumbs down. That's the Rome we'll look at. Our "Caesar Shuffle" begins with the downtown core of ancient Rome, the Colosseum. A logical next stop is the Forum, just next door (and the next chapter), past the Arch of Constantine.

ORIENTATION

Cost: €8 (includes Palatine Hill visit within 24 hours; often a surcharge for special exhibits; also covered by €20 combo-ticket).

Hours: Daily 9:00–19:00, or until an hour before sunset.

Avoid Long Lines: Instead of waiting in line (sometimes as long as an hour) at the Colosseum to purchase a ticket, you have several good alternatives:

1. Buy your ticket at either of the two rarely crowded Palatine Hill entrances near the Colosseum—there's one inside the Forum and another on Via di San Gregorio (facing Forum entry, with Colosseum at your back, go left on street). This €8 ticket includes entry to both the Colosseum and Palatine (valid for 24 hours). With ticket in hand, you can walk

Ancient Rome Sights

right by the long ticket line, through the turnstile, and into the Colosseum.

2. Consider buying a €20 combo-ticket at a less-crowded sight. The combo-ticket covers the Colosseum, Palatine Hill, National Museum of Rome, Museum of the Bath, Baths of Caracalla, and more. Buy it at any of the included sights.

3. Reserve a ticket in advance for an additional €1.50 fee by calling 06-3996-7700 (automated info in English, pay for ticket at side window of Colosseum's ticket office).

4. You can book a tour on the spot from hustlers who rescue individuals from the line by selling tours that include tickets they already have. This will cost you a few euros (€15 for the tour including the €8 ticket), but can save time and comes with a brief guided tour. Beware—American students working for the guides will tell you that there's a long line, when sometimes there is none at all. (It can be hard for you to instantly judge the length of the line because it's tucked into the Colosseum arcade.)

Caution: For a fee, the incredibly crude modern-day gladiators snuff out their cigarettes and pose for photos. They take easy-to-swin-

Colosseum

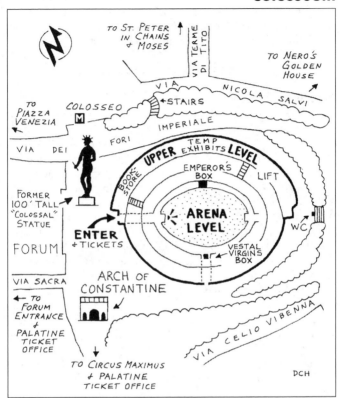

dle tourists for too much money. Watch out if you tangle with these guys (they're armed…and accustomed to getting as much as €100 from naive tourists). Also, be on guard as this is traditionally a happy hunting ground for gangs of children pickpockets.

Getting There: The Metro stop, Colosseo, lets you out just across the street from the monument.

Information: Outside the entrance of the Colosseum, vendors sell handy little *Rome: Past and Present* books with plastic overlays to un-ruin the ruins (marked €11, price soft). A WC is behind the Colosseum (facing ticket entrance, go right; WC is under stairway). Tel. 06-3974-9907.

Tour: A dry but fact-filled audioguide is available at the ticket office (€4 for 2 hours of use). Guided tours in English depart several times per day and last about one hour (€4).

Length of This Tour: Allow 45 minutes.

Cuisine Art: For a quick lunch, climb the steps above the WC and cross the busy street to the cafés with expansive views of the

Colosseum. However, you'll find better values away from the views; consider these two simple eateries at the top of Terme di Tito, a block uphill from the Colosseum: the friendly Caffè dello Studente and, next door, Ostaria da Nerone (both closed Sun).

THE TOUR BEGINS

Exterior of Colosseum

• *View the Colosseum from the Forum fence, across the street from the "Colosseo" subway station.*

Built when the Roman Empire was at its peak (A.D. 80), the Colosseum represents Rome at its grandest. The Flavian Amphitheater (its real name) was an arena for gladiator contests and public spectacles. When killing became a spectator sport, the Romans wanted to share the fun with as many people as possible. They stuck two theaters together to create a freestanding amphitheater. The outside (where slender cypress trees stand today) was decorated with a 100-foot-tall bronze statue of Nero that gleamed in the sunlight. The final structure was colossal—a "coloss-eum," the wonder of its age. It could accommodate 50,000 roaring fans (100,000 thumbs).

The Romans pioneered the use of the rounded arch and concrete, enabling them to build on this colossal scale. The exterior is a skeleton of 3.5 million cubic feet of travertine stone. (Each of the pillars flanking the ground-level arches weighs five tons.) It took 200 ox-drawn wagons shuttling back and forth every day for four years just to bring the stone here from Tivoli. They stacked stone blocks (without mortar) into the shape of an arch, supported temporarily by wooden scaffolding. Finally, they wedged a keystone into the top of the arch—it not only kept the arch from falling, it could bear even more weight above. Iron pegs held the larger stones together—notice the small holes that pockmark the sides.

The exterior says a lot about the Romans. They were great engineers, not artists, and the building is more functional than beautiful. While the essential structure is Roman, the four-story facade is decorated with the three types of Greek columns—Doric (ground level), Ionic (second story), Corinthian, and, on the top, half-columns with a mix of all three. Originally, copies of Greek statues stood in the arches of the middle two stories giving this arena of death a veneer of sophistication. If ancient Romans visited the United States today as tourists, they might send home postcards of our greatest works of "art"—freeways.

Only a third of the original Colosseum remains. Earthquakes destroyed some of it, but most was carted off as easy precut stones for other buildings during the Middle Ages and Renaissance.

• *To enter, join the ticket line or, if you've already purchased a ticket elsewhere, bypass the line, head left up the passage for groups, and go directly to the turnstile. Once inside, find the Vestal Virgins' Box (see map on page 329).*

Interior of Colosseum

You're at the "50-yard line" on arena level. What you see now are the underground passages beneath the playing surface. The oval-shaped arena (280 by 165 feet) was originally covered with boards, then sprinkled with sand (*arena* in Latin).

Like modern stadiums, the spectators ringed the playing area in bleacher seats that slant up from the arena floor. To build these bleachers, they made a shell of brick, then filled it in with concrete. The brick masses around you supported the first small tier of seats, and you can see two larger, slanted supports higher up. Originally, the

bare brick was faced with marble (lower stories) or plaster (cheap seats). A few marble seats have been restored (at the right end). The whole thing was topped with an enormous canvas awning that could be hoisted across by armies of sailors to provide shade for the spectators—the first domed stadium.

"Hail, Caesar! *(Ave, Caesar!)* We who are about to die salute you!" The gladiators would enter the arena from the left end, parade around to the sound of trumpets, acknowledge the Vestal Virgins (where you're standing), stop at the emperor's box (directly opposite), raise their weapons, shout and salute—and the fights would begin. The fights pitted men against men, men against beasts, and beasts against beasts.

A walkway stretches across the arena, allowing you to contemplate the games from a gladiator's-eye view, right in the center of the action. Picture 50,000 screaming people around you (did gladiators get stage fright?), and imagine that they hate you and want to see you die. Find the shafts of little elevators near the center that brought you gnarly surprises.

The games began with a few warm-up acts—watching dogs bloody themselves attacking porcupines, female gladiators fighting each other, or a dwarf battling a one-legged man. Then came the main event—the gladiators.

Some wielded swords, protected only with a shield and a heavy helmet. Others represented fighting fishermen, with a net to snare

opponents and a trident to spear them. The gladiators were usually slaves, criminals, or poor people who got their chance for freedom, wealth, and fame in the ring. They learned to fight in training schools, then battled their way up the ranks. The best were rewarded like our modern sports stars with fan clubs, great wealth, and, yes, product endorsements.

The animals came from all over the world: lions, tigers, and bears (oh my!), crocodiles, elephants, and hippos (not to mention exotic human "animals" from the "barbarian" lands). They were kept in cages beneath the arena floor, then lifted up in elevators. Released at floor level, the animals would pop out from behind blinds into the arena—the gladiator didn't know where, when, or by what he'd be attacked. (This brought howls of laughter from the hardened fans in the cheap seats who had a better view of the action.) Nets ringed the arena to protect the crowd. The stadium was inaugurated with a 100-day festival in which 2,000 men and 9,000 animals were killed. Colosseum employees squirted perfumes around the stadium to mask the stench of blood.

If a gladiator fell helpless to the ground, his opponent would approach the emperor's box and ask: Should he live or die? Sometimes the emperor left the decision to the crowd, who would judge based on how valiantly the man had fought. They would make their decision—thumbs up or thumbs down (or, as some historians say, sideways). When a brave gladiator died, they'd drain his blood and sell it as a tonic.

Did they throw Christians to the lions like in the movies? Christians were definitely thrown to the lions, made to fight gladiators, crucified, and burned alive...but probably not here in this particular stadium. Maybe, but probably not.

Rome was a nation of warriors that built an empire by conquest. The battles fought against Germans, Egyptians, barbarians, and strange animals were played out daily here in the Colosseum for the benefit of city-slicker bureaucrats who got vicarious thrills watching brutes battle to the death. The contests were always free, sponsored by politicians to bribe the people's favor or to keep Rome's growing mass of unemployed rabble off the streets.

• *With these scenes in mind, wander around. Climb to the upper deck for a more colossal view. There are stairs near either long end, and an elevator in the east corner. On the upper level, there's a bookstore at the west corner and temporary exhibits at the northeast end.*

After you exit, head to the Arch of Constantine (between the Colosseum and Forum, at the west corner of the Colosseum).

Arch of Constantine

If you are a Christian, were raised a Christian, or simply belong to a so-called "Christian nation," ponder this arch. It marks one of the great turning points in history—the military coup that made Christianity mainstream. In A.D. 312, Emperor Constantine defeated his rival Maxentius in the crucial Battle of the Milvian Bridge. The night before, he had seen a vision of a cross in the sky. Constantine—whose mother and sister were Christians—became sole emperor and legalized Christianity. With this one battle, a once-obscure Jewish sect with a handful of followers was now the state religion of the entire Western world. In A.D. 300, you could be killed for being a Christian; later, you could be killed for not being one. Church enrollment boomed.

By the way, don't look too closely at the reliefs decorating this arch. By the fourth century, Rome was on its way down. Rather than struggle with original carvings, the makers of this arch plugged in bits and pieces scavenged from existing monuments. The arch is newly restored and looking great. But any meaning read into the stone will be very jumbled.

• *The Roman Forum (Foro Romano) is to the right of the arch, 100 yards away. If you're ready for a visit, see the next chapter.*

ROMAN FORUM

(Foro Romano)

 The Forum was the political, religious, and commercial center of the city. Rome's most important temples and halls of justice were here. This was the place for religious processions, political demonstrations, elections, important speeches, and parades by conquering generals. As Rome's Empire expanded, these few acres of land became the center of the civilized world.

ORIENTATION

Cost: Free. (There's an €8 charge to visit the Palatine Hill above the Forum.)

Hours: Daily 9:00–19:00, or an hour before dark.

Tip: The ancient paving at the Forum is uneven; wear sturdy shoes. Refill your water bottle from the Forum's public drinking fountains.

Getting There: The closest Metro stop is Colosseo. The Forum's main entrance—where this tour begins—is near the Arch of Constantine and the Colosseum.

Information: Street vendors between the Colosseum and Forum sell small *Rome: Past and Present* books with plastic overlays that restore the ruins (marked €11, offer less). Tel. 06-3974-9907.

Tour: A €4 dry but fact-filled audioguide helps decipher the rubble (rent at gift shop at entrance on Via dei Fori Imperiali). Guided tours in English are offered almost hourly (€4); ask for information at the ticket booth at the Palatine Hill (near Arch of Titus).

Length of This Tour: Allow one hour.

The Forum

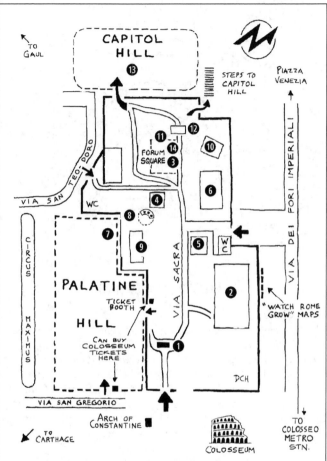

1. Arch of Titus
2. Basilica of Constantine
3. Forum's Main Square
4. Temple of Julius Caesar
5. Temple of Antoninus and Faustina
6. Basilica Aemilia
7. Caligula's Palace
8. Temple of Vesta
9. House of the Vestal Virgins
10. Curia (Senate House)
11. Rostrum
12. Arch of Septimius Severus
13. Temple of Saturn
14. Column of Phocas

THE ROMAN EMPIRE AT ITS PEAK: PAX ROMANA A.D. 100

THE TOUR BEGINS

Overview

• *Walk through the entrance nearest the Colosseum, hiking up the ramp marked "Via Sacra." Stand next to the triumphal Arch of Titus (Arco di Tito) and look out over the rubble-littered valley called the Forum.*

The hill in the distance with the bell tower is Capitol Hill. Immediately to your left, with all the trees, is Palatine Hill. The valley in between is rectangular, running roughly east (the Colosseum end) to west (Capitol Hill). The rocky path at your feet is the Via Sacra, which runs through the trees, past the large brick Senate building, and up Capitol Hill.

Picture being here when a conquering general returned to Rome with crates of booty. The valley was full of gleaming white buildings topped with bronze roofs. The Via Sacra—Main Street of the Forum—would be lined with citizens waving branches and carrying torches. The trumpets would sound as the parade began. First

came porters, carrying chests full of gold and jewels. Then a parade of exotic animals from the conquered lands—elephants, giraffes, hippopotamuses—for the crowd to "ooh" and "ahh" at. Next came the prisoners in chains, with the captive king on a wheeled platform so the people

Rome—Republic and Empire
(500 B.C.–A.D. 500)

Ancient Rome spanned about a thousand years, from 500 B.C. to A.D. 500. During that time, Rome expanded from a small tribe of barbarians to a vast empire, then dwindled slowly to city size again. For the first 500 years, when Rome's armies made her ruler of the Italian peninsula and beyond, Rome was a republic governed by elected senators. Over the next 500 years, a time of world conquest and eventual decline, Rome was an empire ruled by a military-backed dictator.

Julius Caesar bridged the gap between republic and empire. This ambitious general and politician, popular with the people because of his military victories and charisma, suspended the Roman constitution and assumed dictatorial powers around 50 B.C., then he was assassinated by a conspiracy of senators. His adopted son, Augustus, succeeded him, and soon "Caesar" was not just a name but a title.

Emperor Augustus ushered in the Pax Romana, or Roman peace (from A.D. 1–200), a time when Rome reached her peak and controlled an empire that stretched even beyond Eurail—from Scotland to Egypt, from Turkey to Morocco.

could jeer and spit at him. Finally, the conquering hero himself would drive down in his four-horse chariot, with rose petals strewn in his path. The whole procession would go the length of the Forum and up the face of Capitol Hill to the Temple of Saturn (the eight big columns midway up the hill—#13 on map on page 335), where they'd place the booty in Rome's coffers. They'd continue up to the summit to the Temple of Jupiter (no longer exists today) to dedicate the victory to the King of the Gods.

❶ Arch of Titus (Arco di Tito)

The Arch of Titus commemorated the Roman victory over the province of Judea (Israel) in A.D. 70. The Romans had a reputation as benevolent conquerors who tolerated the local customs and rulers. All they required was allegiance to the empire, shown by worshiping the emperor as a god. No problem for most conquered people, who already had half a dozen gods on their prayer lists anyway. But the Israelites' god was jealous and refused to let his people worship the emperor. Israel revolted. After a short but bitter war, the Romans defeated the

rebels, took Jerusalem, sacked their temple, and brought home 50,000 Jewish slaves...who were forced to build this arch (and the Colosseum).

Roman propaganda decorates the inside of the arch, where a relief shows the emperor Titus in a chariot being crowned by the Goddess Victory. (Thanks to the toll of modern pollution, they both look like they've been through the wars.) The other side shows booty from the sacking of the temple—soldiers carrying a Jewish candelabrum and other plunder. The two (unfinished) plaques on poles were to have listed the conquered cities.

The brutal crushing of this rebellion (and another one 60 years later) devastated the nation of Israel. With no temple as a center for their faith, the Jews scattered throughout the world (the Diaspora). There would be no Jewish political entity again for almost two thousand years, until modern Israel was created after World War II.

• *Start down the Via Sacra into the Forum. After just a few yards, turn right and follow a path uphill to the three huge arches of the...*

❷ Basilica of Constantine (a.k.a. Basilica Maxentius)

Yes, these are big arches. But they represent only one third of the original Basilica of Constantine, a mammoth hall of justice. The arches were matched by a similar set along the Via Sacra side (only a

few squat brick piers remain). Between them ran the central hall, which was spanned by a roof 130 feet high—about 55 feet higher than the side arches you see. (The stub of brick you see sticking up began an arch that once spanned the central hall.) The hall itself was as long as a football field, lavishly furnished with colorful inlaid marble, a gilded bronze ceiling, fountains, and statues, and filled with strolling Romans. At the far (west) end was an enormous marble statue of Emperor Constantine on a throne. (Pieces of this statue, including a man-sized hand, are on display in Rome's Capitol Hill Museum.)

The basilica was begun by the emperor Maxentius, but after he was trounced in battle (see page 333), the victor—Constantine—

completed the massive building. No doubt about it, the Romans built monuments on a more epic scale than any previous Europeans, wowing their "barbarian" neighbors.

• *Now stroll deeper into the Forum, down the Via Sacra, through the trees. Many of the large basalt stones under your feet were walked on by Caesar Augustus 2,000 years ago. Pass by the only original bronze door still swinging on its ancient hinges (green, on right) and continue between ruined buildings until the Via Sacra opens up to a flat, grassy area.*

❸ The Forum's Main Square

The original Forum, or main square, was this flat patch about the size of a football field, stretching to the foot of Capitol Hill. Surrounding it were temples, law courts, government buildings, and triumphal arches.

Rome was born right here. According to legend, twin brothers Romulus (Rome) and Remus were orphaned in infancy and raised by a she-wolf on top of the Palatine. Growing up, they found it hard to get dates. So they and their cohorts attacked the nearby Sabine tribe and kidnapped their women. After they made peace, this marshy valley became the meeting place and then the trading center for the scattered tribes on the surrounding hillsides.

The square was the busiest and most crowded—and often the seediest—section of town. Besides the senators, politicians, and currency exchangers, there were even sleazier types—souvenir hawkers, pickpockets, fortune-tellers, gamblers, slave marketers, drunks, hookers, lawyers, and tour guides.

The Forum is now rubble, no denying it, but imagine it in its prime: blinding white marble buildings with 40-foot-high columns and shining bronze roofs; rows of statues painted in realistic colors; chariots rattling down the Via Sacra. Mentally replace tourists in T-shirts with tribunes in togas. Imagine the buildings towering and the people buzzing around you while an orator gives a rabble-rousing speech from the Rostrum. If things still look like just a pile of rocks, at least tell yourself, "But Julius Caesar once leaned against these rocks."

• *At the near (east) end of the main square (the Colosseum is to the east) are the foundations of a temple now capped with a peaked wood-and-metal roof...*

❹ The Temple of Julius Caesar
(Tempio del Divo Giulio, or Ara di Cesare)

Julius Caesar's body was burned on this spot (under the metal roof) after his assassination.

Caesar (100–44 B.C.) changed Rome—and the Forum—dramatically. He cleared out many of the wooden market stalls and began to ring the square with even grander buildings. Caesar's house was located behind the temple, near that clump of trees. He walked right by here on the day he was assassinated ("Beware the ides of March!" warned a street-corner Etruscan preacher).

Though he was popular with the masses, not everyone liked Caesar's urban design or his politics. When he assumed dictatorial powers, he was ambushed and stabbed to death by a conspiracy of senators, including his adopted son, Brutus *(Et tu, Brute?)*.

The funeral was held here, facing the main square. The citizens gathered and speeches were made. Mark Antony stood up to say (in Shakespeare's words), "Friends, Romans, countrymen, lend me your ears. I come to bury Caesar, not to praise him." When Caesar's body was burned, the citizens who still loved him threw anything at hand on the fire, requiring the fire department to come put it out. Later, Emperor Augustus dedicated this temple in his name, making Caesar the first Roman to become a god.

• *Behind and to the left of the Temple of Julius Caesar are the ten tall columns of the...*

❺ Temple of Antoninus Pius and Faustina

The respected Emperor Antoninus Pius (A.D. 138–161) built this temple—originally called the Temple of Faustina—in honor of his late beloved wife. After the emperor's death, the temple became a monument to them both.

The 50-foot-tall Corinthian (leafy) columns must have been awe-inspiring to out-of-towners who grew up in thatched huts. Although the temple has been reconstructed as a church, you can still see the basic layout—a staircase led to a shaded porch (the columns), which admitted you to the main building (now a church) where the statue of the god sat. Originally, these columns supported a triangular pediment decorated with sculptures.

Picture these columns whitewashed, with gilded capitals, supporting brightly painted statues in the pediment, and the whole building capped with a gleaming bronze roof. The stately gray rubble of today's Forum is a faded black-and-white photograph of a 3-D Technicolor era. (Also picture the Forum covered with dirt as high as the green door—as it was until excavated in the 1800s.)

• *There's a ramp next to the Temple of A. and F. Walk halfway up it and look to the left to view the...*

❻ Basilica Aemilia

A basilica was a Roman hall of justice. In a society that was as legal-minded as America is today, you needed a lot of lawyers and a big place to put them. Citizens came here to work out matters such as inheritances and building permits, or to sue somebody.

Notice the layout. It was a long, rectangular building. The stubby columns all in a row form one long, central hall flanked by two side aisles. Medieval Christians required a larger meeting hall for their worship services than Roman temples provided, so they used the spacious Roman basilica (hall of justice) as the model for their churches. Cathedrals from France to Spain to England, from Romanesque to Gothic to Renaissance, all have the same basic floor plan as a Roman basilica.

• *Return again to the Temple of Julius Caesar. Notice the ruts in the stone street in front of the temple—carved by chariot wheels. To the right of the temple are the three tall Corinthian columns of the Temple of Castor and Pollux. Beyond that is Palatine Hill—the corner of which may have been...*

❼ Caligula's Palace (a.k.a. the Palace of Tiberius)

Emperor Caligula (ruled A.D. 37–41) had a huge palace on Palatine Hill overlooking the Forum. It actually sprawled down the hill into the Forum (some supporting arches remain in the hillside), with an entrance from within the Temple of Castor and Pollux.

Caligula was not a nice person. He tortured enemies, stole senators' wives, and parked his chariot in handicap spaces. But Rome's luxury-loving emperors only added to the glory of the Forum, with each one trying to make his mark on history.

Religion in Ancient Rome

Religion in ancient Rome was all about the *pax deorum* (peace or pact with the gods) that guaranteed the prosperity of the incredibly superstitious Romans. To appease the fickle gods, they performed elaborate rituals at lavish temples and shrines. Romans had a god for every moment of their days and each important event in their lives. While the Romans adopted the Greek pantheon, they also embraced the gods from many of the people they came into contact with, sometimes using elaborate ceremonies to persuade these new gods to "move" to Rome. Scholars estimate Romans had about 30,000 gods to keep happy. In this high-maintenance religion, there was Cunina, the goddess who protected cradles; Statulinus to help children stand up; and Fabulina for their first words. Fornax was the oven god, Pomona the fruit-tree goddess, Sterculinus the manure god, and Venus Cloacina the sewer goddess.

Priests interpreted the will of the gods by studying the internal organs of sacrificed animals, the flight of birds, and prophetic books. A clap of thunder was enough to postpone a battle.

Astrology, magic rites, the cult of deified emperors, house gods, and the near deification of ancestors permeated Roman life. But all these gods didn't quite do it for the Romans—the gods were gradually replaced by the rise of monotheistic religions from the East. In A.D. 312, Emperor Constantine legalized and embraced Christianity. By 390, the Christian God was the only legal god in Rome.

• *To the left of the Temple of Castor and Pollux, find the remains of a small white circular temple...*

❽ The Temple of Vesta

This was Rome's most sacred spot. Rome considered itself one big family, and this temple represented a circular hut, like the kind that

Rome's first families lived in. Inside, a fire burned, just as in a Roman home. And back in the days before lighters and butane, you never wanted your fire to go out. As long as the sacred flame burned, Rome would stand. The flame was tended by priestesses known as Vestal Virgins.

• *Around the back of the Temple of Vesta you'll find two rectangular brick pools. These stood in the courtyard of...*

❾ The House of the Vestal Virgins

The Vestal Virgins lived in a two-story building surrounding a central courtyard with these two pools at one end. Rows of statues to the left and right marked the long sides of the building. This place was the model—both architecturally and sexually—for medieval convents and monasteries.

The six Vestal Virgins, chosen from noble families before they reached the age of 10, served a 30-year term. Honored and revered by the Romans, the Vestals even had their own box opposite the emperor in the Colosseum.

As the name implies, a Vestal took a vow of chastity. If she served her term faithfully—abstaining for 30 years—she was given a huge dowry, honored with a statue (like the ones at left), and allowed to marry (life begins at 40?). But if they found any Virgin who wasn't, she was strapped to a funeral car, paraded through the streets of the Forum, taken to a crypt, given a loaf of bread and a lamp...and buried alive. Many women suffered the latter fate.

• *Head to the Forum's west end (opposite the Colosseum). Stop at the big, well-preserved brick building (on right) with the triangular roof. If the door's open, look in.*

❿ The Curia

The Senate House (Curia) was the most important political building in the Forum. While the present building dates from A.D. 283, this was the site of Rome's official center of government since the birth of the republic. Three hundred senators, elected by the citizens of Rome, met here to debate and create the laws of the land. Their wooden seats once circled the building in three tiers; the Senate president's podium sat at the far end. The marble floor is from ancient times. Listen to the echoes in this vast room—the acoustics are great.

Rome prided itself on being a republic. Early in the city's history, its people threw out the king and established rule by elected representatives. Each Roman citizen was free to speak his mind and have a say in public policy. Even when emperors became the supreme authority, the Senate was a power to be reckoned with. (Note: Although Julius Caesar was assassinated in "the Senate," it wasn't here—the Senate was temporarily meeting across town.) The Curia building (A.D. 280) is well preserved, having been encapsulated in an early Christian church for some 1,500 years, until it was freed in a 1930s reconstruction.

A statue and two reliefs inside the Curia help build our mental image of the Forum. The statue, made of porphyry marble in about A.D. 100, with its head, arms, and feet missing, was a tribute to an emperor, probably Hadrian or Trajan. The two relief panels may have decorated the Rostrum. Those on the left show people (with big stone tablets) standing in line to burn their debt records following a government amnesty. The other shows the distribution of grain (Rome's welfare system), intact architecture, and the latest fashion in togas.

• *Go back down the Senate steps to the metal guardrail and find a 10-foot-high wall at the base of Capitol Hill marked...*

⓫ Rostrum (Rostri)

Nowhere was Roman freedom more apparent than at this "Speaker's Corner." The Rostrum was a raised platform, 10 feet high and 80 feet long, decorated with statues, columns, and the prows of ships *(rostra)*.

On this stage, Rome's orators, great and small, tried to draw a crowd and sway public opinion. Mark Antony rose to offer Caesar the laurel-leaf crown of kingship, which Caesar publicly (and hypocritically) refused while privately becoming a dictator. Men such as Cicero railed against the corruption and decadence that came with the city's newfound wealth. In later years, daring citizens even spoke out against the emperors, reminding them that Rome was once free. Picture the backdrop these speakers would have had—a mountain of marble buildings piling up on Capitol Hill.

Nearby (50 feet west) is the Umbilicus Urbis that marked the center of the city. A column at the far end of the Rostrum once told how far it was from here to the distant cities of Rome's vast empire ("Londinium, 851 miles").

In front of the Rostrum are trees bearing fruits that were sacred to the ancient Romans: olives (provided food, light, and preservatives), figs (tasty), and wine grapes (made a popular export product).

• *The big arch to the right of the Rostrum is the...*

⓬ Arch of Septimius Severus

In imperial times, the Rostrum's voices of democracy would have been dwarfed by images of empire such as the huge, six-story-high Arch of Septimius Severus (A.D. 203). The reliefs commemorate the

Rome Falls

Again, Rome lasted 1,000 years—500 years of growth, 200 years of peak power, and 300 years of gradual decay. The fall had many causes, among them the barbarians who pecked away at Rome's borders. Christians blamed the fall on moral decay. Pagans blamed it on Christians. Socialists blamed it on a shallow economy based on spoils of war. (George W. Bush blamed it on Democrats.) Whatever the reasons, the far-flung empire could no longer keep its grip on conquered lands, and it pulled back. Barbarian tribes from Germany and Asia attacked the Italian peninsula and even looted Rome itself in A.D. 410, leveling many of the buildings in the Forum. In 476, when the last emperor checked out and switched off the lights, Europe plunged into centuries of ignorance, poverty, and weak government—the Dark Ages.

But Rome lived on in the Catholic Church. Christianity was the state religion of Rome's last generations. Emperors became popes (both called themselves Pontifex Maximus), senators became bishops, orators became priests, and basilicas became churches. And remember that the goal for the greatest church-building project ever—that of St. Peter's—was to "put the dome of the Pantheon atop the Basilica of Constantine." The glory of Rome remains eternal.

African-born emperor's battles in Mesopotamia. Near ground level, see curly haired Severus marching captured barbarians back to Rome for the victory parade. Despite Severus' efficient rule, Rome's empire was crumbling under the weight of its own corruption, disease, decaying infra-

structure, and the constant attacks by foreign "barbarians."

• *Pass underneath the Arch of Septimius Severus and turn left. On the slope of Capitol Hill are the eight remaining columns of the..*

⑬ Temple of Saturn

These columns framed the entrance to the Forum's oldest temple (497 B.C.). Inside was a humble, very old wooden statue of the god Saturn. But the statue's pedestal held the gold bars, coins, and jewels of Rome's state treasury, the booty collected by conquering generals.

• *Standing here, at one of the Forum's first buildings, look east at the lone, tall...*

⓮ Column of Phocas

This is the Forum's last great monument (A.D. 608), a gift from the powerful Byzantine Empire to a fallen empire—Rome. After Rome's 1,000-year reign, the city was looted by Vandals, the population of a million-plus shrank to 10,000, and the once-grand city center—the Forum—was abandoned, slowly covered up by centuries of silt and dirt. In the 1700s, an English historian named Edward Gibbon overlooked this spot from Capitol Hill. Hearing Christian monks singing at these pagan ruins, he looked out at the few columns poking up from the ground, pondered the "Decline and Fall of the Roman Empire," and thought, "Hmm, that's a catchy title...."

NATIONAL MUSEUM OF ROME

(Museo Nazionale Romano Palazzo Massimo alla Terme)

Rome lasted a thousand years, and so do most Roman history courses. But if you want a breezy overview of this fascinating society, there's no better place than the National Museum of Rome.

Rome took Greek culture and wrote it in capital letters. Thanks to this lack of originality, ancient Greek statues were preserved for our enjoyment today. But the Romans also pioneered an unheard-of path in art—sculpting painfully realistic portraits of emperors and important citizens.

Think of this museum as a walk back in time. As you gaze at the same statues the Romans swooned over, Rome comes alive— from Romulus sucking a wolf's teat to Julius Caesar's murder to Caligula's incest to the coming of Christianity.

ORIENTATION

Cost: €6, covered by €20 combo-ticket.

Hours: Tue–Sun 9:00–19:45, last entry 45 minutes before closing, closed Mon.

Getting There: The museum is about 100 yards from the Termini train station (Metro: Termini). As you leave the station, it's the sandstone-brick building ahead on your left. Enter at the far end, at Largo di Villa Peretti.

Information: Tel. 06-481-4144.

Tours: An audioguide costs €4 (buy ticket first, then get audioguide at bookshop). To see the fresco collection on the second floor, you must reserve an entry time for a free, 45-minute tour led by an Italian- and English-speaking guide. If interested, book the next available tour when you buy your ticket.

National Museum—Ground Floor

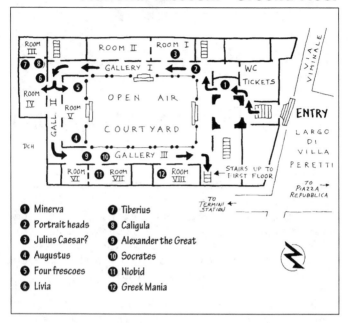

Length of This Tour: Allow two hours.

Starring: Roman emperor busts, *The Discus Thrower*, original Greek statues, and fine Roman copies.

THE TOUR BEGINS

The Palazzo Massimo is now the permanent home of the major Greek and Roman statues that were formerly scattered in other "Museo Nazionales" around town.

The museum is rectangular, with rooms and hallways built around a central courtyard. The ground-floor displays follow Rome's history as it changes from democratic republic to dictatorial empire. The first-floor exhibits take Rome from its peak to its slow fall. The second floor houses rare frescoes and fine mosaics (reservation required for a free tour), and the basement displays coins and every-day objects. As you tour this museum, note that "room" is *sala* in Italian and "hall" is *galleria*.

GROUND FLOOR—FROM SENATORS TO CAESARS

• *Buy your ticket and pass through the turnstile, where you'll find...*

Minerva

It's big, it's gaudy, it's a weird goddess from a pagan cult. Welcome to the Roman world. The statue is also a good reminder that all the statues in this museum—now missing limbs, scarred by erosion, or weathered down to the bare stone—were once whole and painted to look as lifelike as possible.

• *Turning to the right, you'll find Gallery I, lined with portrait busts.*

Gallery I—Portrait Heads from the Republic, 500–1 B.C.

Stare into the eyes of these stern, hardy, no-nonsense, farmer-stock people who founded Rome. The wrinkles and crags of these original "ugly Republicans" tell the story of Rome's roots as a small agricultural tribe that fought neighboring tribes for survival.

These faces are brutally realistic, unlike more idealized Greek statues. Romans honored their ancestors and worthy citizens in the "family" *(gens)* of Rome. They wanted lifelike statues to remember them by, and to instruct the young with their air of moral rectitude.

In its first 500 years, Rome was a republic ruled by a Senate of wealthy landowners. But as Rome expanded throughout Italy and the economy shifted from farming to booty, changes were needed.

• *Enter Room I (Sala I). Along the wall between the doorways, find the portrait bust that some scholars think may be Julius Caesar.*

Julius Caesar? *(Rilievo con Ritratto dalla collezione Von Bergen)*

Julius Caesar (c. 100–44 B.C.)—with his prominent brow, high cheekbones, and male-pattern baldness with the forward comb-over—changed Rome forever.

When this charismatic general swept onto the scene, Rome was in chaos. Rich landowners were fighting middle-class plebs, who wanted their slice of the plunder. Slaves such as Spartacus were picking up hoes and hacking up masters. And renegade generals— the new providers of wealth and security in a  booty economy—were becoming dictators. (Notice the **life-size statue** of an unknown but obviously once-renowned general.)

Caesar was a people's favorite. He conquered Gaul (France), then sacked Egypt, then impregnated Cleopatra. He defeated rivals and made them his allies. He gave great speeches. Chicks dug him.

With the army at his back and the people in awe, he took the reins of government, instituted sweeping changes, made himself the center of power...and antagonized the Senate.

A band of Republican assassins surrounded him in a Senate meeting. He called out for help as one by one they stepped up to take turns stabbing him. The senators sat and watched in silence. One of the killers was his adopted son, Brutus, and Caesar—astonished that even Brutus joined in—died saying, *"Et tu, Brute?"*
• *At the end of Gallery I, turn left, then left again, into the large glassed-in Room V, with a life-size statue of Augustus.*

Room V—Augustus and Rome's Legendary Birth
Statue of Augustus as Pontifex Maximus (*Ritratto di Augusto in Vesta di Offerente*)

Julius Caesar died, but his family name, his politics, and his flamboyance lived on. Julius had adopted his grandnephew, Octavian, who united Rome's warring factions and became the first emperor, Augustus.

Here, Emperor Augustus has taken off his armor and laurel-leaf crown, donning the simple hooded robes of a priest. He's retiring to a desk job after a lifetime of fighting to reunite Rome. He killed Brutus and eliminated his rivals, Mark Antony and Cleopatra. For the first time in almost a century of fighting, one general reigned supreme. Octavian took the title "Augustus" and became the first of the emperors who would rule Rome for the next 500 years.

In fact, Augustus was a down-to-earth man who lived simply, worked hard, read books, listened to underlings, and tried to restore traditional Roman values after the turbulence of Julius Caesar's time. He outwardly praised the Senate while actually reducing it to a rubber-stamp body. Augustus' reign marked the start of 200 years of peace and prosperity, the "Pax Romana."

See if the statue matches a description of Augustus by a contemporary—the historian Suetonius: "He was unusually handsome. His expression was calm and mild. He had clear, bright eyes, in which was a kind of divine power. His hair was slightly curly and somewhat golden." Any variations were made by sculptors who idealized features to make him almost godlike.

Augustus proclaimed himself a god—not arrogantly or blasphemously, as Caligula later did, but as the honored "father" of the "family" of Rome. As the empire expanded, the vanquished had to worship statues like this as a show of loyalty.
• *At this crucial dividing point in Roman history—from republic to*

empire—let's refresh our memory of Rome's legendary origins. At the opposite end of Room V, find...

Four Frescoes of Rome's Mythical Origins (*Fregio Pittorico*, etc.)

These cartoon-strip frescoes (read right to left) tell the story of Augustus' legendary forebears.

1. Upper right fresco: Aeneas (red skin and sword) arrives in Italy from Troy and fights the locals for a place to live.

2. Upper left: His wife (far left, seated, in purple) and son build a city wall around Rome to protect the womenfolk from battles raging outside.

3. Lower right: Several generations later, the God of War (lounging in center, with red skin) lies in wait to rape and impregnate a Vestal Virgin.

4. Lower left: Her disgraced babies, Romulus and Remus, are placed in a basket (center) and set adrift on the Tiber River. They wash ashore, are suckled by a wolf, and finally (far left) taken in by a shepherd. These legendary babies, of course, grow up to found the city that makes real history. (The chisel marks were a preparation designed to help a later fresco (which was never applied) stick.

• *Cross the hallway into Room IV. Find the bust near the doorway of the empress Livia.*

Room IV—The Julio-Claudian Family: Rome's First Emperors (c. 50 B.C.–A.D. 68)

Julius Caesar's descendants ruled Rome for a century after his death, turning the family surname "Caesar" into a title.

Livia

Augustus' wife, Livia, was a major power behind the throne. Her stern, thin-lipped gaze withered rivals at court. Her hairstyle—bunched up in a peak, braided down the center, and tied in back—became the rage throughout the empire, as her face appeared everywhere in statues and on coins. Notice that by the next generation (Antonia Minore, Livia's daughter-in-law, next to Livia), a simpler bun was chic. And by the following generation, it was tight curls. Empresses dictated fashion the way that emperors dictated policy.

Livia bore Augustus no sons. She lobbied hard for Tiberius, her own son by a first marriage, to succeed as emperor. Augustus didn't like him, but Livia was persuasive. He relented, ate some bad figs, and died—the gossip was that Livia poisoned him to seal the bargain. The pattern of succession was established—adopt a son from

within the extended family—and Tiberius was proclaimed emperor.
• *Over your left shoulder, in the corner of the room, is a well-worn...*

Tiberius (*Tiberio,* ruled A.D. 14–37)

Scholars speculate that acne may have soured Tiberius to the world. Shy and sullen but diligent, he worked hard to be the easygoing leader of men that Augustus had been. Early on, he was wise and patient, but he suffered personal setbacks. Politics forced him to divorce his only beloved and marry a slut. His favorite brother died, then his son. Embittered, he let subordinates run things and retired to Capri, where he built a villa with underground dungeons. There he hosted orgies of sex, drugs, torture, really loud music, and execution. At his side was his young grandnephew, who he adopted as next emperor.
• *To your right, in the glass case, is the small bust of...*

Caligula (*Caligol,* ruled A.D. 37–41)

This emperor had sex with his sisters, tortured his enemies, stole friends' wives during dinner and then returned to rate their performance in bed, crucified Christians, took cuts in line at the Vatican Museum, and had men kneel before him as a god. Caligula has become the archetype of a man with enough power to act out his basest fantasies.

Politically, he squandered Rome's money, then taxed and extorted from the citizens. Perhaps he was made mad by illness, perhaps he was the victim of vindictive historians, but still, no one mourned when assassins ambushed him and ran a sword through his privates. Rome was tiring of this family dynasty's dysfunction.
• *Continue down Gallery II and turn left. Busts line Gallery III. Find Alexander and Socrates flanking the entrance into Room VII.*

Gallery III—Rome's Greek Mentors

Rome's legions easily conquered the less-organized but more-cultured Greek civilization that had dominated the Mediterranean for centuries. Romans adopted Greek gods, art styles, and fashions, and sophisticated Romans sprinkled their conversation with Greek phrases.

Alexander the Great (*Alessandro Magno*)

Alexander the Great (356–323 B.C.) single-handedly created a Greek-speaking empire by conquering, in just a few short years, lands from Greece to Egypt to Persia. Later, when the Romans conquered Greece (c. 200 B.C.), they inherited this pre-existing collection of cultured, Greek cities ringing the Mediterranean.

Alexander's handsome statues set the standard for those of later Roman emperors. His features were chiseled and youthful, and this statue was adorned with pompous decorations, like a golden sunburst aura (fitted into the holes). The greatest man of his day, he ruled the known world by the age of 30.

Alexander's teacher was none other than the philosopher Aristotle. Aristotle's teacher was Plato, whose mentor was...

Socrates *(Socrate)*
This nonconformist critic of complacent thinking is the father of philosophy. The Greeks were an intellectual, introspective, sensitive, and artistic people. The Romans were practical, no-nonsense soldiers, salesmen, and bureaucrats. Many a Greek slave was more cultured than his master, reduced to the role of warning his boss not to wear a plaid toga with a polka-dot robe.

• *Enter room VII between Alexander and Socrates.*

Room VII—Greek Beauty in Originals and Copies
Niobid (*Niobide Ferita*, 440 B.C.)
The Romans were astonished by the beauty of Greek statues. Niobid's smooth skin contrasts with the rough folds of her clothing. She twists naturally around an axis running straight up and down. This woman looks like a classical goddess awakening from a beautiful dream. But...

Circle around back. The hole bored in her back, right in that itchy place you can't quite reach, once held a golden arrow. The woman has been shot by Artemis, goddess of hunting, because her mother dared to boast to the gods about her kids. The Niobid reaches back in vain, trying to remove the arrow before it drains her of life.

Romans ate this stuff up: the sensual beauty, the underplayed pathos, the very Greekness of it. They crated up centuries-old statues like this and brought them home to their gardens and palaces. Soon there weren't enough old statues to meet the demand. Crafty Greeks began cranking out knock-offs of Greek originals for mass consumption. In Rooms VII and VIII are originals (like Niobid) and copies—some of extremely high quality, while others were more like cheesy fake *David*s in a garden store. Appreciate the beauty of the world's rare, surviving Greek originals.

Rome conquered Greece, but culturally the Greeks conquered the Romans.

• *We've covered Rome's first 500 years. At the end of the hall are the stairs up to the first floor.*

FIRST FLOOR: ROME'S PEAK AND SLOW FALL

As we saw, Augustus' family did not always rule wisely. Under Nero (ruled A.D. 54–68), the debauchery, violence, and paranoia typical of the Julio-Claudians festered to a head. When the city burned in the great fire of 64, the Romans suspected Nero of torching it himself to clear land for his enormous luxury palace.

Enough. Facing a death sentence, Nero committed suicide with the help of a servant. An outsider was brought in to rule—Vespasian, from the Flavian family.

• *At the top of the stairs, enter Room I. To your right is Vespasian.*

Room I—The Flavian Family
Vespasian (*Vespasianus,* ruled A.D. 69–79)

Balding and wrinkled, with a big head, a double chin, and a shy smile, Vespasian was a common man. The son of a tax collector, he rose through the military ranks with a reputation as a competent drudge. As emperor, he restored integrity, raised taxes, started the Colosseum, and suppressed the Jewish rebellion in Palestine.

• *In the center of the room is...*

Domitian (*Domitianus,* ruled A.D. 81-96)

Vespasian's son, Domitian, used his father's tax revenues to construct the massive Imperial Palace on Palatine Hill, home to emperors for the next three centuries. Shown with his lips curled in a sneering smile, he was a moralistic prude who executed several Vestal ex-Virgins, while in private he took one mistress after another. Until...

• *Over your left shoulder, find...*

Domitia

...until his stern wife found out and hired a servant to stab him in the groin. Domitia's hairstyle is a far cry from the "Livia" cut, with a high crown of tight curls.

• *In the corner opposite Domitia is...*

Nerva (ruled A.D. 96–98)

Nerva realized that the Flavian dynasty was no better than its predecessors. Old and childless, he made a bold, far-sighted move—he adopted a son from outside of Rome's corrupting influence.

• *Entering Room II, Trajan is on the left wall.*

Room II—A Cosmopolitan Culture
Trajan (*Traianus-Hercules,* ruled A.D. 98–117)

Born in Spain, this conquering hero pushed Rome's borders to their greatest extent, creating a truly worldwide empire. The spoils of

National Museum—First Floor

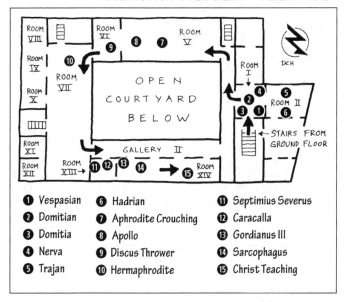

ROOM VIII

ROOM VI

ROOM V

❽ ❼

❾

ROOM IX

❿

ROOM VII

ROOM I

DCH

ROOM X

OPEN COURTYARD BELOW

❹

❺

❷

ROOM II

❸ ❶

❻

← STAIRS FROM GROUND FLOOR

ROOM XI

GALLERY II

ROOM XII

ROOM XIII →

⓫ ⓬ ⓭ ⓮ → ⓯ ROOM XIV

❶ Vespasian

❷ Domitian

❸ Domitia

❹ Nerva

❺ Trajan

❻ Hadrian

❼ Aphrodite Crouching

❽ Apollo

❾ Discus Thrower

❿ Hermaphrodite

⓫ Septimius Severus

⓬ Caracalla

⓭ Gordianus III

⓮ Sarcophagus

⓯ Christ Teaching

three continents funneled into a city of a million-plus people. Trajan could dress up in a lion's skin, presenting himself as a "new Hercules," and no one found it funny. Romans felt a spirit of Manifest Destiny: "The gods desire that the City of Rome shall be the capital of all the countries of the world." (Livy)

• *On the opposite wall...*

Hadrian (*Hadrianus,* ruled A.D. 117–138)

Hadrian was a fully cosmopolitan man. His beard—the first we've seen—shows his taste for foreign things; he poses like the Greek philosopher he imagined himself to be.

Hadrian was a voracious tourist, personally visiting almost every corner of the vast empire, from Britain (where he built Hadrian's Wall) to Egypt (where he sailed the Nile), from Jerusalem (where he suppressed another Jewish revolt) to Athens (where he soaked up classical culture). He scaled Sicily's Mount Etna just to see what made a volcano tick. Back home, he beautified Rome with the Pantheon and his villa at Tivoli, a microcosm of places he'd visited.

Hadrian is accompanied here by the two loves of his life. His wife, **Sabina** (left), with modest hairstyle and scarf, kept the home fires burning for her traveling husband. Hadrian was 50 years old when he became captivated by a teenage boy named **Antinous** (relief behind glass on the left), with his curly hair and full, sensual lips. Together they traveled the Nile, where Antinous drowned. Hadrian wept. Statues of Antinous subsequently went up through the Empire, much to the embarrassment of the stoic Romans.

Hadrian spent his last years at his lavish villa outside Rome, surrounded by buildings and souvenirs that reminded him of his traveling days.

• *Backtrack through room I and turn right, down a hall that leads into the large Room V.*

Rooms V and VI—Rome's Grandeur

Pause at Rome's peak to admire the things the Romans found beautiful. Imagine these statues in their original locations, in the pleasure gardens of the Roman rich—surrounded by greenery, with the splashing sound of fountains, the statues all painted in bright, lifelike colors. Though executed by Romans, the themes are mostly Greek, with godlike humans and human-looking gods.

• *In the center of Room V is...*

Aphrodite Crouching (Afrodite Accovacciata)

The goddess of beauty crouches while bathing, then turns to admire herself. This sets her whole body in motion—one thigh goes down, one up; her head turns clockwise while her body goes reverse—yet she's perfectly still. The crouch creates a series of symmetrical love handles, molded by the sculptor into the marble like wax. Hadrian had good taste—he ordered a copy of this Greek classic for his bathroom.

• *Nearby, find the large statue of...*

Apollo

The god of light appears as a slender youth, not some burly, powerful, autocratic god. He stands *contrapposto*—originally he was leaning against the tree—in a relaxed and very human way. His curled hair is tied with a headband, with strands that tumble down his neck. His muscles and skin are smooth. (The rusty stains come from the centuries Apollo spent submerged in the Tiber.) Apollo is in a reflective mood, and the serenity and intelligence in his face show off classical Greece as a nation of thinkers.

• *At the end of the room is...*

The Discus Thrower (Discobolo)

An athlete winds up, about to unleash his pent-up energy and hurl the discus. The sculptor has frozen the moment for us, so we can examine the inner workings of the wonder called man. The perfect pecs and washboard abs make this human godlike. Geometrically, you could draw a perfect circle around him, with his hipbone at the

center. He's natural yet ideal, twisting yet balanced, moving while at rest. For the Greeks, the universe was a rational place, and the human body was the perfect em-bodi-ment of the order found in nature.

This statue is the best-preserved Roman copy (not one member is missing—I checked) of the original Greek work by Myron (450 B.C.). (The subtle nubs on his head were aids for a measuring device used when making copies.) Statues of athletes like this commonly stood in the baths, where Romans cultivated healthy bodies, minds, and social skills, hoping to live well-rounded lives. *The Discus Thrower,* with his geometrical perfection and godlike air, sums up all that is best in the classical world.

• *Continue into Room VII, where you'll run into a sleeping statue.*

Room VII
Hermaphrodite Sleeping (Ermafrodito Dormiente)
After leaving the baths, a well-rounded Roman may head posthaste to an orgy, where he might see a reclining nude like this, be titillated, circle around for a closer look, and say, "Hey! (Insert your own reaction here)!"

• *Exit Room VII at the far end and turn left. Then turn right into Room XIII, and look to the right to find the bust of Septimius Severus.*

Room XIII—Beginning of the End
Septimius Severus (ruled A.D. 193–211)
Rome's sprawling empire was starting to unravel, and it took a disciplined, emperor-warrior like this African to keep it together. Severus' victories on the frontier earned him a grand triumphal arch in the Forum, but here he seems to be rolling his eyes at the chaos growing around him.

• *Next to Severus is his son...*

Caracalla (ruled A.D. 211–217)
The stubbly beard, cruel frown, and glaring eyes tell us that Severus' son was bad news. He murdered his little brother to seize power, then proceeded to massacre thousands of loyal citizens on a whim. The army came to distrust rulers whose personal agenda got in their way, and Caracalla was stabbed in the back by a man whose brother had just been executed. Rome's long slide had begun.

Room XIV—The Fall
There are a lot of serious faces in this room. People who grew up in the lap of luxury and security were witnessing the unthinkable—the

disintegration of a thousand years of tradition. Rome never recovered from the chaos of the third century. Disease, corruption, revolts from within, and "barbarians" pecking away at the borders were body blows that sapped Rome's strength.

• *At the near end of this long room, find...*

Gordianus III (ruled A.D. 238–244)

By the third century, the Roman army could virtually hand-pick an emperor to be their front-man. (At one point, the office of emperor was literally auctioned to the highest bidder.)

Thirteen-year-old Gordianus, with barely a wisp of facial hair, was naive and pliable, the perfect choice—until he got old enough to question the generals. He was one of some 15 emperors in the space of 40 years who was saluted, then murdered, at the whim of soldiers of fortune. His assassins had no problem sneaking up on him because, as you can see, he had no ears.

Sarcophagus of a Procession
(*Sarcofago con Corteo*, etc., A.D. 270)

A parade of dignitaries, accompanying a new Roman leader, marches up Capitol Hill. They huddle together, their backs to the

wall, looking around suspiciously for assassins. Their faces reflect the fear of the age. Rome would stagger on for another 200 years, but the glory of old Rome was gone. The city was becoming a den of thugs, thieves, prostitutes, barbarians...and Christians.

• *Farther along, on the right-hand wall, find the small...*

Seated Statuette of Christ Teaching
(*Cristo Docente*, A.D. 350)

Christ sits like a Roman senator—in a toga, holding a scroll, dispensing wisdom like the law of the land. The statue comes from those delirious days when formerly persecuted Christians could now "come out" and worship in public. Emperor Constantine (ruled 306–337) legalized Christianity, and within two generations it was Rome's official religion.

Whether Christianity invigorated or ruined Rome is debated, but the fall was inevitable. Rome's once-great legions backpedaled, until even the city itself was raped and plundered by foreigners (410). In 476, the last emperor sold his title for a comfy pension plan, and "Rome" was just another dirty city with a big history. The barely flickering torch of ancient Rome was passed on to medieval Christians: Senators became bishops, basilicas became churches, the

Pontifex Maximus (Emperor) became the Pontifex Maximus (Pope)...and the artistic masterpieces now in this museum became buried under rubble.

THE REST OF THE MUSEUM

The **second floor** (arrange the mandatory guided tour when you arrive at the museum) contains frescoes and mosaics that once decorated the walls and floors of Roman villas. The frescoes—in black, red, yellow, and blue—show a few scenes of  people and animals but are mostly architectural designs, with fake columns and "windows" that "look out" on landscape scenes. The collection is exquisite and the 45-minute tour is in English and Italian.

More interesting stuff is in the **basement,** housing coins and everyday objects from ancient Rome. In A.D. 300, one denar bought one egg. Evaluate Roman life by studying Diocletian's wage and price controls (glass case 21).

Find your favorite emperor or empress on the **coins** using remote-controlled magnifying glasses: Julius Caesar (case 8, #41–44), Augustus (case 8, #65–69; and case 9, #1–38), Augustus' system of denars (case 10), Tiberius (case 10, #1), Caligula (case 10, #17–28), and Nero (case 11, #2–33).

The displays trace Europe's money from denars to euros, including the monetary unit that is now history—*lire.*

PANTHEON

 If your imagination is fried from trying to reconstruct ancient buildings out of today's rubble, visit the Pantheon, Rome's best-preserved monument. Engineers still admire how the Romans built such a mathematically precise structure without computers, fossil-fuel machinery, or electricity. (Having unlimited slave-power didn't hurt.) Stand under the Pantheon's solemn dome to gain a new appreciation for the enlightenment of these ancient people.

ORIENTATION

Cost: Free.

Hours: Mon–Sat 8:30–19:30, Sun 9:00–18:00, holidays 9:00–13:00.

Getting There: Walk (it's a 10- to 15-min walk from the Forum), take a taxi, or catch a bus. Bus #64 carries tourists and pick-pockets daily and frequently between the train station and Vatican City, stopping at Largo Argentina, a few blocks south of the Pantheon. The *electrico* minibus #116 runs between Campo de' Fiori and Piazza Barberini via the Pantheon (daily except Sun).

Information: Tel. 06-6830-0230. Nearest WCs at bars and McDonald's on the square.

Length of This Tour: Allow 45 minutes.

Cuisine Art: You'll find Ristorante da Fortunato a block in front of the Pantheon (closed Sun, Via del Pantheon 55) and perhaps Rome's most exuberant gelato at Gelateria della Palma, two blocks in front of the Pantheon (Via della Maddalena 20).

THE TOUR BEGINS

Pantheon Exterior

The Pantheon was a Roman temple dedicated to all *(pan)* of the gods *(theos)*. First built in 27 B.C. by Augustus' son-in-law (find "M. Agrippa" on the facade), it was completely rebuilt around A.D. 120 by the emperor Hadrian. Some say that Hadrian, an amateur architect, helped design it.

The Pantheon looks like a pretty typical temple from the outside, but this is perhaps the most influential building in art history. Its dome was the model for the Florence cathedral dome, which launched the Renaissance, and for Michelangelo's dome of St. Peter's, which capped it all off. Even Washington, D.C.'s Capitol Building was inspired by this dome.

Back up or step to one side to look above the triangular pediment to the building itself. You'll see the beginnings of a roofline that was abandoned in mid-construction. The pediment was originally intended to be higher, but when the support columns arrived, they were shorter than ordered. Even the most enlightened can forget to "measure twice, cut once."

• *Pass between the enormous, one-piece (too-short) granite columns (most are original) and through the enormous, 2,000-year-old bronze door. Take a seat and take it all in.*

Pantheon Interior

The dome, which was the largest made until the Renaissance, is set on a circular base. The mathematical perfection of this dome-on-a-base design is a testament to Roman engineering. The dome is as high as it is wide—142 feet from floor to rooftop and from side to side. To picture it, imagine a basketball set inside a wastebasket so that it just touches bottom.

The dome is made from concrete that gets lighter and thinner as it reaches the top. The walls at the base are 23 feet thick and made

from heavy travertine concrete, while near the top they're less than five feet thick and made with a lighter volcanic rock (pumice) mixed in. Both Brunelleschi and Michelangelo studied this dome before building their own (in Florence and in the Vatican). Remember, St. Peter's Cathedral is really only "the dome of the Pantheon atop the Basilica of Constantine."

The oculus, or eye-in-the-sky, at the top, the building's only light source, is almost 30 feet across. The 1,800-year-old floor has holes in it and slants toward the edges to let the rainwater drain. The marble floor and wall panels are largely originals.

In ancient times, this was a one-stop-shopping temple where you could worship any of the gods whose statues decorated the niches. Early in the Middle Ages the Pantheon became a Christian church (from "all the gods" to "all the martyrs"), which saved it from architectural cannibalism and ensured its upkeep through the Dark Ages. The only major destruction came in the 17th century, when the pope took the bronze plating from the ceiling of the entry porch and melted it down—some was used to build the huge bronze canopy over the altar at St. Peter's.

About the only new things in the interior are the decorative statues and the tombs of famous people. The artist Raphael lies to the left of the main altar (in the glass case). The Latin inscription on his tomb reads, "In life nature feared to be outdone by him. In death she feared she too would die." You'll also see the tombs of modern Italy's first two kings: Victor Emmanuel II (to the right) and Umberto I (to the left). These are a hit with royalists. In fact there is often a blue-coated guard standing by a guestbook where visitors can register their support for the Savoia family (which recently, with some controversy, returned from exile to the country they once ruled). And finally, under Umberto lies his Queen, Margherita...for whom pizza margherita is named.

The Pantheon is the only ancient building in Rome continuously used since its construction. When you leave, you'll notice how the rest of the city has risen on 20 centuries of rubble.

The Pantheon also contains the world's greatest Roman column. There it is, spanning the entire 142 feet from heaven to earth—the pillar of light from the oculus.

ST. PETER'S BASILICA

(Basilica San Pietro)

St. Peter's is the greatest church in Christendom. It represents the power and splendor of Rome's 2,000-year domination of the Western world. Built on the memory and grave of the first pope, St. Peter, this is where the grandeur of ancient Rome became the grandeur of Christianity.

ORIENTATION

Cost: Free (€5 to climb dome).

Dress Code: The dress code is strictly enforced. No shorts or bare shoulders (applies to men, women, and children), and no miniskirts.

Hours of Church: Daily May–Sept 7:00–19:00, Oct–April 7:00–18:00. Mass is held daily (Mon–Sat 8:30, 10:00, 11:00, 12:00, and 17:00, Sun and holidays 9:00, 10:30, 12:10, 13:00, 16:00, and 17:30). The church occasionally closes on Wednesday mornings during papal audiences. The best time to visit the church is early or late.

Hours of Dome: Daily May–Sept 8:30–18:00, Oct–April 8:30–17:00. The lift to the dome opens daily at 8:30 and closes one hour before the church closes. Allow one hour for the full trip up and down, a half hour to go only to the roof and gallery. The entry to the elevator changes—it's either inside the church (left side of the nave) or just outside the basilica on the north side of St. Peter's. Look for signs to the cupola. For more on the dome, see end of chapter.

Warning: You'll see signs to the crypt

Vatican City

This tiny independent country of just over 100 acres, contained entirely within Rome, has its own postal system, armed guards, helipad, mini–train station, and radio station (KPOP). Politically powerful, the Vatican is the religious capital of 800 million Roman Catholics. If you're not a Catholic, become one for your visit.

Small as it is, Vatican City has two huge sights: St. Peter's Basilica (with Michelangelo's *Pietà*) and the Vatican Museum (with the Sistine Chapel). A helpful TI is just to the left of St. Peter's Basilica (Mon–Sat 8:30–19:00, closed Sun, tel. 06-6988-1662; Vatican switchboard tel. 06-6982, www.vatican.va). The thief-infested bus #64 and the safer #40 express stop right at the basilica. The nearest Metro stops are a 10-minute walk away from either sight: For St. Peter's, the closest stop is Ottaviano; for the Vatican Museum, it's Cipro–Musei Vaticani.

Post Office: The Vatican post, with offices on St. Peter's Square (next to TI) and in the Vatican Museum, is more reliable than Italy's mail service (Mon–Sat 8:30–19:00). The stamps are a collectible bonus. Vatican stamps are good throughout Rome, but to use the Vatican's mail service, you need to mail your cards from the Vatican; write your postcards ahead of time. (Note that the Vatican won't mail cards with Italian stamps.)

Tours: The Vatican TI conducts free 90-minute tours of St. Peter's (depart daily from TI at 14:15, also Mon, Wed, and Fri at 15:00, confirm schedule at TI, tel. 06-6988-1662). Tours are the only way to see the Vatican Gardens; book at least a day in advance by calling 06-6988-4676 (€9, Mon–Sat 10:00–12:00, tours start at Vatican Museum tour desk and finish on St. Peter's Square). To tour the necropolis of St. Peter's and the saint's tomb, call the Excavations Office at 06-6988-5318 (€8, 2 hours, office open Mon–Fri 9:00–17:00), book at least one week ahead.

Seeing the Pope: Your best chances for a sighting are on Sunday and Wednesday. The pope usually gives a blessing at noon

(foundations of old St. Peter's, with tombs) inside the church. It's free, but save it for the end of your visit, because the exit deposits you outside the church.

Getting There: Subway to Ottaviano, then a 10-minute walk south on Via Ottaviano. Several city buses get very near St. Peter's Square. Bus #64 is convenient for pickpockets; the #40 express is less crowded. Taxis are reasonable (Termini train station to St. Peter's is about €10).

Information: The TI on the left (south) side of the square is excellent (Mon–Sat 8:30–19:00, closed Sun, free Vatican and church map, tel. 06-6988-1662). WCs are to the right and left (near TI) of the church and on the roof. Drinking fountains are at

on Sunday from his apartment on St. Peter's Square (except summer, when he speaks at his summer residence at Castel Gandolfo 25 miles from Rome; train leaves Rome's Termini station). St. Peter's is easiest (just show up) and, for most, enough of a "visit." Those interested in a more formal appearance (but not more intimate), can get a ticket for the Wednesday blessing (at 10:30) when the pope, arriving in his bulletproof Popemobile, greets and blesses the crowds at St. Peter's from a balcony or canopied platform on the square (except in winter, when he speaks at 10:30 in the 7,000-seat Aula Paola VI Auditorium, next to St. Peter's Basilica). This requires a ticket—arrange it in advance through your hotel or the Santa Susanna Church (they get it and you pick it up the day before at their church between 17:00 and 18:45, Via XX Settembre 15, near recommended Via Firenze hotels, Metro: Repubblica, tel. 06-4201-4554, www.santasusanna.org). To find out the pope's schedule or to book a free spot for the Wednesday blessing (either for a seat on the square or in the auditorium), call 06-6988-4631. The weekly entertainment guide *Roma c'è* always has a "Seeing the Pope" section. If you only want to see the Vatican—but not the pope—minimize crowd problems by avoiding these times.

Vatican City Overview

the obelisk and near WCs. The post office is next to the TI.

Tours: Ninety-minute tours in English are offered daily at 14:15 and also at 15:00 on Mon, Wed, and Fri; meet at the TI outside the entrance to the basilica (free, confirm schedule at TI, tel. 06-6988-1662).

Length of This Tour: One hour, plus another hour if you climb the dome (elevator plus 323 steps one-way).

Checkroom: Free, usually mandatory bag check is outside at the security check (to the right of the entrance).

Starring: Michelangelo, Bernini, St. Peter, a heavenly host, and, occasionally, the pope.

THE TOUR BEGINS

Old St. Peter's

• *Find a shady spot where you like the view under the columns around St. Peter's oval-shaped "square." If the pigeons left a clean spot, sit on it.*

Nearly 2,000 years ago, this area was the site of Nero's Circus—a huge Roman chariot racecourse. The obelisk you see in the middle of the square stands where the chariots made their hairpin turns. The Romans had no marching bands, so for half-time entertainment they killed Christians. This persecuted minority was forced to fight wild animals and gladiators, or they were simply crucified. Some were tarred up, tied to posts, and burned—human torches to light up the evening races.

One of those killed here, around A.D. 65, was Peter, Jesus' right-hand man, who had come to Rome to spread the message of love. Peter was crucified on an upside-down cross at his own request because he felt unworthy to die as his master had. His remains were buried in a nearby cemetery where, for 250 years, they were quietly and secretly revered.

When Christianity was finally legalized in 313, the Christian emperor Constantine built a church on the site of the martyrdom of this first "pope," or bishop of Rome, from whom all later popes claimed their authority as head of the Church. "Old St. Peter's" lasted 1,200 years (A.D. 329–1500).

By the time of the Renaissance, old St. Peter's was falling apart and was considered unfit to be the center of the Western Church. The new, larger church we see today was begun in 1506 and was actually built around the old one. As the project was completed 120 years later, after many changes of plans, old St. Peter's was dismantled and carried out of the new one. (A few bits survive from the first church: the central door, some columns in the atrium, eight spiral columns around the tomb from "Solomon's Temple," the venerated statue of Peter, and Michelangelo's *Pietà*.)

• *Ideally, you should head out to the obelisk to view the square and read this. But let me guess—it's 95 degrees, right? OK, read on in the shade of these stone sequoias.*

ST. PETER'S SQUARE

St. Peter's Square, with its ring of columns, symbolizes the arms of the church "maternally embracing Catholics, heretics, and the faithless." It was designed by the Baroque architect Bernini, who also did much of the work that we'll see inside. Numbers first: 284 columns, 56 feet high, in stern Doric style. Topping them are Bernini's 140 favorite saints, each 10 feet tall. The "square" itself is elliptical, 660 by 500 feet.

St. Peter's Square

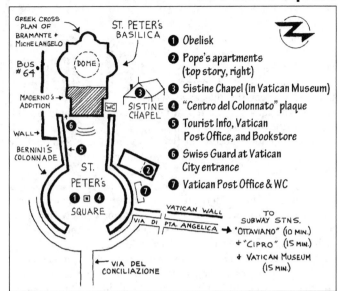

GREEK CROSS PLAN OF BRAMANTE + MICHELANGELO

ST. PETER'S BASILICA

BUS #64

(DOME)

MADERNO'S ADDITION

WC

SISTINE CHAPEL

WALL→

BERNINI'S COLONNADE

❻

❺

ST. PETER'S SQUARE

❶ ▣ ❹

❸

❷

❼

VATICAN WALL

VIA DI PTA. ANGELICA →

TO SUBWAY STNS.
"OTTAVIANO" (10 MIN.)
+ "CIPRO" (15 MIN.)
+ VATICAN MUSEUM (15 MIN.)

← VIA DEL CONCILIAZIONE

❶ Obelisk

❷ Pope's apartments (top story, right)

❸ Sistine Chapel (in Vatican Museum)

❹ "Centro del Colonnato" plaque

❺ Tourist Info, Vatican Post Office, and Bookstore

❻ Swiss Guard at Vatican City entrance

❼ Vatican Post Office & WC

The obelisk in the center is 90 feet of solid granite weighing over 300 tons. Think for a second about how much history this monument has seen. Erected originally in Egypt over 2,000 years ago, it witnessed the fall of the pharaohs to the Greeks and then to the Romans. It was then moved to imperial Rome by the emperor Caligula, where it stood impassively watching the slaughter of Christians at the racecourse and the torture of Protestants by the Inquisition (in the yellow and rust building just outside the square, to the left of the church). Today it watches over the church, a reminder that each civilization builds on the previous ones. The puny cross on top reminds us that our Christian culture is but a thin veneer over our pagan origins.

• *Now venture out across the burning desert to the obelisk, which provides a narrow sliver of shade.*

Face the church, then turn about-face and say *"Grazie, Benito."* I don't make a habit of thanking fascist dictators, but in the 1930s, Benito Mussolini did open up this broad boulevard, finally letting people see the dome of St. Peter's, which had been hidden for centuries by the facade. From here at the obelisk, Michelangelo's magnificent dome can only peek its top over the bulky Baroque front entrance.

The gray building at two o'clock to the right (as you face the church), rising up behind Bernini's colonnade, is where the pope lives. The last window on the right of the top floor is his bedroom. To the left of that window is his study window, where he appears occasionally to greet the masses. If you  come to the square at night as a Poping Tom, you might see the light on—the pope burns much midnight oil.

On more formal occasions (which you may have seen on TV), the pope appears from the church itself, on the small balcony above the central door.

The Sistine Chapel is just to the right of the facade—the small gray-brown building with the triangular roof, topped by an antenna. The tiny chimney (the pimple along the roofline midway up the left side) is where the famous smoke signals announce the election of each new pope. If the smoke is black, a 75 percent majority hasn't been reached. White smoke means a new pope has been selected.

Walk to the right, five pavement plaques from the obelisk, to one marked "Centro del Colonnato." From here, all of Bernini's columns on the right side line up. The curved Baroque square still pays its respects to Renaissance mathematical symmetry.

• *Climb the gradually sloping pavement past crowd barriers and the huge statues of St. Paul with his two-edged sword and St. Peter with his bushy hair and keys. Since 9/11, admission has been limited to one side or the other, but not both at the same time. To avoid a long unnecessary dead-end hike, see which entrance is being used by individuals instead of tour groups before beginning your climb.*

On the square are two entrances to Vatican City—one to the left of the facade, one to the right in the crook of Bernini's "arm." Guarding this small but powerful country's border crossing are the mercenary guards from Switzerland. You have to wonder if they really know how to use those pikes. Their colorful uniforms are said to have been designed by Michelangelo, though he was not known for his sense of humor.

• *Enter the atrium (entrance hall) of the church. You'll pass by the dress-code enforcers and a gaggle of ticked-off guys in shorts.*

THE BASILICA

The Atrium

The atrium is itself bigger than most churches. The huge white columns on the portico date from the first church (fourth century). Five famous bronze doors lead into the church.

St. Peter's Basilica

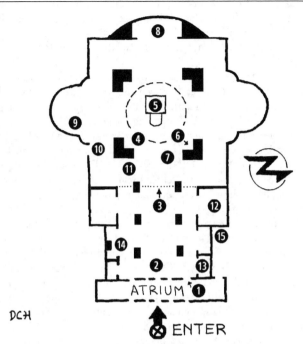

DCH

ENTER

ST.   PETER'S   SQUARE

1. Holy Door
2. Site of Charlemagne's coronation, 800 A.D.
3. Extent of the original "Greek Cross" church plan
4. St. Andrew Statue (view the dome from here)
5. Main altar directly over Peter's Tomb
6. Stairs down to the crypt— the foundation of old St. Peter's, chapels and tombs of popes (the entrance moves around)
7. Statue of St. Peter with irresistibly kissable toe
8. BERNINI—Dove window and "St. Peter's Throne"
9. Site of St. Peter's crucifixion
10. Museum entrance
11. RAPHAEL—Transfiguration mosaic
12. Blessed Sacrament Chapel
13. MICHELANGELO—Pietà
14. Elevator to Roof and Dome-Climb (Possible Indoor Location)
15. Elevator to Roof and Dome-Climb (Possible Outdoor Location)

The central door, made from the melted-down bronze of the original door of old St. Peter's, was the first Renaissance work in Rome (c. 1450). It's only opened on special occasions. The panels (from the top down) feature Jesus and Mary, Paul and Peter, and (at the bottom) how each were martyred: Paul decapitated, Peter crucified upside down.

The far-right entrance is the Holy Door, opened only during Holy Years. On Christmas Eve every 25 years, the pope knocks three times with a silver hammer and the door opens, welcoming pilgrims to pass through. After opening the door on Christmas Eve, 1999, he bricked it up again with a ceremonial trowel a year later to await another 24 years. (A plaque above the door fudges a bit for effect: it says that Pope "IONNES PAULUS II" opened the door in the year "MM"—2000—and closed it in "MMI.") On the door itself, note Jesus' shiny knees, polished by pious pilgrims who touch them for a blessing.

The other doors are modern, reminding us that amid all this tradition, the Catholic Church has changed enormously even within our lifetimes. Door #2 (second from left) commemorates the kneeling pope, John (Giovanni) XXIII, who opened the landmark Vatican II Council in the early 1960s. This meeting of Church leaders brought the medieval Church into the modern age—they dropped outdated rituals, such as the use of Latin in the Mass—and made old doctrines "relevant" to modern times.

• *Now for one of Europe's great "wow" experiences. Enter the church. Gape for a while. But don't gape at Michelangelo's famous* Pietà *(on the right). That's this tour's finale. I'll wait for you at the round maroon pavement stone on the floor near the central doorway.*

The Church

While ancient Rome fell, its grandeur survived. Roman basilicas became churches, senators became bishops, and the Pontifex Maximus (Emperor)...remained the Pontifex Maximus (Pope). This church is appropriately huge.

Size before beauty: The golden window at the far end is two football fields away. The dove in the window has the wingspan of a 747 (OK, maybe not quite, but it is big). The church covers six acres. The babies at the base of the pillars along the main hall (the nave) are adult size. The lettering in the gold band along the top of the pillars is seven feet high. Really. The church has a capacity of 60,000 standing worshipers (or 1,200 tour groups).

The church is huge and it feels huge,

but everything is designed to make it seem smaller and more intimate than it really is. For example, the statue of St. Teresa near the bottom of the first pillar on the right is 15 feet tall. The statue above her near the top looks the same size, but is actually six feet taller, giving the impression that it's not so far away. Similarly, the fancy bronze canopy over the altar at the far end is as tall as a seven-story building. That makes the great height of the dome seem smaller.

Looking down the nave, we get a sense of the splendor of ancient Rome that was carried on by the Catholic Church. The floor plan is based on the ancient Roman basilica, or law-court building, with a central aisle (nave) flanked by two side aisles.

The goal of this unprecedented building project was to "put the dome of the Pantheon atop the Forum's Basilica of Constantine." If you've seen these two Roman structures, you have an idea of this megavision. In fact, many of the stones used to build St. Peter's were scavenged from the ruined law courts of ancient Rome.

On the floor near the central doorway is a round slab of porphyry stone in the maroon color of ancient Roman officials. This is the spot where, on Christmas night in A.D. 800, the French king Charlemagne was crowned "Holy Roman Emperor." Even in the Dark Ages, when Rome was virtually abandoned and visitors reported that the city "had more thieves and wolves than decent people," its imperial legacy made it a fitting place to symbolically establish a briefly united Europe.

St. Peter's was very expensive to build and decorate. The popes financed it by selling "indulgences," allowing the rich to buy forgiveness from the Church. This kind of corruption inspired an obscure German monk named Martin Luther to rebel and start the Protestant Reformation.

The ornate Baroque-style interior decoration—a riot of marble, gold, stucco, mosaics, columns of stone, and pillars of light—was part of the Church's "Counter-" Reformation. Baroque served as cheery propaganda, impressing followers with the authority of the Church, and giving them a glimpse of the heaven that awaited the faithful.

• *Now, walk straight up the center of the nave toward the altar.*

"Michelangelo's Church"—The Greek Cross

The plaques on the floor show where other, smaller churches of the world would end if they were placed inside St. Peter's: St. Paul's Cathedral in London (Londinium), the Florence Cathedral, and so on.

You'll also walk over circular golden grates. Stop at the second one (at the third pillar from the entrance). Look back at the entrance and realize that if Michelangelo had had his way, this whole long section of the church wouldn't exist. The nave was extended after his death.

Michelangelo was 71 years old when the pope persuaded him to take over the church project and cap it with a dome. He agreed, intending to put the dome over Bramante's original "Greek Cross" floor plan (+), with four equal arms. In optimistic Renaissance times, this symmetrical arrangement symbolized perfection—the orderliness of the created world and the goodness of man (who was created in God's image). But Michelangelo was a Renaissance Man in Counter-Reformation times. The Church, struggling against Protestants and its own corruption, opted for a plan designed to impress the world with its grandeur—the Latin cross of the Crucifixion with its nave extended to accommodate the grand religious spectacles of the Baroque period.

• *Continue toward the altar, entering "Michelangelo's Church." Park yourself in front of the statue of St. Andrew to the left of the altar, the guy holding an X-shaped cross. Like Andrew, gaze up into the dome, and also like him, gasp. (Never stifle a gasp.)*

The Dome

The dome soars higher than a football field on end, 430 feet to the top of the lantern. It glows with light from its windows, the blue and gold mosaics creating a cool, solemn atmosphere. In this majestic vision of heaven (not painted by Michelangelo), we see (above the windows) Jesus, Mary, and a ring of saints, more rings of angels above them, and, way up in the ozone, God the Father (a blur of blue and red, without binoculars).

When Michelangelo died (1564), he'd completed only the drum of the dome—the base up to the windows flanked by half-columns—but the next architects were guided by his designs.

Listen to the hum of visitors echoing through St. Peter's and reflect on our place in the cosmos: half animal, half angel, stretched between heaven and earth, born to live only a short while, a bubble of foam on a great cresting wave of humanity.

• *But I digress.*

Peter

The base of the dome is ringed with a gold banner telling us in massive blue letters why this church is so important. According to Catholics, Peter was selected by Jesus to head the church. The banner in Latin quotes from the Bible

where Jesus says to him, "You are Peter *(Tu es Petrus)* and upon this rock I will build my church, and to you I will give the keys of the kingdom of heaven" (Matthew 16:18). (Every quote from Jesus to Peter found in the Bible is written out in 7-foot-tall letters that continue around the entire church.) Peter was the first bishop of Rome. His prestige and that of the city itself made this bishopric more illustrious than all others, and Peter's authority has supposedly passed in an unbroken chain to each succeeding bishop of Rome—that is, the 250-odd popes that followed.

Under the dome, under the bronze canopy, under the altar, some 23 feet under the marble floor, rest the bones of St. Peter, the "rock" upon which this particular church was built. Go to the railing and look down into the small, lighted niche below the altar with a box containing bishops' shawls—a symbol of how Peter's authority spread to the other churches. Peter's tomb (not visible) is just below this box.

Are they really the bones of Jesus' apostle? According to a papal pronouncement: definitely maybe. The traditional site of his tomb was sealed up when Old St. Peter's was built on it in A.D. 326, and it remained sealed until 1940, when it was opened for archaeological study. Bones were found, dated from the first century, of a robust man who died in old age. His body was wrapped in expensive cloth. Various inscriptions and graffiti in the tomb indicate that second- and 3rd-century visitors thought this was Peter's tomb. Does that mean it's really Peter? Who am I to disagree with the pope? Definitely maybe.

If you line up the cross on the altar with the dove in the window, you'll notice that the niche below the cross is just off-center compared with the rest of the church. Why? Because Michelangelo built the church around the traditional location of the tomb, not the actual location—about two feet away—discovered by modern archaeology.

Back in the nave sits a bronze statue of Peter under a canopy. This is one of a handful of pieces of art that was in the earlier church. In one hand he holds the keys, the symbol of the authority given him by Christ, while with the other he blesses us. He's wearing the toga of a Roman senator. It may be that the original statue was of a senator and the bushy head and keys were added later to make it Peter. His big right toe has been worn smooth by the lips of pilgrims and foot-fetishists. Stand in line and kiss it, or, to avoid foot-and-mouth disease, touch your hand to your lips, then rub the toe. This is simply an act of reverence with no legend attached, though you can make one up if you like.

The Main Altar

The main altar beneath the dome and canopy (the white marble slab with cross and candlesticks) is used only when the pope himself says Mass. He sometimes conducts the Sunday morning service when

he's in town, a sight worth seeing. I must admit, though, it's a little strange being frisked at the door for weapons at the holiest place in Christendom.

The tiny altar would be lost in this enormous church if it weren't for Gian Lorenzo Bernini's seven-story bronze canopy (God's "four-poster bed"), which "extends" the altar upward and reduces the perceived distance between floor and ceiling. The corkscrew columns echo the marble ones that surrounded the altar/tomb in Old St. Peter's. Some of the bronze used here was taken and melted down from the ancient Pantheon. On the marble base of the columns are three bees on a shield, the symbol of the Barberini family, who commissioned the work and ordered the raid on the Pantheon. As the saying went, "What the barbarians didn't do, the Barberini did."

Starting from the column to the left of the altar, walk clockwise around the canopy. Notice the female faces on the marble bases, about eye level above the bees. Someone in the Barberini family was pregnant during the making of the canopy, so Bernini put the various stages of childbirth on the bases. Continue clockwise to the last base to see how it came out.

Bernini (1598–1680), the Michelangelo of the Baroque era, is the man most responsible for the interior decoration of the church. The altar area was his masterpiece, a "theater" for holy spectacles. Bernini did: (1) the bronze canopy; (2) the dove window in the apse surrounded by bronzework and statues; (3) the statue of lance-bearing St. Longinus ("The hills are alive..."), which became the model for the other three statues; (4) much of the marble floor decoration; and, (5) the balconies above the four statues, incorporating the actual corkscrew columns from Old St. Peter's said to have been looted by the Romans from the Temple of Herod (called "Solomon's Temple") in Jerusalem. Bernini, the father of Baroque, gave an impressive unity to an amazing variety of pillars, windows, statues, chapels, and aisles.

• *The apse is the front area with the golden dove window.*

The Apse

Bernini's dove window shines above the smaller front altar used for everyday services. The Holy Spirit, in the form of a six-foot-high dove, pours sunlight onto the faithful through the alabaster windows, turning into artificial rays of gold and reflecting off swirling gold clouds, angels, and winged babies. This is the epitome of Baroque—an ornate, mixed-media work designed to overwhelm the viewer.

Beneath the dove is the centerpiece of this structure, the so-called "Throne of Peter," an oak chair built in medieval times for a king.

Subsequently, it was encrusted with tradition and encased in bronze by Bernini as a symbol of papal authority. Statues of four early Church Fathers support the chair, a symbol of how bishops should support the pope in troubled times—times like the Counter-Reformation.

Remember that St. Peter's is a church, not a museum. In the apse, Mass is said daily (Mon–Sat at 17:00, Sun at 17:30) for pilgrims, tourists, and Roman citizens alike. Wooden confessional booths are available for Catholics to tell their sins to a listening ear and receive forgiveness and peace of mind. The faithful renew their faith and the faithless gain inspiration. Look at the light streaming through the windows, turn and gaze up into the dome, and quietly contemplate your deity (or lack thereof).

• *To the left of the main altar is the south transept. At the far end, left side, find the dark "painting" of St. Peter crucified upside down.*

South Transept—Peter's Crucifixion

This marks the exact spot (according to tradition) where Peter was killed 1,900 years ago. Peter had come to the world's greatest city to preach Jesus' message of love to the pagan, often hostile Romans. During the reign of Nero, he was arrested and brought to Nero's Circus so all Rome could witness his execution. When the authorities told Peter he was to be crucified just like his Lord, Peter said "I'm not worthy," and insisted they nail him on the cross upside-down. After he died on this spot, they buried him nearby (where the altar is today).

The Romans were actually quite tolerant of other religions. All they required of their conquered peoples was allegiance to the empire by worshiping the emperor as a god. For most religions, this was no problem, but monotheistic Christians were children of a jealous God who would not allow worship of any others. They refused to worship

Bernini Blitz

Nowhere is there such a conglomeration of works by the flamboyant genius who remade the church—and the city—in the Baroque style. Here's your scavenger-hunt list. You have 20 minutes. Go.

1. St. Peter's Square: design and statues
2. Constantine equestrian relief (right end of atrium)
3. Decoration (stucco, gold leaf, marble, etc.) of side aisles (flanking the nave)
4. Tabernacle (the temple-like altarpiece) inside Blessed Sacrament Chapel
5. Much of the marble floor throughout church
6. Bronze canopy over the altar
7. St. Longinus statue (holding a lance) near altar
8. Balconies (above each of the four statues) with corkscrew, Solomonic columns
9. Dove window, bronze sunburst, angels, "Throne," and Church Fathers (in the apse)
10. Tomb of Pope Urban VIII (far end of the apse, right side)
11. Tomb of Pope Alexander VII (between the apse and the left transept, over a doorway, with the gold skeleton smothered in jasper poured like maple syrup). Bizarre...Baroque...Bernini.

the emperor even when burned alive, crucified, or thrown to the lions. Their bravery, optimism in suffering, and message of love struck a chord among slaves and members of the lower classes. The religion started by a poor carpenter grew, despite occasional pogroms by fanatical emperors. In three short centuries, Christianity went from a small Jewish sect in Jerusalem to the official religion of the world's greatest empire.

This and all the other "paintings" in the church are actually mosaic copies made from thousands of colored chips the size of your little fingernail. Smoke and humidity would damage real paintings. Around the corner on the right (heading back toward the central nave), pause at the copy of Raphael's huge "painting" (mosaic) of *The Transfiguration*, especially if you won't be seeing the original in the Vatican Museum.

• *Back near the entrance to the church, in the far corner, behind bullet-proof glass is the...*

Pietà

Michelangelo was 24 years old when he completed this Pietà of Mary with the dead body of Christ taken from the cross. It was Michelangelo's first major commission (by the French ambassador to the Vatican), done for Holy Year 1500.

Pietà means compassion. Michelangelo, with his total mastery of the real world, captures the sadness of the moment. Mary cradles her crucified son in her lap. Christ's lifeless right arm drooping down lets us know how heavy this corpse is. His smooth skin is accented by the rough folds of Mary's robe. Mary tilts her head downward, looking at her dead son with sad tenderness. Her left hand turns upward, asking, "How could they do this to you?"

Michelangelo didn't think of sculpting as creating a figure, but as simply freeing the God-made figure from the prison of marble around it. He'd attack a project like this with an inspired passion, chipping away to reveal what God put inside.

The bunched up shoulder and rigor-mortis legs show that Michelangelo learned well from his studies of cadavers. But realistic as this work is, its true power lies in the subtle "unreal" features. Lifesize Christ looks childlike compared with larger-than-life Mary. Unnoticed at first, this accentuates the subconscious impression of Mary enfolding Jesus in her maternal love. Mary—the mother of a 33-year-old man—looks like a teenager, emphasizing how Mary was the eternally youthful "handmaiden" of the Lord, always serving Him, even at this moment of supreme sacrifice. She accepts God's will, even if it means giving up her son.

The statue is a solid pyramid of maternal tenderness. Yet within this, Christ's body tilts diagonally down to the right and Mary's hem flows with it. Subconsciously, we feel the weight of this dead God sliding from her lap to the ground.

At 11:30 a.m. on May 23, 1972, a madman with a hammer entered St. Peter's and began hacking away at the *Pietà*. The damage was repaired, but that's why there's a shield of bullet-proof glass today.

This is Michelangelo's only signed work. The story goes that he overheard some pilgrims praising his finished *Pietà*, but attributing it to a second-rate sculptor from a lesser city. He was so enraged he grabbed his chisel and chipped "Michelangelo Buonarroti of Florence did this" in the ribbon running down Mary's chest.

On your right (covered in gray concrete with a gold cross) is the inside of the Holy Door. It won't be opened until Christmas Eve, 2024, the dawn of the next Jubilee Year. If there's a prayer inside you, ask that when it's next opened, St. Peter's will no longer need security checks or bulletproof glass.

Up to the Dome (Cupola)

A good way to finish a visit to St. Peter's is to go up to the dome for the best view of Rome anywhere.

There are two levels, the rooftop of the church and the very top of the dome. An elevator (€5) takes you to the first level, on the church roof just above the facade. Even from there, you have a commanding view of St. Peter's Square, the statues on the colonnade, Rome across the Tiber in front of you, and the dome itself—almost terrifying in its nearness—looming behind you.

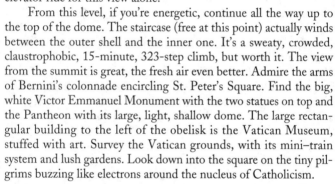

From here, you can also go inside to the gallery ringing the interior of the dome, where you can look down inside the church. Notice the dusty top of Bernini's seven-story-tall canopy far below. Study the mosaics up close—and those huge letters! It's worth the elevator ride for this view alone.

From this level, if you're energetic, continue all the way up to the top of the dome. The staircase (free at this point) actually winds between the outer shell and the inner one. It's a sweaty, crowded, claustrophobic, 15-minute, 323-step climb, but worth it. The view from the summit is great, the fresh air even better. Admire the arms of Bernini's colonnade encircling St. Peter's Square. Find the big, white Victor Emmanuel Monument with the two statues on top and the Pantheon with its large, light, shallow dome. The large rectangular building to the left of the obelisk is the Vatican Museum, stuffed with art. Survey the Vatican grounds, with its mini–train system and lush gardens. Look down into the square on the tiny pilgrims buzzing like electrons around the nucleus of Catholicism.

THE REST OF THE CHURCH

The Crypt: You can go down to the foundations of old St. Peter's, containing tombs of popes and memorial chapels. But you won't see St. Peter's tomb unless you take a tour (€8, call Excavations Office at 06-6988-5318). The staircase entrance varies, but it's usually inside the church, underneath the dome near St. Andrew or one of his three fellow statues. Seeing the crypt is free, but the visit takes you back outside the church, a 15-minute detour. (Do it when you're ready to leave.)

The Museum (Museo-Tesoro): You must pay an admission fee to see an original corkscrew column from Old St. Peter's, the room-sized tomb of Sixtus IV by Pollaiuolo, a big pair of Roman pincers used to torture Christians, and assorted jewels, papal robes, and golden reliquaries (a marked contrast to the poverty of early Christians). The museum is located on the left side of the nave, near the altar.

Blessed Sacrament Chapel: You're welcome to step through the metalwork gates into this oasis of peace reserved for prayer and meditation. It's located on the right-hand side of the church, about midway to the altar.

VATICAN MUSEUM

(Musei Vaticani)

The glories of the ancient world displayed in a lavish papal palace, decorated by the likes of Michelangelo and Raphael...the Musei Vaticani. Unfortunately, many tourists see the Vatican Museum only as an obstacle between them and its grand finale, the Sistine Chapel. True, this huge, confusing, and crowded mega-museum can be a jungle—but with this book as your vine, you should swing through with ease, enjoying the highlights and getting to the Sistine just before you collapse. On the way, you'll enjoy some of the less appreciated but  equally important sections of this warehouse of Western civilization.

ORIENTATION

Cost: €10, free (and packed) on last Sun of each month.

Dress Code: Modest dress (no short shorts or bare shoulders) is appropriate and often required.

Hours: March–Oct Mon–Fri 8:45–16:45, Sat 8:45–13:45; Nov–Feb Mon–Sat 8:45–13:45, closed Sun except last Sun of the month (when it's free, crowded, and open 8:45–13:45). Last entry is about 90 minutes before the closing time.

    The museum is closed on many holidays (mainly religious ones), including—for 2005: Jan 1 and 6, Feb 11, March 19, Easter and Easter Monday (March 27 and 28), May 1 and 5, June 15 and 29, Aug 15 and 16, Nov 1, and Dec 8 and 25–26. Doublecheck these and any other Vatican holidays through www.vatican.va.

    The Sistine Chapel may close 30 minutes before the

museum does. Some individual rooms close at odd hours, especially after 13:00. TV screens inside the entrance lists closures. The rooms described here are usually open. Plan on finishing the Sistine in time to sneak directly into the church to catch a Mass or tour.

Avoiding Lines: The museum is generally hot and crowded. The most crowded days are Saturday, the last Sunday of the month, Monday, rainy days, and any day before or after a holiday closure. Afternoons are best. Most mornings there's a line to get in that stretches around the block. (Stuck in the line? Figure about a 10-minute wait for every 100 yards.)

Getting There: The nearest Metro stop, Cipro-Musei Vaticani, is a 10-minute walk from the entrance. From St. Peter's Square, it's about a 15-minute walk (follow the Vatican Wall). Taxis are reasonable (hop in and say "moo-ZAY-ee vah-tee-KAHN-ee").

Information: In the entry, look for the *i* (it's probably in the bank of windows to your left, under "Special Permits"; some English spoken). You'll find a book kiosk in the lobby, another up the stairs, and others scattered throughout the museum. Some exhibits have English explanations. The museum has signs to four color-coded self-guided visits (A—the Sistine blitz, B—highlights, C—a good tour, D—everything). Tel. 06-6988-4947 or 06-6988-3333 (www.vatican.va). For more on the Vatican City, see page 364.

Exchange windows with sinful rates are in the entry and exit. The post office is upstairs.

Tour: A tour in English is offered once daily at 11:00 (€16.50, 2 hours, call 06-6988-4466 to reserve). You can rent a €5 audioguide (but if you do, you lose the option of taking the shortcut from the Sistine Chapel to St. Peter's, because the audioguide must be returned at the Vatican Museum entrance).

Length of This Tour: Until you expire or 2.5 hours, whichever comes first.

Photography: No photos are allowed in the Sistine Chapel. Elsewhere in the museum, photos without a flash are permitted.

Cuisine Art: A cafeteria is upstairs. Cheaper choices: The great Via Andrea Doria produce market is three blocks north of the entrance (head across the street, down the stairs, and continue straight) and inexpensive Pizza Rustica shops (which sell pizza to go) line Viale Giulio Cesare. Good restaurants are nearby: consider Antonio's Hostaria dei Bastioni (closed Sun, at corner of Vatican wall, Via Leone IV 29) or La Rustichella (closed Mon, good antipasti buffet, near Metro: Cipro-Musei Vaticani, opposite church at end of Via Candia, Via Angelo Emo 1).

Starring: World history, Michelangelo, Raphael, *Laocoön,* the Greek masters, and their Roman copyists.

THE TOUR BEGINS

The Pope's Collection

With the Fall of Rome, the Catholic (or "universal") Church became the great preserver of civilization, collecting artifacts from cultures dead and dying. Renaissance popes (15th and 16th centuries) collected most of what we'll see, using it as furniture to decorate their palace (today's museum). Combining the classical and Christian worlds, they found the divine in the creations of man.

We'll concentrate on classical sculpture and Renaissance painting. But along the way (and there's a lot of along-the-way here), we'll stop to leaf through a few yellowed pages from this 5,000-year-old scrapbook of humankind.

Vatican Museum Overview

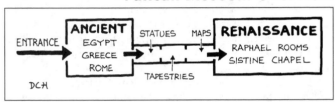

This heavyweight museum is shaped like a barbell—two buildings connected by a long hall. The entrance building covers the ancient world (Egypt, Greece, Rome). The one at the far end covers its "rebirth" in the Renaissance (including the Sistine Chapel). The halls there and back are a mix of old and new. Move quickly—don't burn out before the Sistine Chapel at the end—and see how each civilization borrows from and builds on the previous one.

• *Leave Italy by entering the doors. You may need to go through a security check (like at an airport). Go upstairs (or take the elevator) to buy your ticket, punch it in the turnstiles, then take the long escalator or spiral stairs up, up, up.*

At the top: To your right is the café and the Pinacoteca painting gallery (consider touring the Pinacoteca now if you want the option of

taking the shortcut from the Sistine Chapel directly to St. Peter's; for information on the Pinacoteca, see the end of this chapter). To your left is the beginning of our tour. Go left, then take another left up a flight of stairs to reach the first-floor Egyptian Rooms (Museo Egizio). Don't stop until you find your mummy.

EGYPT (3000–1000 B.C.)

Egyptian art was for religion, not decoration. A statue or painting preserved the likeness of someone, giving him a form of eternal life. Most of the art was for tombs, where they put the mummies.

Mummies

This woman died three millennia ago. Her corpse was disemboweled, and her organs were placed in a jar like those you see nearby. Then the body was refilled with pitch, dried with natron (a natural sodium carbonate), wrapped in linen, and placed in a wood coffin, which went inside a stone coffin, which was placed in a tomb. (Remember that the pyramids were just big tombs.) In the next life, the spirit was homeless without its body, and you wanted to look your best—notice the henna job on her hair.

Painted inside the coffin lid is a list of what the deceased "packed" for the journey to eternity. The coffins were decorated with magical spells to protect the body from evil and to act as crib notes for the confused soul in the netherworld.

• *In the next room are...*

Egyptian Statues

Egyptian statues walk awkwardly, like they're carrying heavy buckets, with arms straight down at their sides. Even in the Romanized versions, they're stiff, two-dimensional, and schematic—the art is only realistic enough to get the job done. In Egyptian belief, a statue like this could be a stable refuge for the wandering soul of a dead man. Each was made according to an established set of proportions. Little changed over the centuries. These had a function and they worked.

Various Egyptian Gods as Animals

Before technology made humans top dogs on earth, it was easier to appreciate our fellow creatures. Egyptians saw the superiority of animals and worshiped them as incarnations of the gods. Wander through a pet store of Egyptian animal gods. Find Anubis, a jackal in a toga. The lioness portrays the fierce goddess Sekhmet. The clever baboon is the god of wisdom, Thot. At the end of the hall is Bes, the patron of pregnant women (and beer-bellied men).

The Ancient World

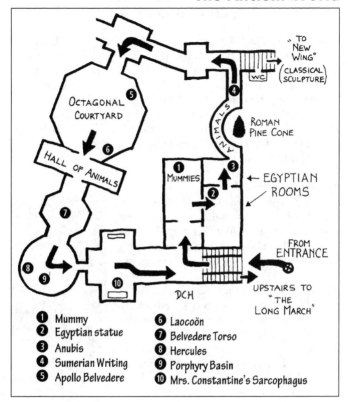

1 Mummy
2 Egyptian statue
3 Anubis
4 Sumerian Writing
5 Apollo Belvedere
6 Laocoön
7 Belvedere Torso
8 Hercules
9 Porphyry Basin
10 Mrs. Constantine's Sarcophagus

• *Continue through a curved corridor of animal gods, then through three more rooms, pausing at the glass case in the third room (Room VIII), which contains brown clay tablets.*

Sumerian Writing

Even before Egypt, civilizations flourished in the Middle East. The Sumerian culture in Mesopotamia (the ancestors of the ancient Babylonians and of Saddam Hussein) invented writing around 3000 B.C. The clay tablets were written on by pressing into the wet clay with a wedge-shaped (cuneiform) pen. The Sumerians also rolled cylinder seals into soft clay to make an impression used to seal documents and mark property.

• *Go with the flow to a balcony with a view of Rome out the window, then turn left into an octagonal courtyard.*

SCULPTURE—GREECE AND ROME
(500 B.C.–A.D. 500)

This palace wouldn't be here, this sculpture wouldn't be here, and our lives would likely be quite different if it weren't for a few thousand Greeks in a small city about 450 years before Christ. Athens set the tone for the rest of the West. Democracy, theater, economics, literature, and art all flourished in Athens during a 50-year "Golden Age." Greek culture was then appropriated by Rome and revived again 1,500 years later, during the Renaissance. The Renaissance popes built and decorated these palaces, re-creating the glory of the classical world.

Apollo Belvedere

Apollo, the god of the sun and of music, is hunting. He's been running through the woods, and now he spots his prey. Keeping his eye on the animal, he slows down and prepares to put a (missing) arrow into his (missing) bow. The optimistic Greeks conceived of their gods in human form...and buck naked.

The Greek sculptor Leochares, following the style of the greater Greek sculptor Praxiteles, has fully captured the beauty of the human form. The anatomy is perfect, his pose is natural. Instead of standing at attention, face forward with his arms at his sides (Egyptian style), *Apollo* is on the move, with his weight on one leg.

The Greeks loved balance. A well-rounded man was both a thinker and an athlete, a poet and a warrior. In art, the *Apollo Belvedere* balances several opposites. He's moving, but not out of control. *Apollo* eyes his target, but hasn't attacked yet. He's realistic but with idealized, godlike features. And the smoothness of his muscles is balanced by the rough folds of his cloak. The only sour note: his recently added left hand. Could we try a size smaller?

During the Renaissance, when this Roman copy of the original Greek work was discovered, it was considered the most perfect work of art in the world. The handsome face, eternal youth, and the body that seems to float just above the pedestal made *Apollo Belvedere* seem superhuman, divine, and godlike, even for devout Christians.

• *In the neighboring niche to the right, a bearded old Roman river god lounges in the shade. This pose inspired Michelangelo's* Adam, *in the Sistine Chapel (coming soon). While there are a few fancy bathtubs in this courtyard, most of the carved boxes you see are sarcophagi—Roman coffins and relic holders, carved with the deceased's epitaph in picture form.*

Laocoön

Laocoön (lay-AWK-oh-wahn), the high priest of Troy, warned his fellow Trojans: "Beware of Greeks bearing gifts." The attacking Greeks had brought the Trojan Horse to the gates as a ploy to get inside the city walls, and Laocoön tried to warn his people not to bring it inside. But the gods wanted the Greeks to win, so they sent huge snakes to crush him and his two sons to death. We see

them at the height of their terror, when they realize that, no matter how hard they struggle, they—and their entire race—are doomed.

The figures (carved from four blocks of marble pieced together seamlessly) are powerful, not light and graceful. The poses are as twisted as possible, accentuating every rippling muscle and bulging vein. Follow the line of motion from *Laocoön*'s left foot, up his leg, through his body, and out his right arm (which some historians used to think extended straight out—until the elbow was dug up early in the 1900s). Goethe used to stand here and blink his eyes rapidly, watching the statue flicker to life.

The *Laocoön* was sculpted four centuries after the Golden Age, after the scales of "balance" had been tipped. Where *Apollo* is a balance between stillness and motion, this is unbridled motion. *Apollo* is serene, graceful, and godlike, while *Laocoön* is powerful, emotional, and gritty.

Laocoön—the most famous Greek statue in ancient Rome and considered "superior to all other sculpture or painting"—was lost for more than a thousand years. Then, in 1506, it was unexpectedly unearthed in the ruins of Nero's Golden House near the Colosseum. The discovery caused a sensation. They cleaned it off and paraded it through the streets before an awestruck populace. No one had ever seen anything like its motion and emotion, having been raised on a white-bread diet of pretty-boy *Apollo*s. One of those who saw it was the young Michelangelo, and it was a revelation to him. Two years later, he started work on the Sistine Chapel, and the Renaissance was about to take another turn.

• *Leave the courtyard. Swing around the Hall of Animals, a jungle of beasts real and surreal, to the limbless* Torso *in the middle of the next large hall.*

Belvedere Torso

My entire experience with statues consists of making snowmen. But standing face to face with this hunk of shaped rock makes you appreciate the sheer physical labor involved in chipping a figure out of solid rock. It takes great strength, but at the same time, great delicacy.

This is all that remains of an ancient statue of Hercules seated on a lion skin. Michelangelo loved this old rock. He knew that he was the best sculptor of his day. The ancients were his only peers—and his rivals. He'd caress this statue lovingly and tell people, "I am the pupil of the *Torso*." To him, it contained all the beauty of classical sculpture. But it's not beautiful. Compared with the pure grace of the *Apollo*, it's downright ugly.

But Michelangelo, an ugly man himself, was looking for a new kind of beauty—not the beauty of idealized gods, but the innate beauty of every person, even so-called ugly ones. With its knotty lumps of muscle, the *Torso* has a brute power and a distinct personality despite—or because of—its rough edges. Remember this *Torso*, because we'll see it again later on.

• *Enter the next, domed room.*

Round Room

This room, modeled on the Pantheon interior, gives some idea of Roman grandeur. Romans took Greek ideas and made them bigger, like the big bronze statue of Hercules with his club, found near the Theater of Pompey (by modern-day Campo de' Fiori). The mosaic floor once decorated the bottom of a pool in an ancient Roman bath. The enormous Roman hot tub/birdbath/vase decorated Nero's place. It was made of a single block of purple por-

phyry stone imported from the desert of Egypt. Purple was a rare, royal, expensive, and prestigious color in pre-Crayola days.

• *Enter the next room.*

Sarcophagi

These two large porphyry marble coffins were made (though not used) for the Roman emperor Constantine's mother (Helena, on left) and daughter (Constanza, on right). They are decorated with a mix of Christian and pagan themes. Helena and Constanza were Christians—and therefore outlaws—until Constantine made Christianity legal in A.D. 312, and they became saints. Both sarcophagi were quarried and worked in Egypt. The technique for working this extremely hard stone (a special tempering of metal was required) was lost soon after this and porphyry was not worked

again until Renaissance times in Florence.

• *See how we've come full circle in this building—the Egyptian Rooms are ahead on your left. Go upstairs and prepare for the Long March down the hall lined with statues, toward the Sistine Chapel and Raphael Rooms.*

Overachievers may first choose to pop into the Etruscan wing— "Museo Etrusco"—located a few steps up from the "Long March" level. (Others have permission to save their aesthetic energy for the Sistine.)

THE ETRUSCANS (800–300 B.C.)

Room I

The chariot is from 550 B.C., when crude Romans were ruled by their more civilized neighbors to the north—the Etruscans. Imagine the chariot racing around the dirt track of the Circus Maximus, through the marshy valley of the newly drained Forum, or up Capitol Hill to the Temple of Jupiter—all originally built by Rome's Etruscan kings.

Room II

The golden breastplate (*Pectoral*, 650 B.C., immediately to the right), decorated with tiny winged angels and animals, shows off the sophistication of the Etruscans. Though not warlike and politically decentralized, these people were able to "conquer" all of central Italy around 650 B.C. through trade, offering tempting metalwork goods like this.

The Etruscan vases done in the Greek style remind us of the other great pre-Roman power—the Greek colonists who settled in southern Italy (Magna Graecia). The Etruscans traded with the Greeks, adopting their fashions. Rome, cradled between the two, grew up learning from both cultures.

A Greek-style bowl (far corner of the room) depicting a man and woman in bed together would have scandalized early Roman farmers. He's peeing in a chamberpot, she's blowing a flute. Etruscan art often showed husbands and wives at ease together, giving them a reputation among the Romans as immoral, flute-playing degenerates.

Room III

This bronze warrior, whose head was sawed off by lightning, has a rare inscription that's readable (on armor below the navel). It probably refers to the statue's former owner: "Aha! Trutitis gave [this] as [a] gift." Archaeologists

understand the Etruscans' Greek-style alphabet and some individual words, but they've yet to fully crack the code. As you look around at beautiful bronze pitchers, candlesticks, shields, and urns, ponder yet another of Etruria's unsolved mysteries—no one is sure where these sophisticated people came from.

Room IV

Most of our knowledge of the Etruscans is from sarcophagi and art in Etruscan tombs. Their funeral art is solemn, but hardly morbid—check out the sarcopha-guy with the bulging belly, enjoying a banquet for all eternity.

The Etruscans' origins are obscure, but their legacy is clear. In 509 B.C., the Etruscan king's son raped a Roman. The king was thrown out, the republic was declared, Etruscan cities were conquered by Rome's legions, and their culture was swallowed up in Roman expansion. By Julius Caesar's time, the few remaining ethnic Etruscans were reduced to serving their masters as flute players, goldsmiths, surgeons, and street-corner preachers, like the one that Caesar brushed aside when he called out, "Beware the ides of March..."

• *Backtrack, returning to the long hall (the Gallery of the Candelabras) leading to the Sistine Chapel and Raphael Rooms.*

The Long March— Sculpture, Tapestries, Maps, and Views

This quarter-mile walk gives you a sense of the scale that Renaissance popes built on. Remember, this building was originally a series of papal palaces. The popes loved beautiful things—statues, urns, marble floors, friezes, stuccoed ceilings—and, as heirs of imperial Rome, they felt they deserved such luxury. The palaces and art represent both the peak and the decline of the Catholic Church in Europe. It was extravagant spending like this that inspired Martin Luther to rebel, starting the Protestant Reformation.

Gallery of the Candelabra— Classical Sculpture

In the second "room" of the long hall, stop at the statue *Diana the Huntress* on the left. Here, the virgin goddess goes hunting. Roman hunters would pray and give offerings to statues like this to get divine help in their search for food.

Farmers might pray to another version of

The Long March

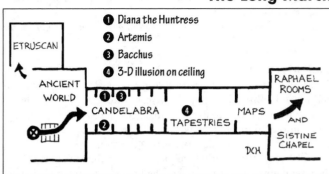

❶ Diana the Huntress
❷ Artemis
❸ Bacchus
❹ 3-D illusion on ceiling

ETRUSCAN

ANCIENT WORLD

RAPHAEL ROOMS

❶❸ CANDELABRA ❹ TAPESTRIES MAPS

❷

AND

SISTINE CHAPEL

DCH

the same goddess, *Artemis,* on the opposite wall. This billion-breasted beauty stood for fertility. "Boobs or bulls' balls?" Some historians say that bulls were sacrificed and castrated, with the testicles draped over the statues as symbols of fertility.

• *Shuffle along to the next "room." On the left is Bacchus with a baby on his shoulders.*

Fig Leaves

Why do the statues have fig leaves? Like **Bacchus,** many of these statues originally looked much different than they do now. First off, they were painted, often in gaudy colors. *Bacchus* may have had brown hair, rosy cheeks, purple grapes, and a leopard-skin sidekick at his feet. Even the *Apollo Belvedere,* whose cool gray tones we now admire as "classic Greek austerity," may have had a paisley pink cloak for all we know. Also, many statues had glass eyes like *Bacchus.*

And the fig leaves? Those came from the years 1550–1800, when the Church decided that certain parts of the human anatomy were obscene. (Why not the feet?) Perhaps Church leaders associated these full-frontal statues with the outbreak of Renaissance

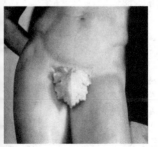

humanism that reduced their power in Europe. Whatever the cause, they reacted by covering classical crotches with plaster fig leaves, the same leaves Adam and Eve had used when the concept of "privates" was invented.

Note: The leaves could be removed at any time if the museum officials were so motivated. There are suggestion boxes around the museum. Whenever I see a fig leaf, I get the urge to pick-it. We could start an organ-ized campaign....

• *Cover your eyes in case they forgot a fig leaf or two and continue to the tapestries.*

Tapestries

Along the left wall are tapestries designed by Raphael's workshop and made in Brussels. They show scenes from the life of Christ, starting with the baby Jesus in the manger. The Resurrection tapestry is curiously interactive…as you walk, Jesus' eyes, feet, knee, and even the stone square follow you across the room.

Check out the beautiful sculpted reliefs on the ceiling, especially the lavender panel near the end of the first tapestry room showing a centurion ordering Eskimo pies from a vendor. Admire the workmanship of this relief, then realize that it's not a relief at all—it's painted on a flat surface! Illusions like this were proof that painters had mastered the 3-D realism of ancient statues.

Map Gallery and View of Vatican City

This gallery still feels like a pope's palace. The crusted ceiling of colorful stucco and paint is pure papal splendor. The 16th-century maps on the walls show the regions of Italy. Popes could take visitors on a tour of Italy, from the toe (entrance end) to the Alps (far end), with east Italy on the right wall, west on the left. The scenes in the ceiling portray exciting moments in Church history in each of those regions. At the far end are Italy's four ports of entry (e.g., Venice) and the maps of Antique Italy (names in Latin, Roman political boundaries in gold) and New Italy.

The windows give you your best look at the tiny country of Vatican City, formed in 1929. It has its own radio station (KPOP), as you can see from the tower on the hill. What you see here is pretty much all there is—these gardens, the palaces you're in, and St. Peter's.

If you lean out and look left you'll see the dome of St. Peter's the way Michelangelo would have liked you to see it—without the bulky Baroque facade.

• *Exit the map room and take a breather in the next small tapestry hall before turning left into the crowded rooms leading to the Raphael Rooms.*

Raphael Rooms

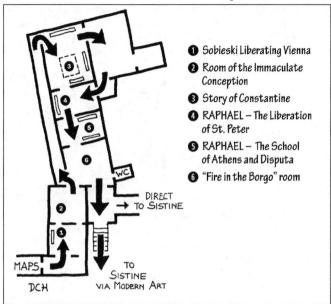

❶ Sobieski Liberating Vienna

❷ Room of the Immaculate Conception

❸ Story of Constantine

❹ RAPHAEL – The Liberation of St. Peter

❺ RAPHAEL – The School of Athens and Disputa

❻ "Fire in the Borgo" room

RENAISSANCE ART

Raphael Rooms—Papal Wallpaper

We've seen art from the ancient world; now we'll see its rebirth in the Renaissance. We're entering the living quarters of the great Renaissance popes—where they slept, worked, and worshiped. The rooms reflect the grandeur of their position. They hired the best artists—mostly from Florence—to paint the walls and ceilings, combining classical and Christian motifs.

• *Entering, you'll immediately see...*

The huge non-Raphael painting shows **Sobieski liberating Vienna** from the Muslim Turks in 1683, finally tipping the tide in favor of a Christian Europe. See the Muslim tents on the left and the spires of Christian Vienna on the right.

The second room's paintings celebrate the doctrine of the **Immaculate Conception,** establishing that Mary herself was conceived free from original sin. This medieval idea wasn't actually made dogma until a century ago. The largest fresco shows how the inspiration came straight from heaven (upper left) in a thin ray of light directly to the pope.

• *Next, you'll pass along an outside ramp overlooking a courtyard (is that the pope's Fiat?), finally ending up in the first of the Raphael Rooms—the Constantine Room.*

Constantine Room

The frescoes (which after Raphael's death were finished by his assistants, notably Giulio Romano) celebrate the passing of the baton from one culture to the next. Remember, Rome was a pagan empire persecuting a new cult from the East—Christianity.

Then, on the night of October 27, A.D. 312 (left wall), as General Constantine (in gold, with crown) was preparing his troops for a coup d'état, he looked up and saw something strange. A cross appeared in the sky with the words, "You will conquer in this sign."

The next day (long wall), his troops raged victoriously into battle with the Christian cross atop their Roman eagle banners. There's Constantine in the center with a smile on his face, slashing through the enemy, while God's warrior angels ride shotgun overhead.

Constantine even stripped (right wall) and knelt before the pope to be baptized a Christian (some say). As emperor, he legalized Christianity and worked hand in hand with the pope (window wall). When Rome fell, its glory lived on through the Dark Ages in the pomp, pageantry, and learning of the Catholic Church.

Look at the ceiling painting. A classical statue is knocked backward, crumbling before the overpowering force of the cross. Whoa! Christianity triumphs over pagan Rome. (This was painted, I believe, by Raphael's surrealist colleague, Salvadorus Dalio.)

Raphael

Raphael was only 25 when Pope Julius II invited him to paint the walls of his personal living quarters. Julius was so impressed by Raphael's talent that he had the work of earlier masters scraped off and gave Raphael free rein to paint what he wanted.

Raphael lived a charmed life. He was handsome and sophisticated, and soon became Julius' favorite. He painted masterpieces effortlessly. In a different decade, he might have been thrown out of the Church as a great sinner, but his love affairs and devil-may-care personality seemed to epitomize the optimistic pagan spirit of the Renaissance. His works are graceful but never lightweight or frilly— they're strong, balanced, and harmonious in the best Renaissance tradition. When he died young in 1520, the High Renaissance died with him.

• *Continue through the next room and bookshop. In the following room, block the sunlight with your hand to see...*

The Liberation of St. Peter

Peter, Jesus' right-hand man, was thrown into prison in Jerusalem for his beliefs. In the middle of the night, an angel appeared and rescued him from the sleeping guards (Acts 1–2). The chains miraculously fell away (and were later brought to the St. Peter-in-Chains Church in Rome) and the angel led him to safety (right) while the guards took hell from their captain (left). This little "play" is neatly divided into three separate acts that make a balanced composition.

Raphael makes the miraculous event even more dramatic with the use of four kinds of light illuminating the dark cell—half-moonlight, the captain's torch, the radiant angel, and the natural light spilling through the museum's window. Raphael's mastery of realism, rich colors, and sense of drama made him understandably famous.

Find Pope Julius II (who also commissioned Michelangelo to do the Sistine ceiling) in the role of Peter in *The Liberation,* and as the kneeling pope in *The Mass of Bolsena* (opposite wall).

• *Enter the next room. Here in the pope's private study, Raphael painted...*

The School of Athens

In both style and subject matter, this fresco sums up the spirit of the

Renaissance, which was not only the rebirth of classical art, but a rebirth of learning, discovery, and the optimistic spirit that man is a rational creature. Raphael pays respect to the great thinkers and scientists of ancient Greece, gathering them together at one time in a mythical school setting.

In the center are Plato and Aristotle, the two greatest. Plato points up, indicating his philosophy that mathematics and pure ideas are the source of truth, while Aristotle points down, showing his preference for hands-on study of the material world. There's their master, Socrates (midway to the left, in green), ticking off arguments on his fingers. And in the foreground at right, bald Euclid bends over a slate to demonstrate a geometrical formula.

Raphael shows that Renaissance thinkers were as good as the ancients. There's Leonardo da Vinci, whom Raphael worshiped, in the role of Plato. Euclid is the architect Bramante, who designed St. Peter's. Raphael himself (next to last on the far right, with the black beret) looks out at us. And the "school" building is actually an early version of St. Peter's Basilica (under construction at the time).

Raphael balances everything symmetrically—thinkers to the left, scientists to the right, with Plato and Aristotle dead center—to show the geometrical order found in the world. Look at the square floor tiles in the foreground. If you laid a ruler over them and extended the line upward, it would run right to the center of the picture. Similarly, the tops of the columns all point down to the middle. All the lines of sight draw our attention to Plato and Aristotle, and to the small arch over their heads—a halo over these two secular saints in the divine pursuit of knowledge.

While Raphael was painting this room, Michelangelo was at work down the hall in the Sistine Chapel. Raphael had just finished *The School of Athens*, when he got a look at Michelangelo's powerful figures and dramatic scenes. He was astonished. From this point on, Raphael began to beef up his delicate, graceful style to a more heroic level. He returned to *The School of Athens*, scraped off a section of plaster, and added one more figure to the scene—Michelangelo, the brooding, melancholy figure in front, leaning on a block of marble.

• *On the opposite wall...*

The Disputa

As if to underline the new attitude that pre-Christian philosophy and Church thinking could coexist, Raphael painted *The Disputa* facing *The School of Athens*. Christ and the saints in heaven are overseeing a discussion of the Eucharist (the communion wafer) by mortals below. The classical-looking character in blue and  gold looks out as if to say, "The pagans had their *School of Athens*, but us Christians (pointing up) have the School of Heaven." These rooms were the papal library, so themes featuring learning, knowledge, and debate were appropriate.

In Catholic terms, the communion wafer miraculously becomes the body of Christ when it's consecrated by a priest, bringing a little bit of heaven into the material world. Raphael's painting also connects heaven and earth, with descending circles: Jesus in a halo, down to the dove of the Holy Spirit in a circle, which enters the communion wafer in its holder. Balance and symmetry reign, from the angel trios in the upper corners to the books littering the floor.

Moving along, the last Raphael Room (called the "Fire in the Borgo" Room) shows work done mostly by Raphael's students, who were influenced by the bulging muscles and bodybuilder poses of Michelangelo.

• *Get ready. It's decision time. From here there are two ways to get to the*

Sistine Chapel. Leaving the final Raphael Room, you'll soon see two arrows—one pointing left to the Sistine (Cappella Sistina) and one pointing right to the Sistine. Left goes directly to the Sistine.

But going right (five minutes and a few staircases longer) leads to quiet rooms at the foot of the stairs with benches where you can sit in peace and read ahead before entering the hectic Sistine Chapel. Also, you get to stroll through the impressive Modern Religious Art collection on the way (signs will direct you to the Sistine). Your call.

THE SISTINE CHAPEL

The Sistine Chapel contains Michelangelo's ceiling and his huge *Last Judgment.* The Sistine is the personal chapel of the pope and the place where new popes are elected. When Pope Julius II asked Michelangelo to take on this important project, he said, "No, *grazie.*"

Michelangelo insisted he was a sculptor, not a painter. The Sistine ceiling was a vast undertaking, and he didn't want to do a half-vast job. But the pope pleaded, bribed, and threatened until Michelangelo finally consented, on the condition he be able to do it all his own way.

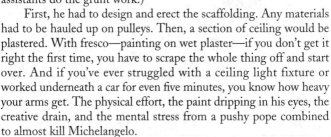

Julius had asked for only 12 apostles along the sides of the ceiling, but Michelangelo had a grander vision—the entire history of the world until Jesus. He spent the next four years (1508–1512) craning his neck on scaffolding six stories up, covering the ceiling with frescoes of Bible scenes.

In sheer physical terms, it's an astonishing achievement: 5,900 square feet, with the vast majority done by his own hand. (Raphael only designed most of his rooms, letting assistants do the grunt work.)

First, he had to design and erect the scaffolding. Any materials had to be hauled up on pulleys. Then, a section of ceiling would be plastered. With fresco—painting on wet plaster—if you don't get it right the first time, you have to scrape the whole thing off and start over. And if you've ever struggled with a ceiling light fixture or worked underneath a car for even five minutes, you know how heavy your arms get. The physical effort, the paint dripping in his eyes, the creative drain, and the mental stress from a pushy pope combined to almost kill Michelangelo.

But when the ceiling was finished and revealed to the public, it simply blew 'em away. Like the *Laocoön* statue discovered six years earlier, it was unlike anything seen before. It both caps the

Renaissance and turns it in a new direction. In perfect Renaissance spirit, it mixes Old Testament prophets with classical figures. But the style is more dramatic, shocking, and emotional than the balanced Renaissance works before it. This is a very personal work—the Gospel according to Michelangelo—but its themes and subject matter are universal. Many art scholars contend that the Sistine ceiling is the single greatest work of art by any one human being.

The Sistine Ceiling—Understanding What You're Standing Under

The ceiling shows the history of the world before the birth of Jesus. We see God creating the world, creating man and woman, destroying the earth by flood, and so on. Along the sides (where the ceiling starts to curve) we see the Old Testament prophets and pagan Greek prophetesses that foretold the coming of Christ. Dividing these scenes and figures are fake niches (a painted 3-D illusion) decorated with nude, statue-like figures with symbolic meaning.

The key is to see three simple divisions in the tangle of bodies:
1. The central spine of nine rectangular Bible scenes
2. The line of prophets on either side
3. The triangles between the prophets showing the ancestors of Christ

• *Ready? Within the chapel, grab a seat along the side (if there's room). Face the altar with the big Last Judgment on the wall (more on that later). Now look up to the ceiling and find the central panel of...*

The Creation of Adam

God and man take center stage in this Renaissance version of creation. Adam, newly formed in the image of God, lounges dreamily in perfect naked innocence. God, with his entourage, swoops in a

The Sistine Schematic

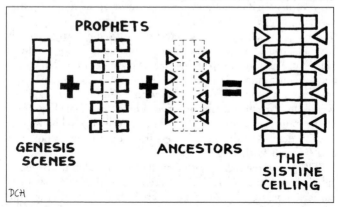

DCH

The Sistine Ceiling

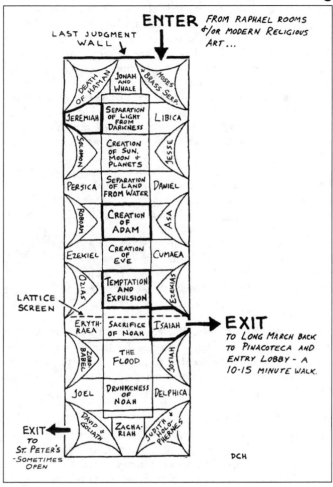

ENTER FROM RAPHAEL ROOMS &/OR MODERN RELIGIOUS ART...

LAST JUDGMENT WALL

DEATH OF HAMAN	JONAH AND WHALE	MOSES & BRASS SERP.
JEREMIAH	SEPARATION OF LIGHT FROM DARKNESS	LIBICA
SOLOMON	CREATION OF SUN, MOON & PLANETS	JESSE
PERSICA	SEPARATION OF LAND FROM WATER	DANIEL
ROBOAM	CREATION OF ADAM	ASA
EZEKIEL	CREATION OF EVE	CUMAEA
OZIAS	TEMPTATION AND EXPULSION	EZEKIAS
ERYTH-RAEA	SACRIFICE OF NOAH	ISAIAH
ZOROBABEL	THE FLOOD	JOSIAH
JOEL	DRUNKENESS OF NOAH	DELPHICA
DAVID & GOLIATH	ZACHA-RIAH	JUDITH & HOLOPHERNES

LATTICE SCREEN

EXIT TO LONG MARCH BACK TO PINACOTECA AND ENTRY LOBBY - A 10-15 MINUTE WALK.

EXIT TO ST. PETER'S -SOMETIMES OPEN

DCH

swirl of activity (which, with a little imagination, looks like a cross-section of a human brain...quite a strong humanist statement). Their

reaching hands are the center of this work. Adam's is limp and passive; God's is strong and forceful, His finger twitching upward with energy. Here is the very moment of creation, as God passes the spark of life to man, the crowning work of His creation.

This is the spirit of the Renaissance. God is not a terrifying giant reaching down to puny and helpless man from way on high. Here they are on an equal plane, divided only by the diagonal patch of sky. God's billowing robe and the patch of green upon which Adam is lying balance each other. They are like two pieces of a jigsaw puzzle, or two long-separated continents, or like the yin and yang symbols finally coming together—uniting, complementing each other, creating wholeness. God and man work together in the divine process of creation.

• *This celebration of man permeates the ceiling. Notice the Adonises-come-to-life on the pedestals that divide the central panels. And then came woman.*

The Garden of Eden: Temptation and Expulsion

In one panel, we see two scenes from the Garden of Eden. On the left is the leafy garden of paradise where Adam and Eve lie around blissfully. But the devil comes along—a serpent with a woman's torso—and winds around the forbidden Tree of Knowledge. The temptation to gain new knowledge is too great for these Renaissance people. They eat the forbidden fruit.

At right, the sword-wielding angel drives them from Paradise into the barren plains. They're grieving, but they're far from helpless. Adam's body is thick and sturdy, and we know they'll survive in the cruel world. Adam firmly gestures to the angel, like he's saying, "All right, already! We're going!"

The Nine Scenes from Genesis

Take some time with these central scenes to understand the story the ceiling tells. They run in sequence, starting at the front:

1. God, in purple, divides the light from darkness.
2. God creates the sun (burning orange) and the moon (pale white, to the right). Oops, I guess there's another moon.
3. God bursts toward us to separate the land and water.
4. *The Creation of Adam*
5. God creates Eve, who dives into existence out of Adam's side.
6. *The Garden of Eden: Temptation and Expulsion*
7. Noah kills a ram and stokes the altar fires to make a sacrifice to God.
8. The great Flood, sent by God, destroys the wicked, who desperately head for higher ground. In the distance, the Ark carries Noah's family to safety. (The blank spot dates to 1793, when a nearby gunpowder depot exploded, shaking the building.)

9. Noah's sons see their drunk father. (Perhaps Michelangelo chose to end it with this scene as a reminder that even the best of men are fallible.)

Prophets

You'll notice that the figures at the far end of the chapel are a bit smaller than those over the *Last Judgment*.

Michelangelo started at the far end, with the Noah scenes. By 1510 he'd finished the first half of the ceiling. When they took the scaffolding down and could finally see what he'd been working on for two years, everyone was awestruck—except Michelangelo. As powerful as his figures are, from the floor they didn't look dramatic enough for Michelangelo. For the other half, he pulled out all the stops.

Compare the Noah scenes (far end) with their many small figures to the huge images of God at the other end. Similarly, Isaiah (near the lattice screen, marked "Esaias") is stately and balanced, while Jeremiah ("Hieremias", in the corner by the *Last Judgment*) is a dark, brooding figure. This prophet who witnessed the destruction of Israel slumps his chin in his hand and ponders the fate of his people. Like the difference between the stately *Apollo Belvedere* and the excited *Laocoön*, Michelangelo added a new emotional dimension to Renaissance painting.

The Cleaning Project

The ceiling and the *Last Judgment* have been cleaned, removing centuries of preservatives, dirt, and soot from candles, oil lamps, and the annual Papal Barbecue (just kidding). The bright, bright colors that emerged are a bit shocking, forcing many art experts to reevaluate Michelangelo's style. Notice the very dark patches left in the corner above the *Last Judgment* and imagine how dreary and dark it was before the cleaning.

The Last Judgment

When Michelangelo returned to paint the altar wall 23 years later (1535), the mood of Europe—and of Michelangelo—was completely different. The Protestant Reformation had forced the Catholic Church to clamp down on free thought, and religious wars raged.

Rome had recently been pillaged by roving bands of mercenaries. The Renaissance spirit of optimism was fading. Michelangelo himself had begun to question the innate goodness of mankind.

It's Judgment Day, and Christ—the powerful figure in the center, raising his arm to spank the

The Last Judgment

1 Christ with Mary at his side
2 Trumpeting Angels
3 The dead come out of their graves, the righteous ascend
4 One of the damned
5 Charon in his boat
6 The demon/critic of nudity
7 St. Bartholomew with flayed skin containing Michelangelo's self-portrait

wicked—has come to find out who's naughty and who's nice. Beneath him, a band of angels blows its trumpets Dizzy Gillespie–style, giving a wake-up call to the sleeping dead. The dead at lower left leave their graves and prepare to be judged. The righteous, on Christ's right hand (the left side of the picture), are carried up to the glories of Heaven. The wicked on the other side are hurled down to Hell, where demons wait to torture them. Charon, from the underworld of Greek mythology, waits below to ferry the souls of the damned to Hell.

It's a grim picture. No one, but no one, is smiling. Even many of the righteous being resurrected (lower left) are either skeletons or cadavers with ghastly skin. The angels have to play tug-of-war with subterranean monsters to drag them from their graves.

Over in Hell, the wicked are tortured by gleeful demons. One of the damned (to the right of the trumpeting angels) has an utterly lost expression, as if saying, "Why did I cheat on my wife?!" Two demons grab him around the ankles to pull him down to the bowels of Hell, condemned to an eternity of constipation.

But it's the terrifying figure of Christ who dominates this scene. He raises his arm to smite the wicked, sending a ripple of fear through everyone. Even the saints around him—even Mary beneath his arm (whose interceding days are clearly over)—shrink back in terror at loving Jesus' uncharacteristic outburst. His expression is completely closed, and he turns his head, refusing to even listen to the whining alibis of the damned. Look at Christ's bicep. If this muscular figure looks familiar to you, it's because you've seen it before—the *Belvedere Torso*.

When *The Last Judgment* was unveiled to the public in 1541, it caused a sensation. The pope is said to have dropped to his knees and cried, "Lord, charge me not with my sins when thou shalt come on the Day of Judgment."

And it changed the course of art. The complex composition, with more than 300 figures swirling around the figure of Christ, was far beyond traditional Renaissance balance. The twisted figures shown from every imaginable angle challenged other painters to try and top this master of 3-D illusion. And the sheer terror and drama of the scene was a striking contrast to the placid optimism of, say, Raphael's *School of Athens*. Michelangelo had Baroque-en all the rules of the Renaissance, signaling a new era of art.

With the Renaissance fading, the fleshy figures in *The Last Judgment* aroused murmurs of discontent from Church authorities. Michelangelo rebelled by painting his chief critic into the scene—in Hell. He's the jack-assed demon in the bottom right corner wrapped in a snake. Look how Michelangelo covered his privates. Sweet revenge.

(After Michelangelo's death, prudish Church authorities painted the wisps of clothing we see today.)

Now move up close. Study the details of the lower part of the painting from right to left. Charon, with Dr. Spock ears and a Dali moustache, paddles the damned in a boat full of human turbulence. Look more closely at the J-Day band. Are they reading music, or is it the Judgment Day tally? Before the cleaning, these details were lost in murk.

The Last Judgment marks the end of Renaissance optimism epitomized in *The Creation of Adam*, with its innocence and exaltation of man. There, he was the wakening man-child of a fatherly

God. Here, man cowers in fear and unworthiness before a terrifying, wrathful deity.

Michelangelo himself must have wondered how he would be judged—had he used his God-given talents wisely? Look at St. Bartholomew, the bald, bearded guy at Christ's left foot (our right). In the flayed skin he's holding is a barely recognizable face—the twisted self-portrait of a self-questioning Michelangelo.

• *There are two exits from the Sistine Chapel. If you exit through the side door next to the screen, you'll soon find yourself facing the Long March back to the museum's entrance (10–15 min away). You're one floor below the long corridor you walked to get here. Or, if you're planning to visit St. Peter's Basilica next, exit out the back corner of the Sistine Chapel. This shortcuts directly to St. Peter's Basilica, saving a 30-minute walk (10–15 min back to Vatican Museum entry/exit, then a 15-min walk to St. Peter's). Though this corner exit is ostensibly only for tour groups, you can often just slide through with the crowds. Note that if you take this shortcut, you'll miss the Pinacoteca art gallery (near the Vatican Museum entrance).*

The Long March Back

Along this corridor, you'll see some of the wealth amassed by the popes, mostly gifts from royalty. Find your hometown on the map of the world from 1529—look in the land labeled "Terra Incognita." The elaborately decorated library that branches off to the right contains rare manuscripts.

• *The corridor eventually spills back outside. Follow signs to the...*

PINACOTECA (PAINTING GALLERY)

Like Lou Gehrig batting behind Babe Ruth, the Pinacoteca has to follow the mighty Sistine & Co. But after the Vatican's artistic feast, this little collection of paintings is a delicious, 15-minute after-dinner mint.

See this gallery of paintings as you'd view a time-lapse blossoming of a flower, walking through the evolution of painting from medieval to Baroque with just a few stops.

• *Enter, passing a model of the* Pietà *(offering a handy close-up look), and stroll up to Room IV.*

Melozzo Da Forli—*Musician Angels*

Salvaged from a condemned church, this playful series of frescoes shows the delicate grace and

Pinacoteca

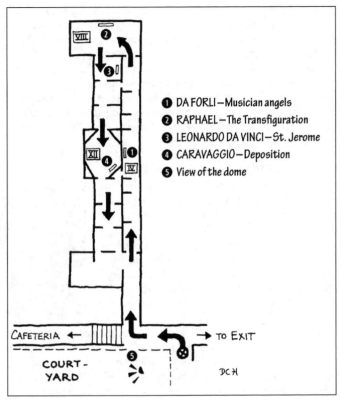

❶ DA FORLI—Musician angels
❷ RAPHAEL—The Transfiguration
❸ LEONARDO DA VINCI—St. Jerome
❹ CARAVAGGIO—Deposition
❺ View of the dome

nobility of Italy during the time known fondly as the Quattrocento (1400s). Notice the detail in the serene faces; the soothing primary colors; the bright, even light; and the classical purity given these religious figures. Rock on.

• *Walk on to the end room (Room VIII) where they've turned on the dark to let Raphael's* Transfiguration *shine. Take a seat.*

Raphael—*The Transfiguration*

Christ floats above a stumpy mountaintop, visited in a vision by the

prophets Moses and Elijah. Peter, James, and John cower in awe under Jesus, "transfigured before them, his face shining as the sun, his raiment white as light" (as described by the evangelist Matthew—who can be seen taking notes in the painting's lower left).

Raphael composes the scene in three descending tiers: Christ, the holiest, is on top, then Peter-James-John, and finally, the nine remaining apostles who try in vain to heal a boy possessed by demons. Jesus is gone, leaving them in disarray, but "Lady Faith" in the center gives them a pep talk.

Raphael died in 1520, leaving this final work to be finished by his pupils. The last thing Raphael painted was the beatific face of Jesus, perhaps the most beautiful Christ in existence. When Raphael was buried (in the Pantheon), this work accompanied the funeral.

• *Heading back down the parallel corridor, stop in Room IX at the brown, unfinished work by Leonardo.*

Leonardo da Vinci—*St. Jerome* (c. 1482)

Jerome squats in the rocky desert. He's spent too much time alone, fasting and meditating on his sins. His soulful face is echoed by his friend, the roaring lion.

This unfinished work gives us a glimpse behind the scenes at Leonardo's technique. Even in the brown undercoating we see the psychological power of Leonardo's genius. Jerome's emaciated body on the rocks expresses his intense penitence while his pleading eyes hold a glimmer of hope for divine forgiveness. Leonardo wrote that a good painter must paint two things: "man and the movements of his spirit." (The patchwork effect is due to Jerome's head having been cut out and used as the seat of a stool in a shoemaker's shop.)

• *Roll on through the sappy sweetness of the Mannerist rooms into the gritty realism of Caravaggio (Room XII).*

Caravaggio—*Deposition*

Christ is being buried. In the dark tomb, the faces of his followers emerge, lit by a harsh light. Christ's body has a death-like color. We see Christ's dirty toes and Nicodemus' wrinkled, sunburned face.

Caravaggio was the first painter to intentionally shock his viewers. By exaggerating the contrast between light and dark, shining a brutal third-degree-interrogator light on his subjects, and using everyday models in sacred scenes, he takes a huge leap away from the Raphael-pretty past and into the "expressive realism" of the modern world.

A tangle of grief looms out of the darkness as Christ's heavy, dead body nearly pulls the whole group with him from the cross into the tomb. After this museum, I know how he feels.

• *Walk through the rest of the gallery's canvas history of art, enjoy one last view of the Vatican grounds and Michelangelo's dome, then follow the grand spiral staircase down. Go in peace.*

MADRID

Madrid is the hub of Spain. This modern capital—Europe's highest, at more than 2,000 feet—has a population of more than four million and is young by European standards. As recently as 1561, King Philip II decided to move the capital of his empire from Toledo to Madrid.

Enjoy the grandeur and intimate charm of Madrid. Saunter from the main square, Puerta del Sol, to the sumptuous Royal Palace. Its gilded rooms and frescoed ceilings rival Versailles. The Prado Museum has Europe's top collection of paintings and highlights the work of Spain's "Big Three": Velázquez, El Greco, and Goya. At the modern art museum, make time to ponder Picasso's moving, anti-war masterpiece, *Guernica*.

Madrid City Walk   **409**

Prado Museum   **419**

Guernica   **449**

Madrid Sights

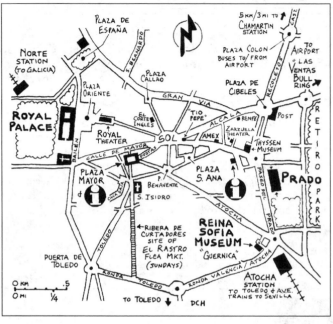

MADRID CITY WALK

From Puerta del Sol to the Royal Palace

One hundred years ago Madrid had only 400,000 people—so 90 percent of the city is modern sprawl surrounding an intact, easy-to-navigate historic core. We'll dive right into it, walking west from the Puerta del Sol, through the 17th-century city, finishing up at the lavish Royal Palace. But aside from historical sights, modern Madrid has enough street-singing, barhopping, and people-watching vitality to give any visitor a boost of youth. Allow an hour for this half-mile walk, and another hour for the Royal Palace.

ORIENTATION

Royal Palace: €7 without a tour, €8 with a tour, April–Sept Mon–Sat 9:00–18:00, Sun 9:30–14:30; Oct–March Mon–Sat 9:30–17:00, Sun 9:00–14:00, last tickets sold one hour before closing, palace can close without warning if needed for a royal function (you can call a day ahead to check, tel. 914-548-700). The palace is most crowded on Wed, when it's free for locals. Metro: Opera.

THE TOUR BEGINS

Puerta del Sol

Start in the center of Madrid, the main square known as the Puerta del Sol. Named for a long-gone medieval gate with the sun carved onto it, Puerta del Sol is ground zero for Madrid. It's a hub for the Metro, buses, political demonstrations, and pickpockets.

Stand by the statue of King Charles III on horseback and

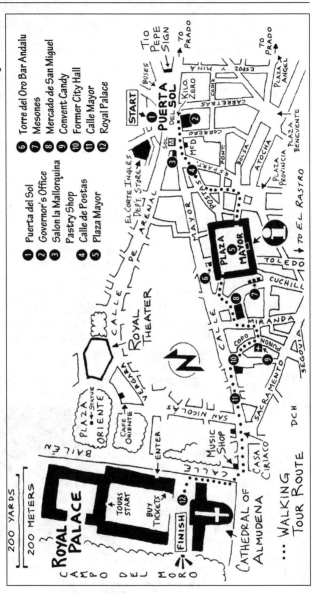

Madrid City Walk

1. Puerta del Sol
2. Governor's Office
3. Salon la Mallorquina Pastry Shop
4. Calle de Postas
5. Plaza Mayor
6. Torre del Oro Bar Andalu
7. Mesones
8. Mercado de San Miguel
9. Convent Candy
10. Former City Hall
11. Calle Mayor
12. Royal Palace

survey the square. Because of his enlightened urban policies, Charles III (1716–1788) is affectionately called the "mayor of Madrid." He decorated the city squares with fountains, got those meddlesome Jesuits out of city government, established the public school system, made the Retiro a public park rather than a royal retreat, and forbid the Madrileños from emptying their chamber pots out the windows.

Behind the king is a statue of a bear pawing a madroño tree. Actual madroño trees stand nearby in the big planter boxes. Bears used to live in the royal hunting grounds outside Madrid. The madroño trees produce a strawberry-like berry that makes the traditional *madroño* liqueur…and that gives the city its name.

Crowds fill the square on New Year's Eve as the rest of Madrid watches the action on TV. As Spain's "Big Ben" atop the governor's office chimes 12 times, Madrileños eat one grape for each ring to bring good luck through the coming year.

Governor's Office

The king faces a red-and-white building with a bell tower. This was Madrid's first post office, established by Charles III in the 1760s. Today it's the governor's office, though it's notorious for having been the police headquarters of Spain's former dictator, Francisco Franco. An amazing number of those detained and interrogated by the Franco police "tried to escape" by jumping out the windows to their deaths. Notice the hats of the civil guardsmen at the entry. It's said the hats have square backsides so the men can lean against the wall while enjoying a cigarette.

Directly in front of the entrance to the governor's office (on the ground by the curb) is the scuffed-up plaque marking "kilometer zero," the center of Spain.

To the right of the entrance, the plaque on the wall marks the spot where the war against Napoleon started. Napoleon wanted his brother to be king of Spain. Trying to finagle this, he brought nearly the entire Spanish royal family to France for negotiations. An anxious crowd gathered outside this building awaiting word of the fate of their royal family. This was just after the French Revolution, and there was a general nervousness between France and Spain. When locals heard that

Napoleon had appointed his brother as the new king of Spain, they gathered angrily in the streets. The French army rode in, blocked the exits to the square, and simply massacred the mob. The painter Goya, who worked just up the street, observed the event and captured the tragedy in his paintings *2nd of May, 1808* and *3rd of May, 1808,* now in the Prado.

• *At the west end of Puerta del Sol, across from McDonald's, is the busy…*

Salon la Mallorquina *Confitería*

The shop is famous for its sweet Napolitana cream-filled pastry (€1) and savory, beef-filled *agujas* pastries (€1.50). Step inside (open daily 9:00–21:00) to see the racks with goodies hot out of the oven. Look back toward the entrance and notice the tile above the door with the 18th-century view of the Puerta del Sol. Compare this with today's view out the door. This was before the square was widened, when a church stood where the *Tío Pepe* sign stands today. The French used this church to detain local patriots awaiting execution. (The venerable *Tío Pepe* sign, advertising a famous sherry for over 100 years, was Madrid's first billboard.)

• *Cross busy Calle Mayor, round McDonald's, and veer left up the pedestrian alley called Calle de Postas.*

Calle de Postas

The street sign shows the post coach heading for that famous first post office. Old-time street signs included pictures so the illiterate could "read" them.

Fifty yards up the street, at Calle San Cristobal, drop into Pans & Company, a popular sandwich chain. Madrileños tend to eat a skimpy breakfast, a huge lunch at 14:00, and dinner after 20:00. Pans & Company's *bocadillos* help fill the times in between. Pick up their translated flier illustrating that Spain is a country of four languages: Catalan (spoken in and around Barcelona), Euskera (Basque), Gallego (a Gaelic language spoken in northwest Spain—Galicia), and Castilian (what we call Spanish).

Hike up Calle San Cristobal. Within two blocks, you'll pass the local feminist bookshop (Librería Mujeres) and reach a small square. At the square notice the big, brick 17th-century Ministry of Foreign Affairs building (with the pointed spire)—originally a jail for rich prisoners who could afford the cushy cells. Turn right and walk down Calle de Zaragoza under the arcade into…

Plaza Mayor

This square, built in 1619, is a vast, cobbled, traffic-free chunk of 17th-century Spain. Each side of the square is uniform, as if a grand palace were turned inside out. The statue is of Philip III, who ordered the square's construction.

Upon this stage, much Spanish history was played out: bullfights, fires, royal pageantry, and events of the gruesome Inquisition. Reliefs serving as seatbacks under the lampposts tell the story. During the Inquisition, many were tried here—suspected heretics, Protestants, Jews, and Muslims whose "conversion" to Christianity was dubious. The guilty were paraded around the square (bleachers were built for bigger audiences, the wealthy rented balconies) with billboards listing their many sins. They were then burned. The fortunate were slowly strangled as they held a crucifix, hearing the reassuring words of a priest as this life was squeezed out of them.

The square is painted a democratic shade of burgundy—the result of a citywide vote. Since Franco's death in 1975, there's been a passion for voting here. Three different colors were painted as samples on the walls of this square, and the city voted for its favorite.

A stamp-and-coin market bustles here on Sundays from 10:00 to 14:00, and on any day it's a colorful and affordable place to enjoy a cup of coffee. Throughout Spain, lesser *plazas mayores* provide peaceful pools in the river of Spanish life. The TI is at #3, on the south side of the square. The building decorated with painted figures, on the north side of the square, is the Casa de la Panadería, which house the Bakers' Guild (interior closed to public).

• *In the northwest corner of the square, to the left of the Bakers' Guild, is the...*

Torre del Oro Bar Andalu

This bar (daily 8:00–15:00 & 18:00–24:00) is a temple to bullfighting. The bar's ambience is "Andalu" (Andalusian). Look under the stuffed head of Barbero the bull. At eye level you'll see a *puntilla*, the knife used to put a bull out of his misery at the arena. This was the knife used to kill Barbero.

Notice the breathtaking action captured in the bar's many photographs. At the end of the bar in a glass case is the "suit of lights" the great El Cordobes wore in his ill-fated 1967 fight. With Franco in attendance, El Cordobes—a working-class hero, the Elvis of bullfighters—went on and on, long after he could have ended the fight, until finally the bull gored him. El Cordobes survived; the bull didn't. Find Franco with El Cordobes at the far end, to the left of Segador the bull. Under the bull is a photo of El Cordobes' illegitimate son, El Cordobes, kissing a bull. Disowned by El Cordobes and using his dad's famous name after a court battle, El Cordobes is one of this generation's top fighters.

Warning: The bar staff push expensive tapas on tourists. A *caña* (small beer) shouldn't cost more than €1.50.

• *Leave Plaza Mayor on Calle Ciudad Rodrigo (far right corner from where you entered the square, and to your right as you exit Torre del Oro). You'll pass a series of fine turn-of-the-20th-century storefronts and shops such as Casa Rúa, famous for its cheap* bocadillos de calamares—*fried squid-ring sandwiches. From the archway you'll see the covered Mercado de San Miguel (green iron posts, on left). Before you enter the market, look left down the street Cava de San Miguel.*

Mesones

If you like sangria and singing, come back around 22:00 and visit one of the *mesones* (such as Guitarra, Tortilla, or Boquerón) that line Cava de San Miguel. These cave-like bars stretch way back and get packed with locals who—emboldened by sangria, the setting, and Spain—might suddenly just start singing. It's a lowbrow, electric-keyboard, karaoke-type ambience, best on Friday and Saturday nights.

Mercado de San Miguel

Wander through the newly renovated produce market and consider buying some fruit (Mon–Fri 9:00–14:30 & 17:15–20:15, Sat 9:00–14:30, closed Sun). The colors, smells, and people-watching are superb. Fully modern Madrileños buy produce in this traditional environment, connecting the old and the new in Madrid.

• *Leave the market on the opposite (downhill) side and follow the pedestrian lane left. At the first corner, turn right, and cross the small plaza to the modern brick convent.*

Convent Candy

Interact with an invisible nun. The door on the right says *venta de dulces.* To buy inexpensive sweets from the cloistered nuns, buzz the *monjas* button, then wait patiently for the sister to respond over the intercom. Say *"dulces"* (DOOL-thays) and she'll let you in (Mon–Sat 9:30–13:00 & 16:00–18:30, closed Sun). When the lock buzzes, push open the door and follow the sign to *torno,* the lazy Susan that lets the sisters sell their baked goods without being seen (smallest quantities: half, or *medio,* kilo). Of the many choices (all good), consider *pastas de almendra* (crumbly) or *mantecados de yema* (moist and eggy).

• *Follow Calle del Codo (where those in need of bits of armor shopped—see the street sign) uphill around the convent to Plaza de la Villa.*

Former City Hall

The statue in the garden is of Don Bazán—mastermind of the Christian victory over the Muslims at the naval battle of Lepanto in 1571. This pivotal battle, fought off the coast of Greece, ended the Muslim threat to Christian Europe.

• *Continue west along…*

Calle Mayor

From here, busy Calle Mayor leads downhill a couple more blocks to the Royal Palace. Halfway down (on the left), there's a tiny square opposite the recommended Casa Ciriaco restaurant (#84). The statue memorializes the 1906 bombing that killed 23 people as the royal couple paraded by on their wedding day. While the crowd was throwing flowers, an anarchist threw a bouquet lashed to a bomb from a balcony of #84 (the building was a hotel at the time). Photos of the event hang just inside the door of the restaurant.

Continue down Calle Mayor. Within a couple of blocks you'll come to a busy street, Calle de Bailen. (The Garrido-Bailen music store is *the* place to stock up on castanets, unusual flutes, and Galician bagpipes.)

Across the busy street is the **Cathedral of Almudena,** Madrid's new cathedral. Built between 1883 and 1993, its exterior is a contemporary mix and its interior is neo-Gothic, with a colorful ceiling, glittering 5,000-pipe organ, and the 12th-century coffin (empty, painted leather on wood, in a chapel behind the altar) of Madrid's patron saint, Isidro. Isidro, a humble peasant, loved the handicapped and performed miracles. Forty years after he died, this coffin was opened and his body was found in perfect condition, convincing the pope to canonize him as the patron saint of Madrid and of farmers, with May 15 as his feast day.

• *Next to the cathedral is the…*

Royal Palace (Palacio Real)

Europe's third-greatest palace (after Versailles and Vienna's Schönbrunn), with arguably the most luxurious original interior, is packed with tourists and royal antiques. After a fortress burned down on this site, King Phillip V commissioned this huge 18th-century palace as a replacement.

Though he ruled Spain for 40 years, Phillip V was very French. (The grandson of Louis XIV, he was born in Versailles, and spoke French most of the time.) He ordered this palace built to be his own Versailles (although his wife's Italian origin had a tremendous impact in the style). It's big—over 2,000 rooms with tons of luxurious tapestries, a king's ransom of chandeliers, priceless porcelain, and bronze decor covered in gold leaf. While these days the royal family lives in a mansion a few miles away, this place still functions as a

royal palace and is used for formal state receptions and tourists' day-dreams.

Touring the Palace: For cost and hours, see page 409. A simple one-floor, 24-room, one-way circuit is open to the public. You can wander on your own (there's a little English information posted in each room) or join an English tour (check time of next tour and decide as you buy your ticket; tours depart about every 20 min). The tour guides, like the museum guidebook, show a passion for mean-ingless data. Your ticket includes the armory and the pharmacy, both on the courtyard and worth a quick look. The €2 audioguides cover only marginally more of interest than what I describe below.

Palace Lobby: In the old days, horse-drawn carriages would drop you off here. Today a sign divides the visitors waiting for a tour and those going in alone.

Grand Stairs: Fancy carpets are rolled down (notice the little metal bar-holding hooks) for formal occasions.

At the top of the first landing, the blue-and-red coat of arms is of the current—and popular—constitutional monarch, Juan Carlos. While Franco chose him to be the next dictator, J. C. knew Spain was ripe for democracy. Rather than become "Juan the Brief" (as some were nicknaming him), he turned real power over to the par-liament. You'll see his (figure) head on the back of the Spanish euro coin. At the top of the stairs (before entering first room, right of door) is a white marble bust of J. C.'s great-great-g-g-g-great-grandfather Phillip V, who began the Bourbon dynasty in Spain in 1700. That dynasty survives today with Juan Carlos.

Guard Room: The guards hung out here. Notice the clocks. Charles IV, a great collector, amassed over 700—the 150 displayed in this palace are all in working order.

Hall of Columns: Originally a ballroom, today this room is used for formal ceremonies. (For example, this is where Spain formally joined the European Union in 1985—see plaque on far wall.) The tapestries (like most you'll see in the palace) are 17th-century Belgian.

Throne Room: Red velvet walls, lions, and frescoes of Spanish scenes symbolize the monarchy in this rococo riot. The ceiling fresco (1764), the last great work by the Venetian painter Giambattista Tiepolo, celebrates the vast Spanish empire—upon which the sun also never set. Find the American Indian (hint: follow the rainbow to the macho, red-caped conquistador). The chandeliers are the best in the house. The throne is only from 1977. This is where the king's guests salute him prior to dinner. He receives them relatively informally...standing rather than seated on the throne. Two rooms later you'll find the...

Antechamber: The four paintings are of King Charles IV (looking a bit like a dim-witted George Washington) and his wife, María Luisa (who wore the pants in the palace)—all originals by Goya. Velázquez's masterpiece *Las Meninas* originally hung here. The clock—showing Cronus, god of time, in marble, bronze, and wood—sits on a music box. The gilded decor you see throughout the palace is bronze with gold leaf.

Gasparini Room: This room, its painted stucco ceiling and inlaid Spanish marble floor restored in 1992, was the royal dressing room. The Asian influence was trendy at the time. Dressing, for a divine monarch, was a public affair. The court bigwigs would assemble here as the king, standing on a platform—notice the height of the mirrors—would pull on his leotards. In the next room, the silk wallpaper is new; notice the J.C.S. initials of King Juan Carlos and Queen Sofía. Passing through the silk room, you reach the...

Charles III Bedroom: Decorated in 19th-century neoclassical style, the bedroom is dominated by a chandelier in the shape of the fleur-de-lis (symbol of the Bourbon family). The thick walls separating each room hide service corridors for servants who scurried about generally unseen.

Porcelain Room: The 300 separate plates that line this room were disassembled for safety during the Spanish Civil War. (Find the little screws in the greenery that hide the seams.) The Yellow Room leads to the...

Gala Dining Room: Up to 12 times a year, the king entertains up to 150 guests at this bowling-lane-size table—which can be extended to the length of the room. Find the two royal chairs. (Hint: With the modesty necessary for 21st-century monarchs, they are just a tad higher than the rest.) The parquet floor was the preferred dancing surface when balls were held in this fabulous room, decorated with vases from China and a fresco depicting the arrival of Christopher Colombus in Barcelona. The table in the next room would be lined with an exorbitantly caloric dessert buffet.

Cinema Room (Sala de Monedas y Medallas): In the early 20th century the royal family enjoyed "Sunday afternoons at the movies" here. Today it stores glass cases filled with coins and medals.

Stradivarius Room: The queen likes classical music. When you perform for her, do it with these precious 350-year-old violins. About 300 Antonius Stradivarius-made instruments survive. This is the only matching quartet: two violins, a viola, and a cello. The next room was the children's room—with kid-sized musical instruments.

Royal Chapel: The Royal Chapel is used for private concerts and funerals. The royal coffin sits here before making the sad trip to El Escorial to join the rest of Spain's past royalty.

Queen's Boudoir: This room was for the ladies, unlike the next...

Billiards and Smoking Rooms: The billiards room and the smoking room were for men only. The porcelain and silk of the smoking room imitates a Chinese opium den, which, in its day, was furnished only with pillows.

You'll exit down the same grand stairway you climbed 24 rooms ago.

Across the courtyard is a fine park view and the **armory** displaying the armor and swords of El Cid (Christian warrior fighting the Moors), Ferdinand (husband of Isabel), Charles V (ruler of Spain at its peak of power), and Phillip II (Charles' son who watched Spain start its long slide downward). Near the exit is a cafeteria and a bookstore, which has a variety of books on Spanish history.

As you leave the palace, walk around the corner to the left along the palace exterior to the grand yet people-friendly Plaza de Oriente. Throughout Europe, energetic governments are turning formerly car-congested wastelands into public spaces like this. Madrid's latest mayor is nicknamed "the mole" for all the digging he's doing. Where's all the traffic? Under your feet.

PRADO MUSEUM

(Museo del Prado)

The Prado Museum is the greatest painting museum in the world. If you like art and you plan to be in Europe, a trip to Madrid is a must. In its glory days, the Spanish Empire was Europe's greatest, filling its coffers with gold from the New World and art from the Old.  While there are some 3,000 paintings in the collection, we'll be selective, focusing on just the top 1,500 or so.

ORIENTATION

Cost: €3, free on Sat after 14:30, all day Sun, and any time if you're over 65. A €7.75 Paseo del Arte combo-ticket covers the Prado, Reina Sofía *(Guernica)*, and Thyssen-Bornemisza Museum.

Hours: Tue–Sat 9:00–19:00, Sun and holidays 9:00–14:00, closed Mon. Most crowded on Tue, Sun, and all mornings.

Getting There: It's located on Paseo del Prado, a 15-minute walk from Puerta del Sol; buses: #9, #10, #19, #27, #34, #45; subway to "Banco de España" or "Atocha" and 10-minute walk; cheap taxis (say "moo-SAY-oh del PRAH-doh").

Information: Good small pamphlets on Flemish art, Goya, and Velázquez on racks in appropriate rooms. Tel. 913-302-800 (http://museoprado.mcu.es).

Length of This Tour: Three hours.

Cloakroom: You're required to leave your day-bag in the cloakroom.

Photography: Allowed without a flash.

Cuisine Art: Good, reasonable cafeteria in basement at south end. For picnicking, the royal gardens are just south, and the huge,

pleasant Retiro park is three blocks east.
Starring: Bosch, Goya, Titian, Velázquez, Dürer, and El Greco.

THE TOUR BEGINS

The Prado is not laid out chronologically, so we'll tour it with a minimum of walking. We'll start briefly with medieval Spanish art, linger in the Italian Renaissance, enjoy more Spanish art (El Greco), and dabble in Northern Renaissance art. Upstairs, we'll go for Baroque and see more Spanish art (Velázquez and Goya).

The Prado's hyperactive curators will likely move the art around. If you can't find a particular work, point to the picture in this book and ask a guard, "*¿Dónde . . . ?*"

• *Enter the museum at the north end through the "Puerta de Goya." There are two entrances here; the first-floor entry is monumental with grand stairs, the ground-floor entry below is unobtrusive with small doors. Our tour starts on the ground floor. If you enter on the first floor instead, head downstairs to begin.*

At either entry, after you pay admission you'll go through a security check (just like the airport) and then check your bag (mandatory). Pick up a free floor plan.

New World Gold—Old World Art

Heaven and earth have always existed side by side in Spain—religion and war, Grand Inquisitors and cruel conquistadors, spirituality and sensuality, holiness and horniness. The Prado has a surprisingly worldly collection of paintings for a country in which the medieval Inquisition lasted up until modern times. But it's just this rich combination of worldly beauty and heavenly mysticism that is so typically Spanish.

Gold from newly discovered America bought the sparkling treasures of the Prado. Spain, the most powerful nation in Europe in the 1500s, was growing rich on her New World possessions just about the time of the world's greatest cultural heyday, the Renaissance.

The collection's strengths reflect the tastes of Spain's cultured kings from 1500 to 1800: (1) Italian Renaissance art (especially the lush and sensual Venetian art which was the rage of Europe); (2) Northern art from what was the Spanish Netherlands; and (3) their own Spanish court painters. This tour will concentrate on these

Prado Overview

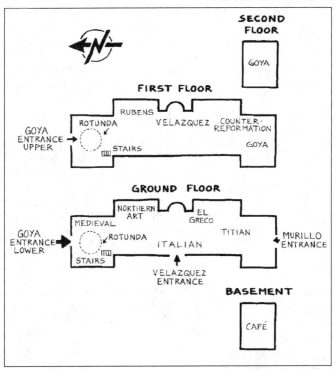

three areas, with a special look at some individual artists who are especially well-represented—Velázquez, Goya, Titian, Rubens, El Greco, and Bosch.

• *Orient yourself from the rotunda on the ground floor. Look through the doorway down the long gallery. The Prado runs north-south. Rooms branch off to the left (east of this long hall). The layout is similar on the floor above. From the rotunda, enter Room 50, packed with medieval Spanish art.*

Medieval Spanish Art

Spanish religious devotion and fanaticism are legendary. Look around. In this whole room, is there even one painting that isn't of saints or Bible stories? I found one once. It showed heretics being punished by the Inquisition during an auto-da-fé—a combination revival meeting and barbecue (coals provided, B.Y.O. sinner). An estimated 2,000 enemies of God were burned alive during the reign of one notorious Grand Inquisitor.

One reason for Spanish fanaticism is that they had to literally fight for their religion. It took centuries of fierce warfare (711–1492) for Spain's Christians to finally drive their Muslim rulers (the Moors) out. Later, in the Counter-Reformation (16th and early 17th century), Catholic Spain had to battle a new set of "infidels," the Protestant threat. The iron-strong Spanish faith was forged in the fires of those wars.

• *Enter the long gallery (Room 49) and belly up to the Annunciation altarpiece on your right.*

ITALIAN RENAISSANCE (1400–1600)

Modern Western civilization began in the prosperous Renaissance cities of Italy during the years 1400 to 1600. Florence, Rome, and Venice led the way out of the Gothic Middle Ages, building on the forgotten knowledge of ancient Rome and Greece.

Unlike the heaven-centered medieval artists, Renaissance artists gloried in the natural world and the human body. They painted things as realistically as possible. For the Italians, "realistic" meant "three-dimensional," and they set out to learn how to capture the 3-D world on a 2-D canvas.

Fra Angélico—*The Annunciation (La Anunciación)*

Fra Angélico combined medieval spirituality with Renaissance techniques. He was a monk of great piety (his nickname means "Angelic Brother") living in the heart of Renaissance Florence.

This is more like two separate paintings in one—medieval on the left, Renaissance on the right. On the left are Adam and Eve in the Garden of Eden just after they've eaten the forbidden fruit. Scrawny and two-dimensional, they seem to float above the foliage. Eve folds her hands nervously, scrunching down, a weak sinner waiting for her punishment from an angry God. The message is medieval, as is the detail work in the flowers—a labor of love by a caring monk who was also a miniaturist. Also medieval are the series of storytelling scenes below illustrating events in the life of Mary for the illiterate faithful.

The Annunciation scene on the right is early Renaissance. The angel tells Mary she'll give birth to the Messiah in a realistic scene set under a three-dimensional porch. The message is upbeat and humanistic, with the angel bringing the news that her son will redeem sinful man from the Fall. (Is it good news to Mary? She doesn't look too thrilled.)

Still, the painting is flat by modern standards, and the study in depth perspective is crude. Aren't the receding bars of the porch's ceiling a bit off? And Mary's hands just aren't right, like she's wash-

Prado—Ground Floor

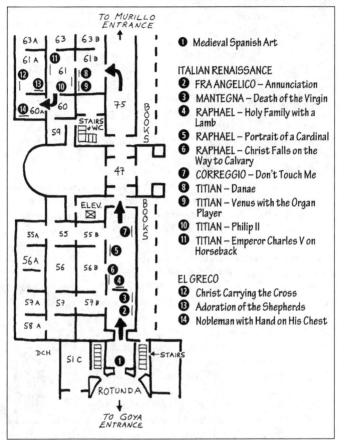

TO MURILLO ENTRANCE

❶ Medieval Spanish Art

ITALIAN RENAISSANCE

❷ FRA ANGELICO – Annunciation
❸ MANTEGNA – Death of the Virgin
❹ RAPHAEL – Holy Family with a Lamb
❺ RAPHAEL – Portrait of a Cardinal
❻ RAPHAEL – Christ Falls on the Way to Calvary
❼ CORREGGIO – Don't Touch Me
❽ TITIAN – Danae
❾ TITIAN – Venus with the Organ Player
❿ TITIAN – Philip II
⓫ TITIAN – Emperor Charles V on Horseback

EL GRECO

⓬ Christ Carrying the Cross
⓭ Adoration of the Shepherds
⓮ Nobleman with Hand on His Chest

ing the dishes with two left-hand rubber gloves.

Notice the serene, spiritual atmosphere of the painting. There are no harsh shadows or strong light sources. Everything is bathed in a pristine, glowing, holy light. The only movement is the shaft of light shooting down from the hands of God, bringing redemption from the Fall, connecting the two halves of the painting and fusing medieval piety with Renaissance humanism.

• *Farther along the same wall, look for...*

Mantegna—*Death of the Virgin (El Tránsito de la Virgen)*

A pioneer of Renaissance 3-D, Andrea Mantegna (mahn-TAYN-yah) creates a spacious setting, then peoples it with sculptural figures.

The dying mother of Christ is surrounded by statue-like apostles with plates on their heads and pots in their hands. The

architectural setting is heroic and spacious. Follow the lines in the floor tiles and side columns. They converge toward the window, then seem to continue on to the far horizon in the lines of the bridge. This creates a subconscious feeling of almost infinite spaciousness, bringing a serenity to an otherwise tragic death scene. You can imagine Mary's soul leaving her body and floating easily out the window, disappearing into the infinite distance.

• *Turn around to see some large Raphael canvases (on opposite wall). Let them overwhelm you, then look left at the partition and refocus your eyes on Raphael's tiny* Holy Family with a Lamb. *The sheer difference in size and scope of these works gives you a sense of the artist's vision.*

Raphael—*Holy Family with a Lamb* (*Sagrada Familia del Cordero*)

Raphael reproduced reality perfectly on a canvas, but also gave it harmony, geometry, and heroism that made it somehow more real than reality. Combining idealized beauty with down-to-earth realism, he was the ultimate Renaissance painter.

Raphael was only 21 when he painted this. He learned Leonardo da Vinci's technique of sfumato, spreading a kind of hazy glow around the figures (this is the technique that gives *Mona Lisa* her vague, mysterious smile). He also borrowed a Leonardo trademark technique—the three figures form a pyramid, with Joseph's head at the peak.

• *Within the same room (#49), find the following paintings:*

Raphael—*Portrait of a Cardinal (El Cardenal)*

Compare the idealized beauty of Holy Family with the stark realism of this gritty portrait of a no-nonsense man. Raphael captures not just his face, but his personality. He's cold, intelligent, detached, and somewhat cynical, the type of man who could become a cardinal at such a young age in the Renaissance Vatican's priest-eat-priest jungle of holy ambition.

Raphael—*Christ Falls on the Way to Calvary* (*Caída en el Camino del Calvario*)

Raphael puts it all together—the idealized grace of the *Holy Family* and the realism of *Portrait of a Cardinal*. Look at the detail on the muscular legs of the guy in yellow (at left) and the arms of Simon, who has come to help Jesus carry his cross. Then contrast that with the idealized beauty of the mourning women. When this painting was bought in 1661, it was the costliest in existence.

Raphael splits the canvas into two contrasting halves. Below the slanting line made by the crossbar is a scene of swirling passion—the sorrow of Christ and the women, the tangle of crowded bodies. Above it is open space and indifference—the bored soldiers and onlookers and the bleak hill in the background where Jesus is headed to be crucified.

• *On the opposite wall (still in Room 49), look for...*

Correggio—*Don't Touch Me (Noli Me Tangere)*

Raphael could paint idealized beauty, but this pushes sweetness to diabetic levels.

It's Easter morning and Jesus has just come back to life. One of his followers, Mary Magdalene, runs into him in the garden near the tomb. She's amazed and excited and reaches toward him. "Don't touch me!" *(Noli me tangere)* says Jesus, though he spoke neither English nor Latin.

The colors accentuate the emotion of the scene. Against the blue-green landscape, Mary Magdalene—the ex-prostitute in a fiery yellow dress and yellow hair—is hot to touch the cool Christ with his blue cloak and pale, radiant skin. The composition also accentuates the action. The painting's energy runs in a diagonal line up the rippling Mary, through Christ and his outstretched arm to heaven, where he will soon go.

• *Head straight to the next long gallery (Room 75). Midway down the gallery, turn left into Room 61b.*

Titian (c. 1490–1576)

Look around. What do you see? Flesh. Naked bodies in various poses; bright, lush, colorful scenes. Many scenes have "pagan" themes, but even the religious works are racier than anything we saw from the Florentine and Roman Renaissance.

Venice in 1500 was the richest city in Europe, the middleman in the lucrative trade between Europe and the Orient. Wealthy, cosmopolitan, and free, Venetians loved life's finer things—rich silks, beautiful people, jewels, banquets, music, wine, and impressive buildings—and Venetian painters enjoyed painting them in bright colors.

The chief Venetian was Titian (they rhyme). Titian (Tiziano in Spain) was possibly the most famous painter of his day—more famous than Raphael, Leonardo, and even Michelangelo. His reputation reached Spain, and he became the favorite portraitist for two kings, who bought many of his works.

Titian—*Danae*

In Greek mythology, Zeus, the king of the gods, was always zooming to earth in the form of some creature or other to fool around with mortal women. Here, he descends as a shower of gold to consort with the willing Danae. You can almost see the human form of Zeus within the cloud. Danae is helpless with rapture, opening her legs to receive him, while her servant tries to catch the heavenly spurt with a towel.

Danae's rich, luminous flesh on the left of the canvas is set off by the dark servant at right and the threatening sky above. The white sheets beneath her make her glow even more. This is more than a classic nude—it's a Renaissance Miss August. How could Spain's ultraconservative Catholic kings have tolerated such a downright pagan and erotic painting?

Titian—*Venus with the Organ Player*
(Venus recreándose en la Música)

A musician turns around to leer at a naked woman while keeping his hands at work on his organ. This aroused King Phillip II's interest. (For more on the king, see below.) The message must have appealed to him—the conflict between sacred, artistic pursuits as symbolized by music, and worldly, sensual pursuits as embodied in the naked lady.

Titian emphasized these two opposites with color—"cool"

colors on the left, hot crimson and flesh on the right. The center of the painting is where these two color schemes meet, so even though the figures lean and the poplar trees in the background are off-center, the painting is balanced and harmonious in the Renaissance tradition.

A century after Phillip's reign, his beloved nudes were taken down from the Escorial and Royal Palace and hidden away as unfit to be seen. For more than a century these great Titians were banned.
• *Continue into Room 61...*

Titian—*Phillip II (Felipe II)*

This is the king who bought Titian's sexy *Danae* and many other paintings of nudes. Phillip had a reputation as a repressed prude— pale, suspicious, lonely, a cold fish; the sort of man who would build the severe and tomb-like Escorial Palace. Freud would have had a field day with such a complex man who could be so sternly religious and yet have such sensual tastes. Here, he is looking as pious and ascetic as a man can while wearing an outfit with a bulging codpiece.

Titian—*Emperor Charles V on Horseback* (*El Emperador Carlos V en la Batalla de Muhlberg*)

Are you glad to be here? If so, then tip your book to that guy on horseback, the father of the Prado's collection.

In the 1500s, Charles was the most powerful man in the world. He was not merely King Charles of Spain, but Holy Roman Emperor with possessions stretching from Spain to Austria, from Holland to Italy, from South America to Burgundy. He was defender of the Catholic Church against infidel Turks, French kings,

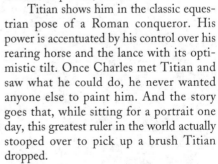

and in this picture, rebellious Protestants.

Titian shows him in the classic equestrian pose of a Roman conqueror. His power is accentuated by his control over his rearing horse and the lance with its optimistic tilt. Once Charles met Titian and saw what he could do, he never wanted anyone else to paint him. And the story goes that, while sitting for a portrait one day, this greatest ruler in the world actually stooped over to pick up a brush Titian dropped.

• *El Greco's art is nearby in Room 60a and 61a.*

El Greco (c. 1540–1614)

The first great Spanish painter was Greek. El Greco (Spanish for "the Greek") was born in Greece, trained in Venice, then settled in Toledo, Spain. The combination of these three cultures, plus his own unique personality, produced a highly individual style. His paintings are Byzantine icons drenched in Venetian color and fused in the fires of Spanish mysticism.

Phillip II, the ascetic king with sensual tastes who bought so many Titians, didn't like El Greco's bizarre style (perhaps because the figures—thin and haunting—reminded him of himself). So El Greco left the Spanish court and moved south to Toledo, where he was accepted. He spent the rest of his life there. If you like El Greco, make the 60-minute trip to Toledo.

• *In Room 61a ...*

El Greco—*Christ Carrying the Cross* (*Cristo Abrazado a la Cruz*)

Even as the blood runs down his neck and he trudges toward his death, Christ accepts his fate in a trance of religious ecstasy. The crossbar points upward. Jesus hugs the cross lovingly and sights along it like a navigational instrument to his destination—heaven.

The upturned eyes are close to tears with humility and sparkle with joyful acceptance. (Warning: Do not get too close to this painting. Otherwise you'll see that the holy magic in the eyes is only a simple streak of white paint.)

• *In the same Room (#61a) ...*

El Greco—*The Adoration of the Shepherds* (*La Adoración de los Pastores*)

El Greco painted this for his own burial chapel in Toledo, where it hung until the 1950s. It combines all of his trademark techniques

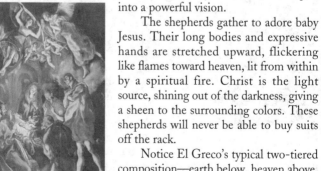

into a powerful vision.

The shepherds gather to adore baby Jesus. Their long bodies and expressive hands are stretched upward, flickering like flames toward heaven, lit from within by a spiritual fire. Christ is the light source, shining out of the darkness, giving a sheen to the surrounding colors. These shepherds will never be able to buy suits off the rack.

Notice El Greco's typical two-tiered composition—earth below, heaven above. Over the Christ Child is a swirling canopy of clouds and angels. Heaven and earth seem to intermingle, and the earthly figures look as though they're about to be sucked up through a funnel into heaven. There is little depth to the picture—all the figures are virtually the same distance from us—so our eyes have nowhere to go but up and down, up and down, linking heaven and earth, God and humankind.

• *Next door in Room 60a ...*

El Greco—*The Nobleman with His Hand on His Chest (El Caballero de la Mano al Pecho)*

Despite the surreal mysticism of many of his paintings, El Greco was not a mystic, but a well-traveled, learned, sophisticated, down-to-earth man who could paint realistic and probing portraits like

this. The sitter is an elegant and somewhat arrogant gentleman, who was obviously trying to make an impression. The sword probably indicates the portrait was done to celebrate his becoming a knight.

El Greco reveals the man's personality in the expressive eyes and in the hand across the chest. The middle two fingers touch—El Greco's trademark way of expressing elegance (or was it the 16th-century symbol for "Live long and prosper"?). Look for it in his other works.

The signature is on the right in faint Greek letters—"Domenicos Theotocopoulos," El Greco's real name.

• *Return to the long gallery (Room 75) and continue straight to the gallery where we started (Room 49, with Italian Renaissance art). Take the last right, just before you reach the rotunda. After entering, take the first left, into Room 58.*

NORTHERN ART

Master of Flemalle (Robert Campin)— *St. John the Baptist (San Jaun Bautista)*

The meticulous detail is the first thing we notice in Northern art. Not only are the wood, the glass, and the cloth done with loving care, but look at the curved mirror in the middle—the whole scene is reflected backwards in perfect detail!

Roger Van Der Weyden—*Descent From the Cross (El Descendimiento)*

Christ is lowered from the Cross by his heartbroken followers. Each of the faces is a different study in grief. Joseph of Arimathea (holding Christ's feet) seems to be asking, "Why do the good always die young?" The bulging veins in his forehead signal his distress. Mary has swooned in the same S-curve as Jesus' body—the death of her son has dealt her a near-fatal blow as well. But the

overwhelming tone of the scene is one of serenity. These are people of Northern piety who know and accept that Jesus must die.

Along with Titian's nudes, this was one of Phillip II's favorite paintings—quite a contrast! Yet this *Descent* and Titian's *Danae* both have the power to send us into ecstasy. Hmm.

• *Continue to Room 56a.*

Bosch (c. 1450–1516)

The work of Hieronymous Bosch can be summed up in one word—wow. It's difficult to be more articulate because his unique vision lends itself to so many different interpretations.

Bosch (rhymes with "Gosh!") was born, lived, and died in a small town in Holland—that's about all we know of him, his life being as mysterious as his work. He was much admired by his contemporaries, who understood his symbolism better than we.

Here are some possible interpretations of Bosch's work. He was: (1) crazy; (2) commenting on the decadence of his day; (3) celebrating the variety of life and human behavior; (4) painting with toxins in a badly ventilated room. Or perhaps it's a combination of these.

Northern Art

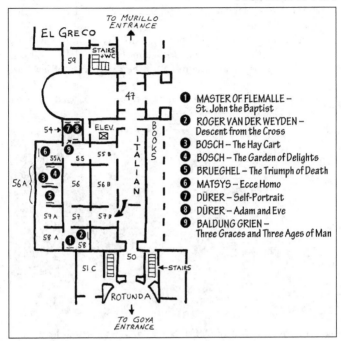

1. MASTER OF FLEMALLE –
   St. John the Baptist
2. ROGER VAN DER WEYDEN –
   Descent from the Cross
3. BOSCH – The Hay Cart
4. BOSCH – The Garden of Delights
5. BRUEGHEL – The Triumph of Death
6. MATSYS – Ecce Homo
7. DÜRER – Self-Portrait
8. DÜRER – Adam and Eve
9. BALDUNG GRIEN –
   Three Graces and Three Ages of Man

Bosch—*The Hay Cart (El Carro de Heno)*

Before unraveling the cryptic triptych *The Garden of Delights,* let's warm up on a "simpler" three-paneled work. Its message is that the pleasures of life are transitory, so we'd better avoid them or we'll wind up in hell.

Center Panel: An old Flemish proverb goes, "Life is a cart of hay from which everyone takes what they can." The whole spectrum of greedy, grabby humanity is here: rich and poor, monks and peasants, scrambling for their share of worldly goods. Even the pope and the Holy Roman emperor (with the sword) chase the cart on horseback. In the very center, a man holds a knife at another man's throat, getting his share by force. Two lovers on top of the cart are oblivious to the commotion but are surrounded by symbols of hate (the owl) and lust (the jug). The cart itself is drawn by Satan's demons.

With everyone fighting for his piece of the pie, it's easy to overlook the central figure—Christ above in heaven, watching unnoticed. Is He blessing them or throwing up His hands?

Left: The left panel tells us where this crazy world of temptation came from. "Read" the panel from top to bottom. At the top, God fumigates Heaven, driving Satan's vermin out and setting them loose on earth. Then God creates Eve from Adam's rib, Eve gets tempted by a (female) serpent, and finally, they're driven from Paradise. It was this first sin that brought a hay-cart's-worth of evil into the world.

Right: Here's the whole point of Bosch's sermon—worldly pleasures lead to hell. Animal-like demons symbolizing various vices torture those who succumbed to the temptation of hay-cart planet Earth.

• *With this traditional Christian interpretation in mind, let's enter the* Garden of Delights *(same room—#56a).*

Bosch—*The Garden of Delights (El Jardín de las Delicias)*

The Garden can be interpreted like the *Hay Cart;* that is, the pleasures of the world are transitory, so you'd better watch out or you'll wind up in hell. With so many figures, the painting is overwhelming. To make it less so, I'd suggest "framing off" one-foot squares to peruse at your leisure.

Central panel: Men on horseback ride round and round, searching for but never reaching the elusive Fountain of Youth. Lower down and to the left are two lovers in a bubble that—like love— could burst at any time. Just to their right is a big mussel shell, a symbol of the female sex, swallowing up a man. My favorite is the kneeling figure in front of the orange pavilion in the foreground— talk about "saying it with flowers!"

Bosch was certainly a Christian, but there's speculation he was a heretical Christian painting forbidden rites of a free-wheeling cult called Adamites. The Adamites were medieval nudists who believed the body was good (as it was when God made Adam) and that sex was healthy. They supposedly held secret orgies. So, in the central panel we see Adamites at play, frolicking across the meadow in two-somes and threesomes, as innocent as Adam and Eve in the garden. Whether or not Bosch approved, you must admit that some of the folks in this garden are having a delightful time.

Left panel: This "Adamist" interpretation makes a lot of sense in the left panel. Here, the main scene, is the fundamental story of the Adamites—the marriage (sexual union) of Adam and Eve. God himself performs the ceremony, wrapping them in the glowing warmth of His aura.

One of the differences between *The Hay Cart* and *The Garden of Delights* is Columbus. Discoveries of new plants and animals in America gave Bosch a whole new continent of sinful pleasures to paint—some real, some imaginary. Check out the cactus tree in the Garden of Eden and the bizarre two-legged dog near the giraffe.

Right panel: Hell is a burning, post-holocaust wasteland of genetic mutants and meaningless rituals where sinners are tortured by half-human demons. Poetic justice reigns supreme, with every sinner getting his just desserts—a glutton is eaten and re-eaten eternally, while a musician is crucified on a musical instrument for neglecting his church duties. Other symbols are less obvious. Two big ears pierced with a knife blade mow down all in the way. A pink bagpipe symbolizes the male and female sex organs (call Freud for details). At lower right a pig dressed as a nun tries to seduce a man. In the center of this wonderful nightmare, hell is literally frozen over. A creature with a broken-eggshell body, tree-trunk legs, and a witch's cap stares out at us—it's the face of Bosch himself.

• *In the same room (#56a), look for Brueghel's work.*

NORTHERN RENAISSANCE (1500–1600)

The sunny optimism of the Italian Renaissance didn't quite penetrate the cold Northern lands. Italian humanists saw people as almost like Greek gods—strong, handsome, and noble—capable of standing on their own without the help of anyone, including God and the Catholic Church. Northern artists concentrated on the flip side of humanism—ordinary folks and their folly and travails.

Brueghel—*The Triumph of Death (El Triunfo de la Muerte)*
The brief flowering of the Renaissance couldn't last. In the 16th century, the bitter break between the Catholic Church and the "Protest"-ants sparked wars across Europe. In Germany alone, a

third of the population died. The battles were especially brutal, with atrocities on both sides—the predictable result when politicians and generals claim God is on their side.

Pieter Brueghel (BROY-gull) the Elder chronicled these violent times. His message is simple and morbid—no one can escape death.

The painting is one big chaotic, confusing battle. Death in the form of skeletons (led by one on horseback with a scythe) attacks a crowd of people, herding them into a tunnel-like building (prescient of a Nazi death camp). Elsewhere, other skeletons dole out the inevitable fate of all flesh. No one is spared. Not the jester (lower right, crawling under the table), not churchmen, not the emperor himself (at lower left, whose gold is also plundered), not even the poor man (upper right) kneeling, praying for mercy with a cross in his hands.

• *Continue to Room 55a.*

Matsys—*Ecce Homo* (*Cristo Presentado al Pueblo*)

The mob—a menagerie of goony faces—razzes the prisoner Christ before his execution. Christ seems quite fed up with it all. The painting is especially effective because of our perspective. We're looking up at Christ on the balcony, making us part of the hooting mob.

• *Stop by Room 54 to meet...*

Dürer—*Self-Portrait* (*Autoretrato*)

Before looking into the eyes of 26-year-old Albrecht Dürer, look first at his clothes and hairdo—they say as much about him as his

face. With his Italian hat and permed hair, he's clearly a mod/hip/fab/rad young guy, a man of the world. The meticulous detail-work (Dürer was also an engraver) is the equivalent of preening before a mirror. Dürer (DEWR-er) had recently returned from Italy, and wanted to impress his bumpkin fellow Germans with all that he had learned.

But Dürer wasn't simply vain. Renaissance Italy treated its artists like princes, not workmen. Dürer learned not only to paint like a great artist, but to act like one as well.

Now look into his eyes, or rather, look up at his eyes, since Dürer literally looks down on us. We see an intelligent, bold, and somewhat arrogant man, confident of his abilities. The strong arms and hands reinforce this confidence.

This is possibly the first true self-portrait. Sure, other artists used themselves as models and put their likeness in scenes (like Bosch in hell), but it was a whole new thing to paint your own portrait to proudly show your personality to the world. Dürer painted probably ten of them in his life—each showing a different aspect of this complex man.

Dürer put his mark on every painting and engraving. Note the pyramid-shaped "A.D." (D inside the A) on the windowsill.

Dürer—*Adam and Eve* (two separate panels)

These are the first full-size nudes in Northern European art. It took the boldness of someone like Dürer to bring Italian fleshiness to the more modest Germans.

The title is *Adam and Eve,* but that's just an excuse to paint two

nudes in the style of Greek statues on pedestals. Dürer splits the one scene into two canvases (Eve is giving Adam the apple, and their hair is blown by the same wind) so that each "statue" has its own niche.

Compared with Bosch's smooth-limbed, naked little homunculi, Dürer's Adam and Eve are three-dimensional and solid, with anatomically correct muscles. They're a bold humanist proclamation that the body is good, man is good, the things of the world are good.

Hans Baldung Grien—*The Three Graces* and *The Three Ages of Man*

Three classical Graces teach a medieval Christian message—that all flesh is mortal and we're all on the same moving sidewalk to the junk pile.

In the left panel are the Three Graces in youth—beautiful, happy, in a playful green grove with the sun shining, and surrounded

by angelic babies. But with grim Northern realism, the right panel shows what happens to all flesh (especially that of humanists!). The Three Graces become the Three Ages of sagging decay—middle age, old age, and death. Death holds an hourglass of that devouring army, Time.

• *Return to the long gallery (Room 49) and head to the rotunda. Go upstairs. Look down the long gallery. To reach Rubens' work, take the first left, into Room 9b. But first, grab a seat in the long gallery and soak in Baroque.*

BAROQUE (1600s)

You're surrounded by Baroque. Large canvases, bright colors, rippling bodies, plenty of flesh, violent scenes. This room contains more rapes per square foot than any gallery in the world.

Baroque art overwhelms. It plays on the emotions, titillates the senses, and carries us away. Baroque was made to order for the Catholic Church and absolute monarchs who used it as propaganda to combat the dual threats of Protestantism and democracy. They impressed the common masses with beautiful palaces and glorious churches, showing their strength and authority.

Rubens (1577–1640)

Peter Paul Rubens of Flanders (Belgium) was the favorite of Catholic rulers. He painted the loves, wars, and religion of Catholic kings. Like Titian before him, he became rich and famous, a cultured, likable man of the world, who was even entrusted with diplomatic missions by his employers.

• *Enter the first Rubens Room (#9b).*

Rubens—*St. George Slaying the Dragon (San Jorge)*

Like a Counter-Reformation king, the Christian warrior fights to save the holy Church from the dragon of Protestantism.

Rubens freezes the action just as George spears the dragon and raises his sword to finish him off. The limp damsel in distress has a lamb, the symbol of Christ and His church.

Baroque art may look like a rippling mess, but it's often anchored in Renaissance-style balance. This painting has an X-like composition, the rearing horse slanting one way and George slanting the other. Above where the X intersects are the two stars of the scene, George with his rippling plumed helmet, and the horse with its rippling mane.

All around these rooms are Rubens paintings of religious subjects. Glance at the series of smaller paintings with titles championing the Catholic cause—*Triumph of the Church, Triumph of the True Catholic,* and so on.

• *In Room 9 (which is back-to-back with Room 9b), look for the following two paintings:*

Rubens—*Diana and Her Nymphs Discovered by a Satyr (Diana y sus Ninfas sorprendidas por Sátiros)*

A left-to-right rippling wave of figures creates a thrilling chase scene. Four horny satyrs (half-man, half-beast—though why mythical

Prado—First Floor

RUBENS
1. St. George
2. Diana and her Nymphs
3. The Three Graces

VELÁZQUEZ
4. The Maids of Honor
5. Jester Portraits
6. The Drinkers
7. Crucifixion
8. Prince Balthasar Carlos on Horseback
9. The Surrender of Breda

SPANISH COUNTER-REFORMATION
10. CANO – St. Bernard and the Virgin
11. ZURBARAN – St. Peter Crucified
12. MURILLO – Immaculate Conception

creatures like this never have their human half at the bottom, I don't know) have crashed a party of woodland nymphos who flee from left to right. Only the Greek goddess Diana, queen of the hunt, turns to face the predatory mutants. She stands with her spear to try to stem the tide of flailing limbs.

All the elements of a typical Rubens work are here—action, emotion, sensuality, violence, bright colors, fleshy bodies, and rippling clothes and hair with the wind machine on high.

Another typical feature is that it wasn't all painted by Rubens.

Rubens was in such demand that he couldn't fill all the orders himself. In his home/studio/factory in Antwerp, he put assistants to work with the backgrounds and trivial details of his huge works, then, before shipping a canvas out the doors, Rubens would bring the work to life with a few final strokes.

Rubens—*The Three Graces (Las Tres Gracias)*

Rubens loved cellulite. The Three Graces have ample, sensual

bodies, glowing skin, rhythmic limbs, grace, and delicacy, set against a pleasant background. His young second wife, the model for the Grace at left, shows up fairly regularly in Rubens' paintings. This particular painting was for his own private collection. Remember that in later, more prudish years, many of Rubens' nudes, like Titian's, were wrapped in brown paper and locked in the closet.

• *Return to the main gallery. Turn left midway down the gallery into the large lozenge-shaped Room 12.*

Velázquez (1599–1660)

For 35 years, Diego Velázquez (vel-LAHS-kes) was the king of Spain's court painters. Scan the room and you'll see portraits in a realistic, down-to-earth style. While El Greco and other Spanish artists painted crucifixions, saints, and madonnas, Velázquez painted what his boss, the king, told him to—mostly portraits.

Unlike the wandering, independent El Greco, Velázquez was definitely a career man. Born in Sevilla, apprenticed early on, he married the master's daughter, moved to Madrid, impressed the king with his skill, and worked his way up the ladder at the king's court. He became the king's friend and art teacher and, eventually, was knighted.

What's amazing in this tale of ambition is that, as a painter, Velázquez never compromised. He was the photojournalist of his time, chronicling court events for posterity.

Velázquez—*The Maids of Honor (Las Meninas)*

Velázquez has made the perfect blend of formal portrait and candid intimate snapshot. It's a painting about the painting of a portrait. Here's what we're seeing:

One hot summer day in 1656, Velázquez (at left), with brush in hand and looking like Salvador Dalí (which is a little like saying that Jesus looked like John Lennon), is painting a formal portrait of King Phillip and his wife. Velazquez stares out at the people he's painting—they would be standing where we are, and we see only their reflection in the mirror at the back of the room.

Their daughter, the Infanta Margarita (the main figure in the center), has come to watch her parents being painted. With her are her two attendants (*meninas,* or girls), one of whom is kneeling, offering her a cool glass of water. Also in the picture is the young court jester (far right) poking impishly at the family dog. A female dwarf looks on, as do others in the background. Also, at that very moment, a member of the court is passing by the doorway in the distance on his way upstairs, and he, too, looks in on the progress of the portrait.

Velázquez knew that the really interesting portrait wasn't the king and queen, but the action behind the scenes. We're sucked right in by the naturalness of the scene and because the characters are looking right at us. This is true Spanish history, and Velázquez the journalist (who is shown wearing the red cross of knighthood, painted on after his death—possibly by Phillip IV himself) has told us more about this royal family than have volumes of history books. The scene is lit by the window at right. Using gradations of light, Velázquez has split the room into five receding planes: (1) the king and queen, standing where we are; (2) the main figures, lit by the window; (3) the darker middle-distance figures (including Velázquez); (4) the black wall; and (5) the lit doorway. We are drawn into the painting, living and breathing with its characters, free to walk behind them, around them, and among them. This is art come to life.

• *Next to* The Maids of Honor, *look for…*

Velázquez—Jester Portraits *(Bufones)*

In royal courts, dwarfs were given the job of entertaining the nobles. But some also had a more important task—social satire. They alone were given free rein to say anything they wanted about the king, however biting, nasty, or—worst of all—true. Consequently, these dwarfs were often the wittiest and most intelligent people at court, and Velázquez, who must have known them as colleagues, painted them with great dignity.

Velázquez—*The Drinkers (Los Borrachos)*

Velázquez's objective eye even turns Greek gods into everyday folk. Here the Greek god of wine crowns a drinker for his deeds of

debauchery. But the focus isn't the otherworldly Bacchus but his fellow, human merry-makers.

This isn't a painting, it's a Polaroid snapshot in a blue-collar bar. Look how natural the guy is next to Bacchus, grinning at us over the bowl of wine he's offering—and the guy next to him, clambering to get into the picture and mugging for the camera! Velázquez was the master at making a carefully composed scene look spontaneous.

• *You'll find more work by Velázquez in Rooms 15 and 16. In Room 15…*

Velázquez—Crucifixion (Cristo crucificado)

King Phillip IV was having an affair. He got caught and, being a

good Christian king, was overcome with remorse. He commissioned this work to atone for his adulterous ways.

Velázquez's *Crucifixion* must have matched the repentant mood of his king (and friend). Christ's head hangs down, humbly accepting His punishment.

Meditating on this Christ would truly be an act of agonizing penance. We see him straight from the front, no holds barred. Every detail is laid out, even down to the knots in the wood of the crossbar.

And the dripping blood! We know how long Jesus has been hanging there by how long it must have taken for that blood to drip ever so slowly down.

• *In Room 16, look for the following two paintings…*

Velázquez—
Prince Balthasar Carlos on Horseback
(El Príncipe Balthasar Carlos, a caballo)

As court painter, this was exactly the kind of portrait Velázquez was called on to produce. The prince, age five, was the heir to the throne. But the charm of the painting is the contrast between the pose—the traditional equestrian pose of a powerful Roman conqueror—with the fact that this "conqueror" is only a cute, tiny tyke in a pink and gold suit. The serious look on the prince's face adds the crowning touch.

While pleasing his king, Velázquez was also starting a revolution in art. Stand back and look at the prince's costume—remarkably detailed, right? Now move up closer—all that "remarkable detail" is nothing but messy splotches of pink and gold paint! In the past, artists painted details meticulously. But Velázquez learned how just a few dabs of colors on a canvas blend in the eye when seen at a distance to give the appearance of great detail. Two centuries later this technique would eventually be taken to its extreme by the Impressionists.

Velázquez—*The Surrender of Breda* (*La Rendición de Breda*)

Here's another piece of artistic journalism, the Spanish victory over the Dutch after a long siege of  Breda, a strongly fortified city. The scene has become famous as a model of fair play. The defeated Dutch general is offering the keys to the city to the victorious Spaniards. As he begins to kneel in humility, the Spanish conqueror restrains him—the war is over and there's no need to rub salt in the wounds. The optimistic calm-after-the-battle mood is enhanced by the great open space highlighted by the 25 lances (the painting is often called "The Lances") silhouetted against the sky.

• *From the cool objectivity of Velázquez, enter the heat and passion of Spain's religious art of the Counter-Reformation. Start with Room 17a.*

COUNTER-REFORMATION ART— FIGHTING BACK WITH BRUSHES (1600s)

Europe was torn in two by the Protestant Reformation. For 100 years, Catholics and Protestants bashed Bibles in what has been called the first "world war." The Catholic Church also waged a propaganda campaign (the Counter-Reformation) to bolster the faith of the confused, weary masses. Art was part of that campaign. Pretty

 pictures brought abstract doctrines to the level of the common man.

Cano—*St. Bernard and the Virgin* (*San Bernardo y la Virgen*)

Here's a heavenly vision brought right down to earth. St. Bernard is literally enjoying the "milk of paradise," a vision he had of being suckled on the heavenly teat of Mary. When God's word was portrayed in this realistic

way, the common folk lapped it up.
• *In Room 18a...*

Zurbarán—*St. Peter Crucified Appearing to Peter Nolasco* (*Aparición de San Pedro a San Pedro Nolasco*)

Zurbarán is like a bitter jolt of café solo. In Spain, miracles are real. When legends tell of a saint who was beheaded but didn't die, that isn't an allegory on eternal life to the Spanish—they picture a real man walking around with his head under his arm.

So, when Zurbarán paints a mystical vision, he gives it to us in photographic realism. Bam, there's the Apostle Peter crucified upside down right in front of us. Nolasco looks as shocked as we are at the reality of the vision. This is "People's Art" of the Counter-Reformation, religious art for the masses. (Zurbarán has the sort of literal-minded religion that makes people wonder things like—"When the Rapture comes, what if I'm sitting on the toilet?")

• *Return to the long gallery. Within the gallery, in section 28 (roughly between the lozenge-shaped room and the far end of the gallery), look for...*

Murillo—*The Immaculate Conception* (*La Inmaculada "de El Escorial"*)

For centuries, the No. 1 deity in the Christian "pantheon" was the goddess Mary. This painting is a religious treatise, explaining a Catholic doctrine that many found difficult to comprehend. The Immaculate Conception of Mary meant that, though all humans are stained by the original sin of Adam, the mother of Jesus was conceived and born pure.

The Spanish have always loved the Virgin. She's practically a cult figure. Common people pray directly to her for help in troubled times. Murillo (mur-REE-oh) painted a beautiful, floating, and Ivory soap–pure woman—the most "immaculate" virgin imaginable—radiating youth and wholesome goodness.

• *Go to far end of gallery and enter the round room (#32).*

GOYA (1746–1828)

Francisco de Goya, a true individual in both his life and his painting style, is hard to pigeonhole, his personality and talents were so varied.

Prado—Goya

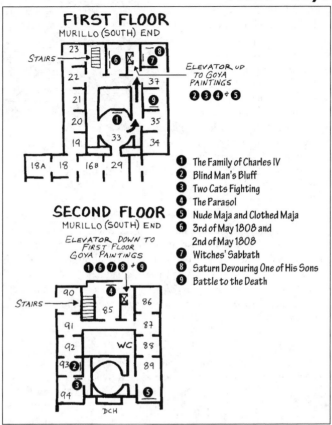

FIRST FLOOR
MURILLO (SOUTH) END

STAIRS

ELEVATOR up
TO GOYA
PAINTINGS

SECOND FLOOR
MURILLO (SOUTH) END

ELEVATOR DOWN TO
FIRST FLOOR
GOYA PAINTINGS

STAIRS

WC

DCH

❶ The Family of Charles IV
❷ Blind Man's Bluff
❸ Two Cats Fighting
❹ The Parasol
❺ Nude Maja and Clothed Maja
❻ 3rd of May 1808 and
   2nd of May 1808
❼ Witches' Sabbath
❽ Saturn Devouring One of His Sons
❾ Battle to the Death

We'll see several different facets of this rough-cut man—cheery apprentice painter, loyal court painter, political rebel, scandal-maker, disillusioned genius. His work runs the gamut, from pretty Rococo to political rabble-rousing to Romantic nightmares.

For convenience, let's divide Goya's life into three stages: the Court Painter (including his early years), Political Rebel, and Dark Stage.

Court Painter

Goya—The Family of Charles IV (La Familia de Carlos IV)

They're decked out in all their finest, wearing every medal, jewel, and ribbon they could find for this impressive group portrait. Goya, the budding political liberal, captures all the splendor of the court in 1800, but with a brutal twist of reality. King Charles, with his ridiculous hairdo and silly smile, is portrayed for what he was—a vacuous, good-natured fool, a henpecked husband controlled by a domineering queen. She, the true center of the composition, is proud and defiant. The queen was vain about the supposed beauty of her long, swan-like neck, and here she stretches to display every centimeter of it. The other adults, with their bland faces, are bug-eyed with stupidity. Catch the crone looking out at us bird-like, fourth from left. The look

in their eyes seems to say "I can't wait to get this monkey-suit off." (I picture Goya deliberately taking his own sweet time making them stand and smile for hours on end.) Underneath the royal trappings, Goya shows us the inner personality—or lack thereof—of these shallow monarchs.

As a tribute to *Maids of Honor* (by Velázquez), Goya painted himself painting the scene at far left. But here Goya stands back in the shadows looking with disdain on the group. Only the children escape Goya's critical eye. Here they're painted with the sympathy he always showed to those lower on the social ladder.

• *Let's look at Goya's early years. Facing the above painting, exit the round room to the left, then turn right down the hall. Go up the stairs to Rooms 90–94.*

The Early Years

Born in a small town, Goya, unlike Velázquez, was a far cry from a precocious painter destined for success. In his youth he dabbled as a

matador, kicking around Spain before finally landing a job in the Royal Tapestry. The canvases in these rooms were designs made into tapestries bound for the walls of nobles' palaces.

Browse through these rooms and watch lords and ladies of the 1700s with nothing better to do than play—toasting each other at a picnic, dancing with castanets, flying kites, playing paddleball, listening to a blind guitarist, walking on stilts, or playing Blind Man's Bluff (in Room 93).

In Room 94, the more serious side of Goya emerges. His *Two Cats Fighting (Gatos Riñendo)* represents the two warring halves of a human soul, the dark and light sides, anger and fear locked in immortal

combat, fighting for dominance of a man's life. We're entering the Age of Romanticism.

Notice—how do I say this?—how BAD the drawing is in some of these canvases, especially the early ones. However, in the few short years he worked in the tapestry department, Goya the inexperienced apprentice slowly developed into a good, if not great, drafts-

man. *The Parasol* (*El Quitasol,* in Room 85) was one of his first really good paintings, with a simple composition and subtle shadings of light. Goya worked steadily for the court for 25 years, dutifully cranking out portraits before finally becoming First Court Painter at age 53.

• *Head to Room 89 (also on second floor).*

Political Rebel
Goya—*Nude Maja (La Maja Desnuda)* and *Clothed Maja (La Maja Vestida)*

Goya remained at court because of his talent, not his political beliefs…or his morals. Rumor flew that he was fooling around with the beautiful, intelligent, and vivacious Duchess of Alba. Even more scandalous was a painting, supposedly of the Duchess in a less-than-devoutly-Catholic pose.

A *maja* was a hip working-class girl. Many of Goya's early tapestries show royalty dressed in the garb of these colorful commoners. Here the Duchess has undressed as one.

The *Nude Maja* was a real shocker. Spanish kings enjoyed the sensual nudes of Titian and Rubens, but it was unheard of for a pious Spaniard to actually paint one. Goya incurred the wrath of the Inquisition, the Catholic court system that tried heretics and sinners. Tour guides explain that the painting caused such a stir that Goya dashed off another version with her clothes on. The quick brushwork is sloppier, perhaps because Goya was in a hurry, or because he was anxious to invent Impressionism. The two paintings may have been displayed in a double frame—the nude could be covered by sliding the clothed *maja* over it to hide it from Inquisitive minds that wanted to know.

Artistically, the nude is less a portrait than an idealized nude in the tradition (and reclining pose) of Titian's *Venus* and the *Organ Player*. The pale body is highlighted by the cool green sheets, à la Titian, as well. Both paintings were locked away in obscurity, along with the Titians and Rubenses, until 1901.

• *Return down the stairs. In Room 39, next to the stairs, you'll find...*

Goya—2nd of May, 1808 and 3rd of May, 1808

Goya became a political radical, a believer in democracy in a world of kings. During his time, the American and French Revolutions put the fear of God in the medieval minds of Europe's aristocracy. In retaliation, members of the aristocracy were determined to stamp out any trace of political liberalism.

Goya admired the French leader Napoleon, who fought for the democratic ideals of the French Revolution against the kings of Europe. But then Napoleon invaded Spain (1808), and Goya saw war firsthand. What he saw was not a heroic war liberating the Spaniards from the feudal yoke, but an oppressive, brutal, senseless war in which common Spaniards were the first to die.

The *2nd of May, 1808* and *3rd of May, 1808* show two bloody days of the war. On May 2, the common citizens of Madrid rebelled against the French invaders. With sticks, stones, and kitchen knives, they rallied in protest at Puerta del Sol, Madrid's main square. The French sent in their fearsome Egyptian mercenary troops to quell the riot. Goya captures the hysterical tangle of bodies as the Egyptians wade through the dense crowd hacking away at the over-matched Madrilenos who have nowhere to run.

The next day the French began reprisals. They took suspected rebels to a nearby hill and began mercilessly executing them. The *3rd of May, 1808* is supposedly a tribute to those brave Spaniards who rebelled against the French, but it's far from heroic. In fact, it's anti-heroic, showing us the irrationality of war—an assembly line  of death, with each victim toppling into a crumpled heap. They plea for mercy and get none. Those awaiting death bury their faces in their hands, unable to look at their falling companions. The central victim in luminous white spreads his arms Christ-like and asks, "Why are you doing this to us?"

Goya goes beyond sympathy for the victims. In this war, even the executioners are pawns in the game, only following orders without understanding why. The colorless firing squad, with guns perfectly level and feet perfectly in step, is a faceless machine of murder, cutting people down with all the compassion of a lawnmower. They bury their faces in their guns as though they, too, are unable to look their victims in the eye. This war is horrible, and what's worse, the horror is pointless.

The violence is painted with equally violent techniques. There's a strong prison-yard floodlight thrown on the main victim, focusing all our attention on his look of puzzled horror. The distorted features, the puddle of blood, the twisting bodies, the thick brushwork—all are features of the Romantic style that emphasized emotion over beauty. It all adds up to a vivid portrayal of the brutality of war. Like the victims, we ask, "How can one human being do this to another?"

Goya was disillusioned by the invasion led by his hero Napoleon. Added to this he began to go deaf. His wife died. To top it off, he was exiled as a political radical. Goya retreated from court life to his own private, quiet—and dark—world.

• *To find the dark paintings, silently flagellate yourself, then go to Room 38.*

Dark Stage

In 1819, Goya—deaf, widowed, and exiled—moved into a villa and began decorating it with his own oil paintings. The works were painted right on the walls of rooms in the villa andlater transferred here.

You immediately see why these are the Dark Paintings—both in color and mood. They're nightmarish scenes, scary and surreal, the inner visions of an embittered man smeared onto the walls as though finger-painted in blood.

Goya—*The Witches' Sabbath (El Aquelarre)*
Dark forces convened continually in Goya's dining room. This dark coven of crones swirls in a frenzy of black magic around a dark, Satanic goat in monk's clothes who presides, priest-like, over the obscene rituals. The main witch, seated in front of the goat, is the very image of wild-eyed adoration, lust, and fear. (Notice the one noble lady sitting just to the right of center with her hands folded primly in her lap—"I thought this was a Tupperware party.")

Goya—*Saturn Devouring One of His Sons (Saturno)*

Fearful that his sons would overthrow him as king of the gods, the Roman god Saturn ate them. Saturn was also known as Cronus, or Time, and this may be an allegory of how Time devours us all.

• *In Room 36…*

Goya—*Battle to the Death (Duelo a Garrotazos)*

Two giants buried up to their knees, face to face, flail at each other with clubs. Neither can move, neither can run, neither dares rest or the other will finish him off. It's a standoff between

superpowers caught in a never-ending cycle of war. Can a truce be reached? It looks bleak. Is this really by the same artist who did the frilly Blind Man's Bluff?

The Dark Paintings foreshadow 20th-century Surrealism with their dream images, and Expressionism with their thick-smeared style and cynical outlook.

Goya was a dying man in a violent world. The destructiveness of war is shown in all its horror by a man unafraid of the darker side.

Like the giants, I'm beat, so let's end our Prado tour.

GUERNICA

Perhaps the single most impressive piece of art in Spain is Pablo Picasso's *Guernica* in the Centro Arte de Reina Sofia, Madrid's slick modern art museum. The monumental canvas is not only a piece of art but a slice of history, capturing the horror of modern war in a modern style. It's one of Europe's must-see sights.

ORIENTATION

Cost: €3, free Sat afternoon, all day Sun, and any time to those under 18 and over 65; covered by €7.75 Paseo del Arte combo-ticket.

Hours: Mon and Wed–Sat 10:00–21:00, Sun 10:00–14:30, closed Tue.

Getting There: It's located three long blocks south of the Prado across the street from the Atocha train station; look for its exterior glass elevators (Santa Isabel 52, Metro: Atocha).

Information: Tel. 914-675-062, http://museoreinasofia.mcu.es

THE TOUR BEGINS

Guernica

• *Ride the fancy glass elevator to the second floor. The painting is in Room 6.*

Guernica is the product of the right artist in the right place at the right time. Pablo Picasso (1881–1973), a Spaniard, was in Paris in 1937, preparing an exhibition of paintings for its world's fair. Meanwhile, a bloody Civil War was being fought in his own country. The legally elected democratic government was being challenged by traditionalist right-wing forces under Francisco Franco. Franco would eventually win and rule the country with an iron fist for three decades.

On April 27, 1937, Guernica, a village in northern Spain, was the target of the world's first saturation-bombing raid. Franco gave

permission to his Fascist ally, Hitler, to use the town as a guinea pig to try out Germany's new air force. The raid leveled the town, causing destruction that was unheard of at the time, though by 1944 it would be commonplace.

News of the bombing reached Picasso in Paris. He scrapped earlier plans and immediately set to work sketching scenes of the destruction as he imagined it. In a matter of weeks he put these bomb-shattered shards together into a large painting (286 square feet). For the first time, the world could see the destructive force of the rising Fascist movement—a prelude to WWII.

The bombs are falling, shattering the quiet village. A woman looks up at the sky (far right), horses scream (center), a man falls from the horse and dies, while a wounded woman drags herself through the streets. She tries to escape, but her leg is too thick, dragging her down. It's like trying to run from something in a nightmare. On the left a bull, a symbol of Spain, ponders it all, watching over a mother and her dead baby—a modern *pietà*. A woman in the center sticks her head out to see what's going on. The whole scene is lit from above by the stark light of a bare bulb. Picasso's painting threw a light on the brutality of Hitler and Franco, and suddenly the whole world was watching.

Picasso's abstract, Cubist style reinforces the message. It's as if he'd picked up the shattered shards and pasted them onto a canvas. The black and white tones are as gritty as the black-and-white newspaper photos that reported the bombing. The drab colors create a depressing, almost nauseating mood.

Picasso chose images with universal symbolism, making the work a commentary on all wars. Picasso himself said that the central horse, with the spear in its back, symbolizes humanity succumbing to brute force. The fallen rider's arm is severed and his sword is broken, more symbols of defeat. Near the bull, the dove of peace can do nothing but cry.

The bombing of Guernica, like the entire Spanish Civil War (1936–39), was an exercise in brutality. As one side captured a town,

Madrid's Museum Neighborhood

it might systematically round up every man, old and young, including priests, line them up, and shoot them in revenge for atrocities by the other side.

Thousands of people attended the Paris art fair, and *Guernica* caused an immediate sensation. They could see the horror of modern war technology, the vain struggle of the Spanish Republicans, and the cold indifference of the Fascist war machine. After the Paris exhibition, *Guernica* was exiled to America until Franco's death. Picasso also vowed to never return to Spain while Franco ruled. (Franco outlived him.)

With each passing year, the canvas seemed more and more prophetic—honoring not just the thousand that died in Guernica, but also the 600,000 of Spain's bitter Civil War, and the 80 million worldwide that perished in World War II. Picasso put a human face on collateral damage.

The Rest of the Museum

Two rooms near *Guernica* display Picasso's preparatory sketches, filled with iron-nail tears, wounded horses, and screaming mouths.

The museum also houses an easy-to-appreciate collection by

other modern artists. On the second floor, follow the room numbers for art from 1900 to 1950. Room 10 has a nice collection of mind-bending works by another 20th-century Spaniard, the Surrealist Salvador Dalí. The fourth floor continues the collection, from 1950 to 1980. Finally, enjoy a break in the shady courtyard before leaving.

MODERN ART

In your travels through Europe, you'll encounter some of the world's best modern-art collections. Just in the cities in this book, you'll find the Tate Modern (London), Pompidou (Paris), Stedelijk (Amsterdam), Peggy Guggenheim Collection (Venice), and Centro Arte de Reina Sofia (Madrid), and lesser museums and contemporary galleries.

Regardless of the museum, the same artists are usually represented: Picasso, Kandinsky, Dalì, and so on. This chapter is not a painting-by-painting tour but a general guide to modern art—the artists, their styles, and the times in which they lived.

A.D. 1900

A new century dawns. War is a thing of the past. Science will wipe out poverty and disease. Rational Man is poised at a new era of peace and prosperity....

Right. This cozy Victorian dream was soon shattered by two world wars and rapid technological change.

The 20th century was exciting and chaotic, and the art reflects the turbulence of that century of change.

Henri Matisse (1869–1954)

Matisse's colorful "wallpaper" works are not realistic. A man is a few black lines and blocks of paint. The colors are unnaturally bright.

The Evolution of Modern Art

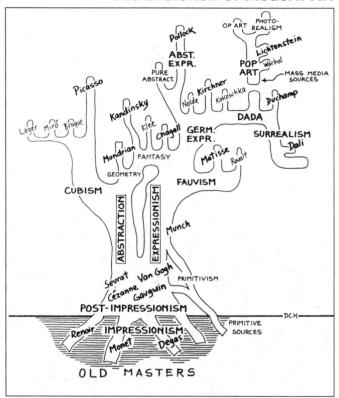

OP ART
PHOTO-REALISM
Pollock
ABST. EXPR.
PURE ABSTRACT.
Lichtenstein
POP ART
Warhol
Picasso
Kandinsky
Nolde Kirchner
Kokoschka
Duchamp
MASS MEDIA SOURCES
Leger Miró Braque
Klee
Chagall
GERM. EXPR.
DADA
SURREALISM
Mondrian
FANTASY
Matisse
Roualt
Dali
GEOMETRY
CUBISM
ABSTRACTION
EXPRESSIONISM
FAUVISM
Munch
Seurat Van Gogh
Cézanne
Gauguin
PRIMITIVISM
POST-IMPRESSIONISM
DCH
Renoir IMPRESSIONISM
PRIMITIVE SOURCES
Monet Degas
OLD MASTERS

There's no illusion of the distance and 3-D that were so important to Renaissance Italians. The "distant" landscape is as bright as things close up, and the slanted lines meant to suggest depth are crudely done.

Traditionally, the canvas was like a window that you looked "through" to see a slice of the real world stretching off into the distance. Now a camera could do that better. With Matisse, you look "at" the canvas, like wallpaper. *Voilà!* What was a crudely drawn scene now becomes a sophisticated and decorative pattern of colors and shapes.

Though fully "modern," Matisse built on 19th-century art—the bright colors of Vincent van Gogh, the primitive figures of Paul Gauguin, the colorful designs of Japanese prints, and the Impressionist patches of paint that only blend together at a distance.

Primitive Masks and Statues

Inspired by African and Oceanic masks and voodoo dolls, European artists tried to inject a bit of the jungle into their civilized world. The result? Modern art that looked primitive: long, mask-like faces with almond eyes; bright, clashing colors; simple figures; and "flat," two-dimensional scenes.

1910—THE MODERNS

The modern world was moving fast, with automobiles, factories, and mass communication. Motion pictures caught the fast-moving world, while Einstein further explored the fourth dimension, time.

Cubism: Reality Shattered

I throw a rock at a glass statue, shatter it, pick up the pieces, and glue them onto a canvas. I'm a Cubist.

Pablo Picasso (1881–1973)

Born in Spain, Picasso moved to Paris as a young man. He worked with fellow painter Georges Braque in poverty so dire they often didn't know where their next bottle of wine was coming from.

Picasso's Cubist works show the old European world shattered to bits. He pieces the fragments back together in a whole new way, showing several perspectives at once—for example, painting a woman's face from the front and in profile, so she ends up with two eyes on one side of her nose.

While newfangled motion pictures could capture several perspectives in succession, Picasso does it on a canvas with overlapping images. A single "cube" might contain both an arm (in the foreground) and the window behind (in the background), both painted the same color. The foreground and background are woven together so that the subject dissolves into a pattern.

Picasso, the most famous and—OK, I'll say it—the greatest artist of the 20th century, constantly explored and adapted his style to new trends. After inventing Cubism, he passed through phases of Synthetic Cubism

(synthesizing the cubes into more colorful and curvy shapes) and Classicism (statues on beaches). As his relationships with women deteriorated, he vented sexual demons by twisting the female body into grotesque balloon-animal shapes (Surrealism, 1925–1931). His *Guernica* put the wreckage of a Fascist air raid on a large canvas for the world to see.

He made collages, ceramic rooster jugs, wood faces, blowtorch garden sculptures, and a bull's head from a bicycle seat and handle-bars. These "multimedia" works, so revolutionary at the time, have become old school.

Marc Chagall (1887–1985)

Marc Chagall, age 22, arrived in Paris with the wide-eyed wonder of a country boy. Lovers are weightless with bliss. Animals smile and wink. Musicians, poets, peasants, and dreamers ignore gravity, tumbling in slow-motion circles high above fiddlers-on-the-roofs. The colors are deep—a pool of mystery with figures bleeding through below the surface. (Chagall claimed his early poverty forced him to paint over used canvases, inspiring the overlapping images.)

Chagall's very personal style fuses many influences. He was raised in a small Russian village, which explains his "naive" outlook. His simple figures are like Russian Orthodox icons, and his Jewish roots produce Old Testament themes. Stylistically, he's thoroughly modern—Cubist shards, bright Fauve colors, Primitive simplicity, and Surrealist dreamscapes. This otherworldly style was a natural for religious works, and so his murals and stained glass, which feature both Jewish and Christian motifs, decorate buildings around the world.

1914—WORLD WAR I

Ankle-deep in mud, a soldier shivers in a trench, waiting to be ordered "over the top." He'll have to run through barbed wire, over fallen comrades, and into a hail of machine-gun fire, only to capture a few hundred yards of meaningless territory that will be lost the next day. This soldier was not thinking about art.

World War I left nine million dead. The war also killed the optimism and faith in mankind that had guided Europe since the Renaissance.

Expressionism: Grosz, Kirchner, Dix, Kokoschka

Cynicism and decadence settled over postwar Europe. Artists

"expressed" their disgust by showing a distorted reality that emphasized the ugly. Using the lurid colors and simplified figures of the Fauves, they slapped paint on in thick brush strokes, depicting a hypocritical, hard-edged, dog-eat-dog world, a civilization watching its Victorian moral foundations collapse.

Dada: Duchamp

Others just laughed. The Dada movement, choosing a purposely childish name, made art that was intentionally outrageous: a moustache on the *Mona Lisa*, a shovel hung on the wall, or a modern version of a Renaissance "fountain"—a urinal (by Marcel Duchamp...or was it I. P. Freeley?).

It was a dig at all the pompous prewar artistic theories based on the noble intellect of Rational Women and Men. While the experts ranted on, Dadaists sat in the back of the class and made cultural fart noises.

Hey, I love this stuff. My mind says it's sophomoric, but my heart belongs to Dada.

1920—ANYTHING GOES

In the Jazz Age, the world turned upside down. Genteel ladies smoked cigarettes. Gangsters laid down the law. You could make a fortune in the stock market one day and lose it the next. You could

dance the Charleston with the opposite sex, and even say the word "sex" while talking about Freud over cocktails. It was almost...surreal.

Surrealism: Dalí, Ernst, Magritte

Artists caught the jumble of images on a canvas. Dripping clocks, Greek statues with sunglasses, a telephone made from a lobster, Venus sleepwalking among skeletons. Take one mixed bag of reality, jumble in a blender, and serve on a canvas—surrealism.

The artist scatters seemingly unrelated things on the canvas, leaving us to trace the connections in a kind of connect-the-dots without numbers.

Surrealists were fascinated with Freud's theories of the "unconscious" mind that thinks dirty thoughts while we sleep. Surrealists let the id speak. The canvas is an uncensored, stream-of-consciousness "landscape" of these deep urges, revealed in the bizarre images of dreams.

Salvador Dalí (1904–1989)

Salvador Dalí, the most famous Surrealist, combined an extraordinarily realistic technique with an extraordinarily twisted mind. He could paint "unreal" scenes with photographic realism, making us believe they could really happen. Dalí's images—dripping clocks, crucifixes, naked bodies—pack an emotional punch.

Abstract Surrealism: Miró, Calder, Arp

Abstract artists described their subconscious urges using color and shapes alone, like Rorschach inkblots in reverse. The thin-line scrawl of Joan Miró's work is like the doodling of a three-year-old, trying to express the most basic of human emotions using the most basic of techniques. Alexander Calder's mobiles hang like Mirós in the sky, waiting for a gust of wind to bring them to life. And there's your primal image—Jean Arp builds human beings out of amoeba-like shapes.

1930—DEPRESSION

As capitalism failed around the world, governments propped up their economies with vast building projects. The architecture style was modern, stripped-down, and functional. Propaganda campaigns champion noble workers in the heroic Social Realist style.

Abstract Art

Abstract art simplifies. A man becomes a stick figure. A squiggle is a wave. A streak of red expresses anger. Arches make you want a cheeseburger. These are universal symbols that everyone from a caveman to a banker understands. Abstract artists capture the essence of reality in a few lines and colors, even things a camera can't—emotions, abstract concepts, musical rhythms, and spiritual states of mind.

With Abstract art, you don't look "through" the canvas to see the visual world, but "at" it to read the symbolism of lines, shapes, and colors. Most 20th-century paintings are a mix of the real world (representation) and colorful patterns (abstraction).

Piet Mondrian (1872–1944)

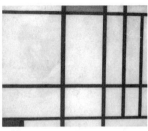

Like blueprints for modernism, Mondrian's T-square style boils painting down to its basic building blocks: black lines, a white canvas, and the three primary colors—red, yellow, and blue—arranged in orderly patterns. (When you come right down to it, that's all painting ever has been. A schematic drawing of, say, the *Mona Lisa* shows that it's less about a woman than about the triangles and rectangles she's composed of.)

Mondrian started out painting realistic landscapes of the orderly fields in his native homeland of Holland. Increasingly, he simplified his style into horizontal and vertical patterns. For Mondrian, who was heavy into Eastern mysticism, "up versus down" and "left versus right" were the perfect metaphors for life's dualities: good versus evil, body versus spirit, Fascism versus communism, man versus woman. The canvas is a bird's-eye view of Mondrian's personal landscape.

Wassily Kandinsky (1866–1944)

The bright colors, bent lines, and lack of symmetry tell us that Kandinsky's world was passionate and intense.

Notice titles like *Improvisation* and *Composition*. Kandinsky was inspired by music, an art form that's also "abstract," though it still packs a punch. Like a jazz musician improvising a new pattern of notes from a set scale, Kandinsky plays with new patterns of related colors as he looks for just the right combination. Using lines and color, Kandinsky translates the unseen reality into a new medium…like lightning crackling over the radio. Go, man, go.

Constantin Brancusi (1876–1957)

Brancusi's curved, shiny statues reduce things to their essence. A bird is a single stylized wing, the one feature that sets it apart from other animals. He rounds off to the closest geometrical form, so a woman's head becomes a perfect oval on a cubic pedestal. Brancusi follows the instinct for order that has driven art from earliest times, from circular Stonehenge and Egyptian pyramids to Renaissance domes and arches.

Paul Klee (1879–1940)

Paul Klee's small and playful canvases are deceptively simple, containing shapes so basic they could be read as if they were universal symbols. Klee thought a wavy line, for example, would always suggest motion, while a stick figure would always mean a human. Children paint things that way intuitively, and so did Klee.

1940—WORLD WAR II

World War II was a global war (involving Europe, the Americas, Australia, Africa, and Asia) and a total war (saturation bombing of civilians and ethnic cleansing). It left Europe in ruins.

Alberto Giacometti (1901–1966)

Giacometti's skinny statues have the emaciated, haunted, and faceless look of concentration-camp survivors. In the sweep of world war and overpowering technology, man is frail and fragile. All he can do is stand at attention and take it like a man.

Francis Bacon (1909–1992)

Bacon's caged creatures speak for all of war-torn Europe when they scream, "Enough!" His genetic experiments gone bad—caged in a claustrophobic room, with twisted, hunk-of-meat bodies and quadriplegic, smudged-mouth helplessness—can do nothing but scream in anguish and frustration. The scream becomes a blur, as though going on forever.

Bacon, largely self-taught, effectively uses "traditional" figurativism to express the existential human predicament—you're caught in a world that is not of your making and you're helpless to change it.

1950—AMERICA THE GLOBAL SUPERPOWER

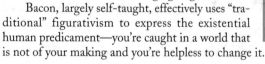

As converted war factories turned swords into kitchen appliances, America helped rebuild Europe, while pumping out consumer goods for a booming population. Prosperity, a stable government, national television broadcasts, and a common fear of Soviet communism threatened to turn America into a completely homogeneous society.

Abstract Expressionism

With Europe in ruins, New York replaced Paris as the art capital of the world. The trend was toward bigger canvases, abstract designs, and experimentation with new materials and techniques. It was called "Abstract Expressionism"—expressing emotions and ideas using color and form alone.

Jackson Pollock (1912–1956)

"Jack the Dripper" attacks convention with a can of paint, dripping and splashing a dense web onto the canvas. Picture Pollock in his

studio, jiving to the hi-fi, bouncing off the walls, throwing paint in a moment of enlightenment. Of course, the artist loses some control this way—over the paint flying in midair and over himself in an ecstatic trance. Painting becomes a whole-body activity, a "dance" between the artist and his materials.

The intuitive act of creating is what's important, not the final product. The canvas is only a record of that moment of ecstasy.

Big, Empty Canvases

With all the postwar prosperity, artists could afford bigger canvases.

But what reality are they trying to show? Every morning, each of us must confront that big, blank, Existential canvas, and decide how we're going to make our mark on it.

Another influence was the simplicity of Japanese landscape painting. A Zen master studies and meditates for years to achieve the state of mind to draw one perfect line. These canvases, again, are only a record of that state of enlightenment. (What is the sound of one brush painting?)

On more familiar ground, postwar painters were following in the footsteps of artists such as Mondrian. The geometrical forms here reflect the same search for simplicity and order, but these artists painted to the 5/4 symmetry of "Take Five."

Patterns and Textures: Jean Dubuffet, Lucio Fontana, and Karel Appel

A painted canvas has lines and colors, but there's a third element: texture. Some works have very thick paint piled on, where you can see the brush strokes clearly. Some have substances besides paint

applied to the canvas, or the canvas is punctured so the fabric itself (and the hole) becomes the subject. Artists show their skill by mastering new materials. The canvas is a tray, serving up a delightful array of different substances with interesting colors, patterns, shapes, and textures. Focus your eyes to look "at" the canvases, not "through" them.

1960—"THE SIXTIES"

The decade began united in idealism—young John F. Kennedy pledged to put a man on the moon, while on earth jet planes, satellites, and Beatles were uniting the world. By decade's end, there were race riots, assassinations, worldwide student protests, and America's floundering war in distant Vietnam. In households around the world, parents screamed, "Turn that down…and get a haircut!"

Culturally, every postwar value was questioned by a rising, wealthy, populous, baby-boom generation.

Pop Art: Andy Warhol (1930–1987)

America's postwar wealth made the consumer king. Pop art is created from the popular objects of that throwaway society—soup can, car fender, tacky plastic statues, movie icons. Take a Sears product, hang it in a museum, and you have to ask, Is this art? Are mass-produced objects beautiful? Or crap? Why do we work so hard to acquire them? Pop art, like Dadaism, questions our society's values.

Andy Warhol (who coined "15 minutes of fame") concentrated on another mass-produced phenomenon—celebrities. He took publicity photos of famous people and reproduced them. The repetition—like the constant bombardment we get from repeated images on TV—cheapens even the most beautiful things.

Roy Lichtenstein (1923–1997)

Take a comic strip, blow it up, hang it on a wall and charge a million

bucks—wham, Pop art. Lichtenstein supposedly was inspired by his young son, who challenged him to do something as good as Mickey Mouse. The huge newsprint dots never let us forget that the painting—like all commercial art—is an illusionistic fake. The work's humor comes from portraying a lowbrow subject (comics and ads) on the epic scale of a masterpiece.

Op Art

Optical illusions play tricks with your eyes, like the way a spiral starts to spin when you stare at it. These obscure scientific experiments in color, line, and optics suddenly became mind-blowing in the psychedelic '60s.

Happenings

Artists staged events where the art was simply what happened when people showed up—Happenings. Artists might do ridiculous things to inspire others to break with convention and be free.

1970—THE "ME DECADE"

All forms of authority—"The Establishment"—seemed bankrupt. America's president resigned in the Watergate scandal, corporations were polluting the earth, and capitalism nearly ground to a halt when Arabs withheld oil.

Artists attacked authority and institutions, trying to free individuals to discover their full human potential. It didn't matter what style emerged, but the status quo had to go in this postmodern period.

"Earth Art"

Fearing for the health of earth's ecology, artists rediscovered the beauty of nature—rocks, dirt, trees, the sound of wind, falling water—and used it to create natural art. A rock placed in a museum or urban square is certainly a strange sight.

1980—MATERIAL GIRL

Ronald Reagan in America, Margaret Thatcher in Britain, and corporate executives around the world ruled over a conservative and materialistic society. Art became big business, with a van Gogh fetching $54 million. Corporations paid big bucks for large, colorful, semiabstract canvases. Marketing was an art form. Gender and sexual choice were popular themes. The crude style of graffiti art demanded to be included in corporate society.

Performance Art

Many artists—who in another day would have painted canvases—have turned to a kind of mixed media of live performance, combining music, dance, theater, poetry, the visual arts, and the performer's own ability to deliver. It's often interactive, dropping the illusion of entertainment and encouraging audience participation. A whole generation of artists was inspired to walk on stage, cluck like a chicken, and stick a yam up themselves.

1990—MULTICULTURAL DIVERSITY

The Soviet-built Berlin Wall was torn down, ending four decades of a global Cold War between capitalism and communism. The new battleground was the "Culture Wars," the struggle to include all races, genders, and lifestyles within an increasingly corporate-dominated, global society.

A new medium arose, the Internet, allowing instantaneous audiovisual communication around the world through electronic signals carried by satellites and telephone lines.

New Media for a New Century

The "modern" world is history. Picasso and his ilk are now gathering dust and boring art students everywhere. Minimalist painting and abstract sculpture are old school. Enter the "postmodern" world as seen through the eyes of current artists.

You'll see fewer traditional canvases or sculptures. Artists have traded paintbrushes for blowtorches (Miró said he was out to "murder" painting) and blowtorches for computer mice. Mixed media work is the norm, combining painting, sculpture, photography, welding, film/slides/video, computer programming, new resins, plastics, industrial techniques, and lighting and sound systems.

Here are some of the trends:

Installations: An entire room is given to an artist to prepare. Like entering an art funhouse, you walk in without quite knowing what to expect (I'm always thinking, "Is this safe?"). Using the latest technology, the artist engages all your senses, by controlling the lights, sounds, and sometimes even smells.

Assemblages: Artists raid dumpsters, recycling junk into the building blocks for larger "assemblages." Each piece is intended to be interesting and tell its own story, and so is the whole sculpture. Weird, useless, Rube Goldberg machines make fun of technology.

The Occasional Canvas: This comes as a familiar relief. Artists of the New Realism labor over painstaking, hyperrealistic canvases to recreate the glossy look of a photo or video image.

Interaction: Some exhibits require your participation, whether you push a button to get the contraption going, touch something,

or just walk around the room. In some cases, the viewer "does" art rather than just stares at it. If art is really meant to change, it has to move you, literally.

Deconstruction: Late-century artists critiqued (or "deconstructed") society by examining our underlying assumptions. One way to do it is to take a familiar object (say, a crucifix) out of its normal context (a church), and place it in a new setting (in a jar of urine). Video and film can deconstruct something by playing it over and over, ad nauseam. Ad copy painted on canvas deconstructs itself.

Conceptual Art: The *concept* of which object to pair with another to produce maximum effect is the key. (Urine + crucifix = million-dollar masterpiece.)

Playful Art: Children love the art being produced today. If it doesn't put a smile on your face, well, then you must be a jaded grump like me, who's seen the same repetitious s#%t passed off as "daring" since Warhol stole it from Duchamp. I mean, it's *so* 20th-century.

2000—?

A new millennium dawns, with Europe and America at a peak of prosperity unmatched in human history...

INDEX

Abbey Museum (London): 86
Abstract Art: 458–461
Accademia (Florence): 283–285
Alexander the Great: 352–353
Amsterdam: 179–233; Anne Frank House, 227–233; City Walk, 181–198; Rijksmuseum, 199–215; Van Gogh Museum, 216–226
Amsterdam City Walk: 181–198; orientation, 181–182
Amsterdam History Museum: 190
Angélico, Fra: *The Annunciation*, 422–423
Anglo-Saxon Sutton Hoo Burial Ship (London): 50
Anne Frank House (Amsterdam): 227–233; orientation, 227–228
Antoninus Pius: 340–341
Appel, Karel: 461
Architecture, tours of: Amsterdam, 181–198; Florence, 279–295; London, 18–28, 78–86; Paris, 89–111; Madrid, 409–418; Rome, 327–333, 334–346, 360–362; Venice, 237–245; Versailles, 160–178
Arch of Constantine (Rome): 333
Arch of Septimus Severus (Rome): 344–345
Arch of Titus (Rome): 337–338
Armory Museum (Venice): 271–272
Art history: 4–9
Articles of the Barons: 74
Artists and dates: 11–15
Artist timeline: 10
Art Nouveau: 158–159
Assyria: 38–43, 133–135
Augustus: 338, 350–352
Avercamp, Hendrick: *Winter Landscape with Ice Skaters*, 203

Bacon, Francis: 460
Banqueting House: 25–26
Barberini family: 374
Bargello (Florence): 316–324; orientation, 316
Baroque: 8, 63–64, 374, 436
Basilica Aemilia (Rome): 341
Basilica of Constantine (Rome): 338–339
Beatles, manuscripts: 77
Begijnhof (Amsterdam): 191–192
Belevedere torso: 385–386

Beowulf: 75
Bernini, Gian Lorenzo: 366, 368, 374, 375, 376
Beurs van Berlage (Stock Exchange, Amsterdam): 184
Bibles: 70–74
Big Ben (London): 18–19
Boadicea, Queen of the Iceni: 21–22
Boccaccio: 294
Bosch: 430; *Garden of Delights*, 432–433; *The Hay Cart*, 431–432
Botticelli, Sandro: 57; *Allegory of Spring*, 303–304; *Birth of Venus*, 304–305; *Slander*, 305
Boucher: *Pan and Syrinx*, 65
Boules: 110
Boulevard St. Michel (Paris): 101
Brancusi, Constantin: 459–460
Braque, Georges: 455
Bridge of Sighs (Venice): 244–245, 275
British Art: 65–66
British Library (London): 69–77; orientation, 69–70; historic maps, 70
British Museum (London): 29–50; orientation, 28–31
Bronze Horses (Venice): 260–261
Brueghel, Pieter: *Triumph of Death*, 433–434
Brunelleschi, Filippo: 286, 320
Byzantine: 6, 246, 252

Cabanel, Alexandre: *The Birth of Venus*, 140–141, 143
Cabinet War Rooms (London): 23
Caesar, Julius: 337, 340, 349–350
Caffé Florian: 242
Caligula: 352, 367; palace, 341–342
Campanile, The (Venice): 241–242
Campin, Robert: *St. John the Baptist*, 429
Canal cruises (Amsterdam): 192
Cano: *St. Bernard and the Virgin*, 441–442
Canterbury Tales, The: 75–76
Caravaggio: *Abraham Sacrificing Isaac*, 315; *Bacchus*, 315; *Deposition*, 404–405; *The Supper at Emmaus*, 64
Cathedral of Almudena (Madrid): 415
Cellini: *Models of Perseus*, 324; *Perseus*, 293

Cenotaph (London): 24

Centraal Station (Amsterdam): 182–183

Centro Arte de Reina Sofia: 449–452; orientation, 449

Cézanne, Paul: *Bathers*, 68; *Self-Portrait*, 151; *The Card Players*, 152

Chagall, Marc: 456

Chapel of King Henry VII (London): 82

Chapel of the Magi (Florence): 286

Charlemagne: 93

Charles I: 25–26

Charles III: 409, 411

Charles IV: 443–444

Charpentier, Alexandre: 158

Chaucer: 75–76

Churches and cathedrals: Begijnhof (Amsterdam), 191–192; Cathedral of Almudena (Madrid), 415; Chapel of King Henry VII (London), 82; Chapel of the Magi (Florence), 286; Church of San Giorgio Maggiore (Venice), 243; De Papegaai Hidden Catholic Church (Amsterdam), 189–190, 192; Duomo (Florence), 286–288; English Church (Amsterdam), 192; Nieuwe Kerk (Amsterdam), 187; Notre Dame (Paris), 93–97; Orsanmichele Church (Florence), 290–291; Royal Air Force Chapel (London), 82–83; Sainte-Chapelle (Paris), 103–107; St. Margaret's Church (London), 22; St. Mark's Basilica (Venice), 239, 240, 246–261; St. Martin-in-the-Fields (London), 26–27; St. Peter's Basilica (Rome), 363–378; St. Séverin (Paris), 100; Westminster Abbey (London), 22, 78–86

Churchill, Winston: 23, 86

Church of San Giorgio Maggiore (Venice): 243

Cigars: 192–193

Cimabue: *Madonna of the Angels*, 121

Cité "Metropolitain" Stop (Paris): 107–108

Civic Guard Gallery (Amsterdam): 190–191

Classical sculpture: 307–308, 310

Claudel, Camille: *Maturity*, 159

Clock Tower, The (Venice): 240–241

Codex Sinaiticus: 71

Colosseum (Rome): 327–333; orientation, 327–330

Column of Phocas (Rome): 346

Conceptual Art: 465

Conciergerie (Paris): 108–109

Conservative Art: 138–140

Constable, John: *The Hay Wain*, 65

Constantine: 386–387, 392

Coronation Chair (London): 83

Coronation Spot (London): 85

Correggio: *Don't Touch Me*, 425

Counter-Reformation Art: 441–442

County Hall building (London): 20–21

Courbet, Gustave: *L'Atelier du Peintre*, 142

Couture, Thomas: *The Romans of the Decadence*, 142

Cranach, Lucas: *Adam and Eve*, 309; *Martin Luther*, 309–310

Crivelli, *Annunciation with Saint Emidius*, 57–58

Crypt Museum (Paris): 93

Crypt, The (Vatican): 378

Cubism: 455–456

Curia: 343–344

Dada Movement: 457

Da Forli, Melozzo: 402–403

Dalí, Salvador: 458

Damrak: 184

Dam Square (Amsterdam): 184–186

Dante: 294

Daumier, Honoré: *Celebrities of the Happy Medium*, 141

David, Jacques-Louis: *The Coronation of Napoleon*, 127–128

Da Vinci, Leonardo: 294; *Adoration of the Magi*, 306; *Annunciation*, 305; *Mona Lisa*, 125–126; notebook, 74; *St. Jerome*, 404; *Virgin, Child, and St. Anne*, 124–125; *Virgin and Child with St. John the Baptist and St. Anne*, 58–59; *Virgin of the Rocks*, 52–53

Deconstruction: 465

Degas, Edgar: *The Dance Class*, 145–146; *In a Café*, 147

Delacroix, Eugène: *Liberty Leading the People*, 129–130

Delaroche, Paul: *The Execution of Lady Jane Grey*, 66

Delft china: 196

Della Robbia, Luca: 321

De Papegaai Hidden Catholic
   Church (Amsterdam): 189–190,
   192
Deportation Memorial (Paris): 97–98
Diamond Center (Amsterdam): 189
Dickens, manuscripts: 77
Dodgson, Charles L.: 77
Doge's Palace (Venice): 243, 244,
   262–275; orientation, 262–264;
   Seventh Column, 244
Donatello: 290, 294; *David*, 319–320;
   Niccolo da Uzzanò, 317–318; *St.
   George*, 318–319
Don Bazán: 415
Drugs: 195–196
Dubuffet, Jean: 461
Duomo (Florence): 286–288
Dürer: *Self-Portrait*, 434–435; *Adam
   and Eve*, 435
Dutch Art, the Golden Age: 201–226
Dutch slice-of-life scenes: 203, 205

Early Renaissance (Florence):
   301–303
Eating: *See* orientation at specific
   destinations
Edward the Confessor: 22, 81
Egypt: 4, 32–38, 382–383
Elgin Marbles, The: 36–50
El Greco: 427–429; *Christ Carrying
   the Cross*, 428
Elizabeth I: 81, 82
English Church (Amsterdam): 192
English literature: 75–77
Etruscans: 387–388
Expressionism: 457

Fabriano, Gentile da: *Adoration of the
   Magi*, 300–301
Fall of Rome: 357–358
Field Marshal Montgomery: 25
Florence: 277–295; Renaissance
   Walk, 279–295; Uffizi Gallery,
   296–315; Bargello, 316–324
Florentine Renaissance: 280–283
Florentine Sculpture: 317–324
Flower Market (Amsterdam): 193,
   195
Fontana, Lucio: 461
Food: *See* orientation at specific
   destinations
Forum (Rome): 339
Fountain spectacles (Paris): 163
Franco: 416, 451

Frank, Anne: 227–233
French Art: 64–65,127–130,136–148,
   151–155, 158–159,
French Rococo: 64–65

Galileo: 294
Gare d'Orsay: 137–138
Gauguin, Paul: *Areaea*, 153–154
Géricault, Théodore: *The Raft of the
   Medusa*, 128–129
Ghiberti, Lorenzo: 320–321; *Bronze
   Doors*, 288–289
Giacometti, Alberto: 460
Giambologna: *Mercury*, 324; *Rape of
   the Sabines*, 293
Giotto: 288, 294; *Madonna and Child*,
   298–299; *St. Francis of Assisi
   Receiving the Stigmata*, 121–122
Gladiators: 331–332
Goldberg, Rube: 464
Golden Age (Dutch): 200–215
Golden Altarpiece (Venice): 257–259
Goya: 417, 442–444; *Nude Maja*,
   445–446; *2nd of May*, 446–447;
   Witches' Sabbath, 447
Grand and Petit Trianon Palaces
   (Paris): 160, 161
Great Sphinx, The: 34
Greece: 4–5, 43–46, 353, 384–386;
   statues, 115–118, 356–357
Grien, Hans Baldung: 308–309, 435
Grosz: 457
Guernica (Madrid): 449–452
Guillotine: 168
Gutenberg Bible (London): 73–74

Hadrian: 353–356, 361
Haig, Earl: 24
Hall of Mirrors: 171–172
Hals, Frans: *The Merry Drinker*,
   203–204
Hammurabi: 132–133
Handel, manuscripts: 77
Henry IV: 110
Henry VII: 82
Henry VIII: 81, 85
High Renaissance: 58; Florence,
   311–315
Historic Paris Walk: 89–111; map,
   90; orientation, 89, 91; timeline, 92
House of Commons (London): 20
House of Hajenius (Amsterdam):
   192–193
House of Lords (London): 20

Houses of Parliament (London): 18–20
Hugo, Victor: 97

Ile St. Louis: 98
Illuminated manuscripts: 72–73
Impressionism: 9; National Gallery collection, 66–68; Orsay collection, 144–148; Van Gogh Museum, 220–226
Ingres: *La Grande Odalisque*, 128; *The Source*, 139–140
Italian Renaissance: 6–7, 57–61, 122, 124, 422–429

Joan of Arc: 96
Juan Carlos: 416
Jubilee Promenade (London): 21

Kalverstraat (Amsterdam): 189
Kandinsky, Wassily: 459
King James Bible: 71–72
Klee, Paul: 460
Kokoschka: 457
Koningsplein (Amsterdam): 195

Laocoön: 385
Latin Quarter (Paris): 100–101
Left Bank (Paris): 98–99
Leidesplein (Amsterdam): 196–197
Leochares: 384
Leo X: 313
Le Potager du Roi (Versailles): 173
Lichtenstein, Roy: 462–463
Lindisfarne Gospels: 72–73
Lindow Man: 50
Lippi, Fra Filippo: 301–302
London: British Library, 69–77; British Museum, 29–50; National Gallery, 51–68; Westminster Abbey, 78–86; Westminster Walk, 18–28
London Eye Ferris Wheel: 20
Louis IX: 106
Louis XIV: 163, 166, 167–174, 175, 177
Louis XV: 169, 177
Louis XVI: 169, 177
Louvre (Paris): 112–120; orientation, 112–114
Luther, Martin: 309–310, 371

Madrid: 407–452; City Walk, 409–418; *Guernica*, 449–452; Prado Museum, 419–448

Madrid City Walk: 409–418; orientation, 409
Magna Carta: 74–75
Magritte: 457–458
Manet: *Luncheon on the Grass*, 144–145; *Olympia*, 142–143; *The Waitress*, 67
Mantegna, Andrea: *Death of the Virgin*, 423–424; *St. Sebastian*, 122–123
Map gallery (Vatican): 390
Marie-Antoinette: 108, 109, 174, 178
Martini, Simone: 300
Mary, Queen of Scots: 83
Mary I: 81
Matisse, Henri: 453–455
Matsys: 434
Max Euweplein (Amsterdam): 197
Medici family: 286, 293, 303
Medici Riccardi Palace (Florence): 286
Medieval: 5–6, 53–56, 99, 121–127, 290–291, 298–299, 421–422
Mercado de San Miguel (Madrid): 414
Mesones: 414
Michelangelo: 59–60, 284–285, 286, 294, 313, 367, 371–372, 376–377, 386; cartoon, 50; *David*, 283–284; *Holy Family*, 311–312; *Pietà*, 376–377; sculptures, 322–323; Sistine Chapel ceiling, 364, 395–402; *Slaves*, 130; *The Last Judgement*, 399–402
Millet, Jean-François: *The Gleaners*, 141–142
Ministry of Defense (London): 24–25
Mint Tower (Amsterdam): 193
Miró, Joan: 458
Modern Art: 9, 453–465; Centro Arte de Reina Sofia (Madrid), 449–452; Peggy Guggenheim Collection (Venice), 453; Pompidou Center (Paris), 453; Stedelijk Museum (Amsterdam), 453; Tate Modern (London), 453
Mondrian, Piet: 459
Monet: *Gare St. Lazare*, 66–67; *Paintings from Monet's Garden at Giverny*, 147–148; *The Water-Lily Pond*, 67
Monteverdi, Claudio: 254
Mosaics: 248–256, 259
Mouth of Truth: 266

Mummies: 37–38, 382
Murillo: 442
Museum policies: 2–3; *See also specific destinations*
Music manuscripts: 77
Mussolini, Benito: 367
Myron: 357

Napoleon: 127, 174, 186, 411–412, 446–447
National Gallery (London): 51–68; orientation, 51–52
National Museum of Rome (in Palazzo Massimo): 347–359; orientation, 347–348
Nazis: 188
Neoclassical: 8, 127–128
Nelson, Admiral Horatio: 26
Nero: 354, 366, 375
Nieuwe Kerk (Amsterdam): 187
Northern Protestant Art: 7, 61–63, 429–433
Northern Renaissance: 308–311, 433–435
Notre Dame (Paris): 91–92, 93–97
#10 Downing Street: 24

Old St. Peter's (Rome): 366
Opéra Exhibit (Paris): 143–144
Oriental antiquities: 130–135
Orsanmichele Church (Florence): 290–291
Orsay Museum (Paris): 136–159; orientation, 136–137

Palais de Justice (Paris): 107
Palazzo Massimo: *See* National Museum of Rome
Palazzo Vecchio (Florence): 291–292
Pantheon (Rome): 360–362; oculus, 362; orientation, 360
Paradiso (Amsterdam): 197
Paris: 87–178; Historic Paris Walk, 89–111; Louvre, 112–135; Orsay Museum, 136–159; Versailles, 160–178
Parliament Square (London): 22–23
Parmigianino: *Madonna of the Long Neck*, 314–315
Parthenon Frieze panels: 118
Performance Art: 463–464
Petrarch: 294
Phillip I: 438–439
Phillip II: 426–427, 428

Phillip V: 415
Photography: 2; *See also specific destination*
Piazzetta, The (Venice): 242–243
Piazza, The (Venice): 239–240
Picasso, Pablo: 455–456; *Guernica*, 449–452
Pinacoteca (Rome): 402–405
Pissarro, Camille: 148
Place Dauphine (Paris): 109–110
Place St. André-des-Arts (Paris): 102
Place St. Michel (Paris): 102–103
Plaza Mayor (Madrid): 412–413
Poets' Corner (London): 83–85
Point Zero (Paris): 93
Pollack, Jackson: 461
Pollaiolo, Antonio: *Hercules and Antaeus*, 321–322; *Labors of Hercules*, 302
Pont Neuf (Paris): 110–111
Ponte Vecchio (Florence): 295
Pop Art: 462–463
Pope: 364–365, 368
Pope Julius II: 392, 395
Pope Leo X: 313
Post-Impressionism: 149–153
Prado Museum (Madrid): 419–448; orientation, 419–420
Praxiteles: *Venus de' Medici*, 307; *Apollino*, 307
Primitives: 153–155
Printing: 73
Prisons: 274
Puerta del Sol (Madrid): 409, 411

Raphael: 362, 376, 391–393, 395, 424–425; *La Belle Jardinière*, 125; *Madonna of the Goldfinch*, 312; *Pope Julius II*, 60; *The Disputa*, 394; *Transfiguration*, 403–404
Realism: 141–144
Redon, Odilon: 152–153
Rembrandt: 207, 209–210; Belshazzar's Feast, 62; *Portrait of Saskia*, 208; *Self-Portrait at an Early Age*, 206; *The Night Watch*, 214–215
Renaissance Art: 391–395
Renaissance (Florence): 294, 303–307
Renaissance Walk (Florence): 279–295; orientation, 279–280
Renoir: *Boating on the Seine*, 67; *Dance at the Moulin de la Galette*, 148
Reservations (Florence): 282

Rijksmuseum (Amsterdam): 197–198, 199–215; orientation, 199–201

Rococo: 8, 64–65

Rodin, Auguste: *Honoré de Balzac*, 159; *The Gates of Hell*, 159; *The Walking Man*, 158–159

Roman Forum: 334–346; orientation, 334

Roman rulers: 354–356

Romanticism: 8, 128–130

Rome: 5, 119, 325–405; Colosseum, 327–333; Roman Forum, 334–346; National Museum of Rome, 347–359; Pantheon, 360–362; St. Peter's Basilica, 353–378; Vatican Museum, 379–405

Rosetta Stone: 32–33

Rostrum: 344

Rousseau, Henri: *War*, 153

Royal Air Force Chapel (London): 82–83

Royal Palace (Amsterdam): 186

Royal Palace (Madrid): 415–418

Rubens: 63, 315, 437; *St. George Slaying the Dragon*, 436; *The Three Graces*, 438

Sainte-Chapelle (Paris): 103–107

St. Isidro: 415

St. Margaret's Church (London): 22

St. Mark's Basilica (Venice): 239, 240, 246–261; exterior, 248–249; mosaics, 248–256; museums, 256–260; orientation, 246, 248

St. Mark's Square (Venice): 237–245; orientation, 237, 239

St. Martin-in-the-Fields (London): 26–27

St. Peter: 372–373, 375–376, 393

St. Peter's Basilica (Rome): 363–378; orientation, 363–365

St. Peter's Square (Rome): 366–368

St. Séverin (Paris): 100

Salle des Fêtes: 155–157

San Marco Museum: 259–261

Sansovino: 243–244

Savonarola: 293, 305

Sculpture: 36–37, 39–50, 115–120, 131–133, 134–135, 158–159, 283–285, 307–308, 310, 317–324, 349–359, 384–390

Seine River: 111

Seurat: *Bathers at Asnières*, 67–68; *The Circus*, 154

Sfumato: 125, 424

Shakespeare: 76, 99–100

Sinterklaas: 187

Sistine Chapel (Rome): 364, 395–402

Socrates: 353

Stadsschouwburg (Amsterdam): 196

Stained glass: *See* Sainte-Chapelle

Steen, Jan: 212–214

Stradivarius Room (Madrid): 418

Sumerian culture: 383

Surrealism: 457–458

Tapestries: 390

Temple of Julius Caesar: 340

Temple of Saturn: 345–346

Temple of Vesta: 342

Thames: 21

Tiberius: 352

Tiepolo, G.B.: *Venice Receiving Neptune*, 267–268

Tiepolo, Giambattista: 417

Tintoretto: *Bacchus and Ariadne*, 268; *Origin of the Milky Way*, 61; *Paradise*, 272–273; *Triumph of Venice*, 269

Tips: 1–3

Titian: *Bacchus and Ariadne*, 60–61; *Danae*, 426; *Venus with the Organ Player*, 426; *Venus of Urbino*, 314

Torre del Oro Bar Andalu: 413–414

Toulouse-Lautrec: *The Clownesse Cha-U-Kao*, 154; *Jane Avril Dancing*, 155

Tours: *See* orientation at specific destinations

Trafalgar Square (London): 26–28

Trajan: 354–355

Transportation: *See* orientation at specific destinations

Treasury (Venice): 256–257

Tretarchs, The: 244

Turner, Joseph: *The Fighting Téméraire*, 65

Uccello, Paolo: *Battle of San Romano* (London panel), 53, 56; *Battle of San Romano* (Florence panel), 301

Uffizi Courtyard (Florence): 294

Uffizi Gallery (Florence): 296–315; orientation, 296–298

Umberto I: 362

Van Der Weyden: 429–430

Van Dyck: *Charles I on Horseback*, 63

Van Eyck: *Arnolfini Marriage*, 56–57
Van Gogh Museum (Amsterdam): 216–226; orientation, 216–217
Van Gogh, Vincent: *Church at Auvers-sur-Oise*, 150–151; *Peasant Woman Near the Hearth*, 149–150; *Potato Eaters*, 219; *Room at Arles*, 150; *Self-Portrait*, 150; *Sunflowers*, 68
Vatican City: 364
Vatican Museum (Rome): 379–405; orientation, 379–380
Velázquez, Diego: 417; *Jester Portraits*, 439; *Maids of Honor*, 438–439; *Rokeby Venus*, 63–64
Venetian Gothic: 242–243
Venetian Renaissance: 60–61
Venice: 235–275; St. Mark's Square, 237–245; St. Mark's Basilica, 246–261; Doge's Palace, 262–275
Venus de' Medici: 307
Venus de Milo: 116
Vermeer: *A Young Woman Standing at a Virginal*, 61–62; *Kitchen Maid*, 211
Veronese, Paolo: 269, 273: *Marriage at Cana*, 126–127; *Rape of Europa*, 268

Verrocchio: 306; *David*, 321
Versailles (Paris): 160–178; gardens, 175–177; orientation, 160–163; touring, 164–165
Vespucci, Amerigo: 294
Vestal Virgins: 343
Via dei Calzaiuoli (Florence): 289–290
Victor Emmanuel II: 362
Victoria, Queen: 23, 80

Warhol, Andy: 462
Wars of the Roses: 82
Westminster Abbey (London): 22, 78–86; map, 80; orientation, 78–79
Westminster Bridge (London): 18–21
Westminster Walk (London): 18–28
Whistler: *Portrait of the Artist's Mother*, 145
Whitehall (London): 23
Wilhelmina, Queen: 192
World War I: 86, 456
World War II: 86, 188, 450, 460

Zurbarán: 442

Start your trip at
www.ricksteves.com

Rick Steves' website is packed with over 3,000 pages of timely travel information. It's also your gateway to getting FREE monthly travel news from Rick — and more!

Free Monthly European Travel News

Fresh articles on Europe's most interesting destinations and happenings. Rick will even send you an e-mail every month (often direct from Europe) with his latest discoveries!

Timely Travel Tips

Rick Steves' best money-and-stress-saving tips on trip planning, packing, transportation, hotels, health, safety, finances, hurdling the language barrier...and more.

Travelers' Graffiti Wall

Candid advice and opinions from thousands of travelers on everything listed above, plus whatever topics are hot at the moment (discount flights, packing tips, scams...you name it).

Rick's Annual Guide to European Railpasses

The clearest, most comprehensive guide to the confusing array of railpass options out there, and how to choo-choose the railpass that best fits your itinerary and budget. Then you can order your railpass (and get a bunch of great freebies) online from us!

Great Gear at the Rick Steves Travel Store

Enjoy bargains on Rick's guidebooks, planning maps and TV series DVDs—and on his custom-designed carry-on bags, wheeled bags, day bags and light-packing accessories.

Rick Steves Tours

Every year more than 5,000 lucky travelers explore Europe on a Rick Steves tour. Learn more about our 26 different one-to-three-week itineraries, read uncensored feedback from our tour alums, and sign up for your dream trip online!

Rick on TV

Read the scripts and see video clips from the popular Rick Steves' Europe TV series, and get an inside look at Rick's 13 newest shows.

Respect for Your Privacy

Ordering online from us is secure. When you buy something from us, join a tour, or subscribe to Rick's free monthly travel news e-mails, we promise to never share your name, information, or e-mail address with anyone else. You won't be spammed!

Have fun raising your Travel I.Q. at
www.ricksteves.com

Travel smart…carry on!

The latest generation of Rick Steves' carry-on travel bags is easily the best—benefiting from two decades of on-the-road attention to what really matters: maximum quality and strength; practical, flexible features; and no unnecessary frills. You won't find a better value anywhere!

Convertible, expandable, and carry-on-size:

Rick Steves' Back Door Bag $99

This is the same bag that Rick Steves lives out of for three months every summer. It's made of rugged water-resistant 1000 denier Cordura nylon, and best of all, it converts easily from a smart-looking suitcase to a handy backpack with comfortably-curved shoulder straps and a padded waistbelt.

This roomy, versatile 9" x 21" x 14" bag has a large 2600 cubic-inch main compartment, plus three outside pockets (small, medium and huge) that are perfect for often-used items. And the cinch-tight compression straps will keep your load compact and close to your back—not sagging like a sack of potatoes.

Wishing you had even more room to bring home souvenirs? Pull open the full-perimeter expando-zipper and its capacity jumps from 2600 to 3000 cubic inches. When you want to use it as a suitcase or check it as luggage (required when "expanded"), the straps and belt hide away in a zippered compartment in the back.

Attention travelers under 5'4" tall: This bag also comes in an inch-shorter version, for a compact-friendlier fit between the waistbelt and shoulder straps.

Convenient, durable, and carry-on-size:

Rick Steves' Wheeled Bag $119

At 9" x 21" x 14" our sturdy Rick Steves' Wheeled Bag is rucksack-soft in front, but the rest is lined with a hard ABS-lexan shell to give maximum protection to your belongings. We've spared no expense on moving parts, splurging on an extra-long button-release handle and big, tough inline skate wheels for easy rolling on rough surfaces.

This bag is not convertible! Our research tells us that travelers who've bought convertible wheeled bags never put them on their backs anyway, so we've eliminated the extra weight and expense.

Rick Steves' Wheeled Bag has exactly the same three-outside-pocket configuration as our Back Door Bag, plus a handy "add-a-bag" strap and full lining.

Our Back Door Bags and Wheeled Bags come in black, navy, blue spruce, evergreen and merlot.

For great deals on a wide selection of travel goodies, begin your next trip at the Rick Steves Travel Store!

Visit the Rick Steves Travel Store at
www.ricksteves.com

Rick Steves

COUNTRY GUIDES 2005

France
Germany & Austria
Great Britain
Greece
Ireland
Italy
Portugal
Scandinavia
Spain
Switzerland

CITY GUIDES 2005

Amsterdam, Bruges & Brussels
Florence & Tuscany
London
Paris
Prague & The Czech Republic
Provence & The French Riviera
Rome
Venice

BEST OF GUIDES

Best European City Walks & Museums
Best of Eastern Europe
Best of Europe

More *Savvy.* More *Surprising.* More *Fun.*

PHRASE BOOKS & DICTIONARIES

French
French, Italian & German
German
Italian
Portuguese
Spanish

MORE EUROPE FROM RICK STEVES

Easy Access Europe
Europe 101
Europe Through the Back Door
Mona Winks
Postcards from Europe

DVD
RICK STEVES' EUROPE

Rick Steves' Europe All Thirty
  Shows 2000–2003
Britain & Ireland
Exotic Europe
Germany, The Swiss Alps & Travel
Skills
Italy

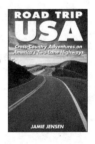

Avalon Travel Publishing
1400 65th Street, Suite 250, Emeryville, CA 94608, U.S.A.

Avalon Travel Publishing
An Imprint of Avalon Publishing Group, Inc.

Printed in the U.S.A. by Worzalla. Second printing November 2004.

Portions of this book were originally published in *Rick Steves' Mona Winks* © 2001, 1998, 1996, 1993, 1988 by Rick Steves and Gene Openshaw

ISBN 1-56691-523-6 • ISSN 1551-1200

For the latest on Rick's lectures, guidebooks, tours, and public television series, contact Europe Through the Back Door, Box 2009, Edmonds, WA 98020, 425/771-8303, fax 425/771-0833, www.ricksteves.com, or rick@ricksteves.com.

Europe Through the Back Door Managing Editor: Risa Laib
Avalon Travel Publishing Series Manager: Roxanna Font
Avalon Travel Publishing Project Editor: Patrick Collins
Copy Editor: Chris Hayhurst
Cover Design: Kari Gim, Laura Mazer
Production & Typesetting: Patrick David Barber
Interior Design: Jane Musser, Laura Mazer, Amber Pirker
Maps & Graphics: David C. Hoerlein, Zoey Platt, Lauren Mills, Mike Morgenfeld
Indexer: Vera Gross
Avalon Travel Publishing Graphics Coordinator: Deb Dutcher
Photography: Rick Steves, Gene Openshaw, Dominic Bonuccelli, and others
Front cover photos: front image, Rome, Vatican Museum, © Robert Frerck/ Getty Images; back image, Italy, Venice, Piazzetta San Marco at dawn, © Will & Deni McIntyre/Getty Images